16A

MOTHER'S
FIRST-BORN
DAUGHTERS

RELIGION IN NORTH AMERICA

Catherine L. Albanese and Stephen J. Stein, editors

MOTHER'S FIRST-BORN DAUGHTERS

Early Shaker Writings on Women and Religion

EDITED BY

Jean M. Humez

INDIANA UNIVERSITY PRESS
Bloomington and Indianapolis

The paper used in this publication meets the minimum requirements of American
National Standard for Information Sciences—Permanence of Paper for Printed
Library Materials, ANSI Z39.48-1984.

⊚™

Manufactured in the United States of America

Library of Congress Cataloging-in-Publication Data

Mother's first-born daughters : early Shaker writings on women and
religion/edited by Jean M. Humez.

    p.   cm.—(Religion in North America)

    Includes bibliographical references and index.

    ISBN 0-253-32870-5 (cloth : alk. paper).—ISBN 0-253-20744-4
(pbk. : alk. paper)

    1. Women, Shaker—History—Sources. 2. Shakers—History—Sources.
3. United States—Church history—19th century—Sources. 4. Lee,
Ann, 1736–1784. 5. Wright, Lucy, 1760–1821. I. Humez, Jean
McMahon, date. II. Series.

BX9789.W7M68   1993

289'.8'082—dc20   92-20920

1 2 3 4 5 97 96 95 94 93

✦ CONTENTS

     CORRESPONDENCE OF SHAKER SISTERS, WEST
     AND EAST, 1805–1835   133

     Introduction   133
     Selected Correspondence   145

4.   "THE HEAVENS ARE OPEN": WOMEN'S PERSPECTIVES
     ON MIDCENTURY SPIRITUALISM   209

     Introduction   209
     The Onset of the Revival (Watervliet Church Family Meeting
     Journal, 1838–1840)   230
     A Visionary Dream Concerning Ann Eliza Goodwin (1840)   238
     Mother Lucy's Word to the Sisters (1841)   239
     Visits from Alien Spirits at Watervliet (Church Family
     Meeting Journal, 1842–1843)   243
     The Hancock Sweeping Gift (1843)   248
     Hancock Mountain Meeting (1843)   250
     Holy Mother Wisdom's Fold (n.d.)   255
     Paulina Bates's *Divine Book of Holy and Eternal
     Wisdom* (1849)   258
     Mary Hazard's "Precious Crumbs of Heavenly Food . . . "
     (1839–1842)   267
     New Year's Verses for the New Lebanon Sisters (1846)   270

     A Selective Bibliography of Published Sources   273
     Index   283

FOREWORD

The revisionist recovery of Shaker history underway today will be aided immensely by the availability of the primary sources in this volume, a number of which have never before appeared in print. Collectively they comprise a persuasive first-order narrative on the women of the Shaker community from the time of its origins during the last three decades of the eighteenth century until the 1850s. Jean Humez, already a significant contributor to Shaker studies by her edition of *Gifts of Power: The Writings of Rebecca Jackson, Black Visionary, Shaker Eldress* (1981) and by her published essays, has selected these documents with an eye to the concerns of those in the fields of religious studies, women's studies, and American studies. Powerful and intrinsically absorbing in their own right, the materials anthologized in this documentary history have been edited with a sensitivity to the social and sociological contexts. Humez, a leader in the effort to reconceptualize Shaker history, also provides a critical but balanced perspective on early Shakerism, avoiding the pitfalls of sentimentality and undue adulation that have trapped many scholars in the field.

In this volume we confront directly the two most important women in the Shaker story, Ann Lee and Lucy Wright. Lee (d. 1784), the founder of the society who wrote nothing herself, is accessible principally through the testimonies of her followers collected many years after her death. Her disciples recounted stories of "Mother Ann," as they called her, traditions that described a powerful leader who was maternal and affectionate as well as stern and demanding. Visionary, prophet, miracle-worker—these, too, Ann Lee was to her followers. By contrast, her opponents denounced her as promiscuous, lewd, and unprincipled. Humez's analysis of the stories concerning Lee helps us to sort out the myths and the nonmyths surrounding this pivotal figure in the early history of Shakerism.

The situation with Lucy Wright (d. 1821) is somewhat different. "Mother Lucy," as she was known, presided over the fortunes of the United Society of Believers for a quarter century. Organizationally gifted, she played a major role in the development of institutional Shakerism and corresponded regularly with subordinates throughout the society. Extant letters from her years of leadership reveal a great deal about her and the situation she and other women occupied in the society. The sayings of Wright were also collected after her death and circulated among the villages. Humez has edited these sources, and through them we encounter perhaps the most powerful female figure in Shaker history.

One theme of central importance in this collection is the question of the status and contribution of women to early Shakerism. This issue has become a topic of increasing scholarly debate over the past several decades. For some time it has been fashionable to identify the Shakers as pioneers of sexual equality. At times, however, the claims for the degree of sexual equality achieved among the Believers have exceeded the evidence. In recent years, thanks in part to the efforts of feminist scholars, a more temperate estimate of the relationship between the sexes has prevailed. The case of Lucy Wright, for example, is very telling in this regard. Despite unparalleled authority and influence as the leader of the Shakers, repeatedly Wright was forced to respond to men who resisted and resented what they called "petticoat government." The principle of sexual equality, as Humez demonstrates, was not uniformly accepted within the society.

The Shaker sisters who took part in the western expansion of the United Society to the Ohio Valley in the first decade of the nineteenth century wrote letters "home" to their fellow Believers on the East Coast, telling of hardship, homesickness, and the host of demands upon them. Theirs was less than a utopian situation. They experienced a sense of isolation and distance from loved ones, feelings shared by other non-Shaker pioneer women also engaged in the task of domesticating the frontier. The Shaker sisters faced the added problem of dealing with difficulties created by hostility to their religious organization. Humez correctly contends that the correspondence from the western Believers provides a rare window into the daily realities confronting Shaker sisters.

The final section of this documentary history underscores the critical function played by ecstatic religion in the lives of Shaker sisters during the antebellum years. Following the lead of anthropologist I. M. Lewis and supported by the work of historians such as Mary P. Ryan and Nancy F. Cott, Humez documents the empowerment that women in the society, especially younger women outside the circle of leadership, derived from ecstatic religion. During the revival period known as "Mother Ann's Work," which began in 1837, spirit communications reported by chosen "instruments" became a major force in the life of the community. At times these spiritualistic mediums were in tension, if not outright opposition, with the society's male ministries. The claim and content of spirit messages brought their recipients power and reputation. The messages themselves were identified as coming from a variety of sources—secular and religious—including the spirits of Ann Lee, Lucy Wright, and other former leaders of the society. These announced communications enabled a new generation of Believers who had not known the formative figures to establish a sense of spiritual relationship with them.

Among the many insights available in this volume is Humez's observation that storytelling was a way of "doing theology" especially congenial to Shaker women who often found themselves on the margin of official religious institutions. During the antebellum years when women had fewer vehicles for self-expression than their brothers, fathers, and husbands, they turned to other forms of expression to seek emotional and psychological satisfactions. Women became "informal theologians" who employed what means were available in an effort to shape their own religious world. Shaker sisters, enfranchised by vision and ecstasy, used storytelling to nurture a distinctive sense of religion and sisterhood within their ranks and to reflect in innovative ways on their conceptions of the nature of God and Christ. These female traditions in literature and the arts are of primary interest in this volume.

Humez's work sets a new standard for a balanced measure of the place of women within early Shakerism. The texts in this anthology invite close scrutiny by those interested in religion, the role of women in American religious history, and the contributions of women to American culture.

Catherine L. Albanese
Stephen J. Stein, Series Editors

ACKNOWLEDGMENTS

During the years in which I have been doing research on nineteenth-century Shaker women, I have received invaluable help and moral support from colleagues and students in women's studies, American studies, and English at the University of Massachusetts at Boston, from friends and family, and from the Shakers themselves. Among those who have generously shared their knowledge of Shakerism with me and provided the colleagial exchanges necessary for sustaining this kind of work, I would especially like to thank: Leonard Brooks, Sister Frances Carr, Jane Crosthwaite, Jerry Grant, Brother Arnold Hadd, Richard Kathmann, Flo Morse, Stephen Paterwic, Daniel Patterson, Marjorie Procter-Smith, Viki Sands, Diane Sasson, and David Watters. I owe a particular debt of gratitude to Stephen J. Stein, who believed in the book from the outset and provided careful readings and extensive comments on earlier versions of the introductory essays.

I would also like to express thanks to Prof. Catherine L. Albanese and to my heroic copyeditor, Lois Crum, for all their efforts to improve the book as it passed through their hands.

Support for my research and writing over the years has come from the National Endowment for the Humanities and from the College of Arts and Sciences at the University of Massachusetts at Boston. I was greatly assisted in completing the project by the award of a Research Associateship in Women's Studies in Religion from the Harvard Divinity School for 1990–91. I am grateful to Constance Buchanan, the Director of the Women's Studies Program there, and to the other research associates and my students, for helping make the year so stimulating and productive.

My research has been assisted on many occasions by the courteous professional staffs of the Berkshire Athenaeum, the Boston Public Library (Microfilm Room), the Dartmouth College Library (Interlibrary Loan Department), the Fruitlands Museum, Hancock Shaker Village, Harvard University Library Government Documents Room, the Library of Congress, the New York State Library at Albany, the New York Public Library (Rare Books and Manuscripts Division), the Philadelphia Museum of Art, the Shaker Museum and Library at Old Chatham, the Shaker Library and Museum at Sabbathday Lake, the University of Kentucky Library, the Healey Library at the University of Massachusetts at Boston, the Western Reserve

Historical Society, the Western Kentucky University Library, the Winterthur Museum Library, and the Williams College Library.

I dedicate the book to the memory of my parents, Lucile Nelson McMahon (1912–1989) and Howard Oldford McMahon (1914–1990). Their support of my choices in life laid the foundation for my present work.

Grateful acknowledgment is made to the Shaker Manuscript Collection, Rare Books and Manuscripts Division, the New York Public Library, Aster, Lenox and Tilden Foundations; to the Manuscripts and Special Collections Division of the New York State Library at Albany; to the Shaker Museum and Library at Old Chatham, New York; to the United Society of Shakers, Sabbathday Lake, Poland Spring, Maine; to the Western Reserve Historical Society; and to the Winterthur Library: The Edward Deming Andrews Memorial Shaker Collection, for permission to reprint manuscript material in their collections. Excerpts from rare Shaker publications are reprinted courtesy of the Massachusetts Historical Society and the Berkshire Athenaeum.

A NOTE ON MANUSCRIPT SOURCES AND ABBREVIATIONS

The bulk of the Shaker manuscripts cited in this book are part of the very large collection at the Western Reserve Historical Society. References to these sources follow the classification system in Kermit J. Pike, *A Guide To Shaker Manuscripts in the Library of the Western Reserve Historical Society* (Cleveland, Ohio: 1974). This collection is available on microfilm, as are those in the Library of Congress and the New York State Library, Albany.

As yet there is no standardized manuscript classification system or central directory of Shaker manuscripts in a dozen major libraries. Two other manuscript finding guides which may be useful to Shaker researchers are Robert F. W. Meader's *Catalogue of the Emma B. King Library of the Shaker Museum* (Old Chatham, New York: 1970) and E. Richard McKinstry's *The Edward Deming Andrews Memorial Shaker Collection* (New York: Garland, 1987).

Shaker manuscript collections are abbreviated as follows in my notes:

DeWint Henry Francis du Pont Winterthur Museum, Winterthur, Delaware

KyBW Western Kentucky University, Bowling Green, Kentucky

MeSl United Society of Shakers, Sabbathday Lake, Maine

MHF Fruitlands Museum, Harvard, Massachusetts

MPH Hancock Shaker Village, Inc., Pittsfield, Massachusetts

MWiW Williams College Library, Williamstown, Massachusetts

N New York State Library, Albany, New York

NN New York Public Library, New York City

NOC Shaker Museum and Library, Old Chatham, New York

OClWHi Western Reserve Historical Society, Cleveland, Ohio

GENERAL INTRODUCTION

After a short time Mother told her to confess her sins, which she did, and from that period till Mother left Harvard for that time her soul seemed to be transported above all earthly things. She said she danced the most of the time during the week, being supported and carried by the power of God. She often leaped so high that her head touched the top of the room and wished that there was nothing in her way to prevent her going as high as the spirit would carry her.

[Jemima Blanchard's conversion story collected by Eunice Bathrick in 1830s, recalling 1780s]

I feel myself to be the seed of the free woman and an heir to the promised inheritance. I have no natural relations with me; but I have spiritual relations, elders, brethren, and sisters, who are dearer to me than any of my natural kindred ever were. In these I can confide and with these I can unite and partake of the true bread of life and drink of the pure waters of life.

[Testimony of Zipporah Cory, 1826]

And in a moment I was caught away in the spirit and the Bride and the Groom stood before me. Her presence brought me to the floor, with my forehead leaning on the instep of Her right foot. . . . And She began to speak to me. Her lips moved, but I heard not Her words. But the interpreter which is in me made known to me the words that She spoke, as fast as they fell from Her holy lips. . . . The first word She said to me was this, "Thou has kept my word, though thou didst not know me and has fought for my truth, and I will own thee in this place and to this people." And many other words the blessed Bride spoke to me, which both comforted and strengthened my soul in the living faith of Christ's Second Appearing.

[Rebecca Jackson, 1843]

I received a draft of a beautiful Tree pencil'd on a large sheet of white paper bearing ripe fruit. I saw it plainly; it looked very singular and curious to me. I have since learned that this tree grows in the Spirit Land. Afterwards the spirit shew'd me plainly the branches, leaves and fruit, painted or drawn upon paper. . . . I entreated Mother Ann to tell me the name of this tree: which she did Oct. 1st 4th hour P.M. by moving the hand of a medium to write twice over Your Tree is the Tree of Life.

[Hannah Cohoon, 1854][1]

These four women all testify to the transformative impact on their spiritual lives of Ann Lee(s) (1736–1784), the charismatic working-class Englishwoman who emigrated to colonial New York State on the eve of the Revolutionary War. Though she lived only ten years in the new land, Lee was to found an Anglo-American religion which still survives today. Based largely on female experience and reflecting "feminine" cultural values, the Shaker religion inspired a communitarian life that has lasted into the twentieth century and has attracted a wide variety of admirers and students throughout its long history. Yet only in very recent years has the world outside Shaker communities begun to look seriously at the enigmatic and multifaceted spiritualism that animated Shaker communalism for two hundred years.[2]

Shakerism's founder, Ann Lee, is acknowledged as a major figure in Shaker history and culture. Less well known are the parts played by other women in the shaping of Shaker religion. There were women among the small cohort of Lee's English followers who formed "the Church"—first, in New York City (1774–1775) and then in log cabins on a swampy tract of land near Albany (1775–1779).[3] Women were among those New Light Baptists from New Lebanon, New York, and surrounding towns, who were drawn to visit the English Shakers in the spring of 1780 to explore their claim to have experienced the Second Appearing of Christ. Women were included in the coterie of American-born converts who joined the original English inner circle of Ann Lee's associate "Elders."[4] During Lee's brief ministry, women participated in many of the functions of her charismatic leadership—including visionary activity, spiritual healing, teaching, and even preaching.

Beyond the perimeter of this inner circle were other women who knew Lee as their spiritual Mother—a whole generation of converts from New Lebanon and from the New England countryside and towns which she and her closest associates visited during an extended missionary tour in 1781–1783. In the years after her death, when Shaker communalism took shape and new communities were formed, this whole first generation came to have a special status in the eyes of younger Believers, because they had known Ann Lee and the Elders in the flesh. The special status of the first generation was remarked on, for example, when Lucy Smith died at the Shaker community in New Lebanon in 1852, and Sally Bushnell noted in a family journal that Smith had been "the last except one of Mother's first born daughters."[5]

This book aims to document the range of contributions to Shaker religion made by women during the first eighty years in America—a period roughly representing the full life spans of the longest-lived of "Mother's first-born daughters." This period (1774–1854) saw Ann Lee's complex legacy as the founder of a new religion fully institutionalized in a network of nineteen separatist celibate communities in eight states.[6] By looking closely at the ways in which women influenced the evolution of Shaker religion during this foundational era,[7] I believe we can both produce a more accurate version of the history of Shakerism and highlight the ways in which gender ideas play an important role in the creation of any new religious institution.

GENDER IN U.S. RELIGIOUS HISTORY

Historians have increasingly come to realize the central role of religion, and especially the Christian religion, in women's historical experience in the United States. At the same time, the importance of women's values and actions in the creation and maintenance of churches and other Christian-influenced social institutions and movements can hardly be overstated.

Though many moderns tend to view traditional Judaeo-Christian religion solely as a source of socially conservative ideology which reinforces the subordination of women, churches attracted women in preindustrial North America in part because they were public places in which there was no question of women's right to appear. As the historian Laurel Ulrich has pointed out, in reference to the northern New England women who were numerically dominant in congregational churches in the eighteenth century,

> Church membership was one of the few public distinctions available to women. Men could be fence-viewers, deacons, constables, captains, hog reeves, selectmen, clerks, magistrates, tithingmen, or sealers of leather. Women could be members of a gathered church. In a society in which church membership had to be earned, this was no small distinction.[8]

Religious ideas and values need to be considered as sources of religion's attraction for women as well. Ulrich continues:

> Just as church membership gave women independent status, religious teaching often ratified traditional female values, supporting old wives in their guardianship of sexual mores, elevating charity over commerce and neighborliness over trade, but, above all, transforming weakness into gentleness, obscurity into humility, changing worldly handicaps into spiritual strengths.

But we cannot fully explain the tremendous appeal of religion to women of the past (and present) without also understanding its spiritual/psychological emancipatory potential. Some recent historical studies informed by anthropological and psychological perspectives on religion have documented and sought to explain the special gravitation of women to the "enthusiastic" forms of Christian religion that emphasize feeling and create and express "disorder."[9] In the context of Protestantism in the United States of the eighteenth and nineteenth centuries, enthusiastic religion included the "heartfelt" conversion experiences that formed an important basis for female bonding among eighteenth-century evangelical women like Esther Edwards Burr; the emotional rebirth experiences encouraged by the dramatic public revivals of the Second Great Awakening; Holiness Methodism's two experiences of divine grace, leading to a state of sanctification or freedom from all sin; and the ecstatic trance states which developed within such unconventional religions as Shakerism and Spiritualism.[10] Although explanations vary according to specific social contexts and periods, almost all emphasize the ways in which ecstatic or "disorderly" religion enables women (and lower-status men and socially subordinate ethnic and racial groups) to express covert rebellion against social domination.[11] Direct contact through trance with the sacred realm allows those excluded from priesthoods to claim alternative sources of authority for religious leadership roles.

SHAKER RELIGIOUS CULTURE IN RELATION TO NEW ENGLAND PROTESTANTISM

In the days of Ann Lee, Shaker religion was an impressively eclectic mix of religious imagery, values, behavior, and ideas, many of these originally drawn from the rich stew of popular British urban Christianity of the eighteenth century by an illiterate, charismatic female leader. Even in the context of the emotionally expressive revivalism of the Second Great Awakening in New England, Shaker religious behavior and teachings were seen from the outset by nonbelieving neighbors as highly eccentric, well outside the Protestant mainstream. Because they required a confession of sins and elevated celibacy over marriage, the English Shakers and their small band of American followers were even accused in the early days of leaning toward Catholicism.[12] After Ann Lee's death, this inchoate religion was modified and elaborated upon by her spiritual heirs as necessary to suit the task of building a permanent church organization in circumstances she could not have foreseen.

During the lifespans of the "first-born daughters," Shaker religion is better described as "feminine" than "feminist." That is, it had no explicit woman's-rights philosophy, but it espoused those Christian moral values—passivity, piety, obedience, and chastity—which were increasingly associated with the "sphere" of women.[13]

Shakerism unconditionally rejected aggressive behavior, including warfare. It emphasized the body as an arena of mystical religious experience and its expression and correspondingly de-emphasized intellectualism, having no educational qualifications for either church membership or leadership. Most radically challenging to patriarchal Protestantism was its rejection of heterosexual intercourse as sinful under all conditions and its fierce criticism of the institution of marriage and of family ties based on "nature" rather than shared values. Marriage and the biological (patriarchal) family were replaced with an ideal of Christian community, as imaged in spiritualized sororal, fraternal, and parent-child relations.

Yet the Shaker religion of Ann Lee's day was no genteel, liberal anti-Calvinist Protestantism of the kind we associate with late-Victorian "feminized" disestablished Protestantism. A vividly imagined hell peopled with evil spirits and lost souls played a central role in early Shaker religion, and the fear of damnation was skillfully used by Ann Lee and the Elders in proseltyzing early converts.[14]

To a large degree the radical, anti-establishment, "feminine" values of early Shakerism reflect the efforts of Ann Lee's followers to honor and build upon the spiritual experience of its female founder. Lee had represented her own process of entering a transformed identity in stories about her spiritual awakening. She was remembered as reporting eloquently through trance behavior and visionary narrative on her subsequent contacts with angels, Christ, and spirits of the dead. Her followers aspired to build a church in which everyone who accepted and acted upon her new gospel message—that sexuality was sinful—would be able to follow her into "the regeneration," a Christlike life of moral purity which would ensure eternal blessedness.

However eccentric or foreign it seemed to some outsiders, early Shaker religious culture inevitably reflected the Anglo-American environment out of which its adult converts came. The first generation of American Shakers converted by Lee and her associates gathered into communities in order to seal themselves off from corrupting contact with the impure "world" of nonbelievers. Yet they necessarily brought with them aspects of that outside world of families and communities which they were rejecting, as they entered into the Shaker life. In succeeding generations, many Shaker leaders were drawn from among those who had been brought up from childhood entirely within the Society's culture. But as a celibate sect, the Shakers continued to depend heavily for survival upon the recruitment of new adult members through revivals and missionary outreach work. Thus despite the stringent rules of separation that created invisible walls between Shaker villages and the outside world, cultural influences from the industrializing and urbanizing northeast United States continually reached the communities and helped shape the religion's nineteenth-century growth. This was as true in the area of thought and feeling about gender as in any other.

It is useful, then, to think of Shakerism's early history as incorporating a dynamic struggle between its original "feminine" (but not feminist) ideals and religious behavior and the Protestant patriarchal value system (itself evolving) into which adult converts to Shakerism had already been socialized. (We will see many examples of this tension between Shakerism's "feminine" and "patriarchal" strains in the literature of the Shaker sisterhood excerpted in this book.)

We can also trace shifting views of feminine spirituality and the meaning of female religious leadership in early Shaker history. Out of the multiple understandings of Ann Lee with which the converts were left at her death, some were considered more appropriate than others by her heirs in the first decades of the nineteenth century—an era when Shakerism was attempting to establish itself in the eyes of the world as a respectable and growing Christian sect with a public, systematic theology. A new exploration of Ann Lee's identity and the meaning of her womanhood was especially in order when a whole generation of younger Shakers was growing up without a firm enough commitment to the ideals of the first leaders.

Over the eighty-year span of time I have proposed as "foundational," Shaker modes of religious expression themselves underwent change. In contrast to the more mainstream Protestantism in the outside world at any given time Shakerism may appear comparatively radical and "disorderly." Yet within its own history there are periods when ordering forces prevail over disorderly impulses, as well as others when the balance shifts in favor of rebellion and ecstasy. During the period of "Mother's first-born daughters," we can see at least two striking examples of important shifts from the disorderly to the orderly mode in worship. The first occurred when the apostolic gifts encouraged during Ann Lee's lifetime were replaced by the ritualized religious dancing and singing of the Wright era (1796–1821). The second such shift happened when an outburst of spontaneous, chaotic visionary trance activity in the late 1830s was largely tamed by the creation of a cohort of official spirit instruments under the control of the leadership.

STUDYING EARLY SHAKER RELIGION THROUGH WOMEN'S LITERATURE

In Shaker history, as in cultural history generally, the recovery of the women's perspectives is an essential step toward a full understanding. The early Shaker sisterhood's religious experience and ideas have not yet been adequately analyzed, in part because of their underrepresentation in early Shaker publications. (This is particularly striking in the foundational period represented in this volume.) The first Shaker publication under a woman's name is from the mid-nineteenth century, Paulina Bates's *Divine Book of Holy and Eternal Wisdom* (1849).

Shaker women's lesser contribution to the more public forms of early Shaker literature is one indication among many of the contradictions inherent in their status in the early years of Shakerism.[15] The hierarchal governance system which developed within the celibate dual-gender religious communities required equal numbers of female and male leaders to oversee both temporal and spiritual realms. Yet a very traditional gender-based division of labor obtained, by which all women, even the leaders, were confined to a "female sphere" of domestic work and administrative concerns—except when very unusual circumstances required an eldress to take up the usual work of an elder, in a temporary violation of the norms.

The women's contribution to the formation of the religion can only be adequately understood through extensive reading in rare early publications by male Shaker leaders and in the ample manuscript writings, such as correspondence and religious testimonials, which have survived, scattered throughout a dozen extensive Shaker manuscript collections.[16] Shaker women's early literature is a rare resource, not just for Shaker historians, but for anyone interested in better understanding the inner lives, and especially the religious imaginations, of women in the American past. From it we can learn something of the values, feelings, thoughts, and social strategies of the sisterhood. It also reflects aspects of the lives of their non-Shaker sisters—the other pious women from rural New England, New York, Ohio, and Kentucky in this era who did not join the Society of Believers in Christ's Second Appearing. The visual designs of the spirit-inspired "gift drawings" created by Shaker sisters at New Lebanon and Hancock in the 1840s and 1850s were clearly influenced by their knowledge of decorative needlework outside the Shaker culture. Similarly, the early writings of the sisterhood are grounded in eighteenth- and nineteenth-century Anglo-American women's self-expressive verbal traditions.[17]

Early Shakerism produced a massive private written record of diaries, journals, correspondence, and testimonials, which is the joy and despair of those engaged in research on Shaker history and culture. This documentation was created in part because a strong pressure for "union" or ideological and social uniformity required close surveillance of all aspects of Believers' spiritual and material lives by the leadership. As the central leadership's emphasis on thorough recordkeeping became increasingly strong in the 1820s, 30s, and 40s, many women contributed to Shaker literature who otherwise would not have left any written record of their lives.

Shaker sisters in the era of Mother's first-born daughters had two occasions for writing: either their leaders were collecting religious testimonial for publication, or, in their administrative capacities as eldresses or deaconesses, they were required to keep careful records of the daily comings and goings of the family, or to correspond with leaders in other communities. During the midcentury spiritualistic revival, the collection of religious testimonials became a vast enterprise when the central leadership required that all religious meetings in which spiritualist events occurred be recorded. Both male and female scribes were appointed in all Shaker families and communities to record the voluminous outpouring of spirit messages generated by spirit instruments over a fifteen-year period.

My aim in this volume is to use early Shaker women's own oral testi-

monial and literature—conversion narratives, correspondence, and spiritualistic forms of expression—to introduce the reader to the many contributions made by women to early Shaker religion. In the introductory
essays accompanying each section of documents, I will provide some context for interpreting the documents included, along with brief discussions
of the ways in which gender questions arising from these writings are
linked with other issues in Shaker religion and history.

Many scholars interested in questions of sexuality and gender in U.S.
history and culture have now begun to discuss the example of Shakerism,
and lively debates go on in conferences, journal articles, and monographs,
about Shaker "feminism." Though this book will draw upon Shaker scholarship—especially that concerned with women's social position and with
gender ideology—I will not attempt to provide the full analysis of these
questions that can now be readily found elsewhere.[18]

A FEMALE EXPERIENTIAL BASIS FOR MALE-GENERATED SHAKER THEOLOGY

Phyllis Bird has argued, in relation to ancient Israelite religion, that

> the question of gender frequently appears to intersect or parallel other
> key issues in the study of religion, such as the distinction between ortho-
> dox and heterodox practice, central and peripheral institutions, "high and
> low" traditions, religion and magic, the sacred and the profane.[19]

This pervasive split between the "masculine" (high, formal, orthodox,
and rational) and "feminine" (low, informal, heterodox, and experiential)
spheres in religion is well illustrated when we look at the relationship of
gender to the production of theology within early Shaker religion. The
contributions of Ann Lee herself and of her "first-born daughters" to the
"new gospel" narrative of early Shakerism provided an essential experiential foundation for the later theological rationalizations penned by a few
male leaders.

Ann Lee was understood by her followers to have embodied in some
way a "second appearing" of Christ, which ushered in a new era of earthly
blessedness, but there were different understandings of exactly what this
meant, especially in the early days.[20] By 1808, Shaker theological writings
revealed to the world that the Christ spirit had come a second time, in the
female form of Ann Lee, as part of a divine plan to complete the work of
redemption begun through the appearing in the male form of Jesus.[21] Ann
Lee had brought a "new gospel," without which no one could really ap-
preciate and act on the full significance of the Christian message. It had
been revealed to her in a vision that the original sin of Adam and Eve had

been the indulgence of lust through sexual intercourse. This allowed humanity's "animal" nature to overwhelm the "spiritual" nature which originally unified it with the divine. She taught that to "enter the redemption" one had to confess all of one's former sins to one's Shaker elder or eldress and renounce sin (including all sexuality), thus beginning a new life in which one could imitate and theoretically achieve the "perfect" sinless life of Christ.

This early Shaker theology was developed after Ann Lee's death by a small number of prominent Shaker male leaders and writers as an aid to missionary activity in the frontier territories of Ohio and Kentucky.[22] They aimed at explaining to an audience largely composed of Baptist and Methodist preachers (and through them, their parishioners) why the Shakers believed that this new sect (founded by someone rumored by hostile neighbors of the Believers to be a "drunken old woman") could possibly be the one true church of Christ. Thus these writers (chiefly Benjamin S. Youngs) combed scripture and Christian history in their effort both to elaborate upon Lee's central insights and teachings and to justify religious practices already in existence to a frequently hostile and always highly skeptical world.

One of the most interesting and problematic results of their efforts was a theory of a fully dual-gender godhead. Ann Lee's nature as a female counterpart to the Savior was mirrored at a higher level by a divine Mother, a "bearing" Spirit (understood by some Christians as the Holy Ghost), the female counterpart of the Father god of Jewish and Christian tradition. One of the functions of the "second appearing in the female" of the Christ spirit had been precisely to reveal for the first time the existence and nature of this Mother Spirit.

Though the concept of Holy Mother Wisdom was strictly a male creation, women are highly visible and audible in the orally based testimonial literature that forms the raw material for early Shaker history and theology. Through their storytelling they make a clear contribution to the creation of Shakerism's "myth of the founder." Ann Lee stories (which continued to be collected after a major anthology was published in 1816) functioned both as sacred history and as community folklore. They anchored a whole panoply of ideas about morality, sexuality, spiritual experience, divine guidance, heaven and hell, and the nature of the spirit world for later generations of Shakers who had not known Ann Lee and her first followers. Many of the most prolific storytellers were women who had known Lee in the early 1780s and heard her tell stories about her experiences in England in the 1760s and 70s. Chapter 1, "A Mother in Divinity," provides a sample of the women's stories from the 1816 *Testimonies* to suggest the multiple meanings Ann Lee had for her first followers and the process by which the women's memories of her contributed to an evolving (and contested) "myth of the founder."

Religious testimonial, it should be remembered, was an important spoken-art form in the late eighteenth and early nineteenth centuries, when Shakerism was taking root in New England. It was a particularly important form of self-expression for women, who were far less likely than their brothers to have literary educations or even bare literacy, and whose confinement to the sphere of home and family did not allow many to conceptualize themselves as imaginative artists.[23]

Chapter 1 also includes some stories of miraculous healing, the first testimonial writings by Shaker women to be published (1808), and some conversion narratives, published in 1827, when Ann Lee and the Elders were under attack from a small number of dedicated anti-Shaker writers.

THE PROBLEM OF FEMALE RELIGIOUS LEADERSHIP IN ANTEBELLUM SHAKERISM

As the female founder and head of a new church that claimed to supersede and displace all other Christian sects and denominations, Ann Lee had to confront much curiosity and open hostility in her own lifetime. The strategies she relied on for claiming authority were convincing to her followers but did not ensure the same unquestioned authority for her "first-born daughters." Female spiritual and political leadership remained a serious problem for early Shakerism, in relating to its neighbors and to prospective converts, and even in its own internal community life for many years. In a variety of different ways, in the different Shaker communities, east and west, over its first seventy-five years, the struggle over how to reconcile Shakerism's dual-gender government system and "feminine" religious values with the patriarchal habits and beliefs of many of its members went on.[24]

Certain Shaker men—most notably Joseph Meacham in the early post-Lee years and Frederick Evans of the New Lebanon community in the later nineteenth century—proved to be strong supporters of the principle that female spiritual leaders were as able as males. It was Joseph Meacham who originally created the dual-gender governance system and appointed Lucy Wright not just his partner at the top of the governance hierarchy, but as his designated single successor as well. On the other hand, there were also many occasions when female leaders were challenged by disgruntled male Shakers, some of whom used the "petticoat government" issue to win support for their broader antiadministration grievances. For example, Lucy Smith (the "first-born daughter" whose death in 1852 in New Lebanon marks the ending of an era for the journalist) had lost her position as the Mother of the Pleasant Hill, Kentucky, community in the 1820s as the result of such a genderized power struggle.

Shakerism's "second Mother," Lucy Wright, herself faced such challenges more than once.[25] In chapter 2, "Your Parent in the Gospel," the letters and sayings of Lucy Wright present some of the problems and strategies of the most influential single female leader of early Shakerism after Ann Lee. Lucy Wright's twenty-five-year administration (1796–1821) brought Shakerism to a high-water mark in population (largely through the missionary activity in Ohio and Kentucky which she actively sponsored). During this period of explosive growth, correspondence between her and Shakers who had been sent west to found and lead new communities reveals an administrative style that was quite different from the charismatic and emotionally transparent Ann Lee's.

Lucy Wright was a cautious and compromising, yet energetic, attentive, and intelligent church leader. Her own personal religious experience is only minimally visible in the self-portrait that emerges from her oral teachings and her letters to other leaders, but her impact on Shaker religion is clear nonetheless. She took an interest in creating new, orderly physical worship forms, such as choreographed religious dance, and in using the idea of "the presence of angels" to teach ethical precepts that would advance community life. As befitted the head of an established communitarian organization, much of her attention was absorbed by her administrative efforts to create harmony, unity, and mutually respectful interdependence among quarrelling, jealous, strong-minded community leaders, east and west. In her correspondence with the leading figures of the new western communities in particular, she writes as the spiritual Mother who mediates their quarrels and responds to their pleas for aid and support in a variety of ways.

The leaders of the sisterhood do not figure as highly visible political actors in the correspondence between male community leaders and Mother Lucy Wright. However, they play a strong role in a more "domestic" correspondence which also survives from the period of western community building. In chapter 3, "Poor Child in a Distant Land," we hear how the western missionary efforts affected the women's sphere of activities—what secular and spiritual work the missionary sisters did under primitive living conditions, and how they maintained relationships with eastern mentors, friends, and relatives over great distances and many years of physical separation. We hear both the formal and informal voices of these female community leaders speaking among themselves, building and maintaining the personal relationships upon which "union" and "order" depended. In so doing, they contributed to a less visible domestic side of Shaker religious culture. Not directly acknowledged in these letters, however, are the tensions endemic to community life in a theocratic society built on an ideology of perfect love among true believers. Such tensions—along with equally important expressions of love—are the subtext of many of the spirit messages from the prolonged midcentury spiritualistic revival.

WOMEN'S PARTS IN THE MIDCENTURY
SPIRITUALISTIC REVIVAL

Shaker religion underwent an extraordinary period of politicization during a spiritualistic revival which began in the 1830s and was quickly institutionalized by the central leadership. Originally spontaneous
spirit-possession activity on the part of low-status young girls and women
(and a few boys) alluded to Ann Lee's theory of missionary contact between
the living Believers and the spirits of the dead. This trance behavior quickly
turned into communal rituals of renewal largely controlled by the leadership and instruments supported by the leadership. Like the spirit possession behavior of young girls that ushered in the witchcraft accusations of
seventeenth-century Salem,[26] these spiritualistic events are especially useful for helping us see covert conflict between the generations, between the
sexes, and between individuals or factions within communal families. Attention to the role of women as spirit mediums both in the earlier, spontaneous phase and in the leadership-controlled period can also illuminate
the changing character of Shaker religion as experienced in the Shaker
sisterhood as the last of "Mother's first-born daughters" disappeared from
among them.
    The revivalistic period of "Mother Ann's work" (1837–1850s) ultimately
produced an immense body of spirit-inspired songs, oral messages, drawings, dramatic enactments, and writings. These are an invaluable though
enigmatic resource for the study of Shakerism's religious culture, as are
the religious meeting journals kept at this time specifically to enable the
leadership to keep track of all spiritualistic events. The meeting journals
allow us to see through Shaker eyes the curious, frequently fantastical
goings-on as different groups of spirits succeeded one another in the collective Shaker imagination.
    In chapter 4, "The Heavens Are Open," we view both the spontaneous
and the leadership-controlled spiritualism, focusing on the ways in which
the sisterhood in particular was drawn to the mediumship roles. We hear
of newly instituted purification rituals on mountaintop "feastgrounds" at
each community and rites in which bands of Shakers with spiritual brooms
marched through the houses and community workplaces miming spiritual
spring cleaning. Examples are also included of the prophetic pronouncements and writings of officially appointed spirit mediums. Women as well
as men gained public prominence through speaking for Shaker ancestors
(including Ann Lee and Lucy Wright), other noteworthy beings in the spirit
world, and even aspects of divinity, such as the Savior, the Heavenly Father,
and Holy Mother Wisdom. Thus, it was during this midcentury revival

that the abstract theological idea of a "Mother Spirit" created by early male Shaker theologians was embodied concretely in the female figure of the spirit instrument who "received" the visiting Holy Mother Wisdom.

Chapter 4 includes some sample pronouncements from Holy Mother Wisdom's book of prophetic utterance, published under the name of the officially appointed female spirit instrument, Paulina Bates, as *The Divine Book of Holy and Eternal Wisdom* (1849). This book was highly edited by the New Lebanon male theocratic establishment, and in particular by the theological and historical writer Calvin Green. It sums up the paradoxical quality of midcentury Shaker gender ideology. A highly honed, orthodox gender dualism made it imperative that Holy Mother Wisdom should speak through a female writer. Yet the content of what Holy Mother Wisdom says about women is profoundly reactionary.

By the 1850s, many Shakers had become disillusioned with the evident manipulation of spiritualism both by the instruments and by the official leadership. Some had left the Society as a result of the political conflicts that went on under the surface of the spiritualistic events. Most of the official ritual which had been created by spirit messages was abandoned. Holy Mother Wisdom ceased her visitations. A more domestic spiritualism, which emphasized the continuation of comforting individual relationships between living and dead Shakers, survived and even flourished in some circles as the official leadership-orchestrated spirit instrumentality waned and disappeared.

A LEGACY OF SPIRITUALISM FOR FUTURE GENERATIONS

The second half of the nineteenth century brought undeniable emotional and material traumas to the communities, as numbers fell off and major financial difficulties occurred. Yet Shaker religion continued to evolve on a strong base of spiritualism, and the sisterhood played an increasingly prominent role in shaping this evolution as the ratio of women to men continued to increase.

In seeking to renew Shaker religion for themselves and others after midcentury, some influential sisters came into conflict with central leadership. Several were perceived as "disobedient," and actually left Shakerism to continue the search elsewhere. Sisters Roxalana and Mary Fidelia Grosvenor of the Harvard community left in 1865, later bringing a lawsuit against the Society, claiming that they were expelled for religious nonconformity—perhaps their incorporation of techniques from "mesmerism" into their spiritual lives.[27] Or again, Eldress Polly Smith of the Groveland, New

York, community, was the leader of a "heresy" in the West Family there in the late 1860s, which ultimately decimated its membership. Drawn to the health reform movement initiated by Sylvester Graham, and refused permission by New Lebanon to go out and preach its truths, she ultimately left the community to associate herself with the "water cure" establishment at Dansville.[28]

Other conscientious Shaker women were more successful in their efforts to renew or reform Shaker spirituality. One notable example is Rebecca Cox Jackson, the black visionary and independent holiness preacher who joined the Watervliet community in the 1840s. She became critical of what she saw as Shaker insularity and left in the 1850s to experiment with spiritualism and found her own Shaker family in her native city of Philadelphia. Ultimately, she was able to return in the late 1850s and win permission to operate the Philadelphia family as a legitimate Shaker community.[29]

There were also some highly influential Shaker sisters in the later nineteenth century who managed to import elements from the philosophical and religious ferment outside the Society into their understanding of "true" Shaker religion. One example is Eldress Anna White of the progressive North Family New Lebanon, coauthor (with Leila Taylor) of the important late volume of Shaker history and theology, *Shakerism: Its Meaning and Message* (1904). After a dramatic healing experience through the help of a Christian Science practitioner, in 1906 White came to see Christian Science as inheriting some truths of early Shaker religion that had been allowed to lapse during the years of declining membership.[30]

Sister Aurelia Mace of Sabbathday Lake, Maine, was another influential Shaker sister who became a tireless publicist for a liberal and ecumenical vision of Shaker religion and community life at the end of the nineteenth century. Like Eldress Anna, she spoke before groups in "the world" that she believed shared some or all of the Shaker philosophy, even if they were not Believers.[31]

Victorian and early modern Shaker spiritual life has never been systematically studied, but we do know that periodic "revivals" came to particular families and communities. Sister Aurelia described in a language of latter-day spiritualism one such intense seven-year period initiated by the sisterhood at Sabbathday Lake in the 1870s:

> Sixteen young Sisters and little girls met together regularly, through summer's heat and winter's cold, hardly ever missed a Wednesday evening. They sung, marched, danced, spoke their lovely thoughts, rejoiced and wept together as occasion required. The great doors were opened and they occupied the room, large as it was. Were they alone? Nay—Many from beyond the veil would come into their midst. They could almost hear the rustle of their garments and a flow of Divine Inspiration would reach their spirits which they would feel at no other time nor place.[32]

THE SISTERHOOD'S CONTRIBUTIONS TO EARLY SHAKER RELIGION

The literature excerpted for this volume brings to the foreground the long-overshadowed agency of "Mother's first-born daughters," the pious women inspired by Ann Lee who helped shape the religious culture of early Shakerism. The women's contributions were frequently made from the less visible, traditionally subordinate and separate "female sphere"— despite the pressure exerted by the Shaker dual-gender ideology to make the roles of the sexes exactly balanced and complementary. To trace the effect of gender ideas on Shaker religion through these writings is to reveal an interlocked series of ironies and paradoxes.

It was a woman, employing the "disorderly" mode of religious ecstasy by which social outsiders typically seek religious authority, who created (and elicited in others) the experiential basis of the religion and articulated its two central behavioral requirements (confession of sins and celibacy). Other women made a crucial contribution to creating a flexible, ambiguous "myth of the founder" which could attract a variety of converts. It was primarily the women's stories of Lee's own spiritual transformation that formed the central theme upon which formal Shaker theology, written by males, elaborated—sometimes quite uneasily. Her personal awakening experience was transformed into the theological concept of Christ's Second Appearing in the Female. Future male leaders were then required to elaborate upon this concept not only to skeptical and hostile audiences in the "world," but to new Shakers brought up with traditional patriarchal values as well.

One result was the creation of Holy Mother Wisdom as a theological abstraction. She was logically necessary if one accepted the premise that gender was an essential aspect of both fall and redemption and believed that creation must be understood as anticipating both. But by the time she was given a voice, in the official ritual of the midcentury revival, she was clearly the tame subordinate of the Father and seemingly of little relevance to the actual spiritual experience of Shaker women or men.[33]

A second apparent gender paradox of early Shaker history is that it was an early male leader, Joseph Meacham, who incorporated women into the Shaker leadership system, even going so far as to appoint a female "first elder" to succeed him. Here again, however, female contributions were crucial. In this case Meacham was influenced both by Ann Lee's teachings about her nature and both his own experience of female leadership, both of Ann Lee and of Lucy Wright.

Wright was a very different kind of female religious leader from Ann

Lee, one whose values and talents were perhaps better adapted than Lee's to the institution-building period over which she presided. Rather than seeking authority and empowerment through ecstatic experience, Wright taught her followers "you need not labor for gifts to dream dreams; if you keep your union together there will be nothing to separate you from Mother." For twenty-five years Wright elevated the values of "order" and "union" over all others, constantly stressing the need to subordinate the demands of the self to the needs of the group. With no access to trance or vision herself, and no direct appointment from Lee, Wright's authority as a woman leader was more open to question than Lee's had been. She presented a significantly more "feminine" (and genteel) model of a woman in authority than had Lee herself. Yet in eschewing the ecstatic mode of female religiosity and in insisting on governing unpartnered, Wright clearly represented the threat of matriarchy ("petticoat government") to some of her male subordinates.

During the midcentury revival, with which the era of the "first-born daughters" ended, Shaker religious culture returned briefly to its original disorderly "feminine" mode, testing the authority of its leaders, its "mothers and fathers," past and present. But the spiritualism that was so powerful a conversion tool in the days when Shakerism was a loosely organized charismatic movement took on a very different meaning in the highly ordered, hierarchical theocracy of nineteenth-century Shaker communalism. It quickly became clear that spirit-inspired instruments could undermine (or bolster) the authority of official leaders and that spiritualism could either release rebellious and destructive impulses within the community, or push lukewarm Shakers toward reform. The leadership acted to bring "order" for the sake of "union." In another irony, the unorthodox ecstatic mode was firmly harnessed to serve the purposes of orthodoxy; and Holy Mother Wisdom was used as the mouthpiece of midcentury "true womanhood" rhetoric.

In its official midcentury spiritualism, Shakerism's orderly, orthodox, "masculine" or patriarchal side temporarily tamed its disorderly "feminine" side—at a high cost to its own spiritual integrity and to its credibility with many Believers, as it turned out. Yet, in a further interesting irony, Shaker leaders were so committed to religious gender dualism by this time that both sexes were compelled to take on less traditional gender roles in this revival. Thus though women spontaneously began it, men who resisted were subjected to heavy pressure to join in the outwardly "disorderly" activities as well. And though a few men spontaneously gravitated to the type of prophetic spirit-instrument role that brought with it a public, policy-making function, women like Paulina Bates were also appointed to take on this function for the female sphere.

A close view of Shaker religion brings many contradictions into focus, yet this sect founded by a woman is of perennial interest to students of

American religion and culture. Continually shaped by both female and male social and spiritual experience, Shakerism has survived and evolved for over two hundred years (numerically dominated by women for most of that time). It has produced an extraordinarily rich spiritualistic culture which is only now beginning to receive the attention Shaker material culture has enjoyed for years. We are fortunate that the leadership emphasized so strongly the gathering and preserving of oral and written testimonial, especially in the dramatic formative years documented in this book.

A NOTE ON THE EDITING OF DOCUMENTS

Shaker manuscripts and early printed documents offer challenging problems to the editor who seeks to establish clear and maximally accessible texts for the nonspecialist modern reader. Many early manuscripts were written by women and men with very little formal education and are consequently unparagraphed, unpunctuated (or punctuated only with dashes), and idiosyncratically (and inconsistently) spelled. (One example of such a manuscript with its original spelling and punctuation preserved is "Holy Mother Wisdom's Fold," included in chapter 4.) Even manuscripts produced by relatively well-educated early leaders reflect very casual late-eighteenth-century stylistic norms (for example, see Joseph Meacham's letter to Lucy Wright, included in its original form as Letter 1 in chapter 2). Correspondence frequently survives only in the form of edited copies of originals produced at a later date by more literate scribes. These employ what were then current Shaker punctuation and spelling conventions. Such conventions themselves changed considerably over the fifty years covered by this volume.

The early printed books from which I chose excerpts also vary in these conventions over time. Moreover, they reflect different degrees of editing by the small number of Shaker brethren responsible for the Society's publications (especially Calvin Green and Seth Y. Wells of New Lebanon). Some were prepared hastily under frontier conditions (such as the 1808 *Testimonies of Christ's Second Appearing*); others were clearly labored over for many months and much changed in the process (as for example Paulina Bates's *Divine Book of Holy and Eternal Wisdom*).

After much internal debate about these issues, I have decided not to attempt to preserve all these individual eccentricities and inconsistencies of style. Rather, in silently normalizing spelling and punctuation, I have sought to make the texts as transparent vehicles of the early Shakers' meaning as possible. I recognize that some scholars might have found exact transcriptions more valuable, but in the present volume my goal is to help early Shaker writing speak to a broader audience. (Original punctuation is retained in quotations from manuscripts that were not edited for inclusion in this volume.)

In excerpting a series of passages from much longer original documents, I have indicated in footnotes the sections of the originals on which I drew. All omissions are marked with ellipses (. . .). In some cases I have added paragraph breaks in order to bring out the narrative logic or central themes more clearly. I have also added some section titles in longer pieces, to help guide the modern reader through a potentially difficult text. My own editorial insertions are indicated in single brackets []; original Shaker footnotes or editorial insertions are provided in double brackets [[ ]].

SHAKERISM'S PRIVATE LANGUAGE

Like all self-enclosed communities and perhaps more than some because of its explicit policy of separating Believers from the moral and spiritual contamination of the "world," early Shakerism developed its own conventional expressions, a jargon of words and phrases with specialized Shaker meanings. As readers of these texts will quickly discover, many of these Shakerisms cluster around central religious ideas. For example, the idea that suffering and hard work are required as part of a continual journey of spiritual growth finds expression in the repeated use of such interlocked terms as "tribulation," "trials," "travail," and "travel." The spiritual family metaphors so important to redefining relationships among celibate women and men, common members and leaders, are another good example of how Shakerism's common language was affected by its religious ideology.

Many Shaker terms probably originally derived from evangelical Protestant theological ideas and usages (particularly from Methodist and New Light Baptist denominations). Others were based on the remembered sayings of Ann Lee and the other first elders. Hearing frequent repetition of such terms by the leaders in exhortations, testimonials and sermons in religious meetings, and in writing, a new Believer would have gradually absorbed the Shaker connotations of such words and phrases. Modern readers of these texts may find themselves going through a similar learning of Shaker language by immersion—though I have provided some glosses in the footnotes to help expedite the process.[34]

NOTES

1. These quotations come from "Testimonies: or the Wise Sayings, Counsel & Instruction of Mother Ann & the Elders . . . Written by Eunice B[athrick]. Book I" (OClWHi VI B 11; the introduction to this volume is dated 1836); Seth Y. Wells and

Calvin Green, *Testimonies* (1827); Jean McMahon Humez, ed., *Gifts of Power: The Writings of Rebecca Jackson, Black Visionary, Shaker Eldress* (Amherst: University of Massachusetts Press, 1981), 169; and Edward Deming Andrews and Faith Andrews, *Visions of the Heavenly Sphere: A Study in Shaker Religious Art* (Charlottesville: University Press of Virginia, 1969), 70.

2. Despite a dramatic population decline beginning in the middle of the nineteenth century, Shakerism evolved throughout the twentieth century and continues today as a living religion in the small Sabbathday Lake Shaker community, Poland Spring, Maine.

3. Arriving in New York City in 1774 were Ann Lee, her husband Abraham Stanley (or Standerin), her brother William and niece Nancy Lee(s), James Shepherd, James Whittaker, John Hocknell and his son Richard Hocknell, and Mary Partington. Hocknell went back to England and returned with his wife, Hannah Hocknell, and daughter Mary Hocknell, and John Partington, in 1775. Abraham Stanley left the Shakers during the year in New York City. Later Nancy Lee married Richard Hocknell; James Shepherd and John Partington left the Society after Ann Lee's death, in 1784, rather than serve under James Whittaker. While most historians assume that the early Shaker use of the term "elders" refers primarily to William Lee and James Whittaker, and perhaps John Hocknell, Marjorie Procter-Smith points out that "several women are also frequently mentioned as close companions to Lee: Mary Partington, Mary Hocknell, Margaret Leland, Hannah Kendall, and Lucy Wright," and sees them as "a kind of court, which was both attendant on Lee, and apprenticed to her" (*Women in Shaker Community and Worship: A Feminist Analysis of the Uses of Religious Symbolism* [Lewiston, Maine: Edwin Mellen Press, 1985], 17).

4. These American-born members of the inner circle included Joseph Meacham, Calvin Harlow, Margaret Leland, Hannah Kendall, and others.

5. Sally Bushnell Journal, North House, New Lebanon, March 12, 1852 (NOC). Lucy Darrow, who died in 1870 at age 91, was called "the last among us at Lebanon who saw Mother Ann," by ministry elder Giles Avery, in "A Register of Incidents and Events" (NN).

6. The major Shaker communities were Watervliet, New York (formerly Niskeyuna), est. 1787; New Lebanon, New York, est. 1787; Hancock, Massachusetts, est. 1790; Enfield, Connecticut, est. 1790–1792; Canterbury, New Hampshire, est. 1792; Tyringham, Massachusetts, est. 1792; Alfred, Maine, est. 1793; Enfield, New Hampshire, est. 1793; Harvard, Massachusetts, est. 1791; Shirley, Massachusetts, est. 1793; New Gloucester (Sabbathday Lake), Maine, est. 1794; Union Village, Ohio, est. 1806; Watervliet, Ohio, est. 1806; Pleasant Hill, Kentucky, est. 1806–1809; South Union, Kentucky, est. 1807–1810; West Union (Busro), Indiana, est. 1810–1811 and disbanded 1827; North Union, Ohio, est. 1822; Whitewater, Ohio, est. 1824–1825; and Sodus Bay (then Groveland), New York, est. 1826. This list is based on Edward Deming Andrews, *The People Called Shakers*, 290–91.

7. I am using the term "foundational" very broadly here, so as to include both the height of population (somewhere between the 1830s and 1860) and the mid-century revival. Shaker historians have yet to agree upon a consistent periodization scheme and terminology. The end date of the era of "Mother's first-born daughters" is somewhat arbitrarily chosen. The year 1854 represents the eightieth anniversary of Ann Lee's arrival in New York, as well as the year of Hannah Cohoon's "Tree of Life" vision and drawing.

8. Laurel Ulrich, *Good Wives: Image and Reality in the Lives of Women in Northern New England, 1650–1750* (New York: Random House, 1982), 216.

9. See, for example, Carroll Smith-Rosenberg, "The Cross and the Pedestal: Women, Anti-Ritualism, and the Emergence of the American Bourgeoisie," in *Disorderly Conduct: Visions of Gender in Victorian America* (New York: Oxford, 1985), 129–64. Smith-Rosenberg argues that what she variously calls "anti-ritualism," "enthusiasm," and "disorderly religion" has demonstrated greater appeal for women than men, not only in Evangelical Protestantism, but also "within Albigensianism and other popular medieval religious movements; within Reform Protestantism in France and Germany in the sixteenth century; in New England during the antinomian controversy; and in England during the Civil War" (135).

10. See Carol F. Karlsen and Laurie Crumpacker, eds., *The Journal of Esther Edwards Burr, 1754–7* (New Haven: Yale University Press, 1984); Nancy F. Cott, "Young Women in the Second Great Awakening," *Feminist Studies* 3, 1/2 (Fall 1975), 15–29; Mary P. Ryan, "A Woman's Awakening: Evangelical Religion and the Families of Utica, New York, 1800–1840," *American Quarterly* 30, 5 (Winter 1978), 602–23; Jean M. Humez, " 'My Spirit Eye': Some Functions of Spiritual and Visionary Experience in the Lives of Five Black Women Preachers, 1810–1880," in Barbara J. Harris and JoAnn K. McNamara, eds., *Women and the Structure of Society: Selected Research from the Fifth Berkshire Conference on the History of Women* (Durham, N. C.: Duke University Press, 1984), 129–43; and Ann D. Braude, *Radical Spirits: Spiritualism and Women's Rights in Nineteenth Century America* (Boston: Beacon Press, 1989).

11. Many students of ecstatic and mystical strands in popular Christian religion draw on I. M. Lewis's classic *Ecstatic Religion: An Anthropological Study of Spirit Possession and Shamanism* (New York: Penguin, 1971) to help explain the relation between these expressions and the social identity of the possessed person. See, for example, Clarissa Atkinson's analytic biography of the fifteenth-century English mystic, *Mystic and Pilgrim: The Book and the World of Margery Kempe* (Ithaca: Cornell University Press, 1983), especially 213–16. Stephen J. Stein, in "Shaker Gift and Shaker Order: A Study of Religious Tension in Nineteenth-Century America," *Communal Societies* 10 (1990), has suggested that the Shaker midcentury revival can be understood in part in the context of Lewis's ideas, p. 111. Also see Carroll Smith-Rosenberg's sophisticated discussion of the relationship between revivalism and women's rights agitation, on the one hand, and the simultaneously developing "cult of true womanhood," on the other, in *Disorderly Conduct*, 161–64.

12. Valentine Rathbun, *Some Brief Hints of a Religious Scheme* (Salem: 1782), as quoted in Edward Deming Andrews, *The People Called Shakers*, 44–46.

13. This is a somewhat modified version of Barbara Welter's well-known list of qualities associated with "true womanhood" by women's magazines and religious literature of the nineteenth century. Welter's "four cardinal virtues" are "piety, purity, submissiveness, and domesticity." See Barbara Welter, "The Cult of True Womanhood 1820–1860," in *Dimity Convictions: The American Woman in the Nineteenth Century* (Athens, Ohio: Ohio University Press, 1976), 21. Many historians have by now discussed what is called the "feminization" of mainstream (Calvinist) Protestant religion in the United States during the nineteenth century—by which different analysts often mean different things. One of the earliest and best discussions is Welter's article, "The Feminization of American Religion: 1800–1860" (1973), in *Dimity Convictions* (83–102). Welter defined feminization "through its results—a more genteel, less rigid institution—and through its members—the increased prominence of women in religious organizations and the way in which new or revised religions catered to this membership" (84). Also see Ann Douglas, *The Feminization of American Culture* (New York: Avon, 1977), especially 1–196.

14. In part in response to the liberalizing of Calvinism in the outside world, male Shaker theological writers and spiritual leaders by the middle of the nineteenth

century were engaged in strenuous internal debate about the origin of evil, specifically the devil. See New Lebanon ministry correspondence, especially January to August, 1854, OClWHi IV B 11.

15. The question of women's "equality" within Shaker communalism has now been much discussed. With some differences in emphases, most historians of Shakerism agree that at least in the early period, Shakerism lacked a feminist philosophy and gave governance roles to women primarily because the separation of the sexes required it. See especially Louis J. Kern, *An Ordered Love: Sex Roles and Sexuality in Victorian American Communes—the Shakers, the Mormons and the Oneida Community* (Chapel Hill: University of North Carolina Press, 1981), and Marjorie Procter-Smith, *Women in Shaker Community and Worship.*

16. One recent comparative study of Shaker women's religious ideas and practices with those of women in other celibate communities, Sally L. Kitch's *Chaste Liberation: Celibacy and Female Cultural Status* (Urbana: University of Illinois Press, 1989), relies primarily on the plentiful publications by prominent Shaker women of the last quarter of the nincteenth century.

17. Edward Deming Andrews and Faith Andrews first noted the indebtedness of the spirit drawings to needlework traditions, in *Visions of the Heavenly Sphere*, 79.

18. Three recent studies which analyze the relationship between Shaker religious ideology and the power relations between the sexes are Marjorie Procter-Smith, *Women in Shaker Community and Worship*; Sally L. Kitch, *Chaste Liberation*; and Linda Mercadante, *Gender, Doctrine, and God: The Shakers and Contemporary Theology* (Nashville: Abingdon Press, 1990). Other useful discussions of gender issues are contained in Priscilla J. Brewer, *Shaker Communities, Shaker Lives* (Hanover, N. II.: University Press ot New England, 1986); Lawrence Foster, *Religion and Sexuality: Three American Communal Experiments of the Nineteenth Century* (New York: Oxford University Press, 1981); and Louis J. Kern, *An Ordered Love.*

19. Phyllis Bird, "Gender and Religious Definition: The Case of Ancient Israel," *Harvard Divinity Bulletin* (Fall 1990), 12.

20. See Clarke Garrett, *Spirit Possession and Popular Religion from the Camisards to the Shakers* (Baltimore: Johns Hopkins University Press, 1987), 231, 237, for a brief discussion of the controversy over the several possible Shaker understandings of the meaning of the "second appearing," in the days immediately following Ann Lee's death.

21. For a fuller discussion of the theological arguments made about the necessity of the second appearing in Benjamin Youngs's *The Testimony of Christ's Second Appearing* (1808), see Linda Mercadante, *Gender, Doctrine, and God*, 76–90.

22. It now seems very clear from the early manuscript records and accounts of early seceders that none of the Shaker sisters had a part in the actual composition of the early Shaker theological publications. Nor is there is any evidence to suggest that Holy Mother Wisdom was a concept promulgated by Ann Lee or any other early Shaker woman.

23. As a religious and communitarian culture, Shakerism did not encourage individual self-expression in secular literary forms, including those (such as the novel or nonreligious poetry) to which women were frequently drawn as writers and readers in nineteenth-century America.

24. Priscilla Brewer discusses the imbalances that developed on the basis of gender within Shakerism's leadership structure in *Shaker Communities, Shaker Lives*, 51–52.

25. See Jean M. Humez, " 'Weary of Petticoat Government': The Specter of Female Rule in Early Nineteenth-Century Shaker Politics," *Communal Societies* (Spring 1992), for more details.

26. There are now many useful interpretations of the spirit possession in Salem, which parallels in several important respects the disorderly onset of midcentury Shaker spiritualism. See especially Paul Boyer and Stephen Nissenbaum, *Salem Possessed: The Social Origins of Witchcraft* (Cambridge: Harvard University Press, 1974); Carol F. Karlsen, *The Devil in the Shape of a Woman: Witchcraft in Colonial New England* (New York: Norton, 1987); and David D. Hall, *Witch-Hunting in Seventeenth-Century New England, A Documentary History, 1683–1692* (Boston: Northeastern University Press, 1991). Several historians of colonial New England, including Karlsen and Laurel Ulrich, have now noted how closely seventeenth-century witchcraft possession and eighteenth- and nineteenth-century preconversion behavior resembled each other. Karlsen puts it succinctly: "Interestingly, the [Great] Awakening produced physical responses in its (mostly young or female) adherents that resembled those of the possessed, but the Awakening's leaders plucked these brands out of the burning without the intermediate step of exorcizing their demons. Resistance to the Lord rather than resistance to the Devil distinguished the agonies of the unconverted from those of the possessed" (255). Also see Ulrich's discussion of the contrasting responses of religious authorities to the role of female "seer" in seventeenth-century Salem and eighteenth-century New Hampshire (223–26).

27. Thomas Hammond's "Church Record," (MHF). Clara Endicott Sears claimed that "after being ardent Shakers for forty-six years Roxalana and Fidelia left the Society to study mesmerism in 1865" (*Gleanings from Old Shaker Journals* [Harvard, Mass.: Fruitlands Museum, 1916], 276).

28. Edward R. Horgan, *The Shaker Holy Land*, 103–104; Giles Avery, "A Register of Incidents and Events," September 29, September 30, October 3, 1868; and March and April 1871 (NN).

29. See my introduction to *Gifts to Power*.

30. She became "a thorough convert," as Leila Taylor wrote in "A Remarkable Statement," in *Christian Science Journal* (December 1907), 543–49.

31. She wrote letters to her local paper, *The Bangor Messenger*, in 1883–1884, as well as to the official organ of Shakerism based in New Lebanon, *The Shaker Manifesto*. A collection of her essays and other writings appeared in 1889 under the title *The Aletheia: Spirit of Truth*. In a 1904 talk before a Ba'hai audience at Greenacre, in Eliot, Maine, she cited the Buddha and Plato as examples of others before Jesus who had manifested the Christ Spirit. See Leonard Brooks, "Sister Aurelia Mace and Her Influence on the Ever-Growing Nature of Shakerism," *Shaker Quarterly* 16, 2 (Summer 1988), 47–60.

32. Aurelia Mace Journal, August 16, 1896 (MeSl).

33. See introduction to chapter 4 for further discussion.

34. Readers may also wish to consult the "Glossary of Shaker Terms" in Priscilla Brewer's *Shaker Communities, Shaker Lives*, xv–xviii.

MOTHER'S
FIRST-BORN
DAUGHTERS

Frontispiece: Group of Shaker sisters, Canterbury, New Hampshire. The Winterthur Library: The Edward Deming Andrews Memorial Shaker Collection, SA 199.

1. "A MOTHER IN DIVINITY"
Ann Lee Imagery and Narrative, 1808–1851

INTRODUCTION

Illiterate herself, Ann Lee is reported to have called her followers "my epistles, read and known of all men."[1] Though her followers were left with vivid memories of their experiences with her and her associate elders when she died, in 1784, it was nearly twenty-five years after her death before the systematic collection of these memories began. It continued while there were any Shakers alive who could tell stories of the early days—through the late 1850s.[2] As a result of this strong commitment to "gather up every crumb," a very large testimonial literature about Ann Lee exists (much of it in unpublished manuscript anthologies). In this chapter, a selection of some of the earliest, most dramatic and most influential images of Ann Lee show something of the multifaceted "myth of the founder" created by Lee's spiritual descendants.[3] Though they were excluded from the arena of formal theology by tradition, early Shaker women were at least as important as Shaker men, and frequently more important, in creating the Ann Lee imagery that was the experiential basis for the theology.

As the charismatic leader of a millennialist movement, Lee probably relied primarily upon the emotional impact of her presence, the dramatic appeal of her message about celibacy, and an ecstatic mode of worship to convince her followers experientially of her authority and the rightness of her leadership. After her death, however, the contradiction between her gender and her role as a head of a new church became a central problem to be solved by her followers. Later male leaders in particular needed to create a myth of the founder that would explain their extraordinary decision to join a church headed by an unknown working woman and would help sustain belief without her presence. They needed to educate and impress would-be converts; to repel, rebut, and chastise enemies of the faith; and to comfort and inspire old and new Believers. Their early nineteenth-century publications wrestle with the problem of creating a coherent understanding of "this extraordinary female whom God had chosen, and in whom Christ did visibly make his second appearance."[4]

Women's Healing Stories in the First Published Testimonials

During the first twenty years after Ann Lee's death, her nature and role in the founding of the sect were not revealed in public discussions of Shaker doctrine.[5] These were the years of gathering the scattered early converts into communities and consolidating a governance system that would enable the communities to survive. These were also the years of persuading Believers that this governance system should include a "Mother" parallel in authority to a "Father" and of dealing with the first major internal rebellion, which led to a "falling away" of members in 1795.

The Shakers did not mention Ann Lee in print until the missionaries to the Kentucky revival in 1806 wrote urgently back to the eastern leadership that they needed a tool for proselytizing and dispelling wild rumors already circulating about the sect's founder. Finally and reluctantly, Lucy Wright authorized the publication of *The Testimony of Christ's Second Appearing* (1808), the first Shaker publication to acknowledge Ann Lee's foundational role in Shaker history and theology.[6] Here for the first time a few influential Shaker males committed the Society in print to the concept of the dual-gender godhead. Here, the necessary existence of a Mother in divinity was inferred from the role played in human salvation by the Christ Spirit's "second appearing," in the person of Ann Lee.

The Testimony of Christ's Second Appearing also contains the first published religious testimonial by Shaker women. Shaker sisters contributed several "affidavits" offering "instances of that miraculous power by which the most stubborn unbelievers were confounded, and the faith of others strengthened, who continue to be living witnesses of the truth, to the present day."[7]

The healing gift was not considered a prerogative of the leadership, but was equally accessible to all as a manifestation of divine power during the early pentecostal period of Shakerism. Though some early Shaker elders like John Hocknell clearly emerged as especially talented healers, it is notable that healing gifts were administered by female believers as well as males. In the stories in this chapter Anna Northrup's touch heals Susannah Cook, and Mary Turner prays for and receives the gift to heal the ax wound of her son.[8] Ann Lee's own role as a healer in the volume is remarkably limited (as is true in later collections as well). She only appears once as healing by the laying on of hands, and that is in the story by Mary Southwick.[9]

Contradictory Images of Ann Lee in the 1816 Testimonies

In 1808, the same year in which *The Testimony of Christ's Second Appearing* was published, an extensive oral history project was launched by Shaker leaders in the eastern communities. First suggested by Rufus Bishop (then one of the elders in the Church at New Lebanon) and approved by Lucy Wright, then the head of the United Society, it aimed (belatedly) at gathering up all eyewitness memories of Ann Lee and her closest associates (Mother Ann and the Elders).[10] To create a volume of "Mother's sayings" for the benefit of future generations of Shakers who would otherwise grow up ignorant of the early days, Rufus Bishop in New Lebanon, Elizur Goodrich in Hancock, Seth Y. Wells in Watervliet, and elders in other communities interviewed "old Believers" who remembered something of the 1780s and 90s.[11] According to the collectors, the older Believers soon "seemed to have their memories refreshed in a remarkable manner, so that they could clearly recollect many things which had been gone from them for nearly 30 years; so that there was an evident gift of God in it. . . . "

The written texts derived from these interviews and other testimonial materials were edited and the stories rearranged into thematic chapters. The testimonial was then supplemented with an introduction and a historical narrative by the editors—primarily Calvin Green. The finished volume, *Testimonies of the Life, Character, Revelations and Doctrines of Our Ever Blessed Mother Ann Lee, and the Elders with Her . . .* , was printed in an edition of 20 copies and sent to the leadership of all Shaker communities, east and west.[12]

Within a very short time, however, the publication of some of these early Ann Lee stories came to seem very dangerous to the eastern Shaker leadership who had worked on the project. By 1818, the New Lebanon Ministry was urgently advising Ohio and Kentucky leaders not to make "indiscriminate" use of Mother Ann's *Testimonies*:

> The contents of the book are a precious treasure given only to the people of God, and too sacred to be polluted by the hands of the wicked. . . . It is felt that the time is not yet come for it to be generally known, even among believers. . . . If once the little record of Mother's gospel should be exposed abroad we should soon have dogs and wolves enough to devour it. . . . It is therefore absolutely necessary, that great care & wisdom be used respecting the little book. Mother [Lucy Wright] says . . . that she would much rather you would commit it to the flames than to expose it to [your people].[13]

The central ministry at New Lebanon was understandably alarmed at the idea of this internal community document falling into the hands of Shaker enemies. Throughout early Shaker history, the communities produced a steady stream of "turnoffs" or seceders—women and men who for a variety of reasons found it impossible to accept the Shaker way of life. Some of these sought to inflame public opinion against Shaker religion and communal life by publishing sensational accounts of scandalous behavior as well as attacks on their heretical doctine. A particularly striking early example is Daniel Rathbun's 1795 "Letter to James Whittaker," which accuses Ann Lee and the Elders of a whole range of improper and hypocritical behavior—including "hard drinking" and naked dancing.[14]

In the second decade of the nineteenth century, Lucy Wright and her associates in the central Shaker leadership had to contend with Mary Marshall Dyer, an energetic woman who made a virtual career as an anti-Shaker propagandist after a brief residence in the Enfield, New Hampshire, community. In an effort to win back the custody of her children from the Shakers, Dyer waged an aggressive campaign aimed at vilifying the religion and its founder. At the very moment that the 1816 *Testimonies* volume was being recalled from circulation, Mary Marshall Dyer was collecting scurrilous affidavits about Ann Lee and the first elders from New Hampshire neighbors of the Shakers, accusing Lee of being a "fortune-teller" and thief. New Lebanon leaders had been informed by New Hampshire leaders that some of the Believers "who have heard these [1816] testimonies have since turned off and spread shocking reports."[15] Some of the more dramatic stories about Ann Lee's sayings and doings in the 1816 *Testimonies* could indeed have been used by active Shaker enemies like Marshall Dyer to support their claims that Lee was a false prophet, a pretended miracle worker, and a disreputable woman.[16]

In addition to the problem of keeping potentially controversial Ann Lee imagery out of the hands of Shaker enemies, the leading Shaker brethren responsible for this volume were concerned about the issue of the text's historical credibility. Supervising editor Seth Y. Wells acknowledged in a letter to Benjamin Youngs in 1822 that

> there were many cases in which I could not satisfy myself as to the identical words, yet I was satisfied as to the substance & therefore wrote them as I found them in the manuscripts of Br. R. & Br. Elizur.

Conscientiously assuring himself and Youngs that he "would not for the world, knowingly write any thing to publish to the world, that she [Ann Lee] would disapprove; for I feel that I must give an account of what I write," Wells rationalized his editorial procedures with reference to New Testament scripture:

> I considered that the words of Jesus Christ were not & could not be given literally; because in the first place it is obvious that the different evangelists often relate the same speeches in different words. . . . And second, . . . because they were spoken mostly, (if not all) in the Hebrew tongue. . . . Hence I have concluded with others whom I have conversed with on this subject, that if the spirit & substance of Mothers words are there, & the language as near as can be recollected, it cannot well be disputed or faulted on the score of words. . . . [17]

Shakerism at this time needed a consistent, credible, and positive understanding of its founder, in order to defend itself from external enemies and internal political problems. Nevertheless, highly contradictory and ambivalent images of Lee emerge in the 1816 *Testimonies*—contradictions which tend to be smoothed out or rationalized in later Shaker historical biography of Lee. She is both endowed with amazing supernatural powers and is said to be "a poor weak woman"; she reports on mystical union with Christ and the angels, yet she threatens her followers with damnation if they disobey her teachings.

The contradictions in Ann Lee imagery derive in part from real tensions within Shakerism at this time over the meaning of her ministry and over the authority of female religious leaders in general. Ann Lee had reportedly convinced the dubious Baptist elder Joseph Meacham of her right to head the church, as a kind of "deputy husband" (to use Laurel Ulrich's term) of the absent Christ.[18] After her death, when Meacham headed the Society, he had elevated Lucy Wright to a position parallel to his own. Yet this did not solve the problem of female authority within Shakerism permanently. Shaker manuscript records for the first thirty years of the nineteenth century abound with evidence of continuing male rebellion against female headship—a sensitive issue once again in the years after Joseph Meacham's death, when Lucy Wright became the undisputed single head of the Society.[19]

An equally important explanation for the highly contradictory quality of the Ann Lee imagery is to be found in the different kinds of orally based narrative included in the volume. Three types of narrative, each having a different claim to historical accuracy and a distinctive literary mode of shaping the reader's impressions of Ann Lee, are represented in the selections from the 1816 *Testimonies* in this chapter.[20]

First is a group of personal experience stories by Ann Lee's first American converts. These recall events which took place in the 1780s, when the original English Shakers were proselytizing in the Albany area and in New England. The tellers of these stories were generally considerably younger than Ann Lee when they knew her, and the stories are frequently about their first meetings with her, or times when they had just been converted to her dramatic new gospel. In such stories, Lee is seen primarily from outside and as it were from a very much lower level. She frequently emerges as a towering, awe-inspiring, and even frightening figure: a strict, even harsh, mother, whose reproofs are remembered clearly for thirty years; or a terrifying seer and prophet, who reported flying with visionary wings through the heavens and the prisons of hell. Some of this material confirms the ex-Shaker Daniel Rathbun's emphasis on terror as a means of winning and holding converts.[21]

A second group of narratives in the 1816 *Testimonies* represent themselves as Ann Lee's personal experience stories. Grouped together in three chapters of the 1816 *Testimonies*,[22] these stories form a kind of embedded oral-historical self-portrait of Ann Lee, largely in first-person speech. This portrait is more internally consistent than that presented in her followers' experience stories, and it also presents a more attractive and consistently sympathetic character. It is based on the memories of a relatively small number of informants, the majority of them women.[23] As these stories demonstrate, Ann Lee's female followers were particularly important carriers of her most impressive metaphors for the spiritual transformation experience which marked her entry into a new life as a religious leader. This group of Shaker sisters was responsible for providing posterity with some of its most powerful and positive images of Ann Lee.

A third kind of narrative provides yet another stream of Ann Lee imagery in this book, one which may seem puzzlingly ambivalent to modern readers. The extended narrative of the journey through New England covers events during the two-year missionary trip undertaken by Lee and her associates, shortly before her death (1781–1783). It suggests a tension between the narrator's ideal for a leader of an embattled religious community and his view of her as a "weak" and persecuted woman. On some occasions she is seen as heroic, able to defend her community against attack. For example, she faces down "a company of unruly men rushing up to the door on horse back" by speaking "with great power and authority" in a way that makes the horses "run backwards." More frequently, through the language used by the narrator, emphasis is placed on her victimization, and particularly on the way her sex makes her vulnerable to such victimization.[24] This narrative clearly reflects the ambivalent attitude toward Lee as a female leader and founder which was developing among male leadership during this period.[25]

Defenses of Lee in the 1827 Testimonies

If the 1816 *Testimonies* was intended primarily as an internal document, an attempt to provide an understanding of Ann Lee for future Believers, the next major collection of Ann Lee imagery, published in 1827, was aimed primarily at a non-Shaker audience and intended as a direct rebuttal of the anti-Shaker propaganda of Mary Marshall Dyer and others. Those providing most of the testimonial material in *Testimonies Concerning the Character and Ministry of Mother Ann Lee* . . . (1827) were in their sixties or older and were remembering a period in their lives now about forty-five years distant.[26] The Ann Lee that emerges from the stories in this volume is, not surprisingly, much less wild and contradictory.

A central purpose of these accounts was to lay to rest the repeated charges about alcohol abuse by Ann Lee and the Elders. Elizabeth Johnson says that while with Mother and the Elders at Hancock and Richmond, she knew of "their being accused of swearing and blasphemy, drunkenness and fighting; but I saw none of these things among them." Hannah Cogswell indignantly rejects the idea that her life could have been inspired by a delusion: "I feel confident that in point of suffering and persecution, sorrow and cries to God day and night for the salvation of lost souls, she came the nearest to the Lord Jesus Christ of any other woman on earth. I have not been following a drunken woman nor a harlot—nay, in no wise."

One of the most spirited defenses of Lee against the alcoholism charge comes from Zipporah Cory, who says that because her own father was "a downright drunkard," she was particularly sensitive to liquor:

> even the very smell of rum has ever been nauseous and disgusting to me from my earliest infancy; and no object ever appeared so odious in my sight as a drunken person, whether male or female. . . . Had Mother or the Elders been given to intoxication, I should most certainly have discovered it and should have quit them at once. I feel confident that the spirit of God which Mother Ann possessed could never abide in the soul of a drunkard.

Several of the extended testimonies in this 1827 volume are well on their way to becoming full-length spiritual autobiographies, centering on conversion experience. They adhere closely to the plot formula developed in the nineteenth-century evangelical conversion narratives so plentifully published and read in the world outside Shaker communities.[27] After brief (if any) accounts of the seeker's childhood, they describe in some detail a period (usually in adolescence) of fruitless seeking for a true Christianity not to be found in the churches. There is a period of "conviction of sin" and fear of damnation, when as Elizabeth Johnson puts it, "my soul grew darker and darker, and became more and more separated from God." Then the New Lebanon revival of 1779 promised "that Christ was near at hand." Visiting the "singular people" near Albany brings the seeker to the Shakers. Frequently there is a strenuous period of opposition from one or another family member, or the seeker's own resistance to conversion by the "strange" Shakers (a strong theme in the account of Zipporah Cory). The culminating emotional transformation experience is described in dramatic, moving (but nonetheless conventional) language, sometimes directly echoing that used in the Ann Lee personal experience stories of 1816. Elizabeth

Johnson's account of her conversion at the touch of Ann Lee is one of the most impressive:

> She came singing into the room where I was sitting, and I felt an inward evidence that her singing was in the gift and power of God. She came and sat down by my side, and put her hand upon my arm. Instantly I felt the power of God flow from her and run through my whole body. I was then convinced beyond a doubt that she had the power of God, and that I received it from her.

Two of the stories excerpted here (Thankful Barce's and Lucy Wight's) begin with a vision, which is later understood to be confirmed by the conversion to Shakerism.[28] Yet there is also a strong emphasis on the authority of everyday experience. Readers are challenged to suspend their anti-Shaker prejudices while they listen to an honest woman's presentation of what she has seen and heard.

Gathering Up the Last Crumbs in the 1840s and 1850s

The collection of oral testimony about Ann Lee continued on a much smaller scale after the publication of the 1827 *Testimonies*, primarily on a grass-roots level in the sisterhood at the Harvard community (to judge from what manuscripts survive).[29] No more new volumes of Ann Lee imagery were ever published. The outpouring of spirit-inspired pronouncements during "Mother's work" beginning in the late 1830s was to absorb much of the attention of Shaker leadership and to produce a massive literature which kept all available writers busy. Much of the testimonial material collected during the 1840s was aimed at defending the authenticity of the spirit inspirations.[30] This chapter ends with some brief examples of efforts by sisters from the Harvard community to "gather up the crumbs" from the last remaining of "Mother's first-born children."

Jemima Blanchard had been interviewed for the 1816 volume, but only one of her stories of Mother Ann appeared there. Over a number of years, beginning in the 1830s, the Harvard sisters Eunice Bathrick and Roxalana Grosvenor collected her entire conversion account. One story collected by Grosvenor describes Sister Jemima's "singular gift" in meeting:

> She saw hell open, and she seemed to be on the brink in imminent danger of falling. In her efforts to keep out of it she crept around the room on her hands and knees uttering the most heartrending cries. Mother stooped to her and in her agony, wringing her hands, she got hold of Mother's apron. She knew not what it was or that Mother was near her but it felt like a comfort and support to her, so she kept winding it around her hands.

The chapter includes a story of "interviews with Mother" gathered from Elizabeth Wood at the Enfield, Connecticut, community in 1851, when she was 82.[31] Her account includes a rare comic moment during a mob attack at Enfield, when a pursuer is caught on the stairs by David Meacham and "spanked"; and a nicely detailed and comparatively mundane depiction of Ann Lee and her early associates visited by other early Shakers at Watervliet in 1782. We see them at work and in meeting. We hear Ann Lee handing out work assignments and giving instructions and telling mothers to take care of their own children; hear her explain the prophetic meaning of her sickness to the young Elizabeth. We watch her behavior in the "laboring" meetings, as she sees angels turning Elizabeth as she whirls, and as "the sisters gathered round her and hugged and kissed her." Unedited and told in plain unrhetorical language, Elizabeth Wood's manuscript narrative nonetheless suggests that it was Ann Lee's integration of ecstatic religion with a shrewd and authoritative domestic management of her converts that laid a strong experiential basis for what later formally developed into Shaker communalism.

NOTES

1. [Rufus Bishop], *Testimonies of the Life, Character, Revelations and Doctrines of Our Ever Blessed Mother Ann Lee, and the Elders with Her . . .* (Hancock: J. Tallcott and J. Deming, Junrs., 1816), 308.

2. Although I have not done a complete survey of the manuscript testimonial literature, the latest date I have found on which elderly Shakers were interviewed about the days of Ann Lee is 1857 (Thankful Goodrich at Hancock) (OClWHi VIII B 188).

3. Parts of my discussion here are based on a more extensive analysis published under the title, " 'Ye Are My Epistles': The Construction of Ann Lee Imagery in Early Shaker Sacred Literature" (forthcoming article in *Journal of Feminist Studies in Religion*, [Spring 1992]).

4. [Benjamin Seth Youngs and Calvin Green, eds.], *The Testimony of Christ's Second Appearing . . .* (1810 ed.), 2.

5. The first official Shaker publication, Joseph Meacham's 1790 *A Concise Statement of the Principles of the Only True Church . . .* did not mention Ann Lee's name. Calvin Green said in his "Biographic Memoir" (OClWHi VI B 28) that the idea that Christ had fully made a second appearing in female form was "offensive" to the "orthodox," and was not preached publicly until the summer of 1808 (50). Also see Clarke Garrett, *Spirit Possession and Popular Religion*, who thinks an explicit policy of downplaying Ann Lee's role in early Shakerism originated with the second male leader to succeed her, Joseph Meacham (231–32).

6. Parts of this story appear in chapter 2, letters 5 and 10. Lucy Wright initially advised the western brethren against revealing the dual-gender godhead in this work. However, when she learned that the 1808 volume did include this doctrine, she proclaimed herself satisfied with it.

7. The eleven miraculous healing stories published in *The Testimony of Christ's*

Second Appearing were collected at the neighboring New Lebanon and Hancock communities in April 1808. A total of six men and ten women told stories over a five-day period in the two communities. The women whose stories are included in this chapter ranged in age from their thirties to their seventies at the time the stories were collected.

8. Six male healers and four female healers are featured in these stories.

9. Also see two of Ann Lee's healing gifts, below, in the 1827 Testimony of Prudence Hammond.

10. Elizur Goodrich, the former husband of Lucy Wright, initially opposed the project, on the ground that too much time had passed for Believers to be able to recall the exact words of Ann Lee. Lucy Wright overruled him, however, and "directed Br. Rufus to go round & speak to the Elders in the different families & let them enquire of their members who had been acquainted with Mother & the Elders, and let them labour for a gift in the matter & see what could be recollected." When the interviews began to bear fruit, Goodrich was convinced that the accounts were accurate and joined the project as a collector (letter from Seth Y. Wells, Watervliet, to David Darrow, Union Village, Ohio, April 25, 1822, OClWHi IV A 78).

11. Diane Sasson points out that the printed versions of the "sayings" probably represent reworkings of other written versions no longer extant and thus are not reliable evidence for studying Shaker speech patterns (Sasson, *The Shaker Spiritual Narrative* [Knoxville: University of Tennessee Press, 1983], 68).

12. Hereafter referred to as the 1816 *Testimonies*. Sources for reconstructing the history of this project are the New Lebanon leadership correspondence for 1818, 1819, 1822, and 1823 (OClWHi IV A 77 and 78) and Calvin Green's retrospective "Biographic Memoir" (OClWHi VI B 28), 152–53.

13. Shaker leadership expressed particular concern with keeping secret certain events that took place at Ashfield (Seth Y. Wells, Watervliet, to Benjamin S. Youngs, South Union, February 22, 1819; OClWHi IV A 77).

14. Clarke Garrett provides a judicious and ultimately convincing discussion of the two primary scandalous accusations made in a number of early Shaker seceders' accounts. He concludes that both naked dancing (as a self-mortifying religious practice) and the alcohol addiction of Ann Lee and her brother William during their very last two years of life probably had some basis in reality. He suggests the possibility, following the seceder William Haskett, that "the practice of using alcohol as a means of generating visions and gifts" may have "developed only gradually," and "become a serious problem only after the leadership's return to the Berkshires" in 1783 (*Spirit Possession and Popular Religion*, 202–12).

15. Draft letter from Seth Wells to Benjamin Youngs, n.d. [1818?] in OClWHi IV A 77. Wells wrote: "We are accountable and responsible to posterity for what we publish concerning Mother Ann & the Elders . . . for this reason, every thing which we publish ought to be well weighed . . . and carefully kept from common scrutiny till the matter is fully examined and finally determined what ought to be preserved and handed down to posterity—and what not—lest something should finally or inadvertantly leak out which may be a dishonor to the testimony."

16. Many of the ecstatic practices and spiritualistic beliefs of the early Shakers from England could have been seen in such a light. For example, Lee depicted herself as a seer with access to the afterworld in which the spirits of the dead were "in prison." She taught that living souls could "bear for the dead," or take on vicarious suffering for the sins of those who died in ignorance of the true gospel. The seceders' accounts say that she and her close associates were understood to have the power to "bind and loose" souls—to damn or to save souls.

17. Seth Y. Wells to David Darrow, April 25, 1822 (OClWHi IV A 77).

18. Laurel Ulrich devotes a chapter of *Good Wives* to colonial New England women's roles as deputies of their husbands, pointing out that "under the right conditions any wife not only *could* double as a husband, she had the responsibility to do so," in order to keep the family business thriving during the husband's absence or in the event of his incapacity or death (*Good Wives*, 35–50).

19. I have developed this argument at greater length in " 'Weary of Petticoat Government': The Specter of Female Rule in Early Nineteenth-Century Shaker Politics."

20. For a more extended discussion of these issues, see my paper, "Ye Are My Epistles." I have organized the excerpts in sections to emphasize these distinct types of narrative.

21. See "Testimonies of Ann Lee's Followers (1816)," below. The seceder Daniel Rathbun claimed that "The Mother's ministration being attended with visions, revelations, unknown tongues and prophecies, as we accepted, we dare not but believe what she said, and that they were what they pretended to be; they often threatened us with damnation, and the loss of our souls, if we disbelieved, or disobeyed them" (Daniel Rathbun's *Letter to James Whittaker*, 1785, as excerpted in Mary Dyer's *A Portraiture of Shakerism*, 81–82).

22. Chaps. VII, VIII, and IX. These excerpts appear under the heading "Ann Lee's Own Personal Experience Narratives, As Remembered by Her Followers (1816)," below.

23. In the 1816 *Testimonies* as a whole, sixty-seven women and fifty-four men are listed as sources of stories. Many more women than men serve as active transmitters of Ann Lee's own personal experience stories. Mehetabel Farrington is singled out by the Shaker editors as a remarkably gifted and accurate source of information.

24. A good example is the episode in which a mob pulled Ann Lee out of hiding "feet foremost" out of a house and drove off with her in a carriage, "committing at the same time, acts of inhumanity and indecency which even savages would be ashamed of," in the narrator's indignant and prurient language.

25. The introduction and much of the narrative surrounding the oral testimonial in the volume were written by Calvin Green and, to a lesser extent, Seth Y. Wells. This narrative is represented by the excerpt titled, "Narrative of the Journey through New England (1816)," below.

26. According to Calvin Green's "Biographic Memoir," the older Shakers initiated this project themselves, and Calvin Green took their testimonial down, while Seth Wells again edited the volume (374). The ages in 1827 of the women whose testimonies I include in part or in full in this chapter are as follows: Thankful Barce (68), Hannah Cogswell (64), Zipporah Cory (62), Prudence Hammond (67), Elizabeth Johnson (78), Anna Matthewson (64), and Lucy Wight (70). (Note that Lucy Wight is not to be confused with Lucy Wright, the Society's Second Mother.)

27. For an analysis of how testimony evolved into formal autobiography within Shaker literature, see Diane Sasson, *The Shaker Spiritual Narrative* (Knoxville: University of Tennessee Press, 1983). A recent book by Virginia Brereton, *From Sin to Salvation* (Indiana University Press, 1991) provides an excellent discussion of nineteenth-century evangelical women's published conversion narratives.

28. Diane Sasson discusses the structural function of the vision in Shaker autobiography, in *The Shaker Spiritual Narrative*, chapter 3, 44–66.

29. Roxalana Grosvenor produced four different anthologies of oral-historical material about Ann Lee and the elders, derived largely from the period of Lee's residences at the Square House in Harvard during the mission to New England, 1781–1783. Brother Arnold Hadd of the Sabbathday Lake Shakers has pointed out in a recent conference paper, "And So Keep My Way Ever Holy: Roxalana Grosvenor

and the Testimonies" (given at the Harvard Shaker Bicentennial, July 20, 1991), that the *Testimonies* published in 1816 have a strong New Lebanon bias, whereas the manuscript testimonies collected by Grosvenor do a better job of representing events from Lee's Harvard residence. One of Grosvenor's manuscript anthologies is scheduled for publication by the Sabbathday Lake Shakers in the near future.

30. Space considerations also entered into my decision not to include 1840s testimonial in the present volume. Linda Mercadante has done an interesting preliminary analysis of some of this testimonial as collected from spirit instruments at Harvard, in order to see whether Shaker women actually experienced deity as dual-gendered during this period. See Mercadante, *Gender, Doctrine and God*, 127–46.

31. Eunice Bathrick and Roxalana Grosvenor each made multiple copies of their anthologies for presentation to different Shaker leaders (well into the late 1860s and early 70s) and there is much overlapping between their work. Four volumes by Eunice Bathrick are in the Western Reserve Collection (VI B 10, 11, 12, and 13) and another is in the New York State Library Collection (Item 324).

Mary Southwick, of Hancock, testifies: That about the beginning of August, 1783 (being then in the twenty-first year of her age), she was healed of a cancer in her mouth, which had been growing two years and which, for about three weeks, had been eating, attended with great pain and a continual running, and which occasioned great weakness and loss of appetite.

That she went one afternoon to see Calvin Harlow to get some assistance. That Mother being at the house, Calvin asked her to look at it. That she accordingly came to her and put her finger in her mouth upon the cancer, at which instant the pain left her and she was restored to health and was never afflicted with it afterwards.

Taken from the mouth of the said Mary Southwick the 23rd day of April, 1808. In presence of Jennet Davis, Rebecca Clark, Daniel Cogswell, Daniel Goodrich, and Seth Y. Wells.

(Signed) Mary Southwick. . . .

Susannah Cook, of Hancock, testifies: That in the spring of the year 1783 (according to the best of her remembrance), she was healed of an issue or fever sore, under which she had suffered very much for the space of seven years, and could find no relief from doctors, though much labor and pains were taken for her recovery.

That having faith to be healed by a gift of God, she went six miles, to Luther Cogswell's, where a number of the brethren and sisters were assembled. That her feelings led her to apply for a healing gift to Anna Northrop, who was then laboring under great power of God. That she received a healing gift from Anna's hand, which instantly restored her.

That previous to her receiving this gift, she was not able to walk one mile without great difficulty and greatly increasing her disorder, but that she was never troubled with her old complaint afterwards. That soon after, she travelled about forty miles on foot [[to Watervliet]] and could travel any distance on foot without any inconvenience.

Taken from the mouth of the said Susannah Cook the 23d day of April, 1808. In presence of Daniel Goodrich, Seth Y. Wells, and others.

(Signed) Susannah Cook

Mary Turner, of New Lebanon, testifies: That her son Jonathan (since deceased), being about nine or ten years of age, was chopping wood at some distance from home and by a stroke of the ax received a very bad wound on the top of his foot. [[His father, *Gideon Turner*, testifies that he could lay his finger at length in the wound.]] That he was brought home and she, seeing it bleed excessively, was greatly troubled, not knowing what to do for him.

That she went into another room, kneeled down and cried to God, and soon felt the power of God run down her arm and into her right hand— instantly her hand seemed to be filled with the power of God, accompanied with such a delicious balsam smell, as she was unable to describe. That, feeling confident that it was a gift of healing for her son, she returned directly into the room and put her hand on the wound, and it instantly ceased bleeding. She then walked the floor, came again and laid on her hand a second time; this she repeated seven times, gently stroking the wound, during which time it closed up and was healed, leaving only a small seam.

That she then bound it up. This being Saturday afternoon, the next morning she unbound it and found no other appearance of the wound than a small white seam resembling a white thread, after which he attended meeting, went forth in the worship of God, was fully restored, and found no inconvenience from the wound afterwards.

Gideon further testifies that while Mary (the child's mother) was stroking the wound, he saw the flesh gradually gather and close up, leaving only a small red streak about the size of a knitting needle, and that he was restored as above described.

Taken from the mouths of the said Mary and Gideon, April 25th, 1808. In the presence of Daniel Goodrich, Seth Y. Wells and others.

(Signed) Mary Turner, Gideon Turner.

NOTE

1. Source: Benjamin Seth Youngs and Calvin Green, eds., *The Testimony of Christ's Second Appearing* . . . (1st ed., Lebanon, Ohio: 1808; 2d ed., Albany: 1810); chapter X, "Evidences accompanying the Second Appearing of Christ," 486–89. (Pagination refers to 1810 edition.)

TESTIMONIES OF ANN LEE'S FOLLOWERS (1816)

Stories of First Meetings[1]

In the time of the first opening of the testimony in this country, the extraordinary intelligence which was circulated abroad concerning this new and strange religion and the mighty power which attended the subjects of it drew many discerning and inquiring minds to search into the truth of these things. Many inquiries were made from time to time by different individuals during their first interviews with Mother and the Elders, concerning many particular things which appeared new and strange to the inquirers.

Joseph Meacham and Calvin Harlow were among the first that visited this little Church for the purpose of searching out the truth of their religion. After much conversation and many critical inquiries, in all which they received plain and satisfactory answers, Joseph sent Calvin to Mother with the following observation and query, namely: "Saint Paul says, Let your women keep silence in the churches; for it is not permitted unto them to speak; but they are commanded to be under obedience, as also saith the law. And if they will learn any thing, let them ask their husbands at home: for it is a shame for a woman to speak in the church. But you not only speak, but seem to be an elder in your church. How do you reconcile this with the apostle's doctrine?"

Mother answered, "The order of man, in the natural creation, is a figure of the order of God in the spiritual creation. As the order of nature requires a man and a woman to produce offspring; so, where they both stand in their proper order, the man is the first, and the woman the second in the government of the family. He is the father and she the mother; and all the children, both male and female, must be subject to their parents; and the woman, being second, must be subject to her husband, who is the first; but when the man is gone, the right of government belongs to the woman: so is the family of Christ."

This answer opened a vast field of contemplation to Joseph and filled his mind with great light and understanding concerning the spiritual work of God. He clearly saw that the new creation could not be perfect in its order without a father and a mother: That as the natural creation was the offspring of a natural father and mother, so the spiritual creation must be the offspring of a spiritual father and mother.

He saw Jesus Christ to be the father of the spiritual creation, who was now absent; and he saw Ann Lee to be the mother of all who were now begotten in the regeneration; and she being present in the body, the power and authority of Christ on earth was committed to her; and to her appertained the right of leading, directing, and governing all her spiritual children. [[Jethro Turner]] . . .

Soon after the gospel began to open, Israel Chauncey, of New Lebanon, went to visit the Church at Watervliet. While he was gone, Elizabeth (his wife) had a remarkable vision, in which she conceived herself at the Church and saw Mother and the Elders, and Israel with them, in the worship of God and under great operations of the power of God. Israel appeared to be in great distress of soul and body, and his flesh was turned to a purple color.

In this situation she saw him put his hands upon Mother's shoulders and heard him say, "Pray Mother forgive me; for thou knowest all the sins that I have committed from my youth up, to this day." Mother answered in these words: "Thy sins are gone, open before hand, to judgment." And immediately he was released from his sufferings, and his flesh returned to its former color. Mother then took Elizabeth by the hand and led her into another room, and immediately her vision ceased, and she found herself at home in her own house.

After Israel returned, Elizabeth opened the vision to him. He said, "It was a true vision of God; these things were shown to you, as plain as if you had been there and seen them with your bodily eyes." On hearing these things, the whole family was filled with the power of God and with great joy went forth and labored under the beautiful operations of the power of God, in which they continued all that night, without sleep.

A few days after this, Israel and Elizabeth both went to see the Church, and when they arrived, Mother came to the wagon, and Elizabeth knew her to be the same woman she had seen in vision; and Mother took her by the hand and led her into the house. After supper, Mother led her into the meeting and said, "Love the mighty power of God." The second night after their arrival, they had a very joyful meeting, in singing, shouting, dancing, leaping and clapping hands.

The following morning, Mother led Israel and Elizabeth out of the house and spoke to them as follows: "Last night, when we were in the worship of God, I saw a number of souls rise from the dead, and come into the resurrection of life. And when you [[Israel]] was here before, I saw your mother [[His mother had been dead thirty years]] and when you was released, and your flesh turned to its natural color again, she was released also and came into the resurrection. And now you must confess all the sins that you have ever committed, one by one." They immediately complied and confessed their sins in the presence of each other.

After they had confessed their sins, Mother said, "Now you must go home and set your house in order, for there will be great numbers of people there to visit you soon." Then addressing herself to Israel, she said, "Israel, you have begun to bear for other souls,[2] and you must never give out, till the last soul is gathered in. When you get home, tell your father and step-mother that your mother is risen from the dead."

They then returned home and shortly after were visited by great numbers of people, according to Mother's words. Israel gave himself wholly to the work of God and was a faithful minister of the gospel until his decease. [[Elizabeth Chauncey]]

Nathan and Hannah Goodrich also came to see the Church in the early part of the opening (June 1780), and arriving just in the time of a sharp testimony against sin, and much company there, the first words they heard were the following: "Strip off your pride and abominations!—We know you; but you do not know us—We have men here that are not defiled with women, and women that are not defiled with men!" These words were from Mary Partington.[3]

The next day Hannah went in to see Mother; and on inquiring after her husband, Mother said, "Let your husband alone—fastening your lust upon him!" Upon this she sat down in a room where Elder Hocknell was under the operation of the power of God. As it appeared strange to her, she prayed in her heart that God would make it known to her whether this was his work or not, and if not, to keep her from delusion. Immediately upon this, one of the elders came and told her her thoughts, just as they had passed through her mind.

These and many other things which they heard and saw soon convinced Nathan and Hannah that this was the work of God and that these people were his witnesses; and according to their faith and conviction, they both confessed their sins. When they had done that, Mother showed them great charity; to Hannah in a special manner. She told her the manner of her own travel in the way of God, from the beginning. [[Hannah Goodrich]] . . .

Mary Knapp, who had already set out to obey the gospel, came also to see Mother and the Elders in prison, and brought her daughter Hannah with her, who was then in obstinate unbelief. Mother spoke to Hannah and said, "Kneel down, you haughty creature, and confess your sins." Then, addressing Mary, she said, "Why did you bring your daughter here? Take her away and make her confess her sins." And as they turned to go to another apartment, Mother said to Hannah, "You shall confess your sins and be a Believer."

Notwithstanding the labors that were made with Hannah, she continued obstinate for some time and told her mother that if there was no other way to be saved, she was sure of going to hell; for she never could join them. Soon after this, on hearing some persons speak of Mother, she in a rage said, "She acted like a drunken squaw."

On uttering these words, she fell under immediate judgment[4] and continued so till she was convicted of her sins and was willing to confess and forsake them and obey the gospel. Soon after that, she went to see Mother again. She confessed her sins to Elder Hocknell but did not get released from the judgment she felt for speaking against Mother.

In the evening they were all called to kneel down, and Hannah among the rest. While on her knees, her words against Mother came into her mind with such weight that she was compelled to cry out, as if it had been for her life, and pray that Mother would forgive her. Upon which, Mother came and took her into her arms and said, "God forgive you child!" Instantly her judgment was taken away, and she has never had a doubt concerning the way of God since. Hannah is still living in the faith and testifies these things. [[Hannah Knapp]]

Memories of Ann Lee's Doings and Sayings[5]

The manifestations of God in and through Mother were exceedingly great and marvelous. That she was an eminent witness of God, no one could doubt that ever heard and felt the authority of her testimony or experienced the heart-searching power of her spirit; and that she was that distinguished person whom she declared herself to be was beyond all dispute in the minds of her faithful followers; for her works plainly testified it.

In the former part of the year 1781, a large assembly of the Believers were gathered at Watervliet, among whom were Joseph Meacham, Calvin Harlow, Nathan, Ezekiel, and Eunice Goodrich. Mother was at that time under great sufferings of soul. She came forth with a very powerful gift of God and reproved the people for their hardness of heart and unbelief in the second appearance of Christ.[6] "Especially," said she, "ye men and brethren! I upbraid you of your unbelief and hardness of heart."

She spoke of the unbelieving Jews in his first appearance. "Even his own disciples," added she, "after he arose from the dead, though he had often told them that he should rise the third day, believed it not. They would not believe that he had risen, because he appeared first to a woman! So great was their unbelief that the words of Mary seemed to them like idle tales! His appearing first to a woman showed that his second appearing would be in a woman!"

So great was the manifestation of the power of God in Mother at that time that many were unable to abide in her presence. Her words were like flames of fire and her voice like peals of thunder. Well said the prophet, *Who shall abide the day of his coming? For he is like refiner's fire, and like fuller's soap.*

After this Mother was released from her sufferings and began to sing with love and great joy and gathered the people around her; and her countenance was glorious and very beautiful. [[Eunice Goodrich]]

At Joseph Bennett's, in Cheshire, many people were gathered together to see Mother. She kneeled down and wept and groaned in spirit and said, "They do not know who I am, nor my calling." She repeated these words three times. Elizabeth, Phebe and Rhoda Chase, Eunice Bennett, and many others were present. [[Elizabeth Chase]]

The first time that Rhoda Hammond visited the Church [[at Watervliet in 1780]] she had considerable conversation with Mother in private. Mother informed her of the wonderful manifestations of God to her and said she spoke with God face to face as Moses did, and saw the glory of God, and had seen wonderful visions. She also said, "It is through great labor and sufferings that the gifts of God come to me." [[Rhoda Hammond]]

When Mother was at Benjamin Osborn's, in Mount Washington, in conversation with Elizabeth Hill, she said, "I am the first Elder in the Church—I have seen God and spoke with him face to face, as we speak one to another."[7] Elizabeth being then young in the faith, these words of Mother had a powerful effect in confirming and establishing her in the faith. [[Elizabeth Hill]]

Again at the same place Mother was under great sufferings and travail of soul. After which she spoke and said, "The Lord, who brought me over the great waters has redeemed my soul. I hear the angels sing!—I see the glory of God, as bright as the sun!—I see multitudes of the dead that were slain in battle arise and come into the first resurrection!—I see Christ put crowns on their heads of bright, glorious, and changeable colors!—I converse with Christ!—I feel him present with me, as sensibly as I feel my hands together!—My soul is married to him!—He is my husband!—It is not I that speak; it is Christ who dwells in me! [[Jonathan Slosson]][8] . . .

Hannah Goodrich, 1st, being at Watervliet with others, saw Mother very full of power, and her face shone with the glory of God. It reminded Hannah of Moses when he came down from the Mount. Mother then took hold of Hannah's hand and raised it to her head and said, "Hannah, I see your face shine with the glory of God." Hannah said, "Mother's hand is there." Mother replied, "I saw it before Mother's hand was there."

Sometimes Mother used to be taken under great sufferings, so that it would seem as though her life must go from her; at other times she was filled with unspeakable joy and triumph and would say, "I feel as terrible as an army with banners!" [[Hannah Goodrich]] . . .

Job Bishop, being with Mother at Watervliet, opened some visions that he had seen of some of the apostles. Mother, turning to Elder James (who was present), exclaimed, "Aha, James! These are great gifts of God; they are ministering spirits. I have often seen Saint Peter and Saint Paul and conversed with them, and with all the apostles, and with Christ Jesus, my Lord and head; for no man is my head, but Christ Jesus; he is my Lord and head." . . . [[Job Bishop]]

The same year David Slosson and many others being at Watervliet were present with Mother and the Elders, when Mother appeared to be clothed in majesty, and her visage was exceeding glorious. She spoke with great power and said, "I am married to the Lord Jesus Christ! He is my head and my husband, and I have no other. I have walked hand in hand with him in heaven! I have seen the patriarchs, prophets, and apostles; I have conversed with them and I know them! I have seen King David with his robes on, which were of vast extent and inexpressibly glorious! I have seen Job, Saint Paul, and others." She also described their statures and their glory and majesty. [[David Slosson]]

While Mother and the Elders were at Nathan Kendall's, in Woburn, Sarah Kendall and some other young sisters being with Mother in the chamber one day, and after she had been walking the floor for a considerable time, the Elders came in and Mother, addressing them, said, "I have been walking in fine valleys with Christ, as with a lover." [[Sarah Kendall]]

At Watervliet, in 1784, in the presence of a large number of people, Mother spoke as follows: "Christ is ever with me, both in sitting down and rising up, in going out and coming in. If I walk in groves or valleys, there he is with me; and I converse with him, as one friend converses with another, face to face." [[Elizabeth Chase]]

Mother often said that Christ was her lover, that he had promised her his love and she had promised him her love, and that they were lovers together. She also said that she saw Christ and conversed with him face to face. Holding out her hand, she said, "Pretty angels touched my hand. O, what shall separate us from the love of God in Christ Jesus!" [[Hannah Prescott]]. . . .

When Mother and the Elders were at Nathan Goodrich's, in Hancock, Joseph Meacham, Hannah Kendall and others being present, Mother was under great power of God; her soul seemed filled with joy and her countenance shone with beauty; and she spoke these words, "I know that the mysteries of God are revealed unto me; and there is no one that can see through me; any more than an infant can see through its mother." [[Thankful Barce]]. . . .

At another time, while the brethren and sisters were worshipping God in the dance, Mother came into the room and sang awhile. After they stopped dancing, Mother spoke and said, "The room over your heads is full of the angels of God. I see them and you could see them too, if you were redeemed from the nature of the flesh." [[Lucy Prescott]][9]. . . .

At Watervliet, in the presence of Cornelius Thayer, William Scales, and others, Mother said, "I saw William Scales in vision, writing that which was not according to the simplicity of the gospel; and the evil spirits hovered round him and administered evil to him. They looked like crows." And Mother reproved William sharply.[10] [[Cornelius Thayer]]. . . .

Again, in meeting at Nathan Goodrich's in Hancock, Mother said, "I see Ezekiel Goodrich, flying from one heaven to another."[11] [[Ezekiel was a beloved brother, who deceased the third year after the gospel opened.]] And turning to the Believers, she said, "Go in and join his resurrection." She then began to sing, and they went forth and praised the Lord in the dance. [[Anna Northrup]] . . .

Again, Mother spoke to Lydia Matthewson and said, "The apostles in their day saw darkly, as through a glass; but now we see clearly, face to face, and see things as they are and converse with departed spirits and see their states." [[Lydia Matthewson]]. . . .

One morning, Mother came into the room and spoke to Eunice Bennett and informed her that she had been under great sufferings the night past but was supported and comforted in her sufferings by the visions of God. She said she saw the glories of God round about her head and pillow like the colors of the rainbow; that she saw twelve angels come into the room, placed in the form of a heart, six males on one side and six females on the other; these, she said, comforted her. [[Eunice Bennett]]

After Mother returned from the eastward, while a number of brethren were sitting in the new meeting room and conversing about Mother's gifts, Mother, being present, said, "I will tell you a vision I saw of myself. I saw a great gulf fixed between God and the world of mankind; and I had two great wings given to me; and my work was to go up that gulf and fan it away." And, speaking in a very joyful manner, she said, "I did go up the gulf, with my two great wings, and did fan it away—I did fan it away with my two great wings, so that poor lost souls could come to God." [[Isaac Crouch]] . . .

Mother and the Elders uniformly taught the doctrine of a free offer of the gospel to all souls, whether in this world or in the world of spirits:[12] That none could be deprived of the offer of salvation because they had unfortunately left the world before Christ made his appearance, or because they had lived in some remote part of the earth where the sound of the gospel had never reached their ears. Their labors in the work of regeneration were not confined to this world, but extended to the world of spirits; and their travail and sufferings for the salvation of departed souls were often distressing beyond description. . . .

Mother spoke oftentimes, when under great sufferings, of seeing the spirits in prison[13] and often spoke to them. Sometimes she used to speak to them in a very powerful manner and sharply reprove them and bid them shake off their bands. At other times she would tell of seeing unbodied souls, laboring for the power of God, and say that such were in a travel— Then she would smile and speak to them, but often spoke in an unknown tongue. [[Hannah Kendall]] . . .

At Ashfield [[in January 1783]] in the presence of many Believers who were there, Mother said, "I have seen a vision: I saw myself flying up a great gulf—I had great wings; and with the ends of my wings I uncovered the dead, who lay on the banks of the gulf." Again she said, "I have seen a great number (who had been dead), laboring in the worship of God. They had come out of great tribulation. There is no danger of these; for they have had hell enough; but man in the flesh is always in danger." [[Joseph Markham, senr.]] . . .

Soon after Jane Kendall departed this life, Mother spoke to Sarah Kendall, her sister, and said, "I have seen Jane in the world of spirits, and she was praising God in the dance." She also said, "I have seen young Jonathan Wood among the dead, and he was like claps of thunder among them, waking them up." [[Jonathan had then lately deceased.]][14] [[Sarah Kendall]]

At Nathan Goodrich's in Hancock, Mother rose one morning and said, "I have been all night with the dead, and I heard the archangel sound the trumpet; and I heard Ezekiel's voice roar from one prison to another, preaching to the dead." This was not long after Ezekiel Goodrich deceased. [[Thankful Barce]] . . .

David Slosson, having visited the Church at Ashfield and being about to return home, went into Mother's room and was placed in a chair before her; the Elders also being present, David felt himself as in the presence of God and under great weight of body and spirit, but knew not the cause. Mother looked him full in the face and then turned and looked on the Elders, without speaking.

After a short pause, she said, "David, you know not what you feel. I see the dead around you, whose visages are ghastly and very awful. Their faces almost touch thine. If you did but see what I see, you would be surprised."

She then labored in the gift of God and again looked David full in the face, and with an air of joy and love, said, "Child, be not discouraged; for I see the glory of God in thy right eye, as bright as the sun; its form is like the new moon. Be of good comfort, and be not cast down; for the dead gather to thee for the gospel, which thou hast received." [[Thankful Barce]]

One day, while Father William was lying on his bed under great sufferings, Abijah Worster went and kneeled down by his bedside; and while on his knees, he was exercised with peculiar operations. Mother and Elder James being present, Abijah made mention of the sensations he felt. "Yea, yea," said Mother, "I understand you." Then turning to Elder James, she said, "Abijah feels many lifeless states, and he don't know what is the matter with him." Then turning to Abijah, she said, "You are not going into the Kingdom without the progeny from which you sprung; and when you labor and obtain gifts of God, they obtain gifts of God; and when you find mortification, they find it too; they travel as you do." [[Abijah Worster]]

One day, Hannah Kendall, being very unwell, went into the room where Mother was; Mother said, "I do not wonder that you feel as you do; for you have been bearing for the dead. I see a tall soul right behind you now." [[Hannah Kendall]] . . .

While Mother and the Elders were at Ashfield, Lydia Matthewson went to see them, in company with her husband, Philip Matthewson. Lydia, in conversation with Mother, spoke concerning Thomas Matthewson, her husband's father, who had been dead a number of years. She told Mother that he was a very senseless man, as to the things of God, and appeared to have little or no sense about his soul, which formerly caused her great tribulation.

Soon after this, Mother spoke to Lydia as follows; "When you spoke to me concerning Thomas Matthewson, I felt his lost state and labored for him, as faithfully as if it had been for my own soul. And one evening, when the people assembled at the meeting house, I stayed in the dwelling house; and I felt the power of God come upon me, which moved my hand up and down like the motion of wings; and soon I felt as if I had wings on both hands; and I saw them, and they appeared as bright as gold. And I let my hands go as the power directed, and these wings parted the darkness to where souls lay in the ditch of hell; and I saw their lost state.[15]

"Elder James was at the same time preaching to a number of the world in the meeting house; and I saw a number of the dead, who were willing to hear; and they arose at the sound of the trumpet of the gospel, through the preaching of Elder James. And Thomas Matthewson arose and went into the meeting house.

"After this, I felt a gift to go into the meeting house, without any knowledge of what I was going for; but being led by the power of God, I went through the assembly and found Philip Matthewson lying on the floor, apparently like a dying man. His father's state had fallen upon him. I took him by the hand and told him to rise up, and he obeyed; but it was some time before he was fully released from that state which had fallen upon him. But his father united with the testimony of the gospel." [[Lydia Matthewson]] . . .

In reproving and condemning sin[16] and all manner of evil, in feelings, words, and actions, Mother's power was beyond description. Though she would often bear with lost, dark souls, who were blinded and corrupted with sin, till her life seemed almost spent through sufferings, yet at times, when she felt a gift of God to reprove their wickedness, the power of her spirit seemed like flames of fire and the words of her mouth more dreadful than peals of thunder; so that the most stubborn and stouthearted would shake and tremble in her presence, like a leaf shaken with a mighty wind. . . .

Jonathan Slosson received a measure of faith and confessed his sins, while Mother was at Poughkeepsie, but was bound in his affections to a young woman who was in a similar condition, for which reason neither of them were able to gain any gospel strength, but were hinderances to each other. In this situation, Jonathan, never having seen Mother, went to Watervliet to see her just after she returned from Poughkeepsie.

Shortly after he entered the house, Mother came into the room. Jonathan, with his back to the fire and the skirts of his coat drawn forward, asked, "How does Mother do?" To which she replied, "If I am your Mother, young man, I'll teach you to turn your face to the fire, not your back; for heating your backside by the fire enrages lust. It shows ill breeding and bad behavior for people to stand heating their backsides by the fire." Jonathan received the admonition and took his seat facing the fire.

Mother then spoke to him as follows: "God will bring down the haughtiness of man and stain the pride of all flesh. Jonathan, do you let that woman alone; you have no business with her. God will break in pieces the man and maid. If you want to marry, you may marry the Lord Jesus Christ. He is my husband, and in him I trust."

After a little pause, she said, "I see the glory of God, both in visions and revelations! I hear the angels sing! I see the dead arise and come to judgment!" Turning again to Jonathan, she said, "Jonathan Slosson, forsake your lust and that woman, and you shall be my son. The marriage of the flesh is a convenant with death and an agreement with hell; forsake it and be my son. I have seen you and all your father's family in the visions of God." [[Jonathan Slosson]] . . .

Again, at Watervliet, the Believers were attending the funeral of Wm. Bigsby, a Believer from Littleton, and a number of the world was present. While Elder James was addressing the assembly on the occasion, there was a man of the world, who made considerable appearance, kept continually coughing. Mother advanced toward him and spoke with authority, saying, "Stop your coughing! It is the devil barking through you—Be still, and hear the word of God!" The man ceased coughing, and Elder James proceeded without any further interruption. After he had done, Mother spoke and said, "We have power to bind and to loose."[17] [[Mercy Bishop 2nd]]

Rebecca Slosson and a number of other sisters being at Watervliet in January 1784, and being one day employed in washing, Mother came into the room and reproved them sharply for their wastefulness and said, "It is a sin to waste soap, or anything else that God has given you. If you knew the torments of hell, you would fear God in all you do and say." [[Rebecca Slosson]] . . .

Soon after Phebe Chase received the testimony of the gospel, she was much wrought upon in outward operations. Feeling somewhat ashamed of her operations, and thinking it would do the world no good to see them, she strove to conceal herself at such times, to avoid being seen by the world, but never opened her feelings to any one about the matter.

About this time she was at Harvard and saw Mother, whom she had never seen before. Mother told her what her thoughts and feelings had been and said, "You ought to let your light shine, that others may see your works, your faith and repentance, that they may take knowledge of the way of God. You ought to stand forth and let the world see the great power of God which you have upon you, and it will convict them." [[Phebe Chase]] . . .

At Harvard, in a time of great mortification, a large number of Believers being assembled together, Mother came into the room with a gift of reproof and said, "You are lacking of faith in the gifts and power of God. When I was in England, the wicked once came with a mob to take me. When I had got out of the house, I felt a gift to sit down on the ground; and the power of God came upon me and stretched out my arm straight from my body, and I could not bring it back again.

"The wicked came to take me up; but they had not power to move me but were obliged to go away and leave me. And I believe that God is as able to preserve me through persecutions and sufferings until my work is done, as he was to stretch out my arm." [[Lucy Prescott]]

At Ashfield, there was once a great collection of people of all sorts, from various and distant places, who came to see Mother, many of them full of unbelief. Mother came forward and addressed them as follows: "Why do you come from such a distance, spending your time and money to see me, while you judge me in your hearts to be a witch?" Then speaking with great authority, she said, "You that are guilty, come forward, and humble yourselves to God, and confess it." Three of the multitude came forward and confessed that they were guilty of that charge. [[Duncan McArthur]] . . .

Some time in November 1783,[18] Jabez and Phebe Spencer, their daughter Mary, and a number of others were on a visit at Watervliet; and just before they came away, they went into Mother's room to take their leave of her. She sat up in her bed under great sufferings and addressed them as follows:

"Be faithful to keep the way of God; if you do, you will be guarded by good angels as really as the wicked are by evil spirits. Every soul is accompanied by good or evil spirits; and the good or evil spirits gather mostly to that part of the body which contains the most sensations and faculties. The head is the ruling and governing part of the whole body; therefore it will contain the most good or evil of any part of the body; and as the whole body is governed thereby, so the good or evil spirits gather there and rule the whole body.

"The head of a wicked man will suck in evil spirits until it is full of them, like a sponge filled with water; so likewise the faithful who are laboring to resist every evil temptation and crying to God for protection will be filled with good spirits and will be guarded by the angels of God, who will protect them day by day."

After Mother had ended her discourse, Phebe went to her bedside and expressed her thankfulness for the privilege that she and her family had had with her. Mother made no immediate reply, but soon after spoke and said, "When you was speaking, I saw two souls standing by you, one at your right hand, and the other at your left. The one that stood at your right hand was a bright, active, glorious soul; but the one on your left was a black, dark, dismal soul; and he laid his head on your left shoulder." [[Mary Spencer]] . . .

At Watervliet, the first winter after the opening of the gospel,[19] Mother and the Elders having been engaged in private labors with some who had opened their minds, Mother came into the meeting room where many young Believers were assembled, and being in the visions of God and under great impressions of mind concerning the wrath of God against sin, she addressed them as follows.

"If you commit sin with beasts, your souls will be transformed into the shape of beasts in hell. I now see some in hell whose souls are in the shape of dogs, horses, and swine. They appear in the shape of such beasts as they committed sin with; and this is laid upon them as a punishment of that sin.[20]

"Men and women in this world can please themselves, by gratifying their lusts; and if they do not overcome their passions by the gospel, they carry them into the world of spirits with them. Death does not destroy these passions, nor make them less powerful; but souls in hell feel their lustful passions rise a thousandfold stronger than in this world; and yet they can find no way to gratify them. Therefore, their lust is their torment; and it torments them in proportion to its rage.

"And more than all this, they have to feel the wrath of God against that filthy nature; and this is still a greater torment to them than the torment of their lusts. The more people give way to the gratification of their lusts in this world, the stronger their passions will grow, and the more their lusts will rise in hell; and their torments and plagues will rise in proportion; they will be bound and tormented in the same parts where they have taken their carnal pleasure.

"I now see in open vision souls in hell under torment for their sins committed through lust, enough to take away your natural lives, if you could see them as I can. They are bound in the prisons of hell, and their torment appears like melted lead, poured through them in the same parts where they have taken their carnal pleasure." [[Mehetabel Farrington]] . . .

Mother, in expressing her love to the brethren and sisters, used sometimes to speak to them in these words; "Ye are my epistles, read and known of all men: Ye are all the interest I have in this world." [[David Slosson]]

Though our blessed Mother was a woman of few words, yet her soul was filled with divine wisdom;[21] and when she spoke, her words were in the demonstration of the spirit, and with power, and always adapted to the occasion. Many precious sentences were occasionally spoken both by her and the Elders to the brethren and sisters individually, which had a powerful effect and left a lasting impression on their memories. . . .

Esther [[Brackett]] again visited Mother at Ashfield, and while there she felt a great desire to receive the gift of vision and believed that if Mother would promise it to her, she should certainly have it. Accordingly she asked Mother for the gift of vision. After a short pause of solemn silence, Mother replied, "If you will labor for it you shall have it."

Esther returned home and after a few days, as she was one morning on her knees at the breakfast table, she felt a great gift of sorrow, and wept with much freedom. In this situation she saw Mother kneeling by her side, but she did not speak to her. After breakfast she kneeled and again saw Mother by her side. After rising from her knees, Mother appeared before her, and raising her hand, she stamped upon the floor, saying, "Be cheerful! be cheerful! be cheerful!"

Esther was then moved upon to laugh and continued laughing all that day, and could not refrain from it. From that time, she was blest with the gift of vision, which continued through Mother's day, so that she could see Mother and converse with her at any time when she labored for it, as well as though they had been present together in the body. . . .

When Anna Northrup first saw Mother,[22] she received faith in the second appearance of Christ in Mother, confessed her sins, and received the power of the Holy Ghost. But feeling a deep sense of her sinful life, she kneeled down in prayer to God that she might be forgiven. Mother said to her, "I freely forgive you, and I pray that God may forgive you; and I will go and prepare a place for you, that where I am, there you may come also." . . .

A number of different times, Mother took Mehetabel Farrington by the hand, and leading her back and forth, often asked her this question; "Mehetabel, will you stand with me and be a witness for God?" Mehetabel as often answered, "Yea Mother I will." [[It is worthy of notice that Mehetabel has had a singular gift to state, with peculiar correctness, the testimonies, speeches, and divine manifestations of Mother and the Elders, as well as other remarkable transactions, which came within her knowledge and observation at that day, by which it appears that Mother's question to her, so often repeated, was very significant.]] . . .

Mother Hannah Goodrich, being at Watervliet a few days before Mother's decease, did not expect ever to see her out of her room again; but as she was one morning sweeping the piazza floor, Mother came out and said, "Sweep clean." "I will, Mother," replied Hannah. Again she said, "Ah, sweep clean, I say." "I will," said Hannah. "But I say, sweep clean," said Mother again. By this time Hannah perceived that Mother had reference to the floor of the heart, and said no more.

Immediately Mother Lucy, who took care of her in her last sufferings, came and took hold of her hand and asked her to go in. Mother answered, "I will; I will be obedient to you Lucy; for I am married to you and I will go with you." [[This speech seems to be strikingly significant of the lot and place that Mother Lucy was destined to occupy in the Church of Christ, and to which she has since attained.]] And they went in together.

As Mary Hocknell was watching with Mother, a little before her decease, she said, "I see brother William coming, in a golden chariot, to take me home." She then spoke to Mary and said, "Molly, poor child! I am about to go home, and after I am gone, you will have many sorrows." Mother's words came to pass; for Mary passed through many scenes of sorrow and sufferings after the decease of her dearest and best friend, who had brought her up from her childhood.

NOTES

1. Source: 1816 *Testimonies*, "First Interviews of Different Individuals with Mother and the Elders" and "The Subject Continued." I have included here chapter iv, paragraphs 1–5, and chapter v, paragraphs 1–10 and 13–16.

2. "Bearing for souls" refers to the idea held by the early Shakers that living souls could help convert relatives who had died without Ann Lee's saving gospel, through sharing their suffering.

3. Mary Partington was one of the original English followers of Ann Lee.

4. To "fall under judgment" here seems to refer to actual physical paralysis or trance, rather than mere feelings of guilt (as in evangelical Protestant conversion terminology).

5. Source: 1816 *Testimonies*, "Great Manifestations of God in Mother; Christ her Head, Lord and Husband" (chap. xxiii, paragraphs 1–9, 13–14, 21, 24–27, and 31).

6. This is an important indication that Ann Lee encountered continuing resistance among her own followers on account of her gender.

7. Marjorie Procter-Smith provides a useful discussion of several strands of Ann Lee's identity for her followers, as Mother, Elect Lady, and Elder, as presented in the 1816 *Testimonies*, in *Women in Shaker Community and Worship*, 10–25. This is a clear instance of Lee's claiming to be the single head of the Church, the First Elder, on the basis of spiritual experience.

8. It is Ann Lee's male followers who remember her as having said Christ was her "husband" or "Lord and head." The women tend to remember her "lover" metaphor.

9. Source: 1816 *Testimonies*, "Prophecies, Visions and Revelations—the Subject Continued" (chap. xxiv, paragraphs 4, 8, 12, 14, 16–17).

10. William Scales was a prominent early Shaker from Maine who contended both with Ann Lee during her lifetime and with James Whittaker over the succession when Ann Lee died. Scales lost out, and in a final chapter of the 1816 *Testimonies*, the followers of Ann Lee record his unhappy fate as a "wandering vagabond . . . struck with blindness" as a judgment on him (392–95).

11. Ann Lee and the early Shakers believed in multiple heavens, and perhaps multiple hells as well, as is suggested below.

12. Source: 1816 *Testimonies*, "The Gospel Preached to Departed Spirits" (chap. xxvii, paragraphs 1, 4, 7, 10–11, 13–17, 19–22).

13. "The spirits in prison" apparently refers to the souls of sinners in hell.

14. Note that while Ann Lee frequently reported on the missionary activities of deceased Shaker brothers, she is not reported as having seen any missionary sisters rescuing the lost spirits in the world beyond death. This accords with Marjorie Procter-Smith's observation that Lee herself seems to have ceded the role of public preacher to her male associates.

15. This final account of a visionary "wings" experiences is notable for its description of the process of entering the visionary state.

16. Source: 1816 *Testimonies*, "Reproof and Instruction" (chap. xxxii, paragraphs 1, 13–16, 26–27, 31–32, and 38–40).

17. Given the apparent claim of Ann Lee and some of the other early Shaker elders to bind and loose evil spirits, it is easy to see why the enemies of Shakerism accused them of witchcraft.

18. Source: 1816 *Testimonies*, "Public Teaching, Doctrinal Speeches, Exhortations &c." (chap. xxxiii, paragraphs 31–34). Note that the "sayings" of Ann Lee are not based on notes taken while she talked (as some of Lucy Wright's "sayings" are),

but rather on memories over a quarter century old, by a variety of informants of different literary abilities. Readers should regard them as sketchy indications of the topics she talked about that most impressed her followers; we have no way of knowing whether any of the exact turns of phrase may have been hers.

19. Source: 1816 *Testimonies*, "The Subject Continued" (chap. xxiv, paragraphs 1–5 and 22).

20. Louis J. Kern, in *An Ordered Love*, assumes from a reading of the 1816 *Testimonies* that bestiality was among the sexual practices most inveighed against by early Shaker texts, because of its metaphoric value—because lust was seen as deriving from one's animal nature, all acts of sex were like bestiality.

21. Source: 1816 *Testimonies*, "Speeches to Individuals on Various Occasions" (chap. xxxv, paragraphs 1 and 26–28).

22. Source: 1816 *Testimonies*, "The Subject Continued" (chap. xxxvi, paragraphs 2, 6, and 23–25).

ANN LEE'S OWN PERSONAL EXPERIENCE NARRATIVES, AS REMEMBERED BY HER FOLLOWERS (1816)[1]

Mother and the Elders, in the course of their labors with the Believers, occasionally related some of their own experience and sufferings in the earlier part of their faith. Mother's experience, in particular, as it evinced her indefatigable zeal and invincible fortitude of soul, was not only very interesting, but very instructive to those who had but just set out in the same faith, and had a great effect in exciting them to zeal and faithfulness in the way of God.

Soon after the gospel opened at Watervliet (1780), in the presence of a number of the young Believers, Mother related some of her experience as follows: "I love the day when I first received the gospel; I call it my birthday. I cried to God three days and nights, without intermission, that he would give me true desires.

"I was sometimes under such sufferings and tribulation that I could not rest in my bed anights, but had to get up and walk the floor. I feared to go to sleep lest I should wake up in hell. When I felt my eyes closing with sleep, I used to pull them open with my fingers and say within myself, I had better open my eyes here, than to open them in hell.

"I labored to feel a sense of the sufferings and torments of hell, that I might keep my soul continually awake to God. I often figured to my mind the excessive and intolerable heat of a furnace or hot oven and thought within my self that if I could not bear the heat of these, how could I bear the torments of hell.

"I felt such a sense of my sins that I was willing to confess them before the whole world. I confessed my sins to my Elders one by one and repented of them in the same manner. When my Elders reproved me, I felt deter mined not to be reproved twice for one thing, but to labor to overcome the evil for myself.

"I had not been in the Church more than six months before it was made known to me by the revelation of God that he would support me through all my trials and establish me an elder in the Church. The man to whom I was married was very kind according to nature; he would have been willing to pass through a flaming fire for my sake if I would but live in the flesh with him, which I refused to do." [[Hannah Cogswell]]

Just before Mother was imprisoned in Albany,[2] many of the Believers, being assembled together at Watervliet, were under considerable tribulation, because it was expected that Mother and the Elders would soon be driven away from that place by the wicked. Mother came into the room and spoke with tears running from her eyes and said, "The wicked are plotting against us; they mean to drive us away from this place, and it is unknown to me whether I shall ever see you again in this world.

"When I set out to serve God, I served him day and night and cried to God day and night for deliverance from all sin. I did not receive a gift of God and then go away and think it was sufficient without travelling any further: but I stood faithful, day and night, warring against all sin and crying to God for deliverance from the very nature of sin. And can you expect to find power over sin without the same labor and travel of soul?" The people were all filled with the gift of God from Mother and were sent away with a blessing. [[Mehetabel Farrington]] . . .

Soon after the gospel began to open at New Lebanon, Hannah Goodrich, with her husband (Nathan Goodrich) went to Neskeyuna, received faith, and confessed their sins, after which, Mother related to them some of her experience as follows.

"When I set out to obey the gospel, I cried to God to bring my sins to remembrance; and I confessed them one by one as I committed them; and I denied myself of every gratification of a carnal nature, of everything which my appetite craved, and ate and drank that which was mean and poor that my soul might hunger for nothing but God.

"I often rose from my bed in the night and walked the floor in my stocking feet, for fear of waking up the people. I did not let my husband know my troubles, lest I should stir up his affections, and I was careful not to lay any temptation before him. I also prayed to God that no man might suffer in hell on my account.

"Thus I labored in strong cries and groans to God day and night, till my flesh wasted away and I became like a skeleton, and a kind of down came upon my skin, until my soul broke forth to God; which I felt as sensibly as ever a woman did a child, when she was delivered of it. Then I felt unspeakable joy in God, and my flesh came upon me like the flesh of an infant." [[Hannah Goodrich, 1st]]

At Enfield, to Mary Tiffany and others, Mother related some of her experience as follows: "After I opened my mind and set out in my travel, I received great power of God; and in my travel it was revealed to me what the loss of man was—that it was the lust of the flesh.

"My husband was opposed to me and went and complained of me to the Church. The Church opposed my testimony and tried to persuade me to give it up; but I had to stand the test against my husband, my relations, and the Church; and I soon received such power of God that my bed would rock under me; and my husband was glad to leave it.

"In my travail and tribulation, my sufferings were so great that my flesh consumed upon my bones, and bloody sweat pressed through the pores of my skin, and I became as helpless as an infant. And when I was brought through, and born into the spiritual Kingdom, I was like an infant just born into the world; they see colors and objects; but they know not what they see; and so it was with me when I was born into the spiritual world. But before I was twenty-four hours old, I saw and knew what I saw." [[Mary Tiffany]] . . .

The first time that Daniel Wood went to see Mother [[Soon after she was released from prison.]] he related to her the conviction he had been under for fifteen years past respecting the flesh, that the works thereof were evil, but confessed that he had not fully lived up to his faith. Mother replied, "You could not live up to that faith, because you had not confessed your sins."

She then related some of her own experience as follows: "Some time after I set out to live up to the light of God manifested to me through James and Jane Wardley,[3] I fell under heavy trials and tribulation on account of lodging with my husband; and as I looked to them for help and counsel, I opened my trials to Jane. She said, 'James and I lodge together; but we do not touch each other any more than two babes. You may return home and do likewise.'

"In obedience to Jane I went to bed with my husband, but could not sleep, seemingly, any more than if I had been in a bed of embers. I quitted the bed in great tribulation and continued laboring and crying to God for the space of twelve days and nights, to know how the creation was fallen and how the restoration should take place.

"While I was in this labor, I saw the Lord Jesus in his Kingdom and glory. He revealed to me the depth of man's loss, what it was, and the way of redemption. Then I was made able to bear an open testimony against that sin which is the root of all evil; and I felt the power of God flow into my soul like a fountain of living water. From that day to this, I have taken up a full cross against the doleful works of the flesh." [[Daniel Wood]] . . .

The severe persecution and cruel abuses which Mother suffered in England, in consequence of her faith and testimony, were occasionally related to some of the Believers in this country, during their intercourse with her and the Elders and others who came with her from England. They are striking evidences not only of the inveterate hatred and malice of a lost world against every increasing manifestation of divine light, but also of Mother's unexampled confidence and resolution in maintaining her testimony against all opposition, and of the wonderful interposition of divine power in protecting and preserving a life which, next to that of Jesus Christ, was the most valuable and important of any that ever was born into this world.

Soon after Mehetabel Farrington believed the gospel, as she was one day sitting in the piazza with Mother and Mary Hocknell and several others, Mother related many trials and persecutions which she had suffered at the hands of the wicked, on account of her testimony. Among others was the following remarkable account of her imprisonment in some particular apartment of the stone prison.

"They put me into the stone prison and there kept me fourteen days where I could not straighten myself. The door was never opened through the whole time. I stayed there two weeks and had nothing to eat nor drink except what I sucked through a pipe-stem that was put through the key-hole of the door once in twenty-four hours.

"After I had been there awhile, one of the Believers came and whispered to me through the key-hole (for he durst not speak a loud word, for fear of being heard), and said, 'Put your mouth to the key-hole, and I will give you drink.' I did so; but the pipe-stem was so big that he could not get it through the key-hole: So I got no drink that night. The next night he came again and put the stem of a pipe through, so that I could just take it into my lips; and I sucked through the pipe-stem till I felt refreshed."

Mehetabel asked, "What could they give Mother that could have much nourishment?" She answered, "It was wine and milk, poured into the bowl of the pipe. This I received as a favor of God. I had no one to look to but God for help. I bore testimony against their sins and told them of their wicked lives, which was the reason of their hating me so. You must be faithful, and they will hate you too: for wicked men will always hate those souls that take up their cross against sin.

"But I was released in God's time. When their appointed time came, they let me out, and I found I could walk off spry and nimble, and felt as well as I did before. So they did not get their design accomplished: for they meant to kill me. They kept me there four days longer than they could reasonably expect that any one could live without food."

Mehetabel asked Mother how she could live so? Mother answered, "When my joints ached and I was in pain all over, the power of God would flow upon me all over, from head to foot, and make me feel comfortable."

Not long before Mother set out on her eastern journey, she related the particulars of the above mentioned imprisonment to some others of the Believers, in the presence of Elder James and Elder Hocknell. After she had told them how she came out of the prison and could walk spry and nimble, Elder Hocknell testified to the truth of what Mother had related and said he was present, adding, "The world were astonished at it and said it must be a supernatural power that attended her; and that they did not believe it was right to confine or oppress her."

Elder James said, "I was young at that time and had but little acquaintance with Mother; but I had a remarkable feeling for her; I could not rest, day nor night. I labored to know whether I had not a duty to do.

"At length, I thought what I could do; so I went and bought a pint flask bottle, which I could carry in my pocket; and at the same store, I bought some wine and carried it home. About milking time, I went and bought a half pint of milk and put it into my bottle. I then considered how I should convey the wine and milk to Mother. At length I thought of a pipe; so I bought one and put it into my hat.

"In the night, after the people were asleep, having mixed wine with the milk, I went to the prison alone and put my mouth to the key-hole and whispered to Mother, and told her to put her mouth to the key-hole and I would give her drink; which she did; but the pipe-stem was so large that I could not get it through. I durst not pare my pipe-stem there, for fear of being discovered: so I returned home very heavy.

"The next day, I went to a store and bought another pipe, which was a yard long, and carried it home in the button-holes of my coat. The next night, I went to bed and waited till all were asleep; I then arose and went to the prison and accomplished my design. This I did as often as I thought I could and not be discovered; and I know that I received a blessing of God in so doing. But no one knew that I ever went to the prison." [[Mehetabel Farrington]]

Shortly after Mother was released from Poughkeepsie jail, Mehetabel Farrington and a number of others being at Watervliet, Mother related to them some of her sufferings through persecution as follows: "I suffered great persecution in England, on account of my faith. Sometimes the power of God operated so mightily upon me that numbers would try to hold me still; but the more they tried to withstand the power of God, the more I was operated upon.

"One of my brothers, being greatly enraged, said he was determined to overcome me. So he brought a staff about the size of a large broom handle and came to me while I was sitting in my chair and singing by the power of God. He spoke to me; but I felt no liberty to answer. 'Will you not answer me?' said he.

"He then beat me over my face and nose with his staff, till one end of it was very much splintered. But I sensibly felt and saw the bright rays of the glory of God pass between my face and his staff, which shielded off the blows so that I did but just feel them. He continued beating till he was so far spent that he had to stop and call for drink.

"While he was refreshing himself, I cried to God for his healing power. He then turned the other end of his staff and began to beat me again. While he continued striking, I felt my breath like healing balsam streaming from my mouth and nose, which healed me so that I felt no harm from his strokes; but he was out of breath, like one who had been running a race." [[While Mother was at Stonington, she related this same circumstance to Phebe Spencer and others.]]

Elder Hocknell, being present, said, "What Mother has related is the truth. Her brother, in beating her, wore his staff till it was not more than so long" (extending his arm, and measuring from the ends of his fingers to his elbow). [Mehetabel Farrington]

At another time, Mehetabel Farrington being at Watervliet, Mother gave her the following information: "When I lived in England, there arose a great mob against me and determined to put an end to my existence. They took me into the high road and ordered me to advance. In submission to their order, I made the attempt but was soon knocked down with clubs; and after I got up and began to walk, I was kicked every few steps nearly two miles. I then felt as if I should faint with thirst and was almost ready to give up the ghost by reason of the cruel abuses which I received from my riotous enemies.

"While I was suffering by the merciless mob, not one friend was allowed to follow me. But God in mercy remembered me and sent a man who was instrumental of my deliverance. A certain nobleman living at some distance, who knew nothing of what was passing, was remarkably wrought upon in his mind and urged by his feelings to go; but where or for what cause he did not know. But he ordered his servant to fetch his horse immediately. The servant went in haste; but the anxiety of the nobleman was so great that he sent a messenger after his servant to hasten him.

"He then mounted his horse and rode as hastily as if it had been to save his own life, as he afterward told me; but for what cause or where he should stop was unknown to him till he came to a large concourse of people. He then inquired what their business was. On being informed, he rode up to the place where I was and commanded the mob to desist their abuse and sharply reproved them for their cruel conduct and ordered them to disperse immediately.

"He then inquired if I had any friends present and told me if I had not, he was determined to take care of me himself. Elder Hocknell appeared and said he was my friend. The nobleman gave him a strict charge to take care of me. Thus God made use of this nobleman, though out of his sight, to do his will. And the earth opened her mouth and helped the woman."

Elder Hocknell was present and testified to the truth of what Mother had related, and also said, "I followed Mother, feeling determined to follow her amidst the crowd. I had not proceeded far before I was taken and thrown into a bulge place as they call it. [[A deep vault of human excrement.]] With much difficulty I got out and went to a fountain of water and washed myself, then went and changed my garments and pursued after Mother.

"When I overtook the mob, they beat and abused me very much and then rolled me in a mud slough; and although I was wounded and my head in a gore of blood, I did not suffer anger to rise in the least degree. After they left me, a poor widow came and bound up my head with a handkerchief.

"I washed myself and went and changed my garments again and went again in search after Mother. When I came to the place where she was, the nobleman was reproving and dispersing the mob. According to the nobleman's orders, I took good care of Mother. We went and refreshed ourselves and returned home in peace." [[Mehetabel Farrington]]

The first time Abigail Babbitt went to see Mother, she was at David Hammond's, in Petersham. Father William and Father James being present, Mother related to her some of her sufferings in England, as follows: "One night, I was told by a friend that there was a mob after me. As the inhabitants were very thick, I knew no better way to make my escape than to run to a man whom I knew to be my friend, and who lived but a few doors from me.

"So I disguised myself by putting an apron over my head and ran to his house as quick as I could and asked him if he could hide me from the mob. He took a candle and bid me follow him. I followed him to the upper loft of the house, where was a large quantity of wool lying under the roof. He pulled out several fleeces and bid me lie down, and he covered me with the wool and I lay safe and comfortable.

"Soon after, I heard the mob come into the house and inquire for me, and asked to search the house. The man gave them liberty; and they came into the loft where I was, and looking round, said, 'She is not here; there is nothing here but wool.' So they departed. Soon after, my friend came up, and told me that my enemies were gone. I then went down and rested in peace that night.

"At another time I was accused of blasphemy. My accusers told me that my tongue must be bored through with a hot iron and that I must be branded on the cheek. I was led before four of the most learned ministers in those parts. They asked me to speak in other tongues. I told them that they must wait for God's power to move me; for it was by the operation of the power of God that I spoke in other tongues.

"Soon after, the power of God came upon me and I spoke to them in many different tongues of the wonderful works of God. These men, being convinced that I spoke by the power of God, told the people not to hurt me. But the mob were not satisfied; their rage increased, and they said we must be stoned to death.

"So they led me, Elder William, Elder James, Daniel Whittaker, and James Shepherd down into a valley; and the mob brought as many stones as two men could carry and placed them down on the side of a hill and then began to cast them at us; but they could not hit any of us (except Daniel, who received a slight wound on one of his temples); upon which they fell into contention among themselves.

"While they were throwing their stones, I felt surrounded with the presence of God and my soul was filled with love. I knew that they could not kill me, because my work was not done; therefore I felt joyful and comfortable, while my enemies felt distress and confusion.

"At another time, I was put into a stone prison that was built over the water.[4] In this prison I could not stretch myself any way. Here I was kept fourteen days without anything to eat except what was conveyed by a pipe through the key-hole; and I felt great joy, knowing that I suffered for Christ's sake.

"At another time, in the evening, I was informed by a friend that there was a mob after me. I soon ran out to the back side of a little hill, where there was a pond covered with ice, and I laid myself down upon the ice, and remained there all night in great peace and consolation, and did not take cold.

"At another time, there came a mob by night and dragged me out of the house by my feet, till they tore the skin off my face." She showed the scars. [[Abigail Babbitt]]

Mother also related to some of the Believers at Harvard that she was once taken by four men, one of whom was her natural brother; that they bound her hand and foot and tried to throw her out of a high loft window; but the power of God protected her, so that they were unable to accomplish their design. [[Lydia Kilbourn]] . . .

Mary Hocknell also relates the following particulars concerning the last imprisonment which Mother suffered in England. It seems that the wicked had forecast their devices with a view to seize Mother and the principal members of the Society upon the sabbath while they were in the worship of God, that they might have a lawful pretense to punish them for a breach of the sabbath. For this purpose, a number of church officers and spies had been previously placed in streets, as watchmen, under a pretense of preventing people from violating the sabbath.

Mother, being forewarned of God, had sent her brother William out of town early in the morning. The Believers assembled and began their worship, which was attended with great power of God and much shouting. The report was heard, the rumor spread, and the spirit of antichrist was roused; for it was the time of their morning service. Several of these church officers came with a strong party to seize the offenders.

Mother and her little family were worshipping God in the garret or third loft of the house. The mob surrounded the house, burst open the doors, ascended the stairs, and seized all in the house, but were greatly disappointed at not finding William Lee. Great search was made for him, but in vain.

Mary, being young, was closely interrogated and threatened by the mob to make her tell where Bill Lee was, as they called him; but she refused to answer or even to speak. After being shamefully abused by the mob, she was carried before the church officers. Here she was again closely examined, threatened, coaxed, flattered, and had money offered to her, but all in vain. At length she escaped from her persecutors and fled to John Townley's, in Cannon Street.

In the meantime, Mother and those with her were conveyed to the stone prison, where they continued under great power of God to sing and shout and glorify God in the prison, so as to be heard at a great distance. In the night, Elder James visited them and carried them drink, which he conveyed to them through the key-hole.

The next morning, they were all released excepting Mother and John Lee,[5] who were conveyed from thence to the house of correction, where they were kept imprisoned several weeks. During this imprisonment, Mary was frequently sent to carry provisions and other things to them.

In this prison and at this time, Mother received great revelations of God. Many deep and important mysteries were there revealed to her; and by the power and authority of the Holy Ghost she was there commissioned to take the lead of the Society, which till then had rested with James and Jane Wardley.

Though she had before received great manifestations of God, had discovered the root of human depravity, had taken up a full cross against the carnal gratifications of the flesh, and testified these things to the Society, many of whom through her testimony and influence had walked in the same faith, yet she had continued to yield obedience to James and Jane Wardley as her superiors and was eminently useful to them in leading, teaching, strengthening, and protecting the Society.

But when she was released from this last imprisonment, she took Mary Hocknell with her, went to John Townley's, collected the Society together, and opened her revelations with the most astonishing power of God. Here it was seen at once that the candle of the Lord was in her hand, and that she was able by the light thereof to search every heart and try every soul among them. From this time, Mother took the lead of the Society and was received and acknowledged as the first pillar of the Church of God upon earth.

NOTES

1. Source: 1816 *Testimonies* "Sketches of Mother's Experience and Sufferings in England . . . " (chap. vii, paragraphs 1–8, 12–18, and 20–23) and "Mother's Persecution in England . . . " (chap. viii, paragraphs 1–35 and 40–48). The primary storytellers contributing to the collection of Ann Lee's personal experience stories are

Hannah Cogswell, Mehetabel Farrington, Hannah Goodrich, Mary Tiffany, Daniel Wood, Phebe Spencer, Abigail Babbitt, Lydia Kilbourn, and Mary Hocknell.

2. Ann Lee, along with her brother William, John Partington, Mary Partington, James Whittaker, and Calvin Harlow, were all imprisoned in Albany, New York, for teaching a pacifist doctrine during the Revolutionary War in the summer of 1780. Ann Lee and Mary Partington, removed to Poughkeepsie by the military authorities, were not released until December.

3. James and Jane Wardley were the leaders of the original English Shakers in Manchester, England. Ann Lee joined their group in 1758.

4. This story occurs twice in the 1816 *Testimonies*.

5. John Lee was Ann Lee's father, at that time a member of the Wardley Society.

NARRATIVE OF THE JOURNEY THROUGH
NEW ENGLAND (1816)[1]

In December (1781) Mother and the Elders made a journey to Petersham. [[About forty miles west from Harvard]] They arrived at Thomas Shattuck's late in the evening and found the family watching and waiting in expectation of their coming. Mother said, "It is good to watch, and you should always watch." Father William said, "Ye watched; for ye knew not the hour we would come." They, however, proceeded to David Hammond's that night.

The next day being sabbath, many people of the world came in to attend meeting. Elder James preached the gospel from these words: *Cleanse your hands, ye sinners; and purify your hearts, ye double minded. Be afflicted, and mourn, and weep.* [[James 4:8–9]] He spoke with great power and energy of the spirit and urged the necessity of confessing, forsaking, and repenting of their sins. "What is cleansing the hands," said he, "but confessing sins? And what is purifying the heart, but forsaking them? And what is being afflicted and mourning and weeping, but repenting of sin?" He continued his discourse about two hours.

This being the first visit that Mother and the Elders made in Petersham, the inhabitants generally manifested a desire to see and hear for themselves, and as they pretended civility, they had full liberty. Accordingly, on Monday evening there came a considerable number of civil people; also a company of lewd fellows from the middle of the town, who styled themselves the Blackguard Committee.

Being all assembled together, Elder James came and gave notice that all who had come with an honest desire to get information might walk into the other room. Accordingly, the more civil part of the assembly went in, leaving the forementioned company, who had evidently come with no good intentions.

Elder James took a Bible and read to the assembly and then began to speak. In the time of speaking the company which had stayed back in the other room began to crowd in and stretched themselves through the room from the door to the bed, where Mother and Elizabeth Shattuck were sitting together upon the bed-side, with a number of other sisters sitting near them.

As people were occasionally coming in, and the attention of the assembly generally engaged in hearing the preacher, this mob had opportunity to arrange themselves through the assembly without being much noticed. Instantly a cry was heard, "Knock out the lights!" The lights were all suddenly extinguished except the one in Elder James's hand; and immediately a passage was made by the mob from the door to the bed where Mother was sitting.

At this instant entered three ruffians painted black, and rushing forward, the foremost one seized hold of Mother and, with the assistance of his comrades, attempted to drag her out; but Elizabeth Shattuck and several other sisters instantly clinched hold of her and held her; and Elizabeth being a large, heavy woman, and the passage narrow, the ruffians were not able to accomplish their purpose; and quitting their hold, they suddenly fled out of the house.

In this struggle, though it was but momentary, they tore a breadth out of a new gown which Mother had on. Their wicked designs being now fully known, Elder James advised to have the remainder of the assembly withdraw, as it was growing late. On being spoken to, they went off, apparently in a peaceable manner. But Mother, in the spirit of prophecy, said the wicked would come again, which caused some labor among the brethren and sisters to devise means to secure her from their cruel hands.

However, as the mob had withdrawn, and all danger apparently at an end, the neighboring Believers returned home, and some of the brethren who accompanied the Elders went with them. Those who remained were about retiring to rest when Mother discovered from the window that her cruel persecutors were near and made some attempts to conceal herself. The house was again assaulted by about thirty creatures in human shape; the doors, being fastened, were burst open and broke, and these ruffians entered.

David Hammond was immediately knocked down and cruelly beaten. Mary, his woman, who had a young child in her arms, was knocked down and received several severe strokes on her head by one Thomas Carter. Elder James was clinched by the collar, knocked down, and left for dead; and several others were knocked down. Father William was also hurt; and all that stood in their way were beaten and bruised more or less.

As their object was to seize Mother, the candles had been previously concealed to prevent their finding her. But this did not hinder them; they seized firebrands and searched the house, and at length found her in a bedroom. They immediately seized her by her feet and inhumanly dragged her feet foremost out of the house and threw her into a sleigh with as little ceremony as they would the dead carcass of a beast, and drove off, committing at the same time acts of inhumanity and indecency which even savages would be ashamed of.

In the struggle with these inhuman wretches, she lost her cap and handkerchief and otherwise had her clothes torn in a shameful manner. Their pretense was to find out whether she was a woman or not. In this situation, in a cold winter's night, they drove nearly three miles to Samuel Peckham's tavern near Petersham meeting house.

Father William feeling great concern for Mother's safety, he and David Hammond followed the sleigh. He told the ruffians that she was his sister and he would follow her; and attempting to hold on by the hind part of the sleigh, they gave him many blows with the butts of their sleigh-whips. He and David, however, followed them to the forementioned tavern. Elder James, being badly wounded, was not able to follow them.

It appears from information that Samuel Peckham, who was a captain of militia, had previously agreed with the ruffians who seized Mother to give them as much rum as they would drink, upon condition that they would bring her to his house. After their arrival, Father William and David Hammond remonstrated against the ungodliness and brutality of their behavior. David represented to them the unlawfulness of such conduct, and how they had exposed themselves to the penalties of the law.

Being by this time ashamed of their conduct and fearful of the consequences, they promised to release Mother upon condition that David would sign an obligation not to prosecute them for what they had done. Being impelled by a sense of feeling for Mother's safety, he reluctantly yielded to their demands and left them to answer at the bar of Divine Justice concerning a species of conduct for which they were unwilling to appear before an earthly tribunal.

This being done, they released Mother, and some time in the night some of them brought her and those with her back to David Hammond's. She came in singing for joy that she was again restored to her children. The men who brought her back appeared to be greatly ashamed of their wicked conduct and confessed that they had abused her shamefully, said they were sorry for it, and desired her forgiveness. Mother replied, "I can freely forgive you; I hold nothing against you, and I pray God to forgive you." So they departed peaceably.

After their departure, Mother related the shameful abuse which she had suffered from these merciless wretches and said, "It really seemed that my life must go from me when they dragged me out of my room and threw me into the sleigh. Besides, they tore my handkerchief from my neck, my cap and fillet from my head, and even tore some of the hair out of my head.

"But I was treated kindly at the tavern where they carried me. The tavern keeper's wife offered me something to drink, as the weather was cold and I almost destitute of clothing. One of the men that took me away gave me his handkerchief to wear on my head; and another gave me his surtout to wear home." [[By this it appears that Mother was ready to acknowledge kindness, even in her worst enemies.]] Elder James, who had been prevented from following Mother by reason of the severe wound which he had received, informed her of his disaster. His face was greatly swelled and his jaw very painful, and he was apprehensive that it was broke. "But," said he "I can pray for them"; and kneeling down, he cried, *"Father forgive them; for they know not what they do."*

It is worthy of remark that many who were considered as the most respectable people in the town of Petersham and people of property were the instigators and leaders of this savage mob. Robert Peckham, Sheriff of the county, David Sanders, son of a deacon of the Presbyterian Church, and John Hawksey were said to be the persons who took Mother in the sleigh and so shamefully abused her. Mother repeatedly said she never was so abused in all her life as she was by this mob in Petersham.

So inveterate were the inhabitants, both priest and people, professor and profane, that it seemed as if nothing was too bad for them to say or do against the Believers in general, but more especially against Mother and the Elders, against whom the most vile and malicious accusations that could be conceived were uttered. Witchcraft and delusion was the general cry; even in their solemn assemblies of worship, the preachers would vent their malicious spleen, and mock and mimic the operations of the power of God which they had seen or heard of among the people. . . .

Mother and the Elders arrived at Ashfield about the first of November. As this was a central place, and convenient for the resort of the Believers from different quarters, and less liable to be disturbed by mobs and riots, Mother felt a gift to take up her residence here during the approaching winter and to give a general liberty for the Believers to come and see her. Accordingly, great numbers resorted here during the winter from all parts where the gospel had been planted. More than sixty sleighs and 600 people were there at one time. [[They were counted by John Farrington, by Mother's order.]]

During this season, the power of God was manifested in a marvelous manner. Extraordinary operations of the power and gifts of God and violent wars of the spirit against the flesh were ministered through Mother to the people. The voice of Mother and the Elders against the filthy, fallen nature of the flesh was like the roaring of thunder. Every heart was searched and every rein tried, which caused great purging and purifying among the people.

The opposition to the work of God in Ashfield was never so great as it had been in most other places; yet the Believers were sometimes disturbed by "lewd fellows of the baser sort," who gathered there for carnal and mischievous purposes. The greatest disturbance that Mother and the Elders met with while they continued in Ashfield was excited by Daniel Bacon, brother to Asa and Moses Bacon.

Daniel and his wife had both received faith and embraced the testimony, but he afterward fell away and became very bitter and moved off into Shelburn; but his wife still desired to obey her faith. Some time in March, Daniel came to the Church in a sleigh and brought his wife and young child; and without going into the house, he put them out of the sleigh in a very rough and churlish manner into the mud before the house and immediately drove off and left them.

When Mother was informed of this circumstance, she said, "This is a snare; he has done this to get occasion; she is his wife and I will not keep her here so." She therefore sent one of the brethren to carry the woman back. Daniel, failing of his purpose to get an occasion in this manner, now openly came forth and showed plainly what he was after; and by spreading slanderous reports, he gave the enemies of the cross a pretext to persecute. . . .

A few days after Daniel Bacon's wife was sent home, a mob of about fifty or sixty men was collected in Shelburn and its vicinity by Daniel's instigation. The inhabitants of the town of Ashfield, being informed of it, were desirous to prevent any riotous proceedings. With this view, they appointed a committee to confer with the mob and inquire into the cause of their coming and to take suitable measures to prevent them from using any violence in the town.

The committee, consisting of Thomas Stocking, a captain of militia, and two other respectable men, came to Asa Bacon's and desired to see Mother. She went to the door to see them, and said, "I am a poor weak woman, and I have suffered so much by mobs that it seems to me as though I could not endure any more." Stocking replied, "You need not be afraid, Ma'am; we have not come to hurt you; but to defend you."

He then informed her that there was a mob coming from Shelburn to disturb her and her people, that they were not willing to have any mobs in Ashfield, that if she and the Elders would go to Philip Philips's, in the center of the town, they should be protected. Mother paused a little, and considering herself under the protection of God, she did not choose to put herself under the protection of man and declined their offer but at the same time invited them in to dinner and treated them kindly.

After dinner, the committee went up to Smith's tavern, about half a mile distant, and met the mob. Here they held a conference with their leaders and found that their pretended object was to search into the truth of some prevailing rumors respecting Mother's character and the character and conduct of the people with her. They had heard many base and infamous reports and concluded that Mother's pretensions were an imposition upon the people and strongly suspected her to be a British emissary dressed in women's habit for seditious purposes.

Though the committee bore testimony of the peaceable deportment and harmless conduct of the people, still the mob could not be satisfied without a full examination of the people themselves, and particularly of the woman. Accordingly the committee agreed that if the mob would proceed no further, Mother should go to Smith's and answer for herself, upon condition that she should not be abused. . . .

Mother and the Elders felt it most prudent to comply and immediately had a sleigh and horses prepared and went, accompanied by Calvin Harlow, Aaron Wood, Ephraim Welch, and several others of the Believers.

Having arrived at Smith's, the leaders of the mob, of whom Col. David Wells of Shelburn, was chief, entered upon their examination; and finding their charges against Mother fully refuted in all other points, they wished to know whether she was a woman or not. Accordingly Smith's wife and another woman were appointed as a jury to examine her, who reported that she was a woman . . .

Having gone through with their examinations, Mother addressed herself to Col. Wells and reproved him, saying, "Is it not a shame for you, who profess to be a gentleman and an officer, to give heed to such scandalous and inconsistent reports and to come here, at the head of a mob, out of your own town, to persecute an innocent people? Is not the authority of the town able to see to the affairs of their own town?"

The Colonel, stung with this reproof, replied in a pet, "If you don't hold your tongue, I'll cane you." "Do you pretend to be a gentleman," said Mother, "and are going to cane a poor weak woman! What a shame it is!" Abashed at this reply, the Colonel attempted no further opposition. . . .

Thus did the earth open her mouth and swallow up the flood of malicious lies and slanderous reports which the dragon had cast out of his mouth against the woman;[2] and thus did God protect his anointed from the snares of the wicked, and no man was suffered to hurt her or destroy her faithful seed. . . .

One evening, while Mother and the Elders were at Nathan Goodrich's and a large collection of Believers assembled in the worship of God, there came a company of unruly men rushing up to the door on horse-back. Mother, on hearing their noise, went to the door and spoke to them and bid them, "Draw back." But the men refusing to obey, she raised her hand and with great power and authority cried aloud, "Draw back, I say, or I'll smite the horse and his rider."

On uttering these words, all the power of resistance seemed instantly to be taken from the men, and their horses immediately ran backward from the house down to the road, which was about ten rods distant; nor did it seem to those who saw it to be in the power of their riders to govern them, till they got quite into the road; and then they peaceably turned their horses and departed.

NOTES

1. Source: 1816 *Testimonies*, "Mother and the Elders visit Petersham . . . " (chap. xii, paragraphs 1–20); "At Ashfield Mother is Visited by Great Multitudes of People" (chap. xvi, paragraphs 1–13, 15–20, 23–24, 28, 29, and 31); and "Mother and the Elders leave Harvard" (chap. xviii,paragraphs 29–30).

2. See Revelation 12:16.

WOMEN'S TESTIMONIES IN DEFENSE OF ANN LEE (1827)[1]

Testimony of Elizabeth Johnson

I was born and brought up in Durham, Connecticut. In my youthful days I became convicted of sin and felt the need of salvation, and at the age of twenty I made a profession of religion, in hopes thereby to find some way of God to save my soul from sin. But I could find no power to keep myself from sin, though I sought earnestly for it; of course I often fell into those sins which brought me under severe condemnation of conscience. At the age of twenty-four, I was married to Samuel Johnson, who was brought up in the same town and was then settled as a Presbyterian preacher in New Lebanon. I was in hopes by marrying a Christian minister (as I considered him to be), I should be able to live nearer to God and enjoy more of the spirit of religion; but I soon found myself disappointed in this expectation. Instead of living more as I believed a Christian ought to live, I found the cares and concerns of a family and the things of the world increased upon me, and my soul grew darker and darker and became more and more separated from God.

In this situation I continued till the year 1779, when a great revival of religion broke out in New Lebanon and the adjacent towns. We then lived in West Stockbridge. We frequently attended the meetings of the subjects of this work in the several towns around us. They appeared to be greatly awakened concerning the things of God and we both became much exercised in mind and felt deeply interested in this revival. The great manifestations of the spirit and gifts of God which attended this work far exceeded any thing of the kind I had ever known before. The signs and operations and the prophetic spirit which prevailed in these meetings clearly intimated that Christ was about to "appear the second time, without sin, unto salvation." This was the general testimony of those who felt the spirit of the work, and it felt like divine truth. I fully united with it and received a good measure of the power of God; and my soul became awakened to such a degree that for some time days and nights seemed all alike to me. I felt a sure manifestation in my soul that Christ was near at hand. But alas! this power left me and behold, I was enveloped in darkness and all in my sins! This caused me great tribulation of soul, and I cried to God day and night for some way of deliverance; but none could I find.

I continued in this situation until the spring of 1780, when Tallmadge Bishop, of New Lebanon, came to Stockbridge to see us and gave us a particular account of a very singular people living in the wilderness above Albany. I listened to this account with great attention. It appeared evident to me that these strangers had gained greater light of God than any people I had ever heard of before, or at least greater than I had ever received. I felt at this time a great sense of my loss from God; indeed I felt myself a very corrupt creature and cried earnestly to God for his mercy. After hearing this account, my husband and I both set out there and then to take up our crosses, according to the testimony of these strangers, as far as we could understand what it was. . . .

Some time in February following, after Mother and the Elders were released from prison, I visited them at Watervliet. Here I saw Mother for the first time. She came singing into the room where I was sitting, and I felt an inward evidence that her singing was in the gift and power of God. She came and sat down by my side and put her hand upon my arm. Instantly I felt the power of God flow from her and run through my whole body. I was then convinced beyond a doubt that she had the power of God and that I received it from her. She did not flatter me nor daub me with "untempered mortar"; but told me I might confess my sins. I felt ashamed of myself; but I went out with her and honestly confessed my sins to God in her presence. I was fully convinced by what I saw and felt that she had the discerning power of God, so that she could discern the state and situation of my mind as easily as I could behold my face in a glass. I sensibly felt that I had come to judgment and that all the sins I had ever committed in my life must be laid open before God, just as I had committed them, or I could never be saved. I confessed my sins with a full determination to leave them off forever. And in obedience to Mother's teaching I found that power which enabled me to keep myself from all sin in my knowledge. . . .

And I can testify with confidence before all mankind that I never saw the least unrighteous action in her; nor did I ever hear an unrighteous word from her lips. And I can say the same of Elder William and Elder James. I know for myself that they lived pure and holy lives; for their fruits have sufficiently proved it. And I know that by my obedience to their testimony, I received that power of God that has saved me from all sin; and that power has never left me from that day to this, but has ever been increasing in my soul and enlightening my understanding in divine things. And though I am now far advanced in years and my bodily strength is decaying, yet that heavenly faith and power which I received from Mother Ann is still living in my soul.

Elizabeth Johnson

New Lebanon, January 9th, 1827

Testimony of Thankful Barce

When I was young, I was in great trouble of mind about my sinful state and was much concerned to know how I should find peace with God; for I often read in the scriptures that there was *no peace for the wicked*. While in these exercises of mind one night on my bed, I saw a very admirable woman. As she advanced along, I saw a very large flock of sheep following her. They appeared to be the most beautiful flock I ever saw and were clothed with the cleanest and whitest wool that ever my eyes beheld. The woman advanced forward till she came to a large plain, where she halted, and I saw her bait the sheep with something that was in her hand. To my view it resembled salt. The sheep all seemed to gather round her and eat. I did not hear a word spoken by the woman; nor did I speak to her; but I viewed her very attentively and wondered what it could mean; for the scene appeared very solemn.

In the spring of 1780, I heard of a strange people living above Albany, who said they served God day and night and did not commit sin. I thought if there was such a people on earth, they must be the people of God. I did not believe the professors of Christianity around me had this power: for they said they lived in sin and I believed it; and I knew I had not found anything that saved me from sin. Under these considerations, I went to see these remarkable strangers; for I was determined to see and know for myself what sort of people they were. When I arrived, Mother Ann met me at the door, took hold of my hand, and led me into the house. Her first salutation to me was in these words: "Being a daughter of Zion, how camest thou hither without a cap on thy head?" She sat down in a chair and I sat down by her side. Her eyes were shut and it appeared that her sense was withdrawn from the things of time. She sung very melodiously and appeared very beautiful. Her countenance appeared bright and shining, like an angel of glory, and she seemed to be overshadowed with the glory of God. The graceful motion of her hands, the beautiful appearance of her countenance, and the heavenly melody of her voice made her seem like a glorious inhabitant of the heavenly world, singing praises to God. As I sat by the side of her, one of her hands, while in motion, frequently touched my arm; and at every touch of her hand, I instantly felt the power of God run through my whole body. I then knew she possessed the power of God, and I saw that she was the very same woman I had seen in my night vision several years before. Could I then dispute the work of God in this woman? Nay, in no wise; I could not but acknowledge God in her; for God was in her of a truth. . . . If I ever saw the image of Christ displayed in human clay, I saw it in Mother Ann. . . .

When the wicked came to take Mother and the Elders to prison, I was present and was an eye witness to the scene; and to us it was truly a mournful scene. She prayed earnestly that they might be able to endure with patience all that should come upon them. She often prayed for her persecutors, when they came to abuse her, in these words: "Father, forgive them; for they know not what they do." I feel under no necessity of asking those who seldom or never saw Mother Ann what kind of person she was, because I know for myself. I was with Mother and the Elders several weeks at Hancock and Richmond and was knowing to their being accused of swearing and blasphemy, drunkenness and fighting; but I saw none of these things among them. . . .

When I first heard of these strange people, I was asked what I thought of them. I replied that I was not able to judge; that if the work they were in was of God, it would stand; but if not, it would fall without any of my help. Many among mankind deprive themselves of a great blessing by speaking against this testimony; for I know by the revelation of God that all souls that ever find salvation must find it by obeying this gospel. This is my testimony, and I have written it in the fear of God and can bear witness to it in truth and soberness before all my fellow creatures, in time and eternity.

Thankful Barce

New Lebanon, January 13th, 1827

Testimony of Prudence Hammond

In my youthful days I often felt greatly exercised in mind about a future state and was very much afraid of going to hell. The exercises of my mind were more than I could express to anyone. I knew I daily lived in sin, and I could find no way out; and I often prayed to God as well as I knew how but found no releasement. These exercises increased upon me as I grew older, so that at the age of nineteen, which was the time of the great revival in New Lebanon, I was exceedingly wrought upon; but I could find no way out of sin, nor could I find any one that could help me or show me the way out. I could not even find one in whom I could place confidence as a Christian leader, because I did not see anyone who manifested by the works of righteousness that the spirit of Christ was formed within, which I believed really necessary in order to be a Christian. I kept house for my father at that time; and though he was a professor of religion, I could find no help from him. Some would tell me I was converted and born of God and try to persuade me to be baptized and join the church: but all this availed nothing; it would not ease my troubled conscience. I felt myself a child of wrath and greatly feared the judgments of God.

I had been in this troubled state of mind about three years when I first saw Mother Ann and the Elders. I visited them in June 1780, being then twenty years of age. Mother asked me if I was sick of sin. I told her I saw no way out of sin. She repeated the question, "Are you sick of sin?" I knew not what to say. She turned to some who were present and said, "This young woman is sick of sin." Then turning to me, she said, "You can find no way out of sin till you confess your sins." She then told me of some circumstances and mentioned a number of the transactions of my childhood and youth, which I knew it impossible for her to know but by divine inspiration. I said within myself, "Is not this the anointed?" Here I felt that I had found somebody that could help me and show me the way out of sin: and truly it proved so. I found no deception nor witchcraft here—nothing but the plain and honest truth, and my conscience bore witness to it. . . .

Having lost my mother in my childhood, I was placed by my father in a distant family, where I was much abused. Once I was struck by the man of the house on the side of my head so severely that it occasioned a gathering in my head and a running sore, which caused deafness in one ear, and I had never been able to find any help for it. This circumstance I mentioned to Mother. She bid me take faith in the power of God and said it would be unto me according to my faith. She said if I would be faithful and obedient, I should never want for bread; "Not natural bread," said she, "I mean the bread of life." I returned home with full confidence in her testimony and a settled determination to maintain it. My head was restored and my ear came to its hearing and has ever remained as good as the other. . . .

I visited Mother at Ashfield at a time when there was a great concourse of people there from various parts of the country and much work to be done, especially on the part of the sisters. Mother sent to me one day to know whether I could wash. A little time before this I had the bone of one of my fingers broken and it was very much swelled, so that I could not use that hand. I mentioned this circumstance. Mother again sent word that if I had faith in the power of God, I might be healed. I immediately unbound my hand and went and washed two days without any inconvenience; my hand was well and remained so. . . .

Prudence Hammond

New Lebanon, June 1826

Testimony of Zipporah Cory

I was born in Plainfield, Connecticut, April 4th, 1765. When I was about eleven years of age, I had very serious reflections concerning the salvation of my soul and often retired alone to cry and pray to God in the best manner I was able. I greatly feared going to hell and often thought that if I had lived when Jesus Christ was upon earth, I should then have known how to be good. When I was twelve, my parents moved up into Cheshire, Massachusetts. At the age of fourteen I began to go into young company and by that means wore off my conviction; but in about two years it returned upon me heavier than ever. In this state of mind I was naturally led to look around upon the professors of religion to see if they lived any better than I did; but I could not see any that I had any confidence in: for they would allow themselves in that which I knew was wicked. I used to tell some of the young people who professed to be Christians that they were no better than I was, and I did not profess any religion.

In the spring of 1781, being then sixteen years of age, I went with a number of young people to attend a meeting of the Believers at Squire Bennett's, in Cheshire, whose family were all in the faith. My mother had visited them before and had received faith; but my father was a great opposer. By what I saw and heard of their doctrine, worship, and manner of life, I was soon convinced that they were of God. While they were in meeting dancing in the worship of God, I saw Joanna Sales in the worship with an infant in her arms. I stepped out toward her and offered to take the child—she gave it to me, and I held it till the dancing ceased. She then came to take the child; I observed that her countenance was very solemn and she wept. This sunk deep into my heart. I believed them to be the people of God and thought I was left to be lost with the wicked. On our return home, some of my companions were very carnal and rude and mocked the exercises they had seen. I desired them not to do so; for I really believed they were the people of God.

But when I got home and came to consider the matter, I did not feel as though I could take up my cross and deny myself, as I knew I must in order to be one with them. I thought I would try to stifle my conviction if it was possible and strove to do it in every way and manner I could think of; but I felt very serious reflections within. . . .

In the spring of 1782, I attended their meeting at Squire Bennett's. At this time I saw Lucy Bennett, his daughter-in-law, laboring in the dance with her infant child in her arms. I went up to her and took the child and held it till the dancing ceased. She then came and took the child. I observed her countenance was solemn and serene, while the tears were running down her cheeks. This filled me with the most serious impressions; and I thought surely such solemnity and sincerity as I saw among these people was certainly of God. But I went home fully determined, if possible, to *kill* my conscience. I went on as light and carnal as I was able, so that it was observed by my friends that they never saw me so light and airy before. And though at times when I was alone I was obliged to give way to a flood of tears, yet I was determined to stifle all conviction if possible; but I found I could not do it, for the spirit of God was evidently at work with me, and I plainly saw that I must yield at last: thus I went on fighting against my own conviction and feeling the smart of it.

In October following . . . I attended their meeting again on the Sabbath. At this time Mother and the Elders were at Squire Bennett's. Elder James Whittaker delivered a lengthy discourse, which sunk deep into my heart. At this time I was fully determined to confess my sins before I returned home. I kept with the Believers all day, but felt so diffident that I had not resolution enough to speak to them and tell them what I wanted. In the evening I happened to be sitting by myself in the same room where Mother was. She was sitting alone in the further part of the room, though I did not then know who she was. Calvin Harlow soon came into the room and advanced toward Mother as though he was going to speak to her; but seeing me sitting by myself, he turned to me and asked me if I loved the Believers. I answered yes. He asked if I had confessed my sins. I told him I had not. He then went out. In a few minutes Mother rose and came and took me by the hand and led me out of the house to another building, singing all the way as we went, and led me into a room where Elder John Hocknell was.[2] "Here" said she "is a young woman who wants to open her mind, and you must hear her"—and then left me with him. I then confessed my sins freely and heartily and was glad of such a privilege and felt greatly released by it. . . .

I was at that time engaged in work at the house of a Quaker preacher. When I returned there, the people of the house discovered an alteration in me and thought I was sick. As I was very bashful and diffident, I felt as if I could not take up my cross and kneel before them; and for this reason I went without my supper and breakfast.[3] But I went to my work; and while I was spinning at my wheel, the power of God came upon me and suddenly brought me upon my knees. The family then discovered that I was a Shaker, and all my acquaintance soon fell upon me to try to reclaim me by their exhortations and warnings against delusion. . . .

I finished my work at this place as soon as I could and went home. There I found still greater troubles to encounter. My father was like a madman, and my oldest brother was not much better. My father abused my mother very much, because of her faith; and I was so persecuted by them that I really stood in fear of my life. Many times when I lay down at night I did not expect to see the light of another day. At one time my fears were so great on acount of their extreme abuse to me and my mother that for six weeks I never took my clothes off, except to change them for washing. I often went out into the woods and cried to God in my extreme sorrow.

All this persecution I suffered, because I had set out to forsake sin and live a godly life. Before this, I was beloved by the family and neighbors and suffered no persecution.

My parents had a child of five years old that could not speak a word nor help himself any more than an infant three months old. One day, feeling great sorrow of soul, I kneeled down in prayer to God near where this child was sitting on the floor. While I was on my knees, the child suddenly rose up and stood on his feet, which he had never done before, and spoke distinctly, saying "Lord God," three times over, and then sat down again. He never spoke before nor afterward to my knowledge. This alarmed my father very much. "The dumb speaks to me," said he; and it convicted him so much that he went and confessed his sins. But in about a month he was as bad or worse than ever. . . .

I lived with my parents about two years and a half after I embraced the gospel: they then moved back into Connecticut. I was then nearly twenty years of age and had my freedom and enjoyed my faith undisturbed. My mother had faith and would gladly have enjoyed a privilege with Believers but could not on acount of my father's opposition. . . .

Though I was a poor girl and of poor parentage, yet I have never seen any difference made on that account, but I have always fared as well among Believers as the daughters of the rich.

In all the opportunities and privileges I have had with Mother and the Elders, I can truly testify that I never saw the least imperfection in them. They taught me to live a life of purity and godliness; and I always found an example of it in them. They were truly an upright and godly people in all things. As to the charges of intemperance, I never saw the least thing of the kind in them, but always considered them very temperate in all things; and they always taught us temperance. My father was a downright drunkard, which was the cause of great affliction and tribulation to my mother and (as I suppose) was the cause of producing in me a constitutional antipathy to ardent spirits: for even the very smell of rum has ever been nauseous and disgusting to me from my earliest infancy; and no object ever appeared so odious in my sight as a drunken person, whether male or female. But I never saw any ardent spirits where Mother Ann was, nor did I ever smell any there; and I am confident I should have smelled it if any had been there. And had Mother or the Elders been given to intoxication, I should most certainly have discovered it and should have quit them at once. I feel confident that the spirit of God which Mother Ann possessed could never abide in the soul of a drunkard.

. . . I certainly know by the evidence of divine truth in my own soul that she was chosen and anointed of God and that the spirit of Christ was revealed through her ministration. I have lived in obedience to her testimony nearly forty-four years and have always found that it does save me from all sin. And I feel thankful that I am now able to bear witness to the purity of that gospel which I received through her ministration and in which I have found peace and solid rest. I feel myself to be the seed of the free woman and an heir to the promised inheritance. I have no natural relations with me; but I have spiritual relations, elders, brethren, and sisters, who are dearer to me than any of my natural kindred ever were. In these I can confide, and with these I can unite and partake of the true bread of life and drink of the pure waters of life and enjoy in heavenly harmony one Lord, one faith, and one baptism.

Zipporah Cory

New Lebanon, June 12th, 1826

Testimony of Lucy Wight

When I was young I used to be much affected with reading about the sufferings and persecutions which Christ and his disciples endured from the wicked; and I often thought if I had lived in that day, I would have been one of Christ's disciples. When I was about nineteen years old, I was taken very sick with a nervous fever, so that my life was despaired of, both by myself and others. In the time of this sickness I fell into a kind of trance and thought I died. Finding myself alone in the world of spirits, as I thought, and no one to help me, I was in great trouble and prayed that some one would come to my assistance and conduct me to a place of happiness. And there appeared to me a very pure, bright-looking man, who conducted me to a house, as it seemed, where I saw a number of people who looked so pure and clean that I began to feel greatly ashamed of myself. Among the rest I saw a man who seemed to be walking the floor under the operations of the power of God.

The sight of such heavenly purity as these people seemed to possess and the sense I felt of my own impurity and unfitness for such a place brought excessive tribulation upon me, and I felt as though I wanted to get away and hide myself. I told the people that when I was in the body, I thought when I died I should go to heaven, but I could not find heaven, because I had come there in my sins; and I asked them if there was not some place where I could go and repent of my sins and be saved and not go to hell. They said there was; and I might go and repent.

About this time my father came to my bedside and took hold of my hand and I awoke from my trance. I asked him if he thought I was dying. He said he thought I was and asked me if I did not think so. I answered, "No." He asked me if I was willing to die. I replied that I was not, for I was yet in my sins; and if I should die in my sins, I could not be saved. My vision in this sickness greatly awakened my feelings and led me to search for some way out of sin. In this search I continued for several years without success—no way appeared; but I did not then know the cause.

In the year 1779, there was a great revival of religion in New Lebanon, in which I received a witness that the time of Christ's second appearance was near at hand; but in what manner it would take place I could not tell: for I believed his second appearance, like the first, would take place in a manner contrary to all human calculation. And I was afraid I should be like the unbelieving Jews and should oppose Christ in his coming.

In the spring of the following year (1780), there were various reports in circulation about a strange sort of people living up above Albany; and I felt a great anxiety to go and search them out and see whether there was anything good among them or not. Accordingly I set out with six or seven others to make them a visit. While on our journey, one of the company asked me if I was going to join them. I replied that I had searched a great deal after religion but had never yet found any that had any solid foundation; and if their religion had no better foundation than any that I had ever found before, I should not join them: "For," said I, "they cannot catch old birds with chaff."

We went to John Partington's and stayed overnight. The next morning being Sabbath, we went on to the place where Mother and the Elders lived and arrived there just before they began their morning worship and attended their meeting, which was unspeakably powerful, solemn, and striking. We also attended their afternoon meeting. The mighty power of God was evidently present in visible operations among the people. I was so affected with a sense of fear, guilt, and shame on account of my own wretched and lost state and my unfitness to be with a people of such purity, that I drew back and kept out of sight as much as possible. Among other extraordinary manifestations of the power of God which I noticed, one of the Elders, while walking the floor under the visible operations of divine power suddenly extended his hand toward me and came directly up to me, saying, "God knows what is there, and so do his servants." This struck me very forcibly; I fully believed what he said and felt as though all my sins were as plain and open to their view as they were to my own; and I felt as much tribulation as I was able to endure.

We again attended the evening meeting, when I again stepped in behind the people and sat down on a bench in hopes of keeping out of sight. Elder James Whittaker soon came and sat down with me and said, "Woman, what do you think of this great work of God?" I answered, "I know it is the work of God." "So you do," said he, "but you are like the Jews of old, who waited too long for a Messiah, but when he came, he was too mean for them; so is this work of God too mean for you." I replied that I did not think there was any way of God for me. Then Mother and the Elders came and kneeled down before me; my head was bowed down into my lap and I was unable to raise it up or to help myself. Mother wept and cried for a few minutes and then began to sing, and sung very melodiously.[4] They then told me that there was a way of God for me, if I would confess and forsake my sins. This I fully believed, and in obedience to the faith I then received, I went immediately out and confessed my sins honestly before Mother; and I found her to be a Mother indeed. I found that releasement from the burden of sin which I had never felt before and which I had never been able to find in any other way, though I had long sought for it.

The vision which I had seen in my sickness more than four years before came fresh to my mind. Here was the house and the people. I remembered the guilt and confusion I had felt in my vision, and now I had realized it. The man who came to me with outstretched hand I found to be Elder John Hocknell; and I knew him to be the same man that I saw in my vision walking the floor under the operations of divine power. All the scenes of that singular vision were this day realized to me in a very striking manner. I now felt as though I had got upon a sure foundation, where I could safely stand. . . .

When we first heard of Mother and the Elders, we found by the report of their neighbors, of whom inquiry was made, that they were considered as a peaceable, honest, and industrious people, having a good name among their neighbors, who were plain, honest, Dutch people and did not meddle with the religion of other people, and of course had no prejudice against the Shakers on that account. But when we came to hear and embrace their testimony and to receive a measure of the spirit of Christ through their ministration and walk according to it; then it was that evil reports began to spread over the country: so that in a short time Mother was charged with every kind of wickedness that the tongue of slander could express. But so far from weakening my faith, these reports strengthened it the more, because the great similarity between the accusations against the Lord Jesus and Mother Ann was thereby made to appear more striking and evident.

It was not long after I embraced this testimony that Mother and the Elders were imprisoned in Albany, as were also most of the leading characters of the work in New Lebanon. When the wicked took Mother and the Elders to convey them to prison, they made their boasts that if they could confine them and get away the principal members of the Society from New Lebanon, they could easily overthrow the rest and put a stop to the work. Accordingly they seized and committed them all to prison; and we poor children were left like sheep without a shepherd. Yet through our humble prayers to God day and night we were protected and strengthened in our faith, and our persecutors failed in their object and were not able to destroy the work of God. . . .

. . . I was with her when she visited Hancock and New Lebanon, where persecution raged without control. In these persecutions she appeared perfectly undaunted and boldly reproved the wicked for their ungodly conduct. They sometimes accused her on such occasions of being drunk or mad; but I never saw her drunk nor mad at any time. She spoke as she was influenced by the spirit and power of God and was no more mad nor drunk than Jesus was when he exclaimed to the wicked, in his day, *"Ye serpents, ye generation of vipers, how can ye escape the damnation of hell?"* (See Matthew 23:33.). But however great or severe their persecutions, Mother and the Elders always bore their sufferings and abuses with meekness and humility. . . .

. . . My mother died while I was quite young, and though I had a kind father, yet I knew not the value and importance of a mother till I found Mother Ann. . . . I feel my faith firmly fixed and grounded on a sure foundation; nor have I any more doubt of Mother's divine mission or of the truth of her testimony than I have of that of Jesus Christ and his apostles: for it has kept me from all sin and all manner of evil and is to this day like the bread of life to my soul. . . .

I have enjoyed many feeling sensations of Mother's spirit and presence since she left the body. In times of tribulation, I have often felt her present with me to comfort me. These things are not fanciful dreams of the imagination, but as real as the light of the sun in a clear day. . . . I never received anything from her but what was good; nor did I ever see any thing but goodness in her from the first day I saw her to the day of her decease.

Lucy Wight

New Lebanon, June 10th, 1826

Testimony of Hannah Cogswell

I received faith in the present testimony of the gospel in the fore part of January, 1781. I was then in my eighteenth year. I went to Watervliet to visit Mother and the Elders and was received into their family. I lived and lodged in the room with Mother Ann more than four months and a half and sometimes slept in the same bed with her. She taught me to confess and forsake and repent of all my sins and take up a daily cross against my carnal nature. In obedience to her teaching I have found salvation from sin and have "escaped the pollutions that are in the world through lust."

. . . . I have been with her in times of persecution and have repeatedly witnessed the wounds and bruises which she received from the hands of her wicked persecutors, who hated her for the testimony which she bore. She was truly "a woman of sorrows, and acquainted with grief." I feel confident that in point of suffering and persecution, sorrow and cries to God day and night for the salvation of lost souls, she came the nearest to the Lord Jesus Christ of any other woman on earth. I have not been following a drunken woman nor a harlot—nay, in no wise . . .

Testimony of Anne [Anna] Matthewson

. . . There have been many false and scandalous reports published and circulated abroad in the world concerning Mother Ann; but I certainly know for myself that she was not such a person as her enemies have represented. So far from being addicted to intemperance, she was the most temperate woman I ever was acquainted with. So far from being a lewd or profane person, she was truly an example of chastity and godliness to all womankind. . . . These things I do know, for I was with her at all times and seasons, in public and in private, by day and by night, in her sorrows and sufferings, as well as in her joy and comfort; and if she or the Elders with her had been guilty of any such conduct as they have been accused of, I certainly should have known it; for it could not have been kept out of my sight. . . . I cannot feel the least doubt or scruple of her being a chosen woman anointed of the Lord, any more than I can doubt her existence.

. . . There are but few in this day who will pretend to deny the agency of the first woman in leading mankind into sin. Why then should it be thought incredible that the agency of a woman should necessarily be first in leading the human race out of sin? Mother Ann's testimony and example and all her fruits evidently show that she was led by a spirit totally opposite to that which led and influenced the first woman. To the truth of this, all who have heard her testimony and seen her example and faithfully followed it can bear witness; because they have in reality been led out of sin thereby; and they are able to testify that "she taught as never *woman* taught before."

NOTES

1. Source: Seth Y. Wells and Calvin Green, eds., *Testimonies Concerning the Character and Ministry of Mother Ann Lee and the First Witnesses* . . . (Albany: 1827), 87–92, 92–96, 50–54, 54–60, 65–71, 28–32, 46–50.
2. This story indicates clearly that the Shakers had not yet begun to insist on the separation of the sexes in such matters as the confession of sins.
3. This suggests that kneeling at mealtimes was widely understood as a Shaker custom in this neighborhood.
4. Ann Lee's ability to use song as an element in religious persuasion is a striking theme in the early converts' testimonies, and it is no doubt the basis for the prominence of song in later Shaker culture.

JEMIMA BLANCHARD'S STORIES AS RECALLED
BY ROXALANA GROSVENOR (1836)

The following was collected from the aged Believers by Roxalana L. Grosvenor.[1]

I often heard Sister Jemima Blanchard speak of Mother's tenderness in dealing with her. She said that she and Sarah Robbins used to talk together about it, and both felt sure that if Mother had dealt with either of them as she did with the other, that neither would have been saved. Jemima said that if Mother had talked as sharp to her as she did to Sarah she should have been frightened away at once; Sarah said that if Mother had been as tender and loving with her as she was with Jemima, it would have made no impression upon her.

Mother never reproved Jemima but on one occasion. She came into the house where she was, just after she had retired to rest, and called for her. Having been broke of her rest a great deal, she was so sleepy that she was rather slow in meeting the call. She heard Mother speak out sharp and say, "What! Sloth!" This grieved her to the heart. She felt as if she was killed outright. She grieved over it all night and the next morning appeared sad and kept rather distant; Mother spoke sharp to her for appearing so, but she could not rise above it.

Just as Mother was going away she again spoke quite sharp and told her to leap. She obeyed as well as she felt as if she could, but was rather clumsy about it and still kept her grief.

Father James and Father Calvin [Harlow] stopped and spoke a few words of comfort to her. Father Calvin told her how bad he felt the first time he was reproved. They took their handkerchiefs from their necks and asked her to do them up as soon as she could and bring them to them. She thought they were afraid she would not go to meeting and did this that she might be obliged to go. They pacified her a little, but none but Mother could heal the wound that Mother had made. Her smile was sunshine, and her frown was perfect darkness to her.

She went to meeting but kept at a distance from Mother, labored out to the other side of the room. Father James watched her movements and, slipping out of the south door of the meeting room, went round to the east door, near which she was laboring. He pushed her toward Mother till she came close to her. Mother put out her arms and embraced her saying, "Come, come, you shall be the least bantling Mother's got."[2] She then felt so much love from Mother that it took away all her grief and she felt nearer to Mother than ever.

Still she felt mortified that she could bear reproof no better, and when she would hear others reproved sharply, who she knew were greatly her superiors, and she remain untouched, she used to feel ashamed of herself; and when Mother would speak sometimes of children being spoiled by indulgence, she would take it and feel reproved.

She used to admire Mother Hannah Kendall's brave spirit in bearing reproof. She was knowing to her being kept on her knees a long time one night under severe reproof and mortification. She could hear a faint groan from her occasionally but did not see, hear, or feel anything like unreconciliation. . . .

Sister Jemima told me that there were very strange operations and signs at the Square House, and Mother would sometimes appear to be in a labor to know what they meant; she heard her say at one time that she never saw anything like it before; "But," said she after a pause, "it is of God, and it is not for me to condemn it." She said this had been an instructive lesson to her, not to judge or condemn any gift because she could not understand it.

At one time Jemima herself had a very singular gift. She saw hell open, and she seemed to be on the brink in imminent danger of falling. In her efforts to keep out of it she crept around the room on her hands and knees, uttering the most heartrending cries. Mother stooped to her, and in her agony, wringing her hands, she got hold of Mother's apron. She knew not what it was or that Mother was near her, but it felt like a comfort and support to her, so she kept winding it around her hands. Mother followed her round the room some time in that position and then took it off and let her have it. This she was told afterward, as she knew nothing at the time of what was passing. Her Sister Phebe afterward fell away, and she thought this gift was the sign of her situation . . .

NOTES

1. Source: "Sayings of Mother Ann and the First Elders Gathered from Different Individuals . . . Collected Together by Roxalana L. Grosvenor," MeSl (first of four anthology manuscripts under this title), 134–47. Only one story of Ann Lee by Jemima Blanchard is included in the 1816 *Testimonies*, a short one in which she confesses having called Mother Ann a "witch," and receives the lesson that witch- craft is a delusion (318–19). Later much material about the days of Ann Lee, includ- ing Blanchard's own conversion testimony, was collected at Harvard by a variety of interviewers, including Eunice Bathrick and Roxalana Grosvenor.
2. "Bantling" means young child.

ELIZABETH WOOD'S TESTIMONY (1851)[1]

I have many times taken great satisfaction in conversing with the aged about Mother Ann and the Elders.

January 18, 1851. I went in to visit Elizabeth Wood, an aged sister in the Church at Enfield, Connecticut. She related the following particulars of her interviews with Mother, etc.

The first time I saw Mother I was out at the side of the road picking strawberries. I heard a wagon coming and I thought it was Mother Ann. Although no one had been expecting her previously. I immediately left my employment and followed the wagon and pulled down the bars to let her through and followed the wagon to the house. Mother dismounted and went to the door and exclaimed, "Where is the old man?" This was grandfather Meacham who visited Mother in prison and opened his mind. He soon came to the door and let her in. This was her first visit at Enfield. This was in June 1781. She took off her things and called for some water to wash. Those who accompanied her were Father William Lee, Father James Whittaker, Elder John Partington, Elder John Hocknell, Joseph Meacham, Samuel Fitch, Molly Partington, and Margaret Leland.

After dinner Mother walked into a room and sat down by herself. I went in and kneeled down before her and told her I had called her a witch and wished she was shot with a piece of silver. "What made you call me so?" said she. "Wasn't it because you have heard others say so?" I told her I did not know. "Well, it was," said she, "and I can forgive you and pray God to forgive you. Get up, child. Have you any parents?" I answered, "Yea." "You have a step-mother, have you not?" I said, "I have a mother-in-law." "Well, that is a step-mother." She said considerable respecting her and related circumstances which I knew was revealed to her by the gift of God.

Mother and the Elders tarried a number of days and many people came to visit them. One man observed that Mother's singing sounded louder to him than any clap of thunder which he ever heard in his life. The world began to oppose Mother and threatened if they were not gone by such a time they would carry her off by force. Mother thought it wisdom to leave as the world were so bitter and constantly watching to see if they were going to leave at the appointed time.

The second time that Mother and the Elders came, there collected a very large concourse of people who surrounded the house and formed a large ring and called for the old Elect Lady to come out. Mother walked out into the ring and said, "What do you want of me?" One man stepped up and said, "We want to know if you are the head of this Church." "Christ is the head of the Church," said she. They asked a number of questions in that way and she answered them in like manner so as they did not make out to their minds. They all withdrew without doing injury to person or property.

When the Elders were about leaving there gathered round quite a collection of the world; after Mother had got into the wagon, one of the men stepped up idly and pulled out the linchpin and threw it one side, but one of the brethren fortunate saw him and found it and put it back, so they went on safely. The brethren, after following the carriage a short distance, returned.

The third and last time that Mother came to Enfield there was a mob collected and followed her through Stafford and Summit and arrived as soon as she did. She went into the house and took off her things and went outdoors. I followed her and told her that the mob had got there. "Have they?" said she. I supposed she would go back into the house, but she went round to the other door which opened into an entry and led upstairs into her room. The crowd was so thick that Mother spread her arms and said, "Stand away and let me come," speaking with authority. They stood back and she passed through and got onto the stairs and they began to think it was Mother and one man said, "There she is; we will have her." David Meacham sprang upon the stairs. The man sprang through his legs to get upstairs. David caught him by his neck and held him fast and spanked him about right. It sounded pretty smart as the chap had on a pair of leather breeches. The rest of the company were more pleased than mad; they haw-hawed and laughed heartily and began to disperse; but in the meantime they caught Molly Partington, the one who rode with Mother, and thought it was the Old Elect Lady sure enough, and they dragged her along and put her onto a horse and one man got on to the same horse behind her to hold her on. David Meacham left the other man and went and hauled her off of the horse and they collared David and pulled his ears till the blood ran down his shirt sleeves. One of the brethren had previously gone to a constable, who came and warned them off and made them pay a fine. This money the brethren kept to donate to the poor exclusively.

In the year '82 I went to Watervliet to see Mother accompanied by three brethren and two sisters. When we arrived we were kindly received, took supper, and attended a meeting which lasted all night till the break of day. Father James read and spoke a great deal. He read in the Bible. When we retired to rest (which time was very short), we had to lay down on the floor, and I put my shoes under my head for a pillow. Father James kept fire for us. He told us all that we need not meddle with it; he would see to that himself. He came in again and fixed the fire, which was in a small fireplace. We had a little straw to lay on and cover over us, but we were so crowded that if one turned over all had to turn also. But we were conveyed as well as we could be in their then present circumstances.

We tarried eight days. In which time we were set to work. Mother told me to go with Molly Hocknell and spin tow on a little wheel. Said Molly should fix the tow on for me, which she did, and I purled and worked till noon and could not make it go. I then went and told Mother I could not make any headway at it at all. Mother said, "Well, I will set somebody at it that can, and you may sit down and knit William a pair of muffets." She brought the needles and yarn and told me to seam them one and one. After I had got them done I carried them to her and she said, "Now you may sit down and make a pair of slippers for Molly Partington." While I was at work (it being in the room where several more sisters were seated on benches sewing), Mother came in and said to Hannah Knapp (who had on a handkerchief which was not hemmed), "Take off your handkerchief and make it. You had never ought to wear a garment before it is made." She went to another sister and asked her what she was at work on and who it was for. Molly [Freedom?] was the reply. "Where is she? Bring her forward." When she came Mother said to her, "We sent for you to come and work for us but you bring work and set others at work, do you? Here, take your work and sit down and do it yourself before you do anything for us."

In this time Elizur Goodrich came in with David Darrow and another brother. Mother said to them, "Sit down and warm your selves." They readily obeyed and sat down on the floor before the fire, for the weather was turned very cold. After they had sat awhile, Mother came in and told them they might take their axes and go to work and be faithful.

One morning Mother said to Thomas Pratt, "Here, you may be a door-keeper; you may stand and keep the door shut the day over."

I was set to washing one day in an out-building. Mother came towards the place and called me to come to her. I went and she said, "See how sick I am and how I have puked? I am under great sufferings for some that are coming here, and they will be here soon." I kept watch as the road was plain in sight and it was but a short time before three or four loads drove up. They were professedly Believers, but some of the company afterward turned away.

After I had done washing, I went in where was at work three sisters tailoring; while there, Mother's niece[2] came and brought her children who were then held in some degree of union. There was a meeting that after-noon and they attended. Father William was sick at the time, but he was so far released as to be able to attend the meeting; but as soon as it was over he had to go to bed again. Mother said, "Here is William under great sufferings, but there are some here now that don't care any more about it than they do for the cocks crowing or the hens cackling."

We attended meeting every night, which lasted till the cocks crew for day. Then retired to rest till the sun rose, then took breakfast, which was broth—also the same for supper.

One time when we had assembled for meeting, Mother called on David Darrow to relate the labor of his mind through the past day. David complied with the requirement and it was quite a lesson of instruction to the assembly. After he had done, Father William said to him, "David praised God with his whole heart, yea his tongue praises God and his hands praise God and his feet praise God. And now his whole body is devoted to praise and worship God." The assembly then went forth in the lively exercise and we all labored all night. I had a gift to turn, and Mother said to Father William, "See the bright angels turning her now." At another time she came in and raised her hands and shouted, and the sisters gathered round her and hugged and kissed her. I got down to her feet and kissed them, for I loved her so well that it seemed like a privilege to touch her garments. She raised her hands and said, "Now let me go."

It was in vain for any one to try to hide their sins from her, for she was able to search them out.

At one particular time which I very well recollect, Mother reproved a woman in public and told her her situation in plain language. She was a very corrupt creature and did not humble herself to the gospel but continued in wickedness. And the children which came with them appeared very bold and disagreeable. Mother took them to Father James and kneeled them down and told him to examine them, which he did by asking them questions. He repeated the conversation to Mother, and she said, "They are old in wickedness; they are almost as old as Methuselah."

At another time Mother came into the meeting room where was some children lying on benches asleep. She said, "Where are their mothers? Tell them to come and take care of their babies." We had no sitting meeting but labored all the time. Only when the Elders were speaking or reading sometimes, when they were reading some would sit down on the floor and others would kneel, but I stood up the whole time and suffered no inconvenience for want of sleep, and I felt anxious to see, hear, and learn all I could.

When the time came for us to leave, Father William came out and spoke to us in a very feeling manner, desiring us to return home and be faithful. He expressed great thankfulness for the way of God, with tears running down his cheeks. We promised him that we would be faithful and returned home with hearts filled with thankfulness for the blessed privilege which we had enjoyed.

Previous to our starting I told Father Hocknell that I wanted to stay. He said he would go and ask Mother, which he did, and she said, "Tell her to go home and be faithful, for I have precious jewels laid up in my bosom for her." I obeyed Mother's word and returned home and was obedient to my parents as long as they lived, and I have labored to be faithful ever since. I have never flinched at the cross but have taken it up with cheerfulness, and I am now eighty-two years of age and I feel perfectly resigned to the will of God to stay longer or shorter.

I am often with Mother in my sleep and daily feel her blessing resting upon me. I have always labored to be in the gift and have ever kept my union to my lead, which has always been a guide to my feet.

The year the Church was gathered at Enfield, Connecticut, Father Calvin Harlow came and sent for all the young people in the place, and there was nine selected to come into the Church. I was one, and now I am the only one remaining in the Church that is living. Father said to me, "Will you be subject to every gift that is or may be felt for you?" I answered "Yea, I will." He repeated the same question three times, and I answered in like manner. Whenever any cross has been presented to me, this has been in my mind, and it has always been a strength to me.

Elizabeth Wood

NOTES

1. Source: "Testimonial given by Elizabeth Wood," OClWHi VI B 1. Elizabeth Wood was born in 1768, and was eighty-two when she told this story. (A fair copy of the first part of this testimony also appears in OClWHi VI B 54, as "Sketches taken from the mouth of Elizabeth Wood of Enfield Ct. Aged 87; by Olive Hatch of Harvard. August 5, 1855.")

2. One of the few references in Shaker literature to Ann Lee's niece, Nancy Lee(s), who left the community to marry Richard Hocknell, according to the seceder Thomas Brown (Garrett, 218).

2. "YOUR PARENT IN THE GOSPEL"
The Sayings and Correspondence of Lucy Wright

INTRODUCTION

"Lucy Faith now stands head of the church," wrote the New Lebanon Shaker Angell Matthewson to his brother Jeffrey in 1797, thirteen years after the death of Ann Lee.[1] After a relatively brief interval of male headship—Ann Lee was succeeded first by James Whittaker and then by Joseph Meacham—the church returned to a de facto "matriarchal" governance system for a quarter century.[2] Lucy Faith[3] or Lucy Wright (Goodrich) presided over a period of turbulent development and explosive growth within the United Society of Believers in Christ's Second Appearing until her death in 1821. Historians are only just now beginning to examine closely her role in the political, social, and religious evolution of Shakerism.[4]

Wright's first biographer, Calvin Green (who had worked as a younger and subordinate elder in the Wright administration), tellingly contrasted Lucy Wright's more feminine maternal character with that of Ann Lee.[5]

> I esteemed her as a perfect Model of a Female character, according to the true Order of Gods Creation; and in this respect doubtless she was never equalled on Earth. Our Blessed Mother Ann was her Mother, & had a higher Sphere to fill—and was greater in the Power & Light of God. But in her peculiar calling, she [Lee] was necessitated to display in part the Male as well as the Female qualities, & hence could not distinctly exhibit the genuine Female Character. I esteem her as the revered Mother of the New Creation of God; & Mother Lucy, as the worthy Mother of the Church of God.[6]

Possessing "the genuine Female Character" did not make her submissive, however, and Lucy Wright did not share her power with a male partner. Never claiming Lee's prophetic and visionary powers, Wright saw herself as the fountainhead of love for a whole people and believed that the communities' continued existence depended upon suppressing selfish conflict and increasing the bonds of union.

Unlike Ann Lee, Lucy Wright was literate. She has left us both oral-historical sayings collected by her followers and letters in her own hand. This literature gives us two angles from which to view her work as the second Shaker Mother. The sayings present her performance as a religious leader who valued and taught self-control as a more reliable route to blessedness than ecstasy. The letters give us access to the leadership politics of this period and help us view the development of early Shaker religion from the first-person perspective of a woman in authority.

Wright's Authority as Mother of the Church

By a revealing irony of early Shaker history, Lucy Wright derived her authority not from the founding mother Ann Lee, but from one of Lee's male successors.

Though Lucy Wright became a Shaker in the early days following the New Lebanon revival, there is no indication of a close relationship between the two during Lee's lifetime, nor any firm evidence that Lee intended for her to play a role in future Shaker governance.[7] When Ann Lee started on her itinerant ministry to the east, May 31, 1781, Wright did not accompany her as one of the inner circle or "church." She was certainly never a close female companion of Lee, as were Mary Partington (one of the original English Shakers), Margaret Leland (the American sister of Daniel Wood), and Hannah Kendall.[8] She attended Ann Lee in her last illness but was not the first sister chosen to do so.[9] Nor was Lucy Wright an important source of reminiscences about Ann Lee when the 1816 *Testimonies* were collected, as might be expected of a close companion.[10]

Contemporary accounts suggest that there were significant class differences (as well as a twenty-five-year age difference) between Ann Lee and Lucy Wright. Lee was an unlettered visionary from a British factory town, whereas Wright was the genteel daughter of a prominent family in western Massachusetts. Calvin Green's biography characterizes Wright's relatives as "among the high order of people," and calls her "a leading character among the high class of young women" in the town of Pittsfield, where she grew up. Her husband Elizur Goodrich, who converted first, had told Ann Lee that because Wright's "relations were a lofty high-minded people . . . it was very doubtful to him whether she would believe and obey the gospel."[11]

The testimony of several seceders characterizes Ann Lee's language as "harsh," and her manner as the opposite of genteel.[12] In contrast, Calvin Green's biography dwells on Lucy Wright's emphasis on "correct & proper Language in speaking," and represents her as "very desirous that Believers should always speak properly, & not use clipped, or low, vulgar words, or expressions—"[13]

At Lee's death in 1784, Lucy Wright's role did not immediately change.[14] Calvin Green specifically says that it was Joseph Meacham who had the revelation, in the winter of 1787, that a "joint parentage" of female and male leadership should be established, with Lucy Wright as the "first Mother."[15] A new gender-balanced and hierarchical governance system replaced James Whittaker's looser "system of fathers & mothers" (whereby all the elderly Shakers had courtesy parental titles).[16] Lucy Wright assumed her place as the female partner of Joseph Meacham early in the year 1788, according to Green, and "upon her the lot devolved to find & gain the true Order of the Female in the Church relation."[17] As yet very little is known about Wright's contributions to the organization of the New England Shaker communities during the eight years when she and Meacham together headed the Society.[18]

Wright was involved in at least one major internal upheaval even before Joseph Meacham's death and her appointment as the next first Elder. According to Calvin Green's autobiography, she played a significant role in attempting to prevent the first serious internal division of the New Lebanon Church, in 1795.[19] The failure to contain the rebellion of a substantial number of dissenting youth took its toll on Joseph Meacham's health. Realizing he would not live much longer, he wrote to Lucy Wright—addressing her as "one whom I esteem my equal in order and Lot." In this letter written in the spring of 1796, Meacham clearly designated her as his successor, as "Elder or first born," several months before his death (Letter 1).

> Inasmuch . . . as both the man & the woman have Equal Rights in order & Lots in the Lord & Governance of the Church according to their sex in this Latter Day & as thee tho of the weaker sex in man will be the Elder or first born after my departure I believe the Greatest measure of the Wisdom & Knowledge of God For the Protection of souls will be Given unto thee Especially in Counsel untill thy Power & strength both intellectual & Corporal shall fail as mine hath done.

By appointing Lucy Wright first elder, in preference to his male assistant, Henry Clough, Meacham reversed the evolution away from female headship that had begun with the death of Ann Lee.

Lucy Wright's authority as a woman heading the United Society was questioned more than once during her administration. The first occasion was immediately after Joseph Meacham's death. Though Henry Clough (like Abiathar Babbitt later on) acknowledged her headship,[20] Angel

Matthewson did not. One of the large group who seceded from the United Society in the late 1790s, Matthewson described Lucy Wright's headship in bitter caricature:

> Lucy Faith is not onley hed of the church at Lebanon but she is the supreem hed of elevn churchis in all whom all look up to her for spiritual gifts. at the same time tis not expeted nither is it hur office or duty to preech or pray sing songs or dance in fact she has nothing to do accept to consult the oricles & giv out orders of God, eat & drink & ride to Waterfleet & back again in a curious pleasure waggon drawn by a compleet span of horses & a driver to wate on hur. She has neither food nor rament to look out for as hur food is cooked in the neetist mannor & brought to hur chamber apartment hur clothing is made up without hur toil washed & ironed & brought to hur room—I have no historical knowlidg of ever aney godis on earth fairing so sumtiously and being so well obeyed as Lucy faith . . . altho Lucy is a godis and is convercant with god, she wanted a man to liv in the meeting house with hur to carrey orders of god from her to the elders of distant churchis who pilgrimage to Newlebanon every year to receiv orders of god from the ministry . . . [21]

Class issues seem clearly to be involved in Matthewson's growing resentment of the hierarchical Shaker governance system. Yet in his account of his departure, he stresses his humiliation as a male at being expected to submit to female leadership, or even to "elders ruled by women."[22] In telling the story of his departure, he includes a scene in which he challenges an elder: "as we have a woman for the hed of the church & are intirely ruled by wimmin & you mention freedom how can you call our church goverment freedom?" He considers it the last straw to be rebuked by eldresses and leaves because "I could not keep my mind so narrowly contracted as to follow every odd whim cungered up by wimmin or elders ruled by a woman."[23]

Lucy Wright's authority was challenged even more seriously in 1815–1816, by the male first ministry elder of the Maine Shaker communities. Again, whatever other issues were involved, gender became a lightning rod. The disaffected Father John Barns of Alfred, Maine, fomented rebellion against the New Lebanon ministry headed by Wright in 1815, accusing some elders of drunkenness and preaching doctrines "such as the male prophecy has ceased, and the lead being in the female brings great distress upon the body, so the famine spoken of by Father James is fulfilled."[24] In July 1816, twenty influential New Lebanon brethren sent a letter to Alfred, rebutting various charges made by Barns, including his report that "we have become weary of petticoat-government":

> Answer. We have for many years been satisfied that, petticoat-government, and breeches-government both belonged to the flesh, and have no part in the government of Christ; and we would to God that all Believers, both male and female, might be so sick of it, as to be willing to be made

free from it by the law and government of Christ, which is neither male nor female separably, but the union of the spirit between them both. Therefore, it is not man, nor woman, that is to govern the Church, but it is Christ: And whether Christ governs us through the medium of man, or woman, it is the same unction from the Holy One, and we are equally satisfied. And as it respects our precious Mother, who is the first visible pillar of the Church of Christ on earth; we feel an unshaken faith & full confidence in her gift, and as well satisfied with her administration, as with any that have preceded it.[25]

After incidents like these, Lucy Wright would have been well aware that male resentment of female headship was a potentially divisive force within Shakerism, and this may partially explain her more "feminine" style of spiritual motherhood. Though we have no direct record of her reactions to these rebellions, Lucy Wright is remembered as instructing the leaders who succeeded her not to "get to be male & female while I am gone."[26] She seems to have taken some care to garner the assent of the influential brethren when making decisions affecting the areas of Shaker life considered their responsibility.[27]

The Work of the Lucy Wright Administration

Lucy Wright presided over the network of Shaker communities during a period of dramatic population growth,[28] internal and intracommunity controversy, persistent apostate agitation, and legal attack. Improvising responses to these challenges, and listening to advice from her associates in the New Lebanon and other Shaker ministries, Wright worked for the promotion of the new gospel in "the world" beyond Shaker communities. Yet much of what she experienced seemingly confirmed her initial conservative view that Believers should maintain a safe separation from the outside world.[29]

A recent historian of Shakerism has asserted that Lucy Wright's "most important decision was to reopen Shaker evangelism in 1798 after a twelve-year hiatus."[30] The founding of seven new communities in Ohio, Kentucky, and Indiana within two decades was the most dramatic result of this decision.[31] Despite the burden it placed on the eastern communities to provide missionary leaders and financial and administrative support, Wright gave the western settlement movement strong support during the crucial early years.

The western settlement movement led Wright to attempt to overcome her initially negative attitude (perhaps inherited from Joseph Meacham) toward the publication of Shaker history and theology. In the process of administering the western missionary venture Wright became convinced of the necessity of the Society's publishing its own accounts of its beliefs and history.[32] She approved the first book, the 1808 *Testimony of Christ's Second Appearing*, when it was already well underway. (At the same time she strongly warned the brethren who were writing it that it would stir up persecution.) She approved the printing of only twenty copies of the 1816 *Testimonies*, for Believers' use only; and she ordered these books collected for safekeeping when, shortly after publication, there was a substantial threat that apostates and other anti-Shakers would use material in them against the communities.[33] She refused Freegift Wells's request to have the newly codifed behavioral rules, the "Millennial Laws," circulated to all Shaker communities.[34]

Wright's best-known contributions to Shaker religion are in the area of worship practices. The Calvin Green biography tells us little about Lucy Wright's theological emphases and nothing about any spiritual experience she may have had.[35] We only hear that "she taught no Universalist sentiments"—that is, like Joseph Meacham, as well as Ann Lee and the English Shakers, she taught that those who heard the true gospel and rejected it "must suffer Eternal loss."[36]

Lucy Wright is generally credited with encouraging the development of choreographed sacred dance and the use of hymns and anthems in Shaker worship. Shortly after the Church was established at New Lebanon, under the Meacham administration, singing was stopped and the only approved religious dancing was a "heavy shuffle" that "grew slower and slower until it became almost impossible to exercise it at all." Finally dancing stopped altogether, and meetings "consisted of singing a solemn song without words, & instruction & reproof. All exercise ceased near the close of 1796 & lasted for about a year and a half."[37] Both Matthewson and Green credit Lucy Wright with bringing dance back into the evening worship service, after Father Joseph's death.[38] Brewer suggests that after the 1807 revival, Lucy Wright responded to "pressure to enliven worship meetings," by "allowing the introduction of hymns in 1808 and anthems in 1812, many of which had western origins."[39]

Over her twenty-five-year term as sole head of the United Society, Wright influenced Shaker domestic culture profoundly simply through her own daily behavior and her face-to-face teachings. She inevitably appropriated some of the Ann Lee legacy in her own life and teachings as the Mother of the Church. But her interpretation of spiritual motherhood was influenced by her experience within Shaker communalism, rather than by ecstatic religious experience or the rigors of proselytizing in the wilderness. The "sayings" literature collected by Lucy Wright's followers pictures a Wright ministry and a Shaker religion which are far less outwardly dramatic than in the days of Ann Lee. This seems entirely appropriate when we remind ourselves that Wright's task was to teach a new generation of Shakers how to find inspiration in the dailiness of life in community.

Sayings of Mother Lucy

The selection of Wright's sayings in this chapter comes from several different manuscripts produced at Watervliet and New Lebanon and includes the earliest dated accounts (from 1815–1816), as well as the extended narrative, "Mother's Last Visit to Watervliet," which was widely circulated among Shaker communities shortly after Wright's death in 1821.[40] Wright herself may have initiated the collection project—there is substantial evidence in the sayings to indicate that she took a strong interest in seeing that some of her precepts were captured for posterity. Isaac N. Youngs was the chief recorder of her public speaking in religious meetings, perhaps both at Watervliet and at New Lebanon.[41]

In the accounts of her public speaking we get an extraordinarily detailed formal portrait of her role as a female head of the Society, authoritatively managing passive or unruly members. In the "last visit to Watervliet," we see her march down the aisle between sisters and brethren, clapping and stamping, trying to ensure that all the attending elders and eldresses and many of the family members testify to their faith. We witness her techniques of exhortation, reproof, and counsel, and we also glimpse the apparent difficulty she had during these years of relatively orderly and restrained religious expression, in her efforts to inspire lively participation in worship meetings.

From Rebecca Landon and other recorders in the sisterhood we get a predictably more domestic image. We glimpse Mother Lucy with her assistant in the ministry, Ruth Landon, in their own room, receiving gift-wrapped candy from some of the sisters on her birthday. We hear her give detailed new rules for cooking and eating. She discusses clothing fashion and proper posture for both women and men. She criticizes shortcomings in the sisterhood's communal spirit and urges them on to greater heights of thrift and cleanliness. And in a classic enunciation of the sexual double standard, she tells the sisters that their greater domestic confinement is a "greater privilege" which brings them a greater responsibility for sexual self-control. (She also admonishes the brethren to set an example for their sisters, it should be noted, and she makes an effort to increase the domestic confinement of the brethren as well, telling the farmers on one occasion that it would be better for them physically and spiritually to "stay at home where you can rest" after harvest, rather than freely roaming the fields on holiday.)

According to Calvin Green, Wright was a frequent and excellent speaker in meetings.

> I heard her speak several times in the young Believers meetings, well adapted to their State. She was the best female speaker I ever heard. Her manner was energetic and forcible—& without prolixity of words. Her

voice was solid & clear, & her language plain and distinct, so that her meaning could be easily understood.[42]

Wright's skills as an exhorter and speaker undoubtedly helped shape Shaker worship as much as her more obvious contributions to the dance. The texts of her exhortations, even though paraphrased or summarized and lacking the impact of her personal presence, still provide a valuable window on her objectives and style as a public religious leader. She spends much energy in exhorting Believers to keep their "union" with one another and to obey their elders and the behavioral rules called the "orders of God" (later codified as the "Millennial Laws"). A few basic principles of Shaker faith are reiterated with variations and often illustrated with metaphors—some of which, such as the "golden chain" metaphor for the rules and orders that were designed to produce unity among Believers, later influenced Shaker culture greatly.[43] Wright stresses the idea that for a Believer, life is travel/travail/trial. The effort to become sinless goes on even after death, even in heaven. Occasionally she attempts to arouse fear, by suggesting that failure to follow the "gospel" may be punished by a calamity, such as the burning of a newly built house. Yet she interprets Ann Lee's legacy as one of "kindness": "Mother's spirit is kind and pleasant and loving to the young as well as to the older ones and labors to comfort all" (July 1816).

There is very little formal theology (or even scriptural quotation) in the texts that represent Wright's public talks. On more than one occasion, both in religious meetings and in more intimate settings, she draws on her own experience to support her advice. One particularly noteworthy case is contained in the account of the May 4, 1816, meeting at Watervliet, when she talks about feeling often that her own tribulation is "unreasonable."[44]

A recurrent theme in Lucy Wright's sayings in meetings is that Believers are in the presence of guardian angels. One of the hand motions we see her introduce into Shaker meeting ritual is an imitation of the "motioning" of the angels. She also urges Believers to copy angelic "bowing." Characteristically reticent about her own spiritual experience, she does not refer to seeing angels herself—she only mentions someone else's vision of Ann Lee surrounded by angels (July 10, 1816). The closest she comes in these sayings to describing her own religious experience is her comment that during the retiring period before the meeting she had a "blessing of God" which tasted sweet in her mouth and stomach and impelled her to speak (July 10, 1916).

The increasingly ritualized nature of Shaker expressions of emotion at this period is revealed in these texts. The sisters come to Wright's room to give her presents on her birthday, and, hearing them giggle, she requires them to laugh heartily and then to "be sober." During an exhortation at a Watervliet meeting of May 4, 1816, she requires all her hearers to weep.

During an 1815 family meeting at New Lebanon, Wright encourages her subordinate ministry elder, Abiathar Babbitt, to enact in a ritualized pantomime the metaphors of spiritual parenthood which are being professed verbally. Addressing a family elder who is present, she asks

> "And do you want Abiathar to take care of you?" said Mother. "Yea," was his reply. "Kiss him," said Mother. Elder Abiathar then taking him by the hand kissed him. "Nurse him," said Mother. "I have just nursed him through Mother," replied Elder Abiathar.

Wright frequently encourages controlled outward (visible, symbolic) expressions of piety. "Laboring," the increasingly choreographed ritual dancing, expressed the Believer's desire for spiritual gifts. She seems to have seen this controlled laboring as a middle ground between excessive reliance on visionary experience and religious lifelessness.[45] "You need not labor for gifts to dream dreams, or see visions," she tells Believers in July 1816, "if you keep your union together as good Brethren and Sisters there will be nothing to separate you from Mother." On the other hand, she tells about a time in her own younger days when she withdrew from physical expression of piety: "I was somewhat weary of laboring so much and was very doubtful whether it was necessary." She soon felt "poor and destitute of the gifts of God" and "was then convinced that it was necessary to be alive in the work of God."

The "Sayings" texts, then, display Wright's public religious leadership behavior and teachings. For a less highly choreographed view of Wright's skills as a political leader, and a glimpse of a more private character, we need to turn to the correspondence.

The Western Correspondence

The majority of Lucy Wright's extant letters are addressed to the leaders of the Ohio and Kentucky Shaker communities which were settled during her administration.[46] The very first letters sent to the West in October 1806 already suggest the major problem that Wright was to confront in administering the rapid growth of the western communities: the difficulty of dealing at a great distance with the rivalries, jealousies, and strong-mindedness of her chief emissaries.

Many essentially political questions are raised in the correspondence of the early years of pioneer western Shakerism. Was it appropriate for the ministry elders in the West to travel as public preachers once communities had formed? To what extent should one community rely on another for aid, in the form of money or labor, if disasters of various kinds struck? What kind of balance of power could strong-minded male and female leaders strike between them? How could status differences between those raised in the church and those from less spiritually "forward" families be resolved? Would all the western communities acknowledge Union Village, Ohio, as their lead ministry in the West, or would they insist on equal relationships to New Lebanon? Should leaders make tremendous efforts to hold on to wavering "poor Believers," or simply let them go? Should the fever-ridden Busro (Indiana) community, which had appeared at first to be so beautiful a location, be resettled after its evacuation or abandoned? And what should be done when irreconcilable conflicts developed between communities and their leaders, or among the leaders of different communities?

In the western leadership correspondence, Lucy Wright listened to a chorus of complaints and requests for aid from the West and decided whether to comfort or chastise, confront or mollify, hold to a strict line or be flexible. She might invoke the authority of Father Joseph Meacham for her opinion on a serious policy issue, but equally often she appealed to her own experience or to basic principles of Christianity or of Ann Lee's Shaker "gospel." Her tone varies from formal and distant to intimate, from teacherly to motherly or sisterly, depending upon the circumstances and the correspondent.

Some of the letters are written for entire communities to share, while others are only for the eyes of one or two correspondents—generally the ranking ministry, especially her trusted missionary brethren David Darrow or Benjamin Youngs, the top leaders of Union Village, Ohio, and South Union, Kentucky, respectively. In the confidential letters between Wright and these trusted subordinate leaders, we find frank admissions of the shortcomings of individuals and discussions of the real internal problems of the communities.

Calvin Green's biography characterizes Wright (eulogistically, from his point of view), as "inflexible in practicing whatever she professed and taught as Principle," but also "generous, liberal, & kind . . . affable, free, friendly & accessible" in conversation—sometimes even "innocently playful." Showing all of these personal qualities, Wright's western letters give us an appreciation of the complexity of the work she had to do as spiritual overseer of the burgeoning Shaker world, as well as a clearer sense of the skills and strategies with which she met the various challenges from the West.

Her strongest-willed and most plain-spoken correspondent was first ministry elder David Darrow. It was Darrow who strongly put the case for publishing an open and full statement of Shaker belief, including the significance of "our first Mother," Ann Lee. Darrow argued forcefully for a tool that would allow the western missionaries to combat the rumors that the Society was founded by a "drunken old woman"[47] (Letter 2). Wright gave approval of the draft text Darrow sent her, explaining that she and Joseph Meacham had talked over this question in the past many times, and "we always felt the time was not come." Wright sent the western missionaries some of Joseph Meacham's writings to aid them in their work and delegated responsibility for the publication to them, not requiring to see any more of it. At the same time she warned them not to print anything but what they were prepared to "live and die by" (Letter 5). When *The Testimony of Christ's Second Appearing* was published, she pointed out that the writers had "varied" from her "counsel in relation to the order of the godhead," but she acknowledged that they were right. Having read the whole she could agree that "it appears altogether necessary that it should be opened more or less" (Letter 10).

In private letters to David Darrow she repeatedly warned that he might lose his gift as elder if he continued travelling and preaching, because too much mixing with "the world" would bring spiritual danger. (She walks a fine line in Letter 9, treating Darrow as an old colleague whom she does not "pretend to be able to teach in particular how you ought to labor," but also asserting her final authority over him, implying her ability to replace him if he should continue to disregard her instructions.)

Benjamin S. Youngs, the principal writer of *The Testimony of Christ's Second Appearing*, was another strong personality who tested Lucy Wright's skills as an administrator. As early as August 16, 1806, Youngs responded to her request for his frank opinions of the other easterners recently sent out to help lead the western settlements. As South Union's first ministry elder from 1811 through 1836, Youngs frequently supplied New Lebanon with his (often critical) perspective on the other western communities.

Lucy Wright often had to listen to the difficulties Darrow and Youngs had with each other. Darrow viewed Benjamin Youngs as capable but overly ambitious. In July 1809, he wrote a confidential letter to Lucy Wright, reacting negatively to the idea of sending Youngs east to work on the second edition of *The Testimony of Christ's Second Appearing*. Through devoting himself too much to writing, Benjamin had already begun to "lose some of his gift," according to Darrow. (Wright took Darrow's advice and Benjamin Youngs did not participate in the revision of the volume—much to his chagrin.) Darrow also reported in 1814 that he had advised Youngs not to keep in his own hands both temporal and spiritual management of the South Union community—but nothing would "satisfy" Benjamin short of "being first."

Youngs expressed his problems with Darrow in somewhat more veiled terms, since Darrow was the acknowledged head of all the Societies in the West. He did make it clear that he felt the western lead ministry was doing a less than fully conscientious job in their parental oversight of the Kentucky (and Indiana) communities. At this point (1813) Wright responded with an unusually warm and intimate letter addressed to "my dear son Benjamin," giving him permission to visit her in the East and ending with a blessing (Letter 12). Evidently she was beginning to realize that Youngs felt jealous, hurt, and isolated as a result of New Lebanon pressure on the

Kentucky communities to channel all their communication with Wright through David Darrow and Ruth Farrington, their lead ministry elders at Union Village. Wright also acted on Youngs's information that the Kentucky Believers needed more attention from the Ohio lead ministry than they were getting. In a letter written June 18, 1818, she urged Darrow and Farrington to visit the Kentucky Believers. If the Kentucky communities needed money, the Ohio Ministry should be generous with them, just as the New Lebanon community had been with the Harvard Believers when they needed help (Letter 15).

Factionalism and disunity in the new western communities ultimately led Wright to remove one of the top ministry elders she had sent to the West. In 1818, in response to urgent requests from David Darrow, Wright wrote to Elder John Meacham at Pleasant Hill, Kentucky, asking him to come to New Lebanon, under the pretext of wishing to see him and other transplanted easterners one more time before her death (Letter 14). Once there he was informed frankly that his "gift was out"; and the remaining Pleasant Hill ministry members were rebuked for spiritual disobedience. They were advised in strong terms to "purge out" materialistic practices like the wearing of silver and gold and to work with their hands as common members did. Most importantly, they were to establish an annual "opening" or confession of sins, in order to conform to standard eastern Shaker religious practices.[48]

One of the most divisive western political issues during Wright's administration was the question of parental titles: whether all the other western communities would acknowledge the Union Village, Ohio, lead ministry as their spiritual (and political) superiors by giving up their own ministry's right to parental titles. This issue was never fully resolved during Lucy Wright's lifetime. Wright expressed a clear desire to have only one set of Shaker parents in the West, but this was ignored by the Pleasant Hill ministry, John Meacham and Lucy Smith. Benjamin Youngs complained to Lucy Wright in December 1818 that Pleasant Hill's continued use of parental titles "hurt the feelings" of the South Union Believers, who had complied with Wright's wishes. Then, when New Lebanon tried to intervene, David Darrow and Ruth Farrington advised them against removing Lucy Smith's "Mother" title, for fear of causing further disunion at Pleasant Hill. The parental title issue in the West was still highly problematic after Wright's death and was a major contributing factor to the conflict that ultimately erupted in the mid-1820s between Elder Samuel Turner and Mother Lucy Smith at Pleasant Hill (ending in Lucy Smith's removal from office and return to the East).[49]

We can see in her letters that Wright was never a highly controlling administrator. She frequently gave only very general advice, expressing confidence in the ability of the western leadership to work out the particulars, using their own best judgment and better knowledge of circumstances there.[50] As the fractiousness of the western communities and the complexity of administering them at a distance increased, Wright and her associates in the New Lebanon ministry attempted to delegate more authority to the Ohio lead ministry. She told David Darrow during the Pleasant Hill crisis leading to John Meacham's removal, "You must look to the protection of all the Believers in the West, and not leave it for me—nor us—to do, for we cannot do it" (Letter 13).

Her letters, like her sayings, are characterized by an emphasis on ethics and the practical realities of religious communities, rather than an interest in the subtleties of theology. When urging David Darrow and Ruth Farrington to help the Kentucky communities (Letter 15), for example, she reminds them that elders must teach liberality by example:

> For could we ever have loved God, unless he had first loved us and thereby drawn us to him?
> I know it is the duty of the younger to seek the union of the elder and to come to him. But if he is purblind and cannot see so far, the elder should come so near to him that he can reach him and not let him be lost. This is the way I have to do with the people. For though I possessed all wisdom and knowledge and positively knew the requirements of God upon his people here, what good would it do, unless they could get hold of it? Not any. Therefore, I strive to bring the people as near to the requirements of God as they are able to come, and then I unite with them and bless them; and in so doing, I am joined to them and they to me, and we travel together and find a blessing. And I think it my wisdom so to do, for if the hand and body be separate, what is either good for?

A fine expression of her sense of personal accountability as a spiritual leader is to be found in her last letter to David Darrow, dated September 21, 1819 (Letter 16). Though ill, she wrote personally to Darrow, perhaps realizing that he would accept criticism of his handling of the western communities' turmoil from no one but herself.

> Now, beloved friend, I feel it my duty to write a few lines to you in simplicity and plainness, since we cannot speak together face to face, for I feel greatly straitened to know my duty in relation to you, and how I shall give an account to God, and how I shall meet you in the days of eternity. . . . You call me Mother, and often call on me to justify or condemn your proceedings according to the gift which I feel. Now if I see you going astray and do not warn you, can I be justified?

We get a glimpse of Wright's own understanding of her role as the spiritual leader of all the Shakers, in a letter to Benjamin Youngs (Letter 12):

> I know that God has and does still own and bless me and my labors in the gospel, and that He has given me health, strength, and wisdom ac-

cording to my day and opened in my soul a fountain of charity, mercy, and love of God, which freely flows like an endless river to all the faithful sons and daughters of Zion throughout the whole Israel of God.

The letters to the western Believers show Lucy Wright attempting to live up to this ideal self-image as the fountainhead of charity to a growing family of Believers. She acknowledged on many occasions that the westerners and the eastern leaders she had sent them still partook of "the fallen nature," and were boisterous, self-centered, and power-seeking. She nevertheless attempted to provide a model of maternal leadership in her dealings with the western societies, encouraging both mutual generosity among the sibling communities and increased independence from the East as the communities grew older.

NOTES

1. Angell Matthewson, "Reminiscences in the form of a series of letters to his brother Jeffrey, 1792–1813" (NN Item 119), Letter 21.

2. Marjorie Procter-Smith has argued that at Ann Lee's death, Shakerism lost its earlier "gynocentric" character (*Shakerism and Feminism: Reflections on Women's Religion and the Early Shakers*, Old Chatham, N.Y.: Center for Research and Education, Shaker Museum and Library, 1991).

3. She was born Lucy Wright in 1760. Married to Elizur Goodrich in 1780, just before his conversion to Shakerism, she seems to have been called Lucy Goodrich among the Shakers until renamed Lucy Faith by Elder James Whittaker in 1785 (Matthewson, "Reminiscences," Letter 8). Calvin Green says in his "Memoir of Lucy Wright" (OClWHi VII B 60.1) that she took back her maiden name when she and Elizur Goodrich dissolved their marriage by mutual consent (81–82). Nevertheless, she signed herself Lucy Goodrich when writing to the apostate Eunice Chapman in 1817.

4. Recent students of Shakerism, especially Priscilla Brewer, Clarke Garrett, and Marjorie Procter-Smith, have begun to look closely at Lucy Wright's administration, using oral testimonial collections, the accounts of the seceders Thomas Brown and Angell Matthewson, Calvin Green's "Biographic Memoir of the Life and Experience of Calvin Green" (OClWHi VI B 28), and some of Wright's own surviving writings. I have drawn particularly on Green's memoir of Wright and his "Biographic Memoir"; the New Lebanon lead ministry correspondence for the years of her administration; early testimonial literature, including Thomas Hammond's "Sayings of Mother Ann and the First Elders, taken from Abijah Worster" (OCLWHi VII B 22); and references in some of the apostate materials.

5. Green's biography of Lucy Wright was the work of his old age, completed in 1864, when he was in his eighties (and she had been dead for more than forty years). At the time she became the head of the United Society, in 1796, he was sixteen and she was thirty-six. When she died in 1821, he was forty-one.

6. Green, "Memoir of Lucy Wright," 116–17. Thomas Brown also comments on the basis of hearsay on Ann Lee's "masculine, sovereign address" (Brown, *An Account of the People Called Shakers* . . . [1812], 330).

7. The 1816 *Testimonies*, which was published during the Wright administration, naturally attempts to show that Wright's role was somehow predicted by Lee, with-

out actually asserting that Lee chose her for leadership. The late Shaker historians and eldresses Anna White and Leila Taylor also include a story in which Childs Hamlin prophesies her future role (*Shakerism, Its Meaning and Message*, 74). But if Lee had actually nominated Wright as a possible successor, it would most certainly have been included both in the 1816 *Testimonies* and in Green's "Memoir of Lucy Wright."

8. Green and Wells state that Margaret Leland and Mary Partington were Ann Lee's female companions on the missionary tour to the east, in *A Summary View of the Millennial Church*, p. x. According to Brown (1812), Hannah Kendall was Ann Lee's travelling companion for this journey (319).

9. "When Mother Ann's health began to decline with that sickness which ended her earthly life, Lucy's time was so occupied that another capable Sister was employed to take care of Mother. But it was not long before she called for Lucy & desired her to remain her Caretaker while she lived, which Lucy was faithful to do" (Green, "Memoir of Lucy Wright," 84). She is mentioned in the 1816 *Testimonies* as being present with Ann Lee three days before the latter's death (234).

10. In the 1816 *Testimonies*, there are two brief reminiscences which are described in the index as "Mother's vision and prophecy concerning" Lucy Wright (223 and 234). Beyond these, we get only the most fleeting glimpses of Lucy Wright (76–77, 115). She is the source of six very brief and unremarkable memories of Ann Lee's sayings (220, 234, 272, 281, 306, 309).

11. 1816 *Testimonies*, 222–23.

12. Brown says that Ann Lee "sang sweetly, with a pleasant voice, but would frequently use the most harsh, satirical language" (330); Matthewson claims that in speeches of chastisement, Ann Lee used "harsh terms with language that would have bin destitute of dilicasy in any other woman" ("Reminiscences," Letter 4).

13. Calvin Green, "Memoir of Lucy Wright," 111–12.

14. "She continued to reside at Watervliet in the capacity of a leading Caretaker among the Sisters, during all of Father James ministration" (Green, "Memoir of Lucy Wright," 85).

15. Green, "Biographical Account of the Life, Character, and Ministry of Joseph Meacham" (1827), reprinted in *The Shaker Quarterly*, 10, 1, 30–31. Anna White and Leila Taylor tell a story in which Childs Hamlin was the one who first received divine knowledge that Lucy Wright was to be the First Mother, in *Shakerism: Its Meaning and Message*, 74.

16. Matthewson, "Reminiscences," Letter 11.

17. Matthewson makes Joseph Meacham's control over ministry appointments sound absolute, however. "Father Joseph at the same time reservs to himself the prerogativ over the whole & the care of the Church at Waterfleet & his homested at New-lebanon the name & title of the mother church so that thare is now four father & mother Establishments under father Joseph this makes him father of fathers & Mother lucy faith mother of mothers yit father Joseph holds the whole power of appointment or remooving & pooting another in command" (Matthewson, "Reminiscences," Letter 16).

18. Priscilla Brewer assumes Wright acted as a full partner with Meacham in selecting the leaders for the other New England Shaker communities that were gathering into gospel order on the New Lebanon model during the years of the Meacham/Wright administration (*Shaker Communities, Shaker Lives* [hereafter *SCSL*], 25–28).

19. "Mother Lucy also labored fervently to prevent as far as possible the sad catastrophy" (Green, "Biographic Memoir," 26).

20. The early sources are unanimous in stating that Clough, though Meacham's

male successor, was never considered equal in power to Lucy Wright. Reuben Rathbun calls Clough "a young man who had labored in the ministry as an assistant to Elder Joseph" and says "he was not first in the ministry, but was subject unto her whom he called his mother, which was the partner of Elder Joseph" (Rathbun, *Reasons Offered for Leaving the Shakers*, 11.) Also see Angell Matthewson, "Reminiscences," Letter 21, and Brown, *An Account of the People Called Shakers* (340–41). Abiathar Babbitt was the sole elder in the New Lebanon ministry from 1798 through 1805. Ebenezer Bishop then served with him for two years, until 1807, when Bishop became Gathering Order Elder at the North House. According to a letter from the New Lebanon ministry to Solomon King at Union Village, dated September 2, 1829, "Elder Abiathar was alone after Elder Ebenezer went to the North House, but he was not first in the lot—neither could any brother go in there to be a Father . . . " (OClWHi IV B 7).

21. Matthewson, "Reminiscences," Letter 22. In the last section of this passage, Matthewson refers to the appointment of the subordinate male ministry elder, Abiathar Babbitt. Matthewson appears to resent the fact that Lucy Wright's former husband, the educated and able Elizur Goodrich, was passed over for the Ministry and the inferior Babbitt selected instead.

22. His other complaints included the exclusivity of the New Lebanon Church in its worship services, the failure of the Society to provide minimal literacy for its young members, and the restrictions on freedom of movement of "mechanics" and farmers.

23. Matthewson, "Reminiscences," Letter 24.

24. Alfred Ministry to Seth Babbit, Harvard, May 4, 1816 (OClWHi IV A 1). "Prophecy" is my best guess at the word in the manuscript here.

25. New Lebanon Brethren to Alfred community, July 30, 1816, (OClWHi IV A 33).

26. Priscilla Brewer noted this testimony by Ruth Hammond, as recorded by Thomas Hammond in his "Sayings of Mother Ann and the First Elders," 86, in her discussion of Lucy Wright's headship (*SCSL*, 51).

27. Brewer points out that Wright experienced opposition from the brethren when she had a gift to have a certain house moved, in the spring of 1814 (*SCSL*, 51). The sayings excerpted in this chapter show an example of her asking for the brethren's public assent when making a speech about the house-building project at Watervliet, July 1, 1816.

28. Brewer says on the basis of careful work with census records that during the twenty years between 1800 and 1820, the eleven eastern communities grew on an average of 42.5% (*SCSL*, 36).

29. Calvin Green's biography notes that she taught that Believers must separate themselves from "the world," and opposed contracting debts outside Shaker communities or hiring laborers from the world. The seceder William Haskett claims that because of "her dignified station in office" she herself "conversed with but few, if any of the 'world' " (Haskett, *Shakerism Unmasked*, 142).

30. Stephen Marini, *Radical Sects of Revolutionary New England*, 133.

31. These were Union Village, Ohio (1806–1912); Watervliet, Ohio (1806–1910); Pleasant Hill, Kentucky (1809–1910); South Union, Kentucky (1810–1922); North Union, Ohio (1822–1889); and Whitewater, Ohio (1824–1907). The West Union (Busro), Indiana, community was a failure (1810–1827).

32. Priscilla Brewer credits Wright's administration with a "publishing campaign leading to five major works" within a decade, even going so far as to characterize it as something Wright "initiated." To my mind this overstates the documented facts somewhat. The five major publications to which Brewer refers seem to be the

two editions of *The Testimony of Christ's Second Appearing*, 1808 and 1810; the *Millennial Praises*, 1813; the 1816 *Testimonies*; and John Dunlavy's *Manifesto* (1818) (Brewer, *SCSL*, 35).

33. See my discussion of the 1816 *Testimonies*, introduction to chap. 1, above.

34. Brewer tells the story of Freegift Wells's compiling the rulebook and showing it to Lucy Wright shortly before her death, only to have her refuse to have it circulated and read aloud to members in meeting (*SCSL*, 40).

35. Green attempts to make the case for Lucy Wright's having a "spirit of prescience" or a "prophetic spirit" but adduces no examples of visionary activity. This is in strong contrast to his procedure in writing Joseph Meacham's biography, where several examples are given of Meacham's having "revelations" or being particularly "filled with the power of God," as at the funeral of James Whittaker.

36. Green also attributes this doctrine to Joseph Meacham, in the Meacham biography. It is worth noting that Green was writing this biography in the 1860s, a time when "liberal" Shakers like Frederick Evans were challenging Shaker orthodoxy on such matters as the existence of the devil and hell. It is perhaps important to Green to stress Lucy Wright's orthodoxy in this context of internal controversy.

37. Green, "Biographic Memoir," 28–29. Clarke Garrett believes that James Whittaker and Joseph Meacham were responsible for bringing "excesses" of ecstatic behavior under control in the years immediately following the death of Ann Lee (1784–1796) (Garrett, *Spirit Possession*, chap. 10).

38. Matthewson says that after Joseph Meacham died, under Lucy Wright, Hannah Kendall, and Henry Clough, dancing was reinstated "as a part of divine worship every night (this was abolished by father Joseph as being unprofitable a number of years back). . . . they also have declared that the gospel is a bout to be opned to the world as it has bin seeled up in mistory during father Josephs Ministry and orginizing the church it is now freely to be preeched to every one & is expected thousands will com forward join the church" ("Reminiscences," Letter 21). According to Green, the choreographed symbolic religious dancing that was to distinguish Shaker worship for nearly a century began in the second year of Lucy Wright's administration, 1798, with the "square step manner" first. But Andrews says that the square order shuffle was seen in New Lebanon as early as 1795, the year before Meacham died (*The People Called Shakers*, 141).

39. Priscilla Brewer, *SCSL*, 35. Also see Daniel Patterson, *The Shaker Spiritual* (Princeton, N.J.: Princeton University Press, 1979), 107–16.

40. I have taken excerpts for this chapter from two manuscript anthologies in the Western Reserve Historical Society collection: "Betsy Bate's Book, Words of Mother Lucy, Spoken at Different Times . . . " (OClWHi VI B 61) and "Elizabeth B. Harrison's Book, Sayings of Mother Lucy, Spoken at Different Times . . . " (OClWHi VII B 60.1). I have also used "Mother Lucy's Last Visit at Watervliet" (OClWHi V A 11, a copy with Harriet Storer's name on it). Rebecca Landon was one of the primary scribes in the sisterhood. My arrangement of selections is chronological whenever I have been able to determine the dates.

41. "Her discourses in the Church meetings were mostly taken down at the time of delivery, by Bro. Isaac N. Youngs" (Green, "Memoir of Lucy Wright," 114). Wright and her associates in the New Lebanon ministry divided their time equally between the two communities of New Lebanon and Watervliet and attended Church Family meetings in both communities.

42. Calvin Green, "Memoir of Lucy Wright," 114.

43. The "chain of union" had been introduced into Shaker religious culture as a metaphor and dramatic ritual at least as early as 1795, according to Matthewson, who quoted Elder John Partington as saying, on a visit to Ashfield, "You must

always keep up a chain of union from the greatest down to the lest you must alway be so nigh to each other in your simpathizing feelings as to tuch & assist each other in times of distress" (Matthewson, "Reminiscences," Letter 8). Lucy Wright may have been the one responsible for making the chain of union "golden."

44. She may have been referring at this time to political struggles documented in the correspondence—perhaps specifically to the events that led to the dismissal of Jethro Turner as the elder of one of the Watervliet families in May 1816 or to the rebellion led by John Barns at Alfred, Maine, against her "petticoat-government," which occurred in the same period.

45. Brewer points to her saying to Beulah Cooper that Believers should not "make a sign of everything" to support the argument that Wright intentionally de-emphasized the authority of vision. Brewer (SCSL, 55) found Cooper's recollection in a manuscript collection of testimonies edited by Eunice Bathrick (OClWHi VI B 10, 13).

46. The letters in this chapter have been selected from manuscript archives to emphasize Lucy Wright's handling of "benchmark" events. The dailiness and domesticity of western Shakerism will emerge more clearly in the sisterhood's correspondence in chapter 3.

47. It was not until the westerners forced the issue that the United Society publicly acknowledged their beliefs about Ann Lee's relationship to Christ and the dual nature of the godhead. During Joseph Meacham's administration these tenets of Shaker faith were kept secret. Calvin Green says in his biography of Joseph Meacham that Father Joseph predicted "in the next opening of the gospel, the Mother would be had in remembrance, her order & office would be brot forward and openly declared," and that he saw the dual nature of God in a vision, "but thro' motives of wisdom did not manifest it publicly" ("Biographical Account of the Life, Character and Ministry of Father Joseph Meacham," 57).

48. Letter dated June 10, 1818 (OClWHi IV A 33). New Lebanon based this rebuke on private information supplied in letters from David Darrow and Ruth Farrington and from the visiting South Union leaders Youngs and Comstock Betts.

49. Ministry and Elders at New Lebanon to David Darrow and Ruth Farrington, March 27, 1819 and to Benjamin S. Youngs, South Union, September 6, 1819 (OClWHi IV A 33). My paper "Weary of Petticoat Government" has more details on the struggle between Lucy Smith and Samuel Turner in 1826.

50. For example, in reference to the complex problems of the failed Indiana community, she wrote to Benjamin S. Youngs in August 1813, "In relation to the settlement of the Busro Believers, I feel to be silent. But if the poor unreconciled part of them falls into your care, labor to do your duty to them according to the best gift given to you" (Letter 12, below).

WORDS SPOKEN BY MOTHER LUCY, AND THOSE WITH HER, IN A MEETING AT THE SECOND FAMILY, NEW LEBANON, MARCH 25TH, 1815[1]

Mother came here on Saturday. The next day after the family had returned from the meeting house we assembled in our new house. Mother assembled with us; being filled with the gifts of God, her countenance was very beautiful, and she spoke as follows:

"I feel a very pleased satisfied feeling here among you. You feel pleased and satisfied in your feelings; and I hope a good degree of thankfulness. And I hope that I may ever find a spirit here that is pleased to keep the way of God in this house. You must remember and consider that you built this house to serve God in, not to commit sin in. And if any has an inclination to commit sin, they ought to go somewhere else to do it. And consider yourselves unworthy of the privilege of living here.

"Each one ought to labor to keep the way of God for themselves. Some of you may think the elders will keep the way of God for you, and you can grow careless and forgetful. And the elders perhaps may labor and speak to you time after time of the way of God till they feel themselves poor and destitute and think they do not know what more can be said than has been said.

"If I was in the elders' places, when I felt so, I would call on some of you to speak."

She then turned to Elder Brother Amos Stower and said, "Is there any among you that is so poor that they would not speak for the way of God, if they were called upon to speak?" "I hope and trust not any," replied Elder Brother. "You do not ought to feel bound and shut, but often speak of the way of God and your faith in it," said Mother.

Then she walked back and forth through the assembly and said, "Get away superstition!" We all repeated these words after her.

"I do not love a nasty fleshly crooked nature."

We repeated these words after her.

"I would not be bound and screwed up in the nature of the flesh." We repeated these words in like manner. "You feel bondage and superstition: and if you can't do nothing else you will lock your hands together and grip them as tight as you can.[2]

"You have the greatest privilege that any people ever had to travel in the gospel.

"I look upon it to be the greatest day that ever was given to souls to travel in the way of God. You may have great faith in the gifts of God in first Mother's day and in Father James's day, but if you are not joined to the present work of God it will do you no good; for your souls need food to nourish and support them as well as your bodies. And you all know that the food you eat then will not nourish your bodies now; no more will the gifts of God which you received then nourish your souls now unless you are joined to the present work of God. But if you are joined to the present work of God, you are joined to all the good that is past.

"Some may feel as though they had a great many trials; but you must expect trials as long as there is any flesh here. Some may hope they shall come to the end of trials, sometime or other. But I hope if any one travels to the end of trials, there will be no flesh there; for if you come to the end of trials, I don't see but you will come to the end of travelling.

"I expect to travel as long as I live in this world; and I don't expect to stop travelling then. I hope I shall travel swifter than I do now. I do not want to fall asleep and feel at ease; but I want to keep travelling; and I expect I shall. I do not expect ever to die. My body will die and I shall leave this earthly tabernacle, which will be returned to the earth like all others: but my spirit will never die. Souls will never stop travelling, if they are faithful; but they will travel and travel till they come to the heaven of heavens and not stop then, for there is no end to the work of God.

"Here is the place where you will show your travel, between the two sexes.[3] If souls are after the gospel and travel in the way of God there will be a kind of tender feeling between brethren and sisters. On the other hand, if any are after the flesh *there* is the first place it shows itself. So this you may know, that if you feel hard feelings or are unkind to each other, it proceeds from a wicked spirit within. You must always overcome evil with good; many times souls receive great help by feeling a kind loving spirit from each other. They will often say, 'Such an one was so kind and loving that I could not feel anything against them.'

"When you have wicked thoughts and feelings, you should say, 'Get thee behind me, Satan.' You ought to be strong in the way of God and be preachers of the gospel, every one of you."

She then called upon Elder Abiathar [Babbitt], who spoke as follows.

"If I was called upon to speak, I would speak; I would take up my cross, if I said no more than 'I will be strong! and feel strong in the way of God.'

"Why will any one let the devil make them ashamed of that which has done them so much good? There is nothing that has done you so much good as the way of God; therefore you ought often to speak of it. It would be a help to you and do you good, if you did not speak more than three words.

"If I were in the elders' places, when I felt worn out I would let you assemble and labor for a gift for yourselves. It would do as much good as to always depend upon the elders for a gift. Everyone ought to feel zealous to keep the way of God. You ought to take up your crosses and speak when you are called upon. Mother called upon me to speak and I took my cross and spoke; and I feel the better for it, and so would you."

Mother then turned to Sister Ruth [[Landon]] and desired her to speak, and she arose and spoke as follows.

"I think the brethren and sisters look very pretty. They look as though they meant to serve God, and I believe they do. But you must remember to keep the orders of God that are given for your protection. It is not all at once that souls fall from the way of God, but it is by doing wrong and going with it covered from time to time; and so by little and little, they lose sight of the work of God; and when a soul has entirely lost sight of the work of God and have fallen away, they are out of the reach of help from any in this world, so they can receive no help as I can see."

Mother then smiled and said, "She has broke through and has had a gift and has spoken very well." Mother then called upon the brethren and sisters to speak, and they did accordingly, which seemed to satisfy Mother very well.

Mother then said to Elder Brother Amos, "I don't know but we shall keep the brethren and sisters here two hours; if we do, I think the time will be spent much better than in talking and chatting together, will it not, Elder Brother?" (Elder Brother answered, "Yea, Mother.") She then said, "It grows toward supper time; what will you do; you will need to eat?" Elder Brother replied, "We are eating the best of suppers with Mother and the ministry, and it is good for us to be here: We have victuals and can eat at any time, but Mother we shall not always have."

Elder Abiathar then walked through the assembly expressing his love to the faithful. As he was speaking he spied a brother that he had not seen before during his stay. He went to him and taking him by the hand asked him where he had been? He replied, "I have been taking care of my lambs." "Taking care of your lambs?" said Elder Abiathar, "You had ought to be a lamb yourself; will you be one?"

"Yea, I will," replied the Brother.

"And do you want Abiathar to take care of you?" said Mother. "Yea," was his reply. "Kiss him," said Mother. Elder Abiathar then taking him by the hand kissed him. ["Nurse him," said Mother. "I have just nursed him through Mother," replied Elder Abiathar.][4] Then turning to the brother he said, "Christ says my sheep hear my voice, and I know them, and they follow me; so you must become a lamb and follow Christ."

Mother then said, "I have noticed (by being with you a while) that your house is very noisy. I think there is much need of you learning to go about the house still and careful. You will then feel the good angels with you. There are evil angels, and they are as faithful to guard those in their kingdoms as the good angels are to guard the people of God.

"Evil angels strive very hard to get in among you, so that if any work of God takes place in a soul they may overthrow it and allure and draw your minds and attention from the gospel and the gifts of God. I hope there is none among you but what wants the good angels with them, but if you go about light and careless and scarcely [[think of]] them from morning till night, how can you expect them to stay with you? I do not know but you are faithful to pray; I do not wish to accuse you, but you ought to pray that the good angels may guard your dwellings. For if you should be left to the judgment of God, such as having your building take fire, you would not feel able to bear it."

Mother then said, "I have now spoken considerable, and I believe you have understood it; but if I had spoken these things to the world of mankind who are lost in sin and wickedness, they would not have understood them, for they are darkened by the flesh; but you are able to understand who have the light of God in you."

NOTES

1. Source: OClWHi VII B 61, "Betsy Bate's Book." Probably taken down by Isaac N. Youngs.
2. Apparently she demonstrated this gesture here, in order to get the assembled Believers to imitate it.
3. In the manuscript, which is clearly a fair copy from an original draft, the phrase reads "show you travel between the two sexes." I have corrected it according to the sense I think it makes, i.e., the relations between the sexes are a kind of litmus test of the Believer's spiritual progress.
4. The passage in brackets is crossed out in the original manuscript.

ACCOUNTS OF TWO VISITS WITH MOTHER LUCY WRIGHT[1]

"The angels make the same motions."

May 14, 1815, Watervliet. When Mother gave us her gift of motioning with our hands, she spoke the following words: "This is a beautiful gift; it feels like a great increase; it is heavenly fruit; it is angel's food. The angels make the same motions; the angels are all around us; we need not think we are alone. Our good brethren and sisters that have left the body make the same motions in their times of rejoicing, and I do not know but that is all the time."

"Everyone must have their faith tried some way or other."

February 5, 1816. This being Mother's birthday, many of the brethren and sisters gave Mother some little presents. Accordingly Philly, Polly, Catherine, and Eliza got some little sugarplums of different sizes and colors and did them up in paper very choice and went to Mother's door and knocked; she immediately bid us come in. There being no seats but those employed, she said she could not invite us to sit down. Then Ruth said, "They want to kneel down around Mother." Then Mother said, "Come," and we all kneeled down. Then Philly said, "Mother's young children have brought some little presents." Then she said, "You may open them and let me see what it is."

We began to open them. Mother said, "It is a cross, is it not?" We said, "It is." Mother said, "You want I should open them, do you not?" We answered, "Yea." Mother said, "This present is in remembrance of my birthday, I suppose." We replied, "Yea." Mother said, "I am fifty-six years old, and thirty-six years I have spent in the gospel."

Mother was very pleasant and cheerful, and these presents being so small, we laughed. Mother immediately bid us laugh as hard as we could. Then we laughed heartily; then Mother bid us be sober.

Then Mother spoke to us in the following manner: "I have no doubt you will have many trials and afflictions, but you must always turn your sense to bless the gospel. It may be easy now, but the time may come when you'll feel that tribulation that it will feel hard for you to bless, but you must bless. I don't mean to bless anything that's wicked but everything that's good, for every one must have the trial of their faith, for faith untried is uncertain. Everyone must have their faith tried some way or other; you may have it in this manner: the world may rise and persecute you, but you must always remember and keep low for if you rise the world can rise higher than you can. Perhaps it may come by your natural relations, but whatever trials you may have to pass through, you must be strong and steadfast, endure to the end. Will you?" said Mother. We all replied, "Yea, Mother, we will." Then we kissed Mother, which ended this most pleasing visit.

NOTE

1. Source: OClWHi V A 9. I have added titles.

SAYINGS OF MOTHER LUCY AT
WATERVLIET (1816)[1]

"I am now going to leave you, and I do not mean to trouble myself about you."

On the 7th of May, 1816, the Elder Brother Jethro [Turner] was released from his office and returned to Lebanon on the 8th; and on the evening of the 9th the ministry came into our meeting, and Mother spoke to us in the following manner:
"Heretofore you have had elders from Lebanon; Jethro Turner came here

to be your elder brother, and now his gift is out, and it is necessary in so large a family as this that you should have elders, some one to call elder brother," and then appointed Samuel Pease to be our elder brother, and called him forward to take his place and said she did not feel willing to have us fall back of our order and earnestly desired to have the gospel kept and honored in this place. She said there was gospel enough here to save every soul both old and young if you will be faithful. "You that are young may think because Jethro is released and gone that you are released from your troubles and that there will be none to search you out, but remember that if you commit sin, that all your dark works will be brought to the light, and your sins will find you out.

"I am now going to leave you, and I do not mean to trouble myself about you."

"You are on slippery ground."

May the 11th, 1816. After Mother had got into her wagon to return to Lebanon, the elder brother and Nathan and a number of the brethren and sisters being present, she spake and said, "Jethro has returned home, and now you may think you can rise out of all your tribulation and not have any more trouble at all, but do not deceive yourselves. The devil stands ready to take advantage; if you are careless and high minded, you will be exposed to lose the gifts of God.

"I do not know but you will be in more danger than ever, if you lose the gift of God; the judgment of God will be upon you in sickness or some other way and sweep half away—you would then feel keen tribulation enough.

"You are on slippery ground, you certainly are, therefore you have need to watch the more to keep you out of evil. I am not agoing to hate the flesh in Jethro and build it up in you; I am not agoing to do any such thing, if you lose the gift of God. I do not know but my spirit will be keener upon you than ever his has been; but I do not say that it will be in the same manner. I feel at liberty now. I never felt really at liberty before; he always had so much of a gift as he thought and chastised so much that I forebore. But now I feel at full liberty and I shall reprove sin wherever I find it, let it be in who it will, and how many of you will keep the way of God I know not. I am now going to leave you, and I do not mean to trouble myself about you. You must labor for yourselves. If you never see my face again, you must remember I had a gift of God in speaking to you as I have."

"Now I want to have you unite and . . . put up your house."

July 1, 1816. The brethren and sisters came together and Mother spake to them in the following manner.

"Brethren and sisters, what we have come to speak to you about at this time is in relation to your earthly house, not the spiritual. You have laid the foundation for your new house; I think it well done so far. The intention of your building it was for the people of God to live in, for you need more room. You have laid it by, and I felt a special gift in it, until your sense could be changed, for you was not united.

"But now we feel if the deacons can purchase boards for you to bring it forward this season to raise it, cover and shingle it, and as much more as you are able to do; and if you do, we think it will be greatly to your honor, and you will be glad you have done it next spring. This season has been backward so far; I think it is likely it will remain so through the season. But you have got your work along beyond my expectation, and now I want to have you unite and bring your work forward and get your haying and harvesting out of the way and then put up your house, for we feel that we can turn and bless it. For I am not called to curse, I am called to a more honorable calling; I am called to bless, and every good Believer will bless, though there may be some weak Believers that may feel to curse, and they will be cursed.

"You have gathered a great deal of that sense that did not much care how things went; and I did not blame you much for it; there was a cause. But now I want to have you all unite and put away that sense and labor to bring things up; if you are faithful you will show it by your fruits; we shall know what tree you are of. And you need not be atelling one another of your afflictions; each one knows their own. But take courage and labor to come up to what the gospel requires and live up to your faith. If you do so you will have faith and feel justification, and no one can take away your justification.[2]

"You can fix up your office, for I desire to see the underpinning put under it before we go to Lebanon. We don't expect to go till the last of next week, and I think you have time enough to do it before we go, and fix up the outside, and clear away the rubbish.

"And what more shall I say? I do not want to speak so much as to weary you."

Then Mother spake and said she would like to have the brethren speak, that she might know if they felt union with what she had said. Elder Abiathar said he felt union with Mother's gift, and a large number of the brethren manifested their feelings in union with Mother's gift.

Then Mother spake to all the brethren and sisters that had not spoken, that they might signify their union to what she had said by bowing, and said, "How beautiful it is to bow; the angels bow, our first Mother has been seen in a vision aspeaking and the angels standing around and at the end of every sentence bow."[3] Then Mother went round to see if they were all in union; then Ruth [[Landon]] spake and said, "Your union is, or will be, your strength. I believe that is what makes the people flourish so at Canterbury and Enfield, because they are built on union."

"There is like to be a great scarcity."

Wednesday evening, July 10, 1816. The ministry came into our meeting and Mother spake to us as follows.

"Brethren and sisters, we have a few words we want to speak at this time. All of us that has received the gospel has been blessed with a great fullness of the things of this life for the comfort of our bodies, and I have thought many times more than we were thankful for. Now we cannot feel nor see but what there is like to be a great scarcity, and it does not appear to us only but to all people as far as we know.[4] Had not we better be a little more saving, and make it hold out some longer? If you keep on having a fullness, it will be too late when it is almost gone to make it hold out then. And if you have faith to take up your crosses and scant a little, I believe you will be as able to go forth and do your duty as you have been with your great fullness."

NOTES

1. Source: Elizabeth B. Harrison's Book; OClWHi VII B 60.1. These excerpts cover two visits from 1816, one in May and the other in July. I have added titles.
2. The theological term "justification" (the condition of being freed from sin and reconciled to God) is frequently used by Lucy Wright in her sayings and writings.
3. Wright seems to refer here to a recent vision of Ann Lee surrounded by bowing angels, but the syntax makes it unlikely that she is speaking of her own visionary experience.
4. This was evidently a time of crop failure in the surrounding communities, as well as at Watervliet. Perhaps in emphasizing this fact Wright is warding off any possible interpretation of the famine as a divine judgment on the Shakers.

SAYINGS OF MOTHER LUCY FROM ELDRESS BETSY HARRISON'S BOOK

"You need not labor for gifts to dream dreams."[1]

July 1816. On the morning of Mother's departure from this place, while seated in the wagon, she spoke in the following manner. (There were two brethren from Tyringham present, who gave the love of their people to Mother and she sent her love in return to all that were good.) "I do not," said Mother, "send my love to any but the faithful." She then addressed us as follows: "I have something to speak to you. You will have feelings that you want to know if you are in union with Mother, but you need not labor for gifts to dream dreams or see visions; if you keep your union together as good brethren and sisters, there will be nothing to separate you from Mother. You ought to go forth in union in all that you do, with a calm

and peaceable spirit—and Mother's spirit will be with you and God will
bless you.

"Speak kind and pretty and labor to comfort each other; then you may
know that you are in union with Mother. If you speak hard and grieve each
other's feelings, Mother's spirit can not bless you. Mother's spirit is kind
and speaks pleasant and loving to the young as well as to the older ones
and labors to comfort all. And if you do this you will have Mother's spirit—
Mother's spirit blesses, it does not curse; I feel to leave that for those who
go out from among us. They can do enough of it. This is suitable for all
and I am willing to have it go through the land."

"If you gather into order and stay at home . . . you will gain by it."

On a particular occasion in the time of harvest Mother spoke to us in
the following manner: "It has been a general custom for the brethren to
have a day of releasement to ramble on the plains after the labor of haying
and harvesting is finished.

"I hope you will now form your sense and feelings so as to be satisfied
to stay at home.

"I am very sensible that it has a bad effect—for if your bodies need rest,
as undoubtedly they do, it is much better to stay at home where you can
rest. You will certainly worry and fatigue yourselves very much by going
out in this manner on the plains after berries. This proceeds from a sense
that is trying to shun mortification, and therefore it is necessary to cross
it. In the time of haying and harvesting, when the bodies are fatigued with
hard labor, the strength of the spirit is certainly diminished—though people are always justified by doing their duty, still it necessarily impairs the
gift of the family, and when you get through I want you should labor to
regain your gift in the spirit. And in order to do this you must gather in
at home as soon as your business will permit.

"You feel lean and destitute and want to get out to throw off uncomfortable feelings.

"But if you gather into order and stay at home, and labor out that way,
you will gain by it and feel the benefit of it."

"The gospel allows us to make use of every good thing which grows."

While one of the brethren was visiting Mother, she ate a peach which
had been given her as a present. While eating the peach, Mother said, "I
am thankful that I have no superstitious notions of religion to prevent my
enjoying the good things which God has created for the benefit of man.

"The gospel allows us to make use of every good thing which grows.
While some are carried away by wild ideas of religion which prevents their
enjoying many things which were evidently created for our comfort and

benefit and ought to be used in a manner to answer the intention of the wise creator who provided these things for our use and benefit.

"In the use of these things people ought to be very careful, for some have very strong appetites for all kinds of fruit—and if they do not govern themselves, they will be exposed to injure their healths as some have already done. I look upon it [as] a very wrong thing to make use of any unripe fruit of any kind, and that which is ripe ought to be used with caution or it sometimes does great injury to people's health. I consider it a wrong thing to eat any kind of fruit, either ripe or unripe, between supper and breakfast. I have known some by giving way to their appetites in this manner injure themselves very much, and for this reason I consider it a very necessary order to be supported among Believers—for no one to eat fruit between supper and breakfast."

"There are many among Believers who have too strong a feeling to follow the fashions of the world."

At a certain time Mother spoke to me[2] of the brethren in this manner—

"I think there are many among Believers who have too strong a feeling to follow the fashions of the world. I have observed that the fashions of the world have a strong influence among some Believers, and in some cases, when they are not sensible of it. They really believe that such fashion is certainly a virtue, whereas if they had originated among Believers, the probability is they would have no feeling for it. Fashions of the world are generally on an extreme one way or the other and frequently change from one extreme to another. But a few years ago they had their trousers almost as tight as their skin, but now they resemble meal bags. I want to have Believers avoid these extremes and keep a proper medium, entirely regardless of the vain fashions of the world. I have no objection to having real improvements introduced among Believers, let its origin be from what quarter it may. But to see Believers anxious for new things merely on account of the fashion of other people is very disagreeable to me and a loss to the people of God."

"People ought to sit straight and handsome in their chairs."

As Mother was in conversation with one of the brethren, he held his hat before him and was drumming with his fingers on the crown. She reproved him and told him that it was an evil spirit in him which always wanted to interrupt good instruction. She said that people ought always to be still and pay attention when their superiors were speaking to them.

At another time Mother observed that people ought to sit straight and handsome in their chairs, "For," said she, "It is very unbecoming for the people of God to sit awkwardly and crooked, wringing in different forms and straddling their legs apart, especially when brethren and sisters are together. And when you sing, be careful not to lean back but always sit erect. When you are in the house, never lean your chair back against the walls, beds, or chests, or any other furniture, but sit up decently. Drumming with the fingers on a chair or whistling about here and there is a mark of idleness and does not belong to the people of God. You ought never to keep your hands behind your back; the proper place for the hands is before, not behind. It appears to me quite ridiculous to see people walking about with their hands behind them, and I hope it may be left off.

"To me it is an evident sign of a heedless, lifeless state of the mind, which ought not to be indulged."

"I was then convinced that it was necessary to be alive in the work of God."

Mother, in speaking of the propriety of laboring in the works of God, made the following observation:

"When I was a young Believer, there was a season that we labored excessively[3] and I was somewhat weary of laboring so much and was very doubtful whether it was necessary and finally concluded that it might probably do as well to be a little more favorable and not quite so severe upon the natural body. Accordingly I was rather indifferent about laboring for a while and careful not to worry myself; but I soon found that this would not do for me. I soon felt myself poor and destitute of the gifts of God, very lean and barren indeed. I was then convinced that it was necessary to be alive in the work of God, that I was laboring for my own soul, and if I was idle the loss would be my own. I then took hold with new zeal and labored for the gifts of God and enjoyed the benefits to my labors, and this I know is necessary for every soul."

"She asked us all, one by one, if we would be good."[4]

In an assembly of sisters one evening, Mother spoke in the following manner: "You have a great privilege to grow good and travel for yourselves. You have a greater privilege than the brethren do. You are more gathered in and not so much exposed to gather lightness, and you ought to be faithful to labor and keep a good substance so that the brethren can feel that you have been faithful in your duty. You ought to be very careful in all your words and actions and by no means do anything to lay any temptation before any one of them. It would be very wrong in any one of you to do anything to draw them out of their order. You ought to labor to be all the strength and help to each other you are able. You ought to be very modest in your behavior and dress and not do anything before your brethren that is not exemplary and modest. I want you should be good and keep the way of God."

Then she asked us all, one by one, if we would be good, with tears in her eyes, and we all promised that we would be good. Then Mother said we should all be her children, and she appeared to feel quite cheerful and pleasant.

NOTES

1. Source: Elizabeth B. Harrison's book, "Sayings of Mother Lucy Spoken at Different Times and under Various Circumstances" (OClWHi VII B 60.1). This is a manuscript anthology, completed in 1864 and probably presented to Eldress Betsy Harrison in that year. The excerpts included here are taken from the first part, "Sayings of Mother Lucy." I have added titles.
2. Perhaps the "me" here is Isaac N. Youngs. Because his trade was tailoring he would have been a likely recipient of these remarks about Shaker men's clothing styles.
3. Wright may be referring to the period during the Meacham-Wright administration when the "slow march" became the dominant physical exercise in the worship and there was a strong emphasis on "mortification of the flesh." See Clarke Garrett, *Spirit Possession and Popular Religion*, chapter 10.
4. The following speech is evidently recorded by one of the sisters, probably an eldress.

COUNSEL AND INSTRUCTION GIVEN BY MOTHER LUCY CONCERNING COOKING, EATING OUR FOOD, ETC. GIVEN AT THE SECOND FAMILY[1]

Mother, Elder Abiathar, and Sister Ruth came to the Second Family. While here Mother felt a gift to instruct the sisters and establish good order in the important branch of cooking.

Mother said we must not eat new baked bread, but have it twenty-four hours old. . . . No wheat cakes or biscuit is to be eaten the same day they are baked; they are very unhealthy, and we ought not to do anything to injure our health or waste anything that God has blessed us with. "For," said Mother, "We cannot make one kernel of grain grow without the blessing of God. Therefore we ought to be very prudent and saving. In such large families there may a great deal be saved or a great deal wasted.

"It is unhealthy to eat hot nut cakes. Let them cool before they are eaten. You need not make any shortcakes; it is a needless thing. You ought not to broil meat for such a large family as there is here. It cannot be done without wasting a great deal. If a person is sick and weak, that is another thing. I do not consider it wrong to broil it for them, if they want it; but to broil it for well people, it is extravagant.

"You ought to take good care of the children and give them wholesome food; they ought to eat bread and milk till they are fourteen years old; milk is for children and they ought to eat it; they will be more healthy than they will to be cooked up with knickknacks such as gingerbread sweet cake and a great many rarities.

"You may give them a suitable dish of bread and milk, and you may give them a suitable piece of bread and butter or a piece of cake or pie and cut it for them and lay it by the side of their dishes; and when they have eat that up, if they have not got enough they may finish their meal with bread and milk. Be careful never to give the children sour milk or mouldy bread; it is certainly hurtful. In the winter season, if you have to give them porridge, have it sweet and good.

"When children come after biting do not give them pie, cake, or gingerbread, for that is strong victuals, and a child is not able to eat such victuals much without injuring them; it will hurt their appetite for more wholesome food. I know it is crossing," said Mother, "not to give a child some such thing, especially when they have been kind and obliging to do chores. But I think I had rather take up some cross than to injure a child. I think it would be much better to give them a piece of rye and Indian bread and cheese, or a piece of cold meat or fish. That will create an appetite, and they will grow up more rugged and healthy. . . .

"A suitable manner of cooking becomes the people of God. I do not believe it is right to be all the time striving to cook something extraordinary nice. I am afraid there is too much of this sense got in among us, a sense of trying to please the natural appetite of somebody or other, or a sense of striving to cook better than others and trying to please each other's natural appetites. I am afraid for me that this sense of pleasing does not please God. It puts me in distress when I go into the kitchen and see the sisters slaving themselves to cook something extraordinary and go beyond what is suitable or needful. I cannot tell you how it makes me feel. It looks to me as though we was agoing to worship and adore this old carcass with all our might and strength. I cannot believe this is right; indeed I know it is not.

"Those that work in the kitchen should have their sense where they are and try to do their work in a suitable manner, such as becomes the people of God . . . "

NOTE

1. Source: OClWHi VII B 61.

MOTHER LUCY'S LAST VISIT TO WATERVLIET[1]

Mother arrived at Watervliet January 10th, 1821. She had before been in the practice of sending word when she was coming, but this time she came very unexpectedly. She appeared to be in better health than she had usually enjoyed of late and was remarkably comfortable in her feelings. The next day she went round among the sisters noticing very attentively what they were employed about. She went into the kitchen, bake-room and dining room and examined the cupboards, pantries, and other by-places in a very critical manner—spoke with everyone she met with in the way and seemed to feel exceeding comfortable and happy. She said to the sisters, "I have come this time like a thief in the night; and for the future I shall always come so; I shall not wait to know whether you are ready, but shall come upon you unawares, whether you are ready or not; but I shall come when I feel a gift." She seemed to observe very particularly what everyone was doing and seemed to take much delight in observing all their works.

The next Sabbath (14th), in the afternoon, she came into the house and attended meeting. . . .

She appeared to feel very comfortable and spoke in a very pleasant loving manner. After we had labored one song, she spoke again and enjoined it upon every one to be alive, to be living souls in the work of God and called upon us to shake, which was instantly obeyed, and we had a very powerful shaking. We then proceeded on in our laboring; and Mother, walking up between the brethren and sisters (which was something very extraordinary to her to do), animated us with powerfully clapping her hands, in which all united. She still continued to animate and encourage us by frequently speaking at the close of the songs, and we had a lively and joyful meeting. After our labors were ended and we had formed into ranks previous to dismission, Mother spoke again. She felt that there was a lack of life and power in our clapping hands. "You clap your hands," said she "as if you had cushions between them," and bid us clap again as we stood in our ranks and again animated us by a powerful clapping of hands, which seemed to fill every soul with the very life and power of her spirit.

Mother continued remarkably comfortable all the week and was very observing of everything that passed and seemed to have a very penetrating gift to see and feel the state of everything among us.

She appeared to be much engaged to increase the spirit of union among the Believers and to gain an increase of order in the Society for that purpose, both in things spiritual and temporal.

On the Saturday following (January 20) one of the brethren (David Hawkins) went in to see her and spoke something to her concerning a particular order which she had lately given for the purpose of increasing the union of the Believers by equalizing, in more particular manner, the temporal income and products of industry in the several orders and departments of the Church.[2] She told him it was the order of God and expressed the feeling sense she then had of their beauty and excellency, how beautiful they appeared to her. She said they appeared like a golden chain that held the people of God together, that every order made a link in that golden chain, "and that order," said she, "makes one more link in the chain." So extraordinary was her gift at this time and so feelingly expressed that it powerfully affected David's feelings, so that he wept very feelingly and Mother right with him. . . .

The next day (Sabbath) she again attended our meeting and appeared still very cheerful and comfortable. In meeting she administered the gift she had felt concerning the golden chain and addressed the brethren and sisters nearly in the following words:

"This family appears at present to be visited with considerable degree of suffering and affliction" (one young sister Sylvina Butler had been buried the Wednesday before, and many of the family were afflicted with a kind of influenza). "But this need not deprive you of the possession and enjoyment of the gifts of God, for outward affliction will not deprive a soul of the comforts and blessings of the gospel.

"You must all labor to keep order, for it is your protection. The orders of God seem hard to a carnal mind, but I should say there are not many, if any, here present so young but that they may see and feel the necessity of keeping good order. To my sense Believers are held together in union by a golden chain. This chain is composed of the gifts and orders of God; and every order is a link in the chain, and if you break any of these orders, you break this chain and are exposed to be led astray. But while you are careful to keep the gifts and orders of God, you are surrounded with this golden chain and are secure from evil; you are on safe ground and nothing can injure you, unless by disobedience you break a link in this chain and so expose yourselves to the enemy without; for the enemy cannot come within to injure you.

"You may see the necessity of order and union by viewing the kingdoms of this world. For if they had not any kind of natural union and order they could not stand, but would soon tumble to pieces and destroy each other, till there would not be a man left upon earth. And this I think may serve as a suitable comparison between the kingdom of Christ and the kingdom of this world.

"How miserable a person must feel without friends. All people want union and friendship, and if we cannot conduct in such a manner as to gain friends, we find a hard travel indeed. Union is more valuable than all earthly things; and you ought always to be careful to support a just union and relation together in the gospel. You ought to be very careful how you speak to each other. Speak kindly and lovingly to each other according to the simplicity of the gospel, and neither give nor take offense.

"I do not feel to speak much at this time, but I hope you will remember what I have said, and if you are careful to observe it, you will certainly be under a blessing."

. . . Friday morning 26th she came into the house again to stir up the brethren and sisters to learn to labor more perfectly and spent the evening.

As she went out of the sisters' dining room of the meeting room she said, "Well, sisters, I don't see that you need anything, only an increase of the same."

She then went into the deaconesses' room and observed to the sisters that she had heard the first Elders say that the time would come when we should be glad to pick up every crumb that ever fell from their mouths; and (referring to the collection of the sayings of our first Mother and Elders)[3] she said we had taken much pains to pick up their crumbs; and (adverting to the gift of laboring) she said, "This is one of Father Joseph's crumbs." "Yea," replied Eldress Ruth, "and next it will be said we are picking up Mother's crumbs." "Yea," said Mother. "I hope," said Tabitha Shapley, one of the deaconesses, "it will be a great while first." "I don't know," replied Mother in a tone, which at the time struck Eldress Ruth and others with a serious impression that Mother then thought it would not be long first.

Saturday 27th she still continued very comfortable and at noon came into the house to eat her dinner; though she seldom ate but very little at a time, she now ate uncommonly hearty for a person of her abstemious habit, which Eldress Ruth noticed with some concern and spoke to her about it. She replied that she did not think it would hurt her, that she felt very well, and the victuals tasted very good. After dinner she returned to her shop and never came into the house again.

The same evening about meeting time, as she and Eldress Ruth were in Elder Abiathar's room in the meeting house and they three were engaged in their little meeting, singing and kneeling, she was suddenly seized with cold chills and soon after went to be sick. But by a proper application of suitable medicine, which seemed to operate very favorably, she appeared the next week to be on the recovery and continued through the week and was remarkably comfortable in her feelings all the week.

Sabbath February 4th, Mother had a particular gift concerning her successors in the ministry. This she opened to Eldress Ruth alone and named those who were to take the lead in the ministry after her decease.[4] It is worthy of remark that during her sickness in the summer of 1819, when many expected her to be very near her end, she felt no gift on this subject, though she was several times questioned about it.

Monday 5th (being her birthday) she felt as well as to be able to walk over to the office. She had for several days felt a desire to go to the office and see the deaconesses and had agreed to go at ten o'clock; but before the time came she began to feel an inward pain and distress and therefore was the more urgent to go to the office, lest she should not be able if she did not go soon. She accordingly went about half past nine. But her pain and distress still increasing upon her, she tarried till nearly twelve o'clock and then was led back to the meeting house; her disorder still continued to increase, with occasional intermissions, till her decease.

Tuesday, 6th. She again spoke to Eldress Ruth concerning those she

had named as her successors in the ministry, expressed her confidence in
them, and said she could feel safe in leaving her charge with them. On
Wednesday she seemed to fail very fast. After dinner the chief part of the
brethren and sisters went to see her. She was dying; her senses appeared
clear and bright; she was unable to speak; but by her countenance, the
motion of her lips, and other signs when questioned, she clearly manifested
that she knew all the brethren and sisters around her, particularly those
who spoke to her. She appeared calm, patient, and resigned, and her smiling spirit seemed to depart in peace and love. She expired a quarter before
three o'clock, February 7, 1821 [[Aged 61 years and 2 days]].

The following circumstance is worthy of remark. The first Sabbath after
Mother came to Watervliet, in the afternoon, being then in the deaconesses'
room, she sent for two of the brethren who expected to set off the next
morning on a long journey of business.

After giving them some good counsel and advice for their protection in
their absence, in which she told them that if they were faithful to keep the
gift of God, they would be under a blessing and would be protected by the
angels of God, that they must pray that the angels of God might go with
them and protect them, they requested that she would pray for them, which
she promised to do and expressed a desire that they might be under a
blessing and return in peace. Morrell desired to know whether he should
see her on his return. She asked him how long he expected to be gone; he
said between three and four weeks; she said, "If you return in three weeks
and three days, you will see me, but I have no promise beyond that."

Morrell went to the meeting house and saw her dying in just three
weeks and three days to the hour. She manifested that she knew him but
was unable to speak to him.

The brethren had returned some days before, but on account of her
sickness had not been to see her.

Morrell has often been employed in journeys, but says he never was
sensible of such a peculiar blessing on a journey in his life.

NOTES

1. Source: OClWHi V A 11.
2. This appears to refer to a process of readjusting the internal economic and
industrial affairs of the Church family at Watervliet.
3. This refers to the 1816 *Testimonies*.
4. In naming her successors, Lucy Wright apparently excluded Abiathar Babbitt,
who had for many years been the only male in the lead ministry. Immediately after
her death, the New Lebanon ministry wrote to Job Bishop, the lead ministry elder
at Canterbury, New Hampshire, asserting that as the last surviving "Father" in the
east, he had the right to be first in the New Lebanon lead ministry if he wished.
Apparently he refused, because shortly thereafter Ebenezer Bishop, Rufus Bishop,
Ruth Landon, and Asenath Clark became the next lead ministry at New Lebanon.

SELECTED CORRESPONDENCE

Letter 1. "I desire to write to thee in Few words as one whom I esteem my Equal." Joseph Meacham to Lucy Wright, 1796.[1]

> [Shortly before his death, Joseph Meacham writes to Lucy Wright about their mutual labor for the "gathering and building of the Church." He clearly sees her as the "first Elder" after his death; and believes she will be given "the greatest measure of the Wisdom & knowledge of God," to compensate for her being "of the weaker sex in man."]

Joseph to Lucy Greeting—Beloved sister in Christ

As it appears at present that I have almost finished my Course & done my work in this Life I desire to write to thee in Few words as one whom I esteem my Equal in order & Lot according to thy sex

As it hath pleased God to Create me for & Call me to the First Lot of Care in my sex & thee in thine in the present Travel of the Church—It was necessary that we should Support a Greater measure of the union of the spirit and that we should Labour more to be mutual helps to Each other then any of the Rest of the members Not for our own privit Good but for the Good of the Whole that now do & shall hereafter believe in the Present which is the second appearing of Christ It is & Ever will be a matter of Consolation to us both that God hath Greatly Blessed His Church both in things spiritual & Temporal By our union & mutual Labours with them and that although he hath Called us for the Good of others to support Immediate union In spirit with Each other & to abundant Labour together he hath Kept us from all sin With Each other which hath Laid the foundation In & by us for the Gathering & Building of the Chh according to our order & Lots in the present which Is the second Generation or Travel of the Chh in this Latter day

Christ Jesus our Lord & Mother are the two Chief anointed ones that stand before God in Relation to the salvation of all souls & as god hath Fulfilled his Promise in them both the Foundation is Laid in the headship of man For the Restitution of all things—tho' they Were Rejected & dispised of man in this world yet they are Chosen of God & Precious & no soul can find Salvation in this latter day without Faith in the Latter as well as in the Former or First as the Counsel of Peace for man between them both. Inasmuch therefore as both the man & the woman have Equal Rights in order

& Lots & in the Lord & Governance of the Church according to their sex in this Latter Day & as thee tho' of the weaker sex in man will Be the Elder or first born after my departure I believe the Greatest measure of the Wisdom & Knowledge of God For the Protection of souls will be Given unto thee Especially in Counsel untill thy Power & strength both intellectual & Corporal shall fail as mine hath done. I believe the Late & present troubles among the young In the Church is the Chief Cause of my Present Weakness & sufferings—as they were young & not able to Receive that Planting of faith in their understanding When gathered into the Chh. as the adult[2] I always Expected there would be more trouble with Them as Come to Ripe age & as the Foundation Principles of Gods Grace to man in the Present day Were not Planted in them many may depart from the Faith unless the older who are Established are able to Protect them untill they are Either planted or Grafted into the present or succeeding Travel of the Church

It hath ben & is still my hope & Expectation that the greater Number of the young will Keep their Faith & if Weak in the present travel Compared with the older They may be more useful in the next & we be Compensated For our Labours & troubles with them

NOTES

1. Source: OClWHi IV A 30. This letter has been transcribed exactly as it appears in the manuscript, as a sample of the spelling and punctuation of some of the earliest correspondence.
2. Twenty out of 180 members of the New Lebanon Church Family returned to the world in 1795–1796, according to statistics provided by Priscilla Brewer (*SCSL*, 28).

Letter 2. "We also express our desires . . . to request the privilege of opening to the world the first foundation and pillar of the present appearing of Christ." David Darrow and the Ohio Brethren to Lucy Wright, New Lebanon, August 16, 1806. [1]

> [David Darrow, speaking for all the western brethren in the leadership, urges Lucy Wright to authorize the publication of a full and clear statement of Shaker belief—including the central tenet which the New Lebanon ministry expected to be very controversial, that a second appearing of Christ had occurred through Ann Lee, a woman.]

Elder David and the brethren that are with him at Lebanon in the country of Miami, unto their spiritual and most beloved Parent at Lebanon in Canaan, who is over the household of God.

Kind Parent, we have for some time past from prevailing circumstances been greatly pressed in our minds to publish our faith to the world by letter. All the particular causes of our feelings would at this time be very tedious as well as difficult to relate, but we can say at once that in relation to other souls we could neither feel satisfied nor justified without coming into some labor concerning it, and have therefore brought to pass what is now sent by the hands of the beloved Elder John.[2]

It would also be difficult to communicate a spiritual sense of the real difference between the religious minds of men in these parts and those in the northern states. They are not generally speaking like that people in their outward manners, but much more unlike them in their religious pursuits. Those who have been in the spirit of the late revival are people of great light as well as many of them are men of natural understanding and penetration. Thousands of those who have seen a great light coming on the earth and have felt its rays are now perishing for the want of knowledge and are prevented from coming even to the sound gospel by reason of incredible heaps of false and ungodly teachers who turn the truth of the gospel into reports of lasciviousness to blind the minds of the simple. And when it is so that any of them come to a hearing, by that time their prejudices are so strongly rooted and their sense so darkened by false and ungrounded reports, that it is not the work of an hour nor a day to remove the stumbling blocks [out] of the way even of the truly honest and seeking soul.

It appears to us that thousands of precious and sincere souls are losing their former light and going to destruction for the want of nothing but a fair statement of naked truth respecting the testimony of the gospel.

Whatever the truth of the matter may appear to be hereafter, so it is that from a present and increasing sense which we feel of these things, our souls are truly pained and in distress from day to day. And it really appears that if the gospel justice [is] to be done to souls that we cannot be justified in forbearing any longer.

It is true that the work of God in this land appears already sufficiently extensive for so few of us to take proper care of without loss. But it is also true that all within the limits of the work are not permitted from wicked and unjust statements of things to get an understanding of what the testimony really is. Neither is there sufficient and proper strength personally to give that understanding of the work of God, which appears really necessary to preserve that light which has already been given in the land. And because it is already extended to our ability of protection, must the work of God stop here? Shall an understanding of what God is doing in the last and greatest dispensation of his goodness be confined to the testimony of a few children, and the work of God lie so much hid from the world till there is no more light on the earth? nor belief of a God? Is it not high time that the world knew that God has a foundation now on the earth? That the scriptures might once be fulfilled, *where the body is, there shall the eagles be gathered together.*

These are a few of our feelings out of many, and we must say that they feel to us very weighty. And to make a publication to a lost and gainsaying world of a testimony which, though it be for the salvation of their souls, yet goes to supplant all the wisdom and generations of the earth, is a matter of still greater moment. But if it can be done in a gift of God though it should be through tribulation, it is our faith that the understanding and researches of all the sincere would be more justly dealt with, the truth of the gospel honored, and our souls on that account greatly released.

Some part of what we have written is divided into the order of chapters and verses, that thereby not only each dispensation, but each head, or even each sentence, if necessary, may be the more easily examined and weighed by itself, or in connection with the rest. At any rate the order of it will be found to be very convenient till the work is finished.

We have thought that if the publication still continues to be felt both at New Lebanon and here, that it would be sent out unto the world from under the hands of four of our young brethren whom we love, to wit, Malcolm Worley, Richard McNemar, and John Dunlavy of this state and Matthew Houston of Kentucky, who all appear to be men of good and simple faith, as well as men of learning who will be able to see that the work is finished acording to good sense and the perfect order of the letter.

We have labored to be as short and as comprehensive as possible and at the same time to leave nothing of any former dispensation on which souls could build their hopes of salvation, and also carefully and tenderly as well as pointedly to show the loss of man and the nature and degree of the work of God in every dispensation and how it pointed to the end.

Time would fail to show why we were so particular. We can therefore only say that it is because the matter feels to be of infinite importance and that the sensations of men are alive in their loss concerning those things whereof we have written.

With this statement, we also express our desires, and we think we feel a gift in it, to request the privilege of opening to the world the first foundation and pillar of the present appearing of Christ.[3] It truly feels to us that so long as the foundation of our faith in the present day is kept concealed, the testimony of the gospel will ever be under weakness. Must it be hid from the world till the eye witnesses of her power and majesty are all gone and none left to strengthen the testimony of their children? But why should it be concealed any longer, seeing the foundation of God in relation to the great and last dispensation is now laid and stands sure? We think we feel a gift in our souls to state clearly the order of God's work in this particular.

As far as the sound of the gospel is gone, it is also gone and established that the foundation of our faith is built on the fables of a drunken old woman, and the world has nothing to the contrary to believe. How long shall we suffer these things without having confidence enough to let the world know that the present work of God is not built on fables? We truly think that we feel a gift of God in relation to these matters, and that which feels hastening and pressing, and we can see no way to get over it and be justified. But as Christ said, *of myself I can do nothing*, so we say. We feel therefore a desire of counsel and that the communication of our minds may be received as from those who ever esteem the counsel and union of their spiritual parent as the greatest blessing.

P.S. Elder John will be able to state more particulars than what may be written, but we should be glad to have a short statement of these things in writing. And it would be a great help to us if a correct copy of these writings might be sent back by Elder John (on account of our time) for we have nothing here but the first rough draft—by this means a proper communication may be kept, as it is likely that we shall make alterations wherever it is necessary till we are fully satisfied. But we think that we shall be best able to determine where anything is written unnecessarily when the whole of the work is put together.

NOTES

1. Source: OClWHi IV A 66.
2. Apparently John Meacham carried along with this letter a draft statement which became the basis for the fuller explication of Shaker faith, *The Testimony of Christ's Second Appearing.*
3. This refers to the doctrine that a second appearing of Christ had occurred in Ann Lee. According to Calvin Green's "Biographic Memoir," it was not until 1809 that public preaching of the doctrine of the dual divinity occurred in the East (OClWHi VI B 28, 50–51).

Letter 3. "I am satisfied you all may feel Elder David your first elder." Lucy Wright, New Lebanon, to David Darrow and company, Ohio, October 9, 1806. [1]

> [Lucy Wright addresses the western Believers, confirming the appointment of David Darrow as first elder in the lead ministry in the West. She warns against too much emphasis on the "outward work" of religion—the "great noise" of ecstatic manifestations of divine grace.]

Beloved Elder David and brethren and sisters that are with thee,

I received your letters dated August by our beloved brother Elder John and am glad to hear that you are in usual health. Likewise I enjoy a small measure of health and strength.

In reading your letters, I feel thankful for the gift of God that called you

to go into that distant land to preach the gospel of peace, life, and salvation
to a poor needy people that never heard there is a way that God has opened
for souls to travel out of all sin. I remember the day the three first brethren
that were sent, Elder John [Meacham], Benjamin [S. Youngs], and Issachar
[Bates], in a cold, distressing season of the year and have not repented of
it. Likewise I remember the day the next three brethren were sent, Elder
David [Darrow], Solomon [King], and Daniel [Mosely], and yet have not
repented. Also I remember the day the three last brethren that were sent,
Peter [Pease], Samuel [Turner], and Constant [Mosely], with six of our
beloved sisters and have not repented. Nay, but I feel thankful for the
world['s] sake, likewise for your faith and obedience to the call and gift of
God to you and for your zeal and love for the opening and spread of the
gospel.

For I feel the special notice of God toward you all and am sensible that
Christ in his first and second appearance is with you; saints and angels
surround you with a ministration of the gospel of peace. We are all benefited by the sufferings of Christ in his first as well as in his second appearance and by all the saints and martyrs that have suffered for their testimony.
Look at this, you writers.

As some of you have answered me according to my desire in relation
to your faith, I am satisfied you all may feel Elder David your first elder,
counsellor, and protector there in that distant land, which is a great comfort
and satisfaction to me and I think it may be to you all. I am sensible you
have diversity of gifts, but by the same spirit I desire you may build upon
and strengthen each other in the gift of God. You may consider you could
not be so complete if you was all a head or an arm or a foot. Therefore
labor to bring your gifts into subjection to the work of God that you are
called to in that land. If any of you should rise too high by reason of having
great gifts of God, I desire you would labor to creep down the best way
you can, for if you should fall it might hurt you.

I desire you may not be deceived so as to feel your justification in making
a great noise or sound, although I believe the people must have an outward
work before they are able to have an inward as a body. But the work of
mortification must increase as they travel. That will be coming down into
the work of God, not rising above. If they do, they rise above their protection and of consequence must suffer loss. What I have written is my intention of doing you good.

I have labored in relation to Somes going with Brother John when he
returned,[2] but found it brought such distress upon me that I should not
be able to endure such a labor, therefore could not feel any gift. But I feel
you stand in need of further help in temporal things in order for you to
gather suitable support and strength to do your duty, those of you that are
already there.

If there should be any letters or presents sent to the young Believers there, I desire you may not feel bound, for I feel it will not be profitable for us nor them to support that manner of relation. It appears to me it will have a bad effect. I desire to hear in relation to the letter that was sent soon after Brother John come to see us, whether it was profitable and suitable for the occasion or not.

I have been a journey (June 2nd and returned June 28th) to the eastward with Elder Abiathar, Ebenezer, and Ruth—first to Shirley then to Harvard, Canterbury, and New Enfield—and found the people under a good degree of blessing, health, and protection. Likewise they remember you and feel for you according to the best of their understanding. We returned home over the Green Mountains, which caused me to think of you often.

My kind love and remembrance to you all in the gospel. Likewise Elder Abiathar, Ebenezer, and Ruth sends their kind love and remembrance to you all.

This from your Parent in the gospel.

NOTES

1. Source: OClWHi IV A 31. This and the other letters in this group dated October 9, 1806, are the earliest writings of Lucy Wright's to survive, so far as I am aware.
2. Apparently the western Shakers had asked for a particular New Lebanon brother to be sent west with Elder John Meacham when he returned, and Wright is denying the request.

Letter 4. "It is my faith that thee is called to stand as the first pillar or elder . . . in that land." Lucy Wright, New Lebanon, to David Darrow, Ohio, October 9, 1806. [1]

To Elder David,

I thank thee for thy kind and respectful letter that thee has wrote to me; likewise am thankful if I have been or may be any help in giving counsel to those that is called to the work of the ministry in the present opening of the gospel.

I make no doubt but there has been many feelings in the Church as ye have signified for lack of understanding, but now they have further sight and feeling of the work of God. As to myself, when I felt willing (but it was a labor) to give thee up, the way was clear before me for I believed thee could do more good there than thee could here in the present state and travel of the Church. It is my faith that thee is called to stand as the first pillar or elder in relation to the present opening of the gospel in that land. I desire ye may have grace to walk according to thy lot and calling.

In relation to the Believers' feelings to go into that land, I believe it is chiefly those that are tinctured with heresy and have a lead in themselves.

I look upon them to be very unsuitable persons to go to such a place. I feel union with thy feelings and understanding of the work thee is called to. It was not my understanding to have thee labor for a gift to speak to the world when thee left the Church, but to labor to protect those that have that gift and them that might believe. It does not belong to the first elder to labor for a gift to the world but on occasion. It appears to me there is a sufficient number gone out of the Church to lay a foundation for the present opening of the gospel (in the present state of things). If there should be need of more help will it not do to send them that has not had so great a privilege? I think it will make it easier for me, and will it not also be easier for thee?[2] If thee should need more help, I desire thee would tell how many and who, and state the gifts and faculties that they need for such a place, and then I will labor to feel how it will bear. Thee may consider my sense is very different from thine, yet I believe thine is as suitable for thy calling as mine is for my calling.

I feel that Brother John has found a great increase since he left these parts. He feels like a worthy man of God and is much more free and sociable in conversation than what he had used to be, which is great satisfaction to me and others. It appears to me he will be more free there when he feels released in relation to writing.[3]

I remember hearing Father Joseph say that when the gospel opened again, the door would never be shut any more as what it has been in our travel. If that is the will of God, I pray it never may. If what I have written may be of service to thee I am thankful.

If there should be any letters or presents sent to the young Believers there I desire thee may not feel bound, for I feel it will not be profitable for us nor them to support that manner of relation. It appears to me it will have a bad tendency.[4] I desire to hear in relation to the letters that was sent soon after Brother John came to see us whether it was profitable and suitable for the occasion or not.

I have given Brother John copies of some writing that was Father Joseph's.[5] I think they may be of great service to those that is called to write our faith in Christ in his first and second appearance. There is one writing I feel confident I gave to thee when thee left the Church, but Brother John said he has not seen any such, therefore I felt to give it to him.

This from thy Mother, sister, and fellow laborer in the gospel.

NOTES

1. Source: OClWHi IV A 31.
2. She seems to indicate here that there had been some problems with the eastern Shakers sent from the relatively more secluded and higher-status Church Family.
3. This refers to some anxiety on John Meacham's part with regard to writing.

Perhaps Wright is excusing him from participating in the preparation of *The Testimony of Christ's Second Appearing*.

4. Wright is instructing David Darrow not to pass on any letters or gifts sent by easterners to new converts in the West.

5. Wright was passing on Joseph Meacham's writings to the western brethren who were writing *The Testimony of Christ's Second Appearing* at this time.

Letter 5. "I have felt and experienced considerable with Father Joseph in relation to writing." Lucy Wright, New Lebanon, to the brethren in Miami County, Ohio, October 9, 1806. [1]

> [Lucy Wright responds to the plea from the western brethren with full approval of their project to write down the Shaker faith. But she anticipates that such a publication will stir up "the wicked," and warns the brethren not to "get any thing printed but what you are willing to live and die by."]

Beloved Brethren,

I have perused your writings that you have sent by our beloved Brother Elder John with care and satisfaction. I am sensible that what you have written is the gift of God that you have received by your faith and obedience to the true and genuine gospel.

I have felt and experienced considerable with Father Joseph in relation to writing and making more fully known to the world the foundation of our faith. We always felt the time was not come. But now I feel satisfied the time is come, and the gift is in you and with you to accomplish this work.

I am sensible your gift and calling that you are called to in the present opening of the gospel brings every gift clear and plain that is necessary for the full accomplishment of this work.

I am with you and the Church also and can strengthen you in the work. Therefore, I think it not necessary for you to send any further respecting it, for I commit the whole to the wisdom and gift you may feel in union there.

I hope and trust my life may be spared to see this work accomplished.

It will not be unexpected to me if the wicked should write against the circulation of such books.

These few lines from your Parent in the gospel.

N.B. I trust you will labor to have it printed free from all involvements, so that it may have free circulation. I hope and trust you will consider well and not get anything printed but what you are willing to live by and die by.

NOTE

1. Source: OClWHi IV A 31. This letter is a direct response to Darrow's request of August 16, 1806 (Letter 2, above).

Letter 6. "Mother, we have not had one day of rest since we left New Lebanon." Ruth Farrington, Martha Sanford, Lucy Smith, Prudence Farrington, Molly Goodrich, and Ruth Darrow, Miami County, Ohio, to Lucy Wright, Abiathar Babbitt, Ebenezer Bishop, and Dolly Sanford, New Lebanon, August 16, 1806. [1]

> [The first six eastern sisters to travel to Ohio
> write to Lucy Wright, expressing dutiful feelings
> as well as a strong sense of shock at their primi-
> tive surroundings and onerous duties as west-
> ern missionaries.]

To our beloved Mother and tender Parent in the gospel,

We now embrace this opportunity and privilege to write to thee as dear children in the gospel, being absent in body but present in spirit we trust. We should [[have]] been thankful to have written before, but circumstances would not admit; it feels to us like a long time since we parted with thee, our Mother. But we do not feel that we have lost our union and relation to our Mother and the Church of Christ; neither have we forgotten the good exhortation to us, but we well remember the gifts and privileges which we received when we were present with thee, yea and gifts in particular which yields us great strength, comfort, and consolation in the gospel.

Mother, we desire to manifest our feelings as far as we are able. And these are our feelings, we feel like poor needy children desiring to be remembered and not forgotten, but it is our full faith that our Mother will remember us and strengthen us in every good thing. For we are sensible that no one knows how it feels to go out of the Church where there is so much order and go into such a distant land where there is so much evil and so little good but those that have experienced it. But we do not feel discouraged, for we are sensible that good is increasing and evil decreasing, and it is all the comfort that we have to see the gospel increasing and souls acoming into the work of God having the gifts and power of God. For we are sensible that there is a number that has received the gospel and the gifts and power of God in the same manner that the people did in the first opening, and their gifts and operations in the power of God is something of the same—powerful gifts of shaking, turning, leaping. And some of these when they get unreconciled, they have what they call the jerks so powerful that they are thankful to come down and seek their relation again. This has been fulfilled in our eyes in some measure. Mother, we feel great tribulation yet not discouraged, for it is our faith to be in that work and gift of God that is allotted for us and do all the good we can both in things spiritual and temporal, and we find as much to do as we can possibly have strength to endure.

Mother, we have not had one day of rest since we left New Lebanon, but we have our hands and hearts full continually either in things spiritual or temporal. And Sabbath day we have long heavy meetings, and when we are not in public meeting we are in private labors continually. And we [at]tend a meeting with them every week in the afternoon and sometimes evening meetings, and we have a great many young Believers that comes to see us of necessity, especially them that comes from a distance for they have need to be with us in order to gather strength. And we have them to cook for and wait on continually. And our work in temporal things comes very hard upon us indeed, and our circumstances is so that we do not see that we can gather any helps from the young Believers at present. For our cabin is very small and poor and inconvenient, and we do not know when we shall be able to move into the new house, for it goes on very slow. But we expect that the brethren will speak more particular about that than we can write.

We have all been very unwell more or less since we left home, for everything being so different that it did not agree with our health. But we think that we rather gain in health and strength. Our journey was long and tedious and very wearisome, but we have had a measure of strength given us to carry us through to this present time, for we feel sensible that we were under a measure of protection and blessing of God in the whole of our journey. And we feel thankfulness and gratitude to God for his goodness and mercy toward us in protecting and keeping us from all danger. Furthermore when we met with our brethren they all received us kindly, and we found Elder David much easier than we expected, for he has got that gift of wisdom and charity that we feel thankful for. We do not feel able to communicate our feelings as we should be glad to do. But this one thing we know and that is we have a Mother, and we remember her and feel her and receive from her. For we feel her so perceptibly and so near many a time that it really makes the tears fall from our eyes. And it is our desire that we may be so wise and faithful as to keep our union and relation to our Mother and to the Church and to all the people of God.

We should be thankful to receive a letter from our Mother or only hear from her would give us great satisfaction. We think that when we see our Mother again, that Joseph's meeting his father Jacob will be nothing to be compared to that meeting, no more than a natural relation is to a spiritual relation. But we remember before we came from home that five years was mentioned,[2] and we do not expect to forget it. We likewise desire the prayers of our Mother and those that live with her and all our brethren and sisters in the gospel. This letter is written from the sisters with their whole hearts in the tears of love to their beloved Mother. This letter is closed with our love and remembrance to our beloved Mother, Elder Abiathar, Ebenezer, Dolly.

Ruth   Prudence   Martha   Molly   Lucy   Ruth

P.S. The particulars of our journey and the temporal affairs we have written in a letter to the sisters,[3] for we did not think it proper to write it in the letter that we wrote to Mother.

NOTES

1. Source: OClWHi IV A 66.
2. This suggests that western missionaries originally believed they were commit-ting themselves to five years in the West.
3. See chapter 3 of this volume.

Letter 7. "You must not seek now to please yourselves." Lucy Wright, New Lebanon, to Ruth Farrington, Ohio, October 9, 1806. [1]

> [Lucy Wright reminds Eldress Ruth and the other
> eastern sisters that they have "gone out to labor
> for others," and somewhat sternly warns them to
> "take courage and press on for the prize."]

Beloved Eldress Ruth and the sisters that are with thee,

I thank you for your kind and dutiful letter which you wrote to me. I feel in some measure able to sense the sudden change which you have had to pass through, but there was no way to avoid it and for you to have the privilege you now have. I remember you and feel that you have taken up your cross so far in a great measure cheerfully for the gospel sake. Therefore you must not seek now to please yourselves but to please God that has called you to that work and protected and guarded you through so many perils and dangers and landed you safe to the place appointed, where you found our beloved brethren that had prepared the way so far for you.

I pray for you. I ask all the people of God to pray for you that you may have strength and patience and wisdom and grace to do the work that you are called to in that distant land. You may consider you have had a long privilege in the Church to labor for yourselves, but now you have gone out to labor for others. As you signified in your letter that good is increasing

and evil decreasing, I think you have great reason to take courage and press
on for the prize of your calling which is [[in Christ Jesus]]. I believe you
may all find a gift therein that will be profitable if your patience and
strength does not fail you, which I pray it may not, for it brings much labor
and tribulation and sufferings upon me and also on the Church in sending
you forth to labor in so distant a vineyard. I do not feel anxious though I
never should see your faces any more in the body, but I feel anxious that
you may find a gift of God where you are sent, and if you do you will
honor your privilege and calling which will be a full compensation for my
trouble and sorrow. I think, Sisters, you have been very particular in writing. Sometimes you make me weep, sometimes smile, but you never will
cause me to repent for sending you there if you are faithful.

As to your manner of living, I think it may serve to make you all more
healthy. Look at Solomon and take courage in the cross.

I must close my letter, not for want of paper, neither for lack of feeling,
but my head and eyes is much pained and it wears upon me to labor to
write.

This from your friend and Parent in the gospel.

NOTE

1. Source: OClWHi IV A 31.

Letter 8. "Our first Mother is publicly preached in her order and lot." David
Darrow, Turtle Creek, Ohio, to Lucy Wright, New Lebanon, January 12,
1807.[1]

> [David Darrow writes to Lucy Wright, express-
> ing general satisfaction with the new missionar-
> ies—though also some reservations about two
> of the sisters. He reports on the missionary
> activities of all the eastern Shakers, claiming that
> "the gospel is preached more clear and in the
> demonstration of the spirit and power than ever
> it was on earth before."]

Beloved Mother,

I cannot feel satisfied without sending a few lines to thee at this time,
particular relating to our family. First, I thank Mother for her kind and
good letters she wrote to me. I am satisfied with Mother's gift in not sending any more members with Brother John, but believe it was for the best.
I expect Mother knows that creatures are apt to have a craving disposition

in them. Although we have as much labor as we are able to do and sometimes a little more, and I expect we should if we had two or three members
more, I agree with Mother that if any more should come it will be easier
for them that are aback in their travel,[2] allowing their faith and talents are
equal—although it is my judgment it is not so much in having a great
privilege or less as it is in their talents or faith and dispositions and sense.
Yet the further creatures travel, the further they have to come down to
come to lost souls. But the wise soul that feels it to be the gift and call of
God to them will endure and suffer it patiently, although it may feel ever
so filthy to them. The disciple ought not to be above his master.

I shall now give a short relation of our family. I am satisfied that the
sisters are helps in the gospel as well as the brethren. Eldress Ruth is a
wise woman of God and has gained the faith and love of the Believers. The
other sisters are all able and are great helps. Prudence and Molly their
sense was too high and sometimes would rise against their elders,[3] but
they have gained and I think they will be more simple. But they are all
stronger both in body and spirit than they was when they came here. I
believe that Solomon, Samuel, and the sisters are twice as strong in a gift
of God as they was at first, and our songs are great conviction and strength
to the people.

Beloved Mother, I am truly thankful to God for his special grace and
goodness to us and the union we have yet been able to keep; it is more
than one could expect in our situation. The brethren are all peaceable and
feel subject. Brother John felt more union and freedom in the family since
he returned than he did before. I am sensible it is through the prayers and
intercessions and labors of the Church and people of God that we are made
partakers of such gifts and blessings, for which I ever feel to return thanks.

We have gathered one young man and two young women to live with
us. They are likely active people and [have] faith enough to give themselves
and services for the support and increase of the gospel and feel happy in
so doing, which has taken off some burden from the sisters. The sisters
have not been on long journeys yet. Eldresses Ruth, Prudence, and Ruth
went with me and Solomon and Daniel to Beulah, about 24 miles, last
September. The other sisters have visited the people here for ten miles
round, and it is great strength to the people.

I have lately been a journey to Eagle Creek and Limestone in Kentucky.
The state of the people was such that they could not be satisfied unless I
visited them. Solomon, Issachar, and Richard went with me; Richard and
John Dunlavy went on to the southern parts of Kentucky to preach the
gospel to the world to a people that had a desire to hear the truth, and also
to visit the Believers in them parts. Solomon, Issachar, and myself returned
home on Christmas evening after being absent 17 days. The Believers where
we went increase in strength, and eight grown persons opened their minds,
and the wife of Daniel Runnels, which I mentioned in our last letter, was
one, and Daniel himself stands strong in the faith.

I believe it is the wisdom of God that the gospel has not spread no faster, for there has as many believed as we have been able to take care of as our circumstances has been. For it would not be wisdom for a man to go into the wilderness and clear land and sow it to wheat and leave it without fence for the beasts to devour it, and then go and clear and sow more and leave it in like manner. He would lose his labor. So it is in the gospel. After the seed is sown, if it is not cultivated and taken care of, the wicked one will come and devour it, so that it will bring forth no fruit to perfection. I think it better for souls to die in their ignorance than after they have received the truth to be lost for the want of protection.

I desire Mother's charity and patience with us. I believe without all doubt the gospel is preached more clear and in the demonstration of the spirit and power than ever it was on earth before, both in Christ's first and second appearing. Our first Mother is publicly preached in her order and lot, so plain as to say her name was Anne Lees, and proved in the most clear manner by the scriptures of truth that Christ's second appearing was to be in the woman. And it is great light and strength to the people. Richard is full of faith, light, life, and power, and the truth is to work like leaven among the people in these parts.

Beloved Mother, my ardent desire is that God may continue thy life to be a long and lasting blessing to us, to lead and guide the Church by thy wisdom and counsel and every branch of the work of God—which I esteem to be one of the greatest blessings. I am sensible as the work of God grows more extensive it will increase thy sufferings and labors. I pray God to comfort and strengthen Mother through all her trials and labors. I desire Mother to remember her poor children in this distant land so far from their Parent and brethren and sisters.

I send my kind love to Elder Abiathar, Ebenezer, and Ruth. I desire all my elders and brethren and sisters in my absence would labor to strengthen and comfort Mother by their love and obedience. It is my desire and labor to honor my parents in the gospel from this time henceforth and forever—

This from Mother's son.[4]

David

N.B. Since I have been able to separate more from the people and shut them more off,[5] I feel stronger in body and spirit.

NOTES

1. Source: OClWHi IV A 67.
2. "aback in their travel": Shakers who are "behind," spiritually—that is, not members of the Church Family. Darrow is agreeing with Wright's suggestion that no more missionaries be sent west from the Church Family.
3. David Darrow's initially critical view of Molly Goodrich is of interest, in the

light of her long subsequent career as the first eldress at South Union, Kentucky. For a selection of her correspondence, see chapter 3.

4. Note that although Lucy Wright calls herself David Darrow's "Mother, sister and fellow laborer," he refers to himself only as her "son," thus acknowledging her undisputed headship of the Society.

5. At this time living arrangements were shifted to allow David Darrow and the others in the Ohio ministry more privacy.

Letter 9. "Beware therefore lest you get darkened and lose sight of your own lot and calling." Lucy Wright, New Lebanon, to David Darrow, Ohio, July 11, 1807.[1]

> [Lucy Wright cautions David Darrow in a private letter to refrain from travelling and public preaching and to stay with his assigned role as first elder or spiritual leader in the West.]

To Elder David,

Beloved brother and fellow laborer in tribulation and travel for the increase of the gospel, I wish grace, mercy, and truth to remain and abide with you, as we are heirs together of the promise of life in Christ if we remain firm in obedience unto the end, however distant from each other the fields may be that we labor in.

I have for some time past felt a weight on my mind in relation to you, and as I have the present good opportunity I embrace it to send this private letter, wherein I desire to signify a few things by way of caution which I desire you may receive as from a faithful friend—although I do not pretend to be able to teach in particular how you ought to labor, for I do not know particular circumstances. But this I feel, that it ought to be your first and greatest labor to lay a foundation for the support and protection of a family in that place and to gather them into that order and union that they may find protection so as to be able to go forth and help others. As you have a number of brethren with you that are able to labor in word and doctrine to others, but you have not many that are able to be first in laying a foundation—and as it is a truth that we do well often to consider that we are forever indebted to God for the everlasting gospel of salvation which has separated us from our former sins and made us able to be helps in the increase of the work of God in this day of the second appearance of Christ— therefore we ought to give earnest heed that we are always found in the gift of God not doing our own will but the will of him that hath called us to his work.

As I have sometimes had fears lest you would have too much feeling to go journeys to visit the Believers at a distance and thereby get darkened and lose the gift of God—furthermore since I have heard of your going after the Indians, I have felt some tribulation on that account[2]—although I do not know the cause of your going and therefore cannot judge whether you went in the gift of God or not, or whether it would not [have] been better to have sent some of the young Believers than to have gone yourself—I leave you to judge. But this I know, that as you are the first in your order, your gift is to bear and suffer the most for the increase of the gospel. And the increasing weight of years that you must feel would admonish you that a careful consideration of the above lines would be a means of prolonging your gift in your present lot in that country.

Although I do not write this letter to bind you in any measure from what you feel to be the gift of God, yet I feel ardent desires and prayers to God that you may feel the importance of improving your strength and talents in laboring in the work of the root, rather than to be occupying in the work of the branches, lest your strength should fail before you have effected that work of God for which you were sent.

Beware therefore lest you get darkened and lose sight of your own lot and calling and thereby become unable to purge, protect, and counsel the ministers and leaders of the people.

What I have written is my sincere intention of doing good, and I desire you may receive it as such.

This from your faithful friend, sister, and Parent in the gospel.

NOTES

1. Source: OClWHi IV A 31.
2. Another letter bearing the same date, apparently in the same handwriting but signed "Ministry," was sent from New Lebanon to "Elder David and Brethren," concerning the Indian mission. It advised the western brethren of the ministry's opinion that the Shawnee "prophet & Elder has the revelation of God & may be able to lead and protect them in their own order & Nation by receiving a small measure of council from some of the Believers." Further Shaker missionary work to the Shawnees was to be done "by some of the young Believers . . . that have not much gift in relation to white people, and then leave them to act for themselves, & by no means gather them. For they are Indians & will remain so, therefore cannot be brought into the order of white people, but must be saved in their own order & Nation" (OClWHi NL IV A 31).

Letter 10. "You have varied from my counsel in relation to the order of the godhead." Lucy Wright, New Lebanon, to David Darrow and Ruth Farrington, Ohio, April 12, 1809.[1]

> [Lucy Wright acknowledges the "heavy burden"
> being felt in both eastern and western Shaker
> communities as a result of the publication of *The
> Testimony of Christ's Second Appearing* (1808). She

reminds Darrow and Farrington that she had advised a more conservative approach to the subject of the godhead. She also comments on
several of the eastern Shakers now being considered for leadership roles in the newly forming
Kentucky communities.]

Beloved Elder David and Eldress Ruth,

I now sit down to write some of my feelings unto you in answer to a
letter that Brother Constant brought. Although Eldress Ruth's name was
not in the letter, yet I believe she has borne a heavy burden in relation to
the publication, and therefore must have a part in this also. Respecting
your trial in relation to the publication, I believe it has been very heavy
and trying, beyond what you ever can fully express. But I can say you have
not been altogether alone in it, for I have experienced the same in my
measure and do not expect to be released but in part until I can see the
effect it has upon the Believers and also the world. Admitting the time is
fully come, we cannot escape the trial, since we are called to defend whatever we publish to mankind.

As you acknowledge, you have varied from my counsel in relation to
the order of the godhead,[2] I give you my reason why I was unwilling it
should be published. It was because I did not know but it would be too
much like casting pearls before swine. But according to the channel the
book runs in, it appears altogether necessary that it should be opened more
or less, and I think it is opened very clear and plain to any whose understanding is fruitful.

As you have observed in your letter, you believe the time is come for
the order, light, and glory of the Church to be opened to mankind, and to
begin to take off the veil of covering from all flesh that the shame of their
nakedness may appear, etc. I also believe the time is come. Furthermore,
you have manifested your faith in the preparatory work of God which he
hath been carrying on for many years past, that it has been for the further
opening of the gospel in America. And that God hath put it into the hearts
of the rulers to frame and establish a constitution which gives all mankind
free liberty of conscience to serve God, speak, or publish their sentiments.
I believe so too. And it feels to me like the work of a merciful God, for it
really appears that through the medium of earthly rulers *the earth hath
opened her mouth to help the woman,* etc.

But in relation to our political sentiments, I feel it is our wisdom to keep
them to ourselves, for *our Kingdom is not of this world.*

As you spoke of the uncertainty of your making us a visit at Lebanon,
I inform you that I should be very glad and thankful to see you once more
in this world, if it is the will of God. But it appears to the contrary to me
at present. As I have labored much upon the matter, it appears to me that

your journey here, then back home again would take nearly the whole of your gift that you have not already spent. Therefore, if it should prove according to this statement, it would be unprofitable to you and likewise to the people that you are called to protect. But I submit the matter to your gift, as you know your own strength best and also the need you have of coming.

Respecting Elder John's going to Kentucky to gather his gift there, I feel union with it and believe that Lucy Smith is the most suitable sister to have the first gift with Elder John of any that has gone from these parts.[3] But according to my understanding he is a very backward man and Lucy is a very forward-spirited woman, and therefore they may be mutual helps to each other. I look upon Lucy to be a likely woman and think she may be very suitable to go to such a place.

I think it will be best to speak a little concerning Brother Comstock [Betts], as he is a clever man and is gifted in both spiritual and temporal things. And as his feeling appeared to turn from the place that he was in to the work of God in Ohio, Elder Nathaniel [Deming] feels it best for him to go, since there is a brother called for, and he has our union in it. Perhaps you may remember he is a man of a forward spirit and a high sense. Therefore I think it will not do for him to go to Kentucky at present, on this account: he will be liable to run over Elder John and hurt his gift. It may do for him to go and do a certain job of work if it is found needful, and then return back to Ohio. I desire you may labor for his protection, and likewise for all the brethren and sisters. Brother Comstock and the three sisters that are now preparing to come and see you are taught they must not visit you in a sense of being ministers or elders,[4] but with this sense, (viz.) to put their hands to work and be reconciled to every gift that is for them.

I believe those three sisters are capable, well-minded women and able to do good either in things spiritual or temporal, although Mercy [Pickett] has not so much gift in spiritual things as the other two.

We do not consider it best for us to establish their lots before you have proved them, lest it should prove as hard for you and them as it has been for those in general, or at least some of them, who have gone in a sense of being ministers heretofore.[5] I think here is as much wrote as it [is] profitable for this time, so farewell

Beloved and loving Elder David and Eldress Ruth,

From Mother

NOTES

1. Source: OClWHi IV A 31.
2. A fuller statement of the Shaker theory of the dual-gender godhead, which was being developed at this time, occurs in a letter written August 26, 1809, from

David Darrow and Benjamin S. Youngs to the New Lebanon ministry and elders: "The everlasting Father was revealed by the Son, through the energy of the Holy Ghost; & the everlasting Mother was revealed by the Daughter, through the energy of the same; & the Holy Ghost one in essence with the Word, was the joint influence proceeding from the everlasting Father & Mother. . . . But the truth of the matter is, that the second appearing of Christ, is strictly speaking, not the 'Revelation of the Holy Ghost,' but the Revelation of Wisdom. Let the attribute of Mother be more particularly applied to the title of Wisdom, & let the title of Wisdom be more generally applied to the everlasting Mother, & then the distinction of these various attributes in the order of God may appear clear & familiar, & the whole stand in harmony & in a reasonable connection together" (OClWHi IV A 67).

3. This refers to David Darrow's appointment of John Meacham and Lucy Smith as first elder and eldress of the newly forming community at Shawnee Run, in Mercer County (later to be named Pleasant Hill). John Meacham and Lucy Smith took their places as first lead ministry there in January 1809, and 128 members signed the covenant in June 1814.

4. A further group of eastern Shakers sent to help in the West at this time were Comstock Betts, Hortency Goodrich, Mercy Pickett, and Hopewell Curtis. Lucy Wright suggests here that the first two stay in Ohio, while the second two go to Kentucky (letter from the New Lebanon ministry to the Ohio ministry, dated February 23, 1809, OClWHi IV A 31).

5. Some eastern Believers had been sent west with the understanding that they would take their places as western ministry, it seems. Lucy Wright is here explicitly amending the practice, by giving David Darrow and Ruth Farrington the responsibility for appointing the best people to the positions, once a probationary period is over.

Letter 11. "I am sorry to hear that any who have been sent out to be helps with you in the gospel should fail of answering the purpose." Lucy Wright, New Lebanon, to David Darrow and others in the West, August 1, 1812.[1]

> [Lucy Wright sends a circular letter to all the eastern Shakers in the West, through David Darrow, about the recent return of three of their company to New Lebanon. She clearly reiterates the hierarchy of leadership in the West and sets policy governing the return of those who "lose their gift."]

Beloved and much respected children in the gospel,

I now sit down to write some of my feelings to you, and whenever you read these lines you may remember that you are not forgotten by me, but that I labor and pray to God night and day for his blessing on your behalf and that he would own you and your labors and make you prosperous in the truth, as there is nothing that will abide unless it is built on the truth. I am sorry to hear that any who have been sent out to be helps with you in the gospel should fail of answering the purpose for which they were sent. But whenever this becomes the case, I believe they had better return to their former homes and labor to gather there for protection, as this was the liberty which was given to all that went from here, that if they could not find a gift there to be useful in the gospel, they might return home, and our doors should be open to receive them if they had labored so faithfully as to keep themselves from all sin. [[I thought it proper to remind you of that liberty which still remains good.]]

In relation to Lucy Bacon, I believe that sending her home was the wisest thing you could have done, and I do not believe it will be any final loss to her, but hope it may be great gain, seeing she went out in obedience and has returned according to the liberty that was given.

And likewise our good brother Daniel [Mosely]—we are glad to have him return home and gather his union and relation with his brethren. We believe that he has had a gift and has been a help to many souls, but in the increase of the work of God his gift and manner of labor must necessarily decrease. And I think it is likely that he has not returned any too soon for his own good and the good of others. And as he has been faithful and laborious in doing good according to his faith and the best measure of wisdom which was given unto him, he is justly entitled to receive his reward among the faithful.

And now if any of the brethren or sisters (that still remain in the West) should come to the end of their gift in that land, I desire they may return home with thankful hearts to God for the gospel and for their privilege in this blessed gospel which saves from all sin every soul that will obey. While writing these lines my spirit flows with thankfulness to God for his protecting hand over us and you as his chosen and faithful followers. I likewise feel thankful for your labor, patience, and charity for the poor lost children of men. And what you have already gained in a spiritual line (if protected) will be a foundation for souls to gather to and an everlasting treasure to you and me and to all the people of God far and near, as the true children of God are always laboring for the union of the spirit and not so much to please themselves, but to please God in those that have travelled before them. But I have not learned (to my full satisfaction) your feelings in relation to the center of your union. Therefore I feel to write my feelings in short, as a word to the wise is sufficient.

Everything that will abide has a center. Therefore it becomes necessary that there be a center of union among those who have been instruments in the hand of God to open the gospel in the West, as really as there is here in the East. And as Elder David and Eldress Ruth were given up to go to that land it was (and still is) my faith and expectation that where they abide, there would be the center of union for the rest to gather to for counsel and instruction and for examples of patience, godliness, meekness, littleness, and the most power over *GREAT I* and *little u* which so often beset the poor people of God in this day of Christ's second coming. It is without doubt that there is a great heap of darkness and blindness that prevents you from coming to your faith in the true line of gospel order and therefore shuts out many blessed gifts and blessings of God from you. You will all own that it is very natural for creatures to seek to please themselves, and by so doing they displease God, the giver of all good.

As Daniel [Mosely], Constant [Mosely] and Lucy [Bacon] have heretofore been called to stand as helps with you in your labors in the gospel and have returned home—and it is likely they will spend the remainder of their days with us—therefore I think it will not be for their comfort or strength for you or the young Believers to send them separate letters, as it may have a tendency to separate them from us. But in order for their feeling comfortable in their present travel, they must leave that labor which they have been in heretofore and gather with the present gift where they now belong. You may write to the ministry, elders or deacons or doctors as you have occasion, and they may see all that is suitable for them to see with the family where they belong.[2]

I send my kind and particular thanks to Elder David and Eldress Ruth for the little girl which you have sent to me. She has faith and love, which will produce good works if wisely attended to.

On reading the letter which you wrote to Daniel Mosely, I was thankful to hear of the wise counsel which Elder David sent to Archibald [Meacham] relative to the present distress of the Believers at Busro, for it is evident that if the young Believers' faith in the doctrines of the gospel is not sufficient to restrain them from fighting in their own defense, it would be dangerous for the old Believers to counsel them much on this subject.[3] But if they are left to the free exercise of their own faith and consciences and should suffer the loss of lives or property, they will have no just cause of reflection upon the old Believers, whether they keep their faith or not.

Elder David—poor child! As my lot and calling here is among a great body of old Believers who are called to support a deep and weighty travel—and likewise there are a large number of young Believers of different ages and in different stages of travel, which occasions much labor and bearing—considering these things I conclude you will not reasonably expect me to write much (nor often) to individuals in the West. Therefore it is my desire that this short epistle may circulate to all the brethren and sisters that went from the East—indeed I should choose that Elder John, Archibald, and Benjamin might (each of them) have a copy thereof.

I do not feel to fill this letter with a sense of your outward afflictions, for tribulations will certainly accompany you if you are faithful, as they have ever been promised to the true children of God. But I do not believe that God will suffer any final harm to come upon you, if you are followers of that which is good. But all these afflictions which ye have to pass through on account of the wicked will yet serve to increase your consolation and be an everlasting seal to your testimony and a standing monument against the workers of iniquity.

Tribulation is truly necessary for the people of God, and I am not able to lay out what way is best for it to come nor how much will be profitable. But O my children, remember this: if you are faithful, you will receive everlasting life and a crown of immortal glory that fadeth not away.

I shall now draw my letter to a close and bid you all a kind and hearty farewell, in the everlasting bonds of true gospel love. And in well doing, I will assure you of the present and future love and good will of a

Mother

Abiathar and Ruth likewise desire to send their best love and remembrance to you all, in particular.

Also all the brethren and sisters in the Church, understanding that I was about to write, unanimously requested to send their sincere love and remembrance to you all. This they manifested in their evening meeting by uplifted hands, and here it is deposited, that when you read these lines, you may all receive a part and know for certainty that it is from those who esteem you very near and dear.

Again, I say farewell, little flock.

P.S. A letter from Kentucky from Elder John and others dated April 13th, 1812, we received May 23rd.

NOTES

1. Source: OClWHi IV A 32. This text is reconstructed from the two partial copies in the folder. One copy is annotated: "A true Copy from Mother's own hand taken Mon. Sept. 27." In the text of the letter, she instructs David Darrow to make separate copies for John Meacham, Archibald Meacham, and Benjamin S. Youngs, and this was evidently done.
2. I.e., like any other eastern Shakers, they will have access only to western correspondence that is written for a general audience.
3. Apparently not all the recent western converts were committed to pacifism, and Wright here counsels against pressuring them on this issue.

Letter 12. "Be assured, my dear son, that I shall feel freedom in writing to thee." Lucy Wright, New Lebanon, to Benjamin S. Youngs, South Union, Kentucky, August 21, 1813. [1]

[Lucy Wright answers Benjamin Youngs's letter in an intimate style, yet without directly re-

sponding to his request for guidance from New
Lebanon on the future of the Busro, Indiana,
Believers. She gives him permission to return,
provided he can do so in union with David Darrow and without jeopardizing the spiritual welfare of the people of South Union.]

My dear son Benjamin,

Your letters of May were taken out of the post office at Lebanon on the
2nd of June. I was then at Harvard on a visit, where I had an opportunity
of seeing the ministers from each Church in the East. The day following,
your letters (one to me, another to the ministry, and one to Father Job
[Bishop])[2] were sent on by private conveyance and came safe to my hand
on the 6th, and thankful indeed was I to receive them. Father Job was also
much pleased to receive his. When I had opened and read their contents,
my spirit was refreshed. It comforted my soul to receive such good fruit
from a distant land. But it matters not to me whether the land in which
you live is nigh by or afar off—but it is a true, sound, and immoveable
faith, manifested by every good word and work, that will cause a near
union and relation to the Church of God here and bring your soul near to
mine both now and forever. It is a matter of great consolation to me to hear
that you have consecrated your soul, body, time, and talents, as a free-will
offering to God, to be in whatever lot you may be of most importance in
the upbuilding of Zion. And I fear not to promise you that if you keep this
faith and abide by it and in it, you will still enjoy a composed mind and
through all your trials and afflictions that rich and boundless peace of
conscience which is unknown to them who take their own ways—whether
you ever see me again in this world or not.

Concerning your request to return here on a visit, I think it is very
reasonable, provided you can see your way clear in union with Elder David
and in safety to the people with whom you are entrusted as an elder. But
as they are yet children, if you should prove to be their Father, it must be
binding on you to see that they do not suffer. But if the way should open
with safety for you to come, I shall be as thankful to see you here as I
should any one that has gone to the West. And I am persuaded it would
be pleasing to all your friends in this part of the vineyard.

In relation to the settlement of the Busro Believers, I feel to be silent.[3]
But if the poor unreconciled part of them falls into your care, labor to do
your duty to them according to the best gift given to you. Then you will
have a right to look for justification, whether they are saved or lost. If you
make good Believers of them, it will be to your honor and you will be
rewarded for all your toil.

Your sending to Brother Seth an answer to my request respecting Freemasonry was immaterial to me—I think it was not strange considering all circumstances. It was satisfying to me to understand the reasons for which you altered the name of your settlement. I think the name you have adopted is not only proper but very beautiful, and I hope the people and place may prove equal to the name.

Be assured, my dear son, that I shall feel freedom in writing to thee, and if I had found anything disagreeable in thy letters, I should let thee know it. But I am thankful to say I find no fault in them, but have taken abundant satisfaction in reading them and feeling your good faith and love of counsel. O! Benjamin, what a precious blessing of God it is to have a firm unshaken faith in the true line and order of God. This I know thou hast received. If thou therefore dost keep the same undefiled unto the end, thou wilt do well.

O! how thankful I was to hear that my little son Benjamin was yet alive and laboring to be little and simple enough to receive the blessing of God in abundance. God's people always had a lead, and they that owned and blessed that lead were owned and blessed of God. As God said to Abraham, *"I will bless them that bless thee; and curse them that curse thee."* I know that God has and does still own and bless me and my labors in the gospel and that he has given me health, strength, and wisdom according to my day and opened in my soul a fountain of charity, mercy, and love of God, which freely flows like an endless river to all the faithful sons and daughters of Zion throughout the whole Israel of God. And now, my son Benjamin, as you have been bountiful in bestowing your blessing upon me, my heart is enlarged and my soul is open to return my blessing upon you; and I pray that God may give you wisdom, strength, and patience equal to your day, lot, and membership—that you may be everlasting honor to the gospel and to the testimony—that you may, through all your afflictions, possess that inward treasure of peace and joy which the wicked cannot give nor take away; and I pray that you may shine as a light in the world, in the midst of a crooked and perverse generation. This is the blessing of Benjamin, bestowed on him by his

Mother

P.S. In relation to the manner in which you have directed your letters, we find no fault. If we should hereafter see occasion for you to direct them different, we will endeavor to inform you. We are at a loss how to superscribe our letters to you. We desire you would give us information the next time you write. It is not likely that we shall write again till we hear from you.

Note: we shall put a letter into the office for Elder David with yours.

NOTES

1. Source: OClWHi IV A 32.
2. Job Bishop was the lead ministry elder in the Canterbury, New Hampshire, bishopric, and probably an old friend of Youngs's.
3. This seems to be an indication of Lucy Wright's reluctance to give advice on political matters which involved several of the western communities in potential or actual conflict. The Busro, Indiana, settlement (later named West Union) had been evacuated in 1812 because of an imminent battle between the Shawnee Indians and white settlers, and Youngs was evidently concerned about the future of the displaced Believers from Busro. (It was resettled in the summer of 1814, but debate continued among the male western leaders afterwards, about whether to keep it going despite yellow fever and internal controversy.)

Letter 13. "It is not likely that John will be either willing or able to tell the whole truth about himself or others." Lucy Wright, New Lebanon, to David Darrow, Union Village, Ohio, February 13, 1818.[1]

> [In response to disturbing information from David Darrow and Ruth Farrington about the spiritual disobedience of Pleasant Hill's lead ministry, Lucy Wright informs Darrow of her decision to recall John Meacham to the East.]

Beloved Elder David,

Your packet of January 6th was taken out of the post office at Lebanon on the 5th of February. I was then at Watervliet. However, the elders sent it up on the 7th (or Saturday), but I could not consistently return till the 10th. So you will understand the reason why I have not answered your letter sooner.

You may better judge of the feelings of my soul when reading those letters than I am able to inform by writing; therefore I shall not make the attempt. But I am thankful that you have used such freedom in writing and hope you will always continue free and open, especially in such important matters. My natural disposition would not crave such an irrepressible burden as this, but God forbid that I should shun the cross or shrink from my duty for the sake of living a few more days in this troublesome world. Nay, let me be up and be doing, that I may finish my work in justification and peace with God. I could write much about these things, but for want of time, I forbear.

The enclosed[2] is a copy of a letter which I have wrote to John. You will understand my mind by reading it. It is possible that you will not think best for those two brethren to come with him (if he does come)—this I could not tell. I have wrote to him as well as you and Elder Benjamin in great haste. If you have objections to one or both and choose to have somebody else come, act your own gift, and I think I shall be agreed with you.

Do write as soon as you can after you receive this, and let me know who you wish to have come with him and who, or how many, you wish to have detained here (if we are able to detain them)—also their state as far as you can and the state of the elders and people. For it is not likely that John will be either willing or able to tell the whole truth about himself or others. I hope you will write often, whether he comes or not, and send all the necessary information in your power that may be any help to us in this woeful case; for after all the information we can obtain, our burden will doubtless be heavy and disagreeable.

I hope and trust that you will have wisdom to appoint some one or more to mend the breach who esteems the wisdom and power of God preferable to letter learning and the meek, quiet, and gentle spirit of Christ far superior to pride, tyranny, and lust.

Beloved friend, we feel very unwilling that you should wax old or fail in such a trying time as this, for we don't know how to spare you.

The elders here wrote you a letter the 23rd of January which gave a general statement of our affairs, so I shall omit particulars and close with my warmest and best love to you and Eldress Ruth and to all the faithful with you that went from here.

Likewise, Elder Abiathar and Sister Ruth and also the elders wish to send their best love in the same manner with mine—farewell,

From Mother

Note: If there is any other brother or sister that you think had better come away, be free and let me know it that I may invite them back. You must look to the protection of all the Believers in the West, and not leave it for me—nor us—to do, for we cannot do it. So you must build with such materials as you have there, for there is no suitable members here for such lots, that can be spared to go there.[3]

NOTES

1. Source: OClWHi IV A 33. This is the first of three letters written on the same day by Lucy Wright to western brethren Darrow, Meacham, and Youngs. See the introduction to this chapter for a brief discussion of Pleasant Hill's departures from orthodox Shakerism and Meacham's recall.
2. This refers to her letter to John Meacham of the same date (letter 14 below.)
3. Here Wright makes it clear that no more easterners will be sent west.

Letter 14. "The sooner you come the better it will suit me." Lucy Wright, New Lebanon, to John Meacham, Pleasant Hill, Kentucky, February 13, 1818.[1]

[Lucy Wright summons John Meacham east
from Pleasant Hill, Kentucky, along with other
male western leaders.]

Respected Elder John,

I feel it my duty to write a few lines to you at this time and let you
know some of my feelings, which bear with great weight on my mind.
God's work appears to increase in these parts with more rapidity than it
has before since the first gathering of the Church. Many souls are awakened
to everlasting life, while many others are plotting by deep and subtle means
to undermine and overthrow the present work of God. There has been a
goodly number gathered to the faith the year past, so that we are greatly
thronged, both by those who embrace the testimony and those who do not.
These things necessarily occasion a heavy weight and bearing, and of
which I have to bear according to my lot and place, which exhausts my
bodily strength to that degree that I feel as though the time of my departure
drew nigh. But I do not feel as though I was ready to be offered up, or to
leave this world, till I can see some of you who stand as principal pillars
in the West face to face. And since Elder David is so far advanced in years,
I think it would be too much for him to undertake so long a journey.
Therefore, I feel a great desire that you may come for one, and the sooner
you come the better it will suit me. I hope nothing will hinder you from
granting my request, for the least delay might be of weighty importance.
But this is not the whole of my request. I want very much to have Elder
Comstock and Elder Benjamin come with you,[2] for I should be very glad
to see them here once more in this world. Again I say, I hope nothing will
hinder you from granting my request as soon as possible.
I shall send a few lines to Benjamin S. Youngs, requesting him to come
with you to Lebanon. I shall likewise send a short letter to Elder David,
informing him of my request [[they will both be put in the Post Office with
this]], so that nothing may be left in the way to obstruct your coming soon
after you receive this. If your intended publication is completed, be so kind
as to bring some of them, for we should be very glad to see them.[3]
Your letters of September 14th and December 21st have been received—
the former on the 10th of October and the latter on the 12th of January,
1818. You mentioned in your last that we might look for another in two or
three weeks. We have looked for it but do not find it.
There has been considerable sickness the fall and winter past—some
fevers, heavy colds, etc. Also, there has been some deaths—. . . .
At present it is nearly a middling time of health (with few exceptions).
I shall now close by sending my best love together with Elder Abiathar's and
Sister Ruth's. Also, the elders wish to send their love with ours—farewell.

From Mother

N.B. I should be very glad if you would write immediately after receiving this, if it be but a few lines, so that I may be able to attend to my duties in regularity. I have been strongly solicited to go a journey to the eastward, if God spared my life and health, but I would much rather forego that journey than miss of seeing you. My anxiety to see you is considerably increased by hearing so much from you about Eldress Lucy's sufferings.[4] Furthermore, I have greatly desired to see the book which you are publishing ever since you informed us of the principal subjects which it treats upon. These are subjects of weighty importance, both to Believers and the world. Therefore, I should be very glad to receive them from your own hand before they spread among Believers or the world,[5] as you would be able to give all necessary information or explanation required better than those who have not been in the work. But if you cannot let me see them first, without breaking your engagements with subscribers, etc., it will alter the case. Be that as it may, I hope you will not fail to come in the spring and bring some, whether they are bound or not, for they may be bound here without any difficulty.

M

NOTES

1. Source: OClWHi IV A 33.
2. Comstock Betts, second ministry elder with John Meacham at Pleasant Hill, also visited New Lebanon in the spring and early summer of 1818. According to other New Lebanon ministry correspondence with Union Village, Betts told the New Lebanon ministry that though he often disagreed with John Meacham, he did not feel he ought to oppose his superior in the ministry.
3. The publication referred to is evidently John Dunlavy's *The Manifesto, or A Declaration of the Doctrine and Practice of the Church of Christ* . . . (Pleasant Hill, Kentucky: 1818).
4. Lucy Smith, first ministry eldress at Pleasant Hill, had a twenty-foot tapeworm at this time, according to a letter from South Union leaders to Mother Lucy and the New Lebanon elders, dated April 20, 1817 (OClWHi IV A 60).
5. Lucy Wright probably felt the need for great caution in publishing any more books of Shaker doctrine at this time, as a result of anti-Shaker activities by seceders among Shaker neighbors, east and west, during this decade.

Letter 15. "If you want the elders in each society should be liberal, you must be liberal first." Lucy Wright, New Lebanon, to David Darrow and Ruth Farrington, Union Village, Ohio, June 18, 1818.[1]

> [Lucy Wright advises the Union Village ministry
> to support the Kentucky societies, through do-
> nations if necessary. She also suggests a new
> leadership configuration for Pleasant Hill.]

Father David and Mother Ruth,

There has already been considerable wrote to you, but my mind is not
fully released; therefore I must talk a little to you one side of the rest.
Doubtless you have it in your understanding that God requires you to look
for the protection of all the societies of Believers in that country. It really
is so, and I hope you will keep a good watch over each society, that there
may be peace and harmony throughout the whole. If you visit the Believers
in Kentucky (as I hope you will) this season, you will have a good opportunity to find out whether they are united together and whether there is
good union between society and society and whether there is good union
between those societies and the Church at Union Village. And if you find
any stumblingblocks, I hope you will roll them out of the way. And if a
covetous, selfish feeling has got into any society, I hope you will nip it in
the bud (if it is not too late), if you have to do as we have done—that is,
to turn out hands and money to help others who stand in need.

You know that while you was here, we had to assist the Believers at
Harvard considerable in money. So we have continued to the present time,
and God has blessed us in it. *The liberal shall live by liberal things,"* and "it
is more blessed to give than to receive." When the Church was gathering here
(you may remember) we had help in building from other places; so, when
the Church was gathering at Watervliet and Enfield, they had help from
here. Last year there were four brethren from Lebanon, Hancock, and
Enfield, who were sent to help the Shirley brethren in building. And we
find that such liberal acts of kindness are a great help in shutting out disunion and covetousness [[if there is no reflections afterward from those
who perform the liberality]].

I know these are temporal things and will perish in the using, and I as
well know that almost all evil surmisings, jealousies, covetousness, etc.,
originate in and about temporal things; and great care should be taken lest
the union of the spirit is laid waste. And you may remember that covetousness will never purge out covetousness; if it is ever purged out, it must
be done by union and liberality. If you want the elders in each society
should be liberal, you must be liberal first. And if they want their respective
societies should be liberal, they must set them the example. For could we
ever have loved God, unless he had first loved us and thereby drawn us
to him?

I know it is the duty of the younger to seek the union of the elder and
to come to him. But if he is purblind and cannot see so far, the elder should
come so near to him that he can reach him and not let him be lost. This is
the way I have to do with the people. For though I possessed all wisdom
and knowledge and positively knew the requirements of God upon his
people here, what good would it do, unless they could get hold of it? Not
any. Therefore, I strive to bring the people as near to the requirements of

God as they are able to come and then I unite with them and bless them; and in so doing, I am joined to them and they to me, and we travel together and find a blessing. And I think it my wisdom so to do, for if the hand and body be separate, what is either good for?

Notwithstanding all that has been wrote about the future arrangements of the elders at Pleasant Hill, if you think best for Comstock and Samuel to abide there, will not Comstock be the most suitable to stand first? He appears to be a very steady and exemplary man.[2] We do not believe there can be any great ministration supported to a people who have believed so long as they have, and it is hard for us to believe that Samuel T[urner] will do for the first.

Now since Elder Benjamin's lot has fallen among a people who have not yet gained so much temporal conveniences as some others have, we have made him some presents according to our own feelings, and we hope no one will reflect on him or us on that account.[3]

Receive with this private letter my particular love to you—farewell.

From Mother

N.B. Please to inform me what arrangements you make at Pleasant Hill and South Union among the elders, when you have a convenient opportunity.

NOTES

1. Source: OClWHi IV A 33. This letter was one of several written at this time, to be carried west by the departing western visitors.
2. Comstock Betts was visiting at New Lebanon with Benjamin Youngs at this time.
3. See Molly Goodrich's letter expressing thanks for these gifts, in chapter 3. The Union Village ministry did act on Mother Lucy's advice to be more charitable to the South Union community. The next year, when Eldress Molly Goodrich visited Union Village, she left with wagons loaded with gifts and one hundred dollars in gold, "very comfortable and satisfied," according to a letter from Union Village dated November 1, 1819.

Letter 16. "If I see you going astray and do not warn you, can I be justified?" Lucy Wright, New Lebanon, to David Darrow, Union Village, Ohio, September 21, 1819.[1]

> [Lucy Wright chides David Darrow for allowing the western Believers to become "high and boisterous." Using scriptural arguments, she reminds him that those who invite persecution in order to suffer martyrdom are not acting accord-

ing to the gospel of Ann Lee. She also tells him
confidentially that she has asked Peter Pease to
return to New Lebanon permanently, unless he
can find a more harmonious relationship to Darrow.]

Respected Father David,

If you have received our letter of August 26th, you will understand why
Brother Peter has tarried with us so long—that it was on account of my
sickness, which I am not yet released from, so as to get out of the meeting
house. Soon after that letter was wrote he was taken sick himself, so that
he has not yet been able to start on his journey homeward. However, we
have been hoping that he would in a few days be able and accordingly
wrote our letters and sealed them up and felt our minds measurably answered.

After this (on September the 7th) we received your packet of August
30th and were thankful to hear from you once more—yea, we were all
thankful to hear from our good friends once more. And I can truly say that
I should have been much more thankful if some part of the news had been
more agreeable.

Now, beloved friend, I feel it my duty to write a few lines to you in
simplicity and plainness, since we cannot speak together face to face, for
I feel greatly straitened to know my duty in relation to you and how I shall
give an account to God, and how I shall meet you in the days of eternity.
You have been gone from here a great while and have been necessarily
joined to those who are a great ways back in their travel; therefore I do not
know how much you can bear; and if I should give you stronger meat than
you were able to bear, it would do you hurt instead of good.

You call me Mother and often call on me to justify or condemn your
proceedings according to the gift which I feel. Now if I see you going astray
and do not warn you, can I be justified? If I discover the enemy, shall I not
warn the people, that I may be clear of their blood? [[See Ezekiel 3:17, etc.,
and 33:7, etc.]] When I read your letters of August 30, I could not help
thinking that the sense of the people was too high and boisterous and that
they had too much of the wind, earthquake, fire, and whirlwind; and that
was in a great measure governed by their sense. But if the Lord was not
in the earthquake, fire and whirlwind in the days of Elijah, I think it is in
vain to look for him there now, under the peaceable reign of the Prince of
Peace. It feels to me that Believers in this day (and especially such as are
called to labor for Church relation) ought to feel after the gifts and power
of God in the *still small voice.*

Now as you have so far advanced in years that you cannot reasonably
expect to continue a great while longer in this world and are called to stand

as the first pillar and center of union to all Believers in that western country, it is of great importance that you establish a right manner of faith and sense among that people. For if it is not gained and established in your day, it will be very hard for Mother Ruth or any of your successors to do it, and then they will have, as it were, to lay a new foundation for the people to build upon.

As long as there is any of the fallen nature left in Believers, they will be more or less exposed (when they have the power in their own hands) to exercise arbitrary government over their inferiors; and this is not all. They believe without all doubt that Christ has come the second time to set up his everlasting kingdom and to rule and reign upon earth; and that they are agoing to reign with him; and feel as though they could govern or crush the wicked world and bring them to terms by power and might! But this is not the work of the day for the people of God. *"Not by might, nor by power, but by my Spirit, saith the Lord of hosts."* Our first Parents said that the wicked would break and dash each other to pieces, but the people of God would have nothing to do with it.

It is true we read that Christ said, *"I have overcome the world"*! But where did he overpower the world, except in his own person, or at the most in those who had full faith in him? And this was done by a work of self-denial and not by self's taking the government and subduing all others thereto. But the unmortified man may plead that he has enlisted in a good cause. He can also read about *"contending earnestly for the faith"* and how Christ is to *"rule the nations with a rod of iron,"* etc., and feel as though they had power to call fire down from heaven to consume their enemies. Yet such have not wisdom to discern *"what manner of spirit they are of."*

I think it is probable that many since the first appearance of Christ have willingly stirred up the rage of the wicked in hopes that they might have the honor of suffering persecution and even martyrdom! And if this has been the case, self must have been measurably at the bottom, and the old man[2] would naturally crave the honor and glory of such a sacrifice! And how many there are in this day who have a measure of the same sense, I will not undertake to judge. But this one thing I do know, i.e., the people of God in this day ought to *"be wise as serpents, and harmless as doves."* They might *"conquer the spirit of the world within,"* and then they may be able to overcome it without *"by the blood of the Lamb, and . . . the word of their testimony."*

I hope you will not induce by this letter that I am regardless of your late afflictions by the hands of the wicked; nay, by no means, for I feel with you and for you, that you may be kept and preserved from evil, within and without, and from the rage and malice of the wicked and that you and all with you and under your care may be so far protected and blessed with wisdom that you may never suffer as evildoers or bring upon yourselves unnecessary persecution through a [illegible] which is not according to knowledge or through a desire for vainglory. And that you may forever be an honor to the gospel and stand as a living pattern of meekness and godliness before all men, professor and profane, is the desire and fervent prayer of your best friend and Parent in the gospel.

Receive with this my best love, also Elder Abiathar's and Sister Ruth's.

N.B. Brother Peter knows nothing about your last letter to me, nor about this. But I have given him the best counsel that I was able, i.e., to return to Union Village and sell all his business in peas and onion, so that he may be able to bless you, and you him, and then for him to return back to New Lebanon to live as soon as might be consistent. Nevertheless, if you and he can find a door opened there whereby he can do good one, two, or three years or more, and whereby he can find a sufficient gift to satisfy himself and can gain his union and relation to you, so as to find nourishment and protection for his needy soul, I am as willing he should abide there as any of you. But I strictly charged him to come back if he did not gain more of a gift to join him there than he had felt for some time past. For he or anyone else would be greatly exposed to be lost, unless he was joined to the body of Christ somewhere. If he returns to live with us, we desire that he may not rove about any more, either to West Union or to Kentucky, for we think it will be a loss to him.[3]

As for poor Sister Tency [Hortency Goodrich], her complaint is such that I should not think strange if she should get distracted before she leaves this world. If she is yet living, I hope you will not labor for high gifts for her, for they will not save her earthly tabernacle from death. But labor for the greatest gift, which is charity, and extend it to her, and you may save her soul by gathering her into the union and to the work of God. I think you must know that as little company as can consistently answer for a patient in her situation is the best and easiest for the patient.

NOTES

1. Source: OClWHi IV A 33. This is the last lettter I have been able to locate in Shaker archives bearing Lucy Wright's signature. The quotations from scripture in this letter are not always exact, which suggests that Wright (perhaps in consultation with her colleagues in the New Lebanon lead ministry) was quoting from memory.

2. "The old man" or "the Old Adam" are traditional Protestant terms for unredeemed human nature.

3. This comment about Peter Pease's "roving about" suggests that he may have had a role in spreading information about the controversies among the western leaders.

3. "POOR CHILD IN A DISTANT LAND"

Selected Correspondence of Shaker Sisters, West and East, 1805–1835

INTRODUCTION

"I have long had a desire to see you although unworthy of the privilege," wrote Jennie Luckie McNemar from Turtle Creek, Ohio, to the New Lebanon Shaker sisterhood in September 1805. "I should exceedingly rejoice to see some of you here." Just under a year later, the first six Shaker sisters arrived in Ohio, sent by Lucy Wright to help the missionary brethren build new communities in the West.[1] The westerners expressed their joy at the arrival of the sisters in the ecstatic physical language of the Kentucky revival:

> The Young Believers—especially the females—when their eyes met the Sisters coming in at the door were very deeply affected being greatly filled with joy and wonder—Some fell flat on the floor—others shouted or cryed out and the greater part were immediately in tears . . . one of the Brethren informed us that he observed that the tears were forced from the eyes of some of our most stout hearted & bitter opposers—"[2]

In all, twelve eastern Shaker sisters came over a three-year period to provide guidance to the growing numbers of western Shaker converts living in scattered settlements throughout Ohio and Kentucky.[3] Like other nineteenth-century Anglo-American women who left written accounts of their travels to the West, the Shaker sisters were appalled at the hardships of travelling and of pioneer living conditions.[4] Their first letters home are filled with descriptions of mud and potholes, perilous river crossings, and the unaccustomed physical endurance required as they crossed the Allegheny mountains, largely on foot.

When the first Shaker sisters arrived in Ohio in June 1806, the communal family dwelling house, a log structure of two stories, was nearing completion. It was a far cry from what the easterners were used to. Their longing for space, light, privacy, and proper equipment for their heavy domestic labors comes through clearly in their first letters:

> Our chamber is very full of large cracks, much more open than your barns. . . . We have one window in the house which contains six lights, but two of them was broken out. . . . Our conveniences for cooking is small but our family is large; and besides our own family we have workmen to cook for continually that works on the new house. . . . We have wrote our letter in our cabin chamber where light comes in only through the cracks and a little hole cut out through the logs about a foot square, and our table was a box cover laid in the lap. This is the sisters' lodging chamber and when it rains it comes in by streams through every direction. . . . (Letter 2)

> The first of our house is finished . . . four smoky fireplaces on each loft. Our garret we have for a lodging room with seven beds chiefly on the floor. There is neither door nor partititon upon the loft. We have some blankets hung up between the brethren's beds and ours. The middle loft is all open. They are to work on it. And there is people coming and going frequently from east, west, north, and south . . . (Letter 4)

The Shaker pioneer sister was constantly in the company of other women and men for whom she had responsibility, both Believers and visitors from "the world." She did not face the loneliness and isolation from other women so frequently experienced by her non-Shaker pioneer counterpart.[5] Moreover, the collective labor system of the growing western Shaker communities, assisted by infusions of money and gifts from the East, helped ameliorate the rough living conditions relatively quickly.[6] Nonetheless, the longing for the "home" in the East and for old friends was as central a theme in the Shaker sisters' early letters as it was in westering women's letters generally.

In the first decades in Ohio, Kentucky, and Indiana, the fledgling Shaker communities were frequently threatened with epidemics of disease, outbreaks of hostility between the U.S. and state authorities and the Shawnee Indian population, and anti-Shaker mob activity. As late as 1825, Benjamin S. Youngs of South Union bemoaned the impact on the Shakers of the chaotic political environment in the new state of Kentucky:

> There is no Court of Appeals except what receives its authority from the caprice of party.—The old Court abolished and constitution broken.—The treasury worse than bankrupt.—The State is in complete convulsion.—Unjust men & persecutors—Mobs & rioters have but little to fear from existing Authority—and Believers must suffer more or less under such a disorganized and disorganizing state of affairs.

The domestic sphere of the Shaker sisterhood was no protection against disease, political turmoil, and anti-Shaker mob violence during these early years. The Youngs letter quoted above goes on to tell of an attack led by a furious western mother hoping to regain a daughter who had been attracted to the Shaker way of life:

> In the night the woman collected the Mob and came at the head with a loaded Pistol.—They tried to break into the house where Olive was with a large company of girls, mostly nearly grown under the care of a particular Sister. . . . The Sister who had the charge of the girls, stood looking out of an upper window & talking to the woman,—in the mean time the woman presented her pistol at her, and snap't it 3 times, the sparks flying from the flint every time, but the pistol would not go off; she then threw a brick bat in at the Window with all vengeance among a large room full of girls, but none got hurt. The Sister who stood in the window, was asked why she stood there so coolly when the pistol was fired at her; she answered that she meant to dodge when she saw the smoke come! The pistol was well loaded with powder and five balls of lead.[7]

The eastern Shaker sisters were also confronted from the outset with the wild and unsettled spiritual experience of the converts from the Kentucky revival, who were still "shaking, turning, leaping, and clapping their hands and shouting, and some has the gift of tongues" (Letter 2). Rachel Johnson's 1807 note home suggests an impatience with the revivalistic enthusiasm of the westerners, a feeling that such emotion was yet another obstacle to the goals of the eastern sisterhood:

> We have great meetings, public meeting twice a week when the young sisters are under exercise. Sometimes they get us into their arms and make us hardly fit to be seen. It is so hot and so many people here. . . . (Letter 4)

It had been many years since ecstatic religious gifts of this intensity had been characteristic of eastern Shaker worship. The easterners came from the increasingly well-organized, orderly, and prosperous Shaker communities in New Lebanon or Watervliet, New York, or nearby Hancock, Massachusetts. All but one of the missionary sisters had lived within the relatively cloistered environment of the Church Family in these communities.[8] The sisters' lesser interest in outpourings of wild spirituality in the West may also reflect their different roles as missionaries.

The primary task of Issachar Bates, John Meacham, and Benjamin S. Youngs in the first year in the West had been to ride or walk from settlement to settlement, preaching and explicating Shaker theology to potential converts. The first sisters, on the other hand, were not sent for until a year later, and their work was primarily to teach those already converted how to live the orderly, communal, hierarchical Shaker life that had been established in the eastern communities.

The eastern sisters may have come west expecting only to stay for four or five years,[9] but they soon had to come to terms with an exile in the West that was likely to be much longer—and in some cases, permanent. One of the original twelve sisters did in fact return within the first decade, and two others died.[10] The other nine stayed at their tasks for between twenty and thirty years, all serving as first or second eldresses in the Kentucky or Ohio communities.[11] Only one of the eastern sisters who became a leader in the West, Molly Goodrich, revisited the East during her term of service—and this was after twenty years in the West, during which she begged strenuously in letter after letter to be granted permission to come home.[12]

Though only western lead ministry eldress Ruth Farrington was already appointed to office before leaving the East, all the eastern sisters probably went west expecting to assume positions of leadership there. They were under close scrutiny during the first years, when decisions about leadership appointments were being made. David Darrow, John Meacham, and Benjamin Youngs were all explicitly given an opportunity to veto any of the first group of sisters sent from the East.[13] They were also requested to send frank opinions to Lucy Wright and her colleagues in New Lebanon on the perceived strengths and weaknesses of the new arrivals as potential candidates for spiritual and temporal leadership positions at the first four communities to be gathered, Union Village, Pleasant Hill, South Union, and Busro.[14] The Ohio lead ministry, especially David Darrow and Ruth Farrington, were ultimately responsible for leadership appointments at the other communities.[15]

The role of first lead ministry Eldress Ruth Farrington in organizing the western sisterhood is difficult to assess. Most of the surviving correspondence from Union Village was written by her partner, David Darrow, and his views predominate. We are frequently in the position of inferring that her judgments and wishes must have been consulted in matters directly affecting the organization of the sisterhood. For example, a letter to New Lebanon penned by David Darrow in November 1809 but signed by Darrow and Farrington compares the different talents of the sisters Molly Goodrich and Hortency Goodrich: "Tency is a woman of much more patience and fortitude than Molly: yet Molly has the most gift to labor with young Believers."[16] More explicitly, a letter from John Meacham to Lucy Wright the next year attributes to Ruth Farrington a strong preference for keeping Hortency Goodrich with her at Union Village.[17]

At least one of the eastern sisters did write directly to Lucy Wright in an attempt (though unsuccessful) to influence the selection of her companion leaders. Lucy Smith, the first eldress in the Pleasant Hill ministry, sent "a few lines to my most kind and tender parent in the gospel" on August 12, 1810, correcting a previous report by Brother Constant Mosely on her views of the comparative merits of Martha Sanford and Mercy Pickett.[18]

The Gender-Based Division of Correspondence Duties

When we are aware of the tumultuous political history of western Shakerism that is documented in the correspondence between western male leaders and the Lucy Wright administration (see chapter 2), the surviving correspondence of the leading western sisters at first seems strikingly apolitical.[19] With very few exceptions, it is the male leaders who report to New Lebanon on intercommunity conflicts, rivalries, and rebellions against authorized leaders. A division of labor by gender clearly applied to the duties of intercommunity correspondence, as it did in the realm of work in general. While there were able ministry brethren to do it, the leading ministry sisters were not the primary correspondents for their communities, though they were always expected to play an important supporting role.

Adding to the impact of this unwritten rule was the fact that some of the leading sisters were intimidated by the prospect of writing. Both western and eastern lead ministry eldresses, Ruth Farrington and Ruth Landon, refer to a feeling of inadequacy as writers, in letters included in this selection.[20] Ruth Farrington acknowledges that she has "been very prudent of pens, ink, and paper since I have been here. And it has not been for the want of love to my good sisters in the East . . . but for the lack of letter learning" (Letter 15).

However, ministry and family eldresses were clearly expected to act as "deputy elders," dealing with public and political affairs to some extent in their letters if the elder who usually corresponded with other community leadership was incapacitated or absent.[21] Molly Goodrich was clearly knowledgeable enough about intercommunity Shaker politics to function very effectively as the chief South Union leader when necessary, for example. In the absence of her partner, Benjamin S. Youngs, in 1818, she answered a letter from Elder Archibald Meacham of West Union, diplomatically but decisively refusing to send South Union brethren to help with brickmaking, because she knew they were needed to work on a mill at Drake's Creek (Letter 12). She took over the correspondence with the New Lebanon ministry brethren about political affairs when Youngs was ill in September of 1831 (Letter 20). And when Youngs was making an extended visit to the East in the summer of 1835, she sent him reports on the state of the South Union community every two weeks, ably discussing in one letter the progress of the agricultural work and the sisterhood's silkworm cocoon crop (Letter 23).

Whenever changes in leadership on the female side were required, it was clearly the business of the lead ministry eldress to deal directly with the problem. So, for example, when the conflict between Samuel Turner and Lucy Smith at Pleasant Hill had become serious enough to justify New Lebanon's removal of Lucy Smith as Mother of Pleasant Hill, Ruth Landon of New Lebanon was the one to notify her of the decision.[22]

In general, however, once the eastern sisters were settled in leadership positions in their own western communities, their letters home were concerned primarily with expressing affectionate and dutiful feelings, maintaining relationships, and discussing matters of shared concern in the day-to-day management of the sisterhood. As in their daily lives, so in their correspondence, it was a vital part of the work of the women to construct and maintain the friendship networks that would help tie the western and eastern communities together through difficult times ahead.

Themes in the Sisterhood's Correspondence

The theme of exile emerges strongly and poignantly in the correspondence, particularly in the many surviving letters of Molly Goodrich of South Union, Kentucky.[23] After Goodrich had been only a year in the West, she wrote to Lucy Wright of her feeling like "a poor child in a distant land."[24] In other letters to the East included in this collection, she writes of her desire to have friends "step over the mountains" into the West, or wishes she herself had the "wings of a bird" to fly home (Letters 14, 21). She and her correspondents playfully compare the New Lebanon community to a "hive" where endless "honey" is to be had from the Queen Bee, Mother Lucy Wright (Letters 10, 13). In one letter, Goodrich even likens herself to the Old Testament patriarch Jacob, who served seven years for Rachel (Letter 8).

In her efforts to maintain close contacts with childhood friends and natural siblings (several of whom were themselves eastern Shaker leaders), Goodrich repeatedly requests detailed descriptions of life in eastern Shaker communities. Perhaps as part of her lobbying effort to win an invitation to visit New Lebanon, she asked especially for information on Mother Lucy's activities and appearance:

> Now my dear sister I have one little request to make—that is, if the request is not too bold. I want you to be so kind as to send us particular word about our precious Mother, about her health and just how she looks and how large she is and her exact age and just what clothes she wears and how she lives and how much she has altered since we saw her—yea, how she walks about and visits her pretty children. And when you tell us all about it it will make us laugh and cry too, both. (Letter 7)

In return, she provided in several letters unusually detailed pictures of her own daily life. A particularly good example is the tour she conducts in imagination for her correspondents, Elizabeth Youngs and Ann Bowser, in Letter 18:

> Immediately before you, in the southwest corner of the hall, you see a small room taken off about ten feet square, but you see no door as yet

into this little room. To your right hand is a door; come, let us go in
here. . . . This is the room little Molly lives in, and you are welcome here,
my good sisters, yea, welcome a thousand times.

In the Goodrich letters, as in the sisterhood's east-west correspondence
generally, the material realities of women's domestic work lives figure
largely. Torn between their practical need to adapt to new conditions in
the West and their desire to conform to eastern Shaker practices, the transplanted sisters asked anxiously for detailed information about the eastern
sisterhood's clothing styles—for patterns for caps and aprons, for example.
In Letter 10 Molly Goodrich expresses relief at the discovery that an inno-
vation forced on her by the western climate had not violated correct practice
in the East:

> I feel much pleased to hear that Mother wears thin caps in warm weather,
> for I have felt much need of them in this warm country and have worn
> them some but have felt straitened, but now feel released in the matter.

She also made sure to send home news of her own work and that of
her partner, Mercy Pickett, in domestic manufacture:

> Sister Mercy is very industrious indeed; I tell her sometimes she is too
> worldly minded. She spins nearly 100 runs every year; besides, she hunts
> up all the old rags she can find and cuts them up for carpets and gives
> them to the little school girls to sew and then to the big girls to weave,
> and then she has them sold to get such like things as we stand in need
> of. Likewise little me does a heap of work. I have spun thirty runs of wool
> this season, besides a heap of knitting and sewing and a plenty of other
> employments . . . (Letter 7)

It was important to report on the physical reality of illness. Yet this was
a topic that could not be discussed at too great length, lest one be thought
to "complain." Writing to her older sister Cassandana, then ministry eldress at the Hancock community in Massachusetts, Molly Goodrich acknowledges

> my weakness of body is a great discouragement to me, although I cannot
> complain at this time for I have had better health this winter past than I
> have had for three years past. I think I have said sufficient on this subject.
> (Letter 6)

One could elaborate at greater length on physical debility, perhaps, if
the purpose was to report and celebrate its miraculous cure. Elder Sister
Elizabeth Goodrich of the Second Order, Watervliet, writing to her younger
sister Molly Goodrich in 1817, gives a detailed account of her painful af-

fliction in her arms, as a prelude to a story of Lucy Wright's agency in
healing (Letter 11).

In the east-west correspondence we get a rare glimpse of experienced
women religious leaders training up a new generation, through both precept and example. Several of the eastern eldresses gave explicit advice to
their younger friends in the West who were now embarking on careers of
leadership. For example, shortly after Molly Goodrich became lead eldress
at South Union, she received a letter from her sister Cassandana Goodrich,
urging her to think of her work in the spiritual vineyard as requiring great
patience—"perhaps it may feel to you like waiting for the growth of a tree"
(Letter 5).

Other eastern leading sisters taught by example and were capable of
some humor in their description of their own busy lives as eldresses. Anna
Cogswell of the Gathering Order at New Lebanon wrote to Molly Goodrich
about her own ministerial work in 1818, including a particularly lively account of a visit to a group of recent converts not yet gathered into community:

> . . . it is time for somebody to go on the tiptop of the mountains to see
> some young Believers there. . . . I went there last February in a sleigh
> when the snow was about four feet deep upon a level or theareabouts,
> so that we went riding about the lots to shun the snow banks. . . . The
> family where we stayed mostly being rather poor on it for knives, the
> same knife they stirred their victuals with when cooking often fell to my
> lot to eat without being washed, and not a little of whatever was cooked
> froze onto the blade; whether it was pudding, turnips, or onions, it made
> no difference to me as long as it there stuck. (Letter 13)

There are many issues that must have arisen as the western leading
sisters learned on the job about spiritual and social governance. Not all of
these are discussed explicitly in the correspondence, of course. One omis-
sion may strike a modern reader as a particular loss: the question of how
the separate African American family at South Union was integrated into
the life of the broader community there. We hear about little more than the
existence of this family from Molly Goodrich herself (Letter 8).[25]

It would be of great interest to understand the experience of white and
black Shakers with each other in this frontier community in which Shawnee
Indians were also powerful neighbors. Unfortunately, the sisterhood's surviving correspondence contributes only fragments that are difficult to in-
terpret with any confidence. For example, one of the letters in this selection
from Molly Goodrich tells the story of a young white woman Believer who
gave birth to a "mulatto" child and died leaving the child for the Shakers
to raise. She refers to the child as a "yellow papoose," with what would
seem a mixture of condescension and affection. Yet the "blame" in the story
clearly falls on the young woman's "cruel mother," who had refused to let

her daughter come to Believers for several years and who threatened to "abuse" the child (Letter 8). In another letter, Goodrich comments obliquely on the difficulty of seeing to the spiritual and temporal welfare of Believers in a slave state (Letter 14).

Modern readers may also hope to use this correspondence to help understand power relations between male and female Shaker leaders, from the sisters' perspective. Here again, we must often make inferences from relatively scanty evidence. In at least one case, however, the surviving east-west correspondence presents a strong picture of a respectful and loving male-female partnership, that between Molly Goodrich and her lifetime associate in the South Union ministry, Benjamin S. Youngs. Their success is all the more intriguing because in the very first years in the West, David Darrow had frankly warned Lucy Wright that Benjamin Youngs and Molly Goodrich might be a poor match as leadership partners:

> Benjamin and Molly have not found the spiritual order of the gospel—to know which shall be lead—Molly was brought up in the Church—Benjamin was not—& after the most serious labors & plain teaching to them & solemn injunction that we laid upon them—I do not know yet—whether they have settled it to know which shall be the Elder to bear rule—have the lead . . . [26]

To the extent that the modern reader can presume to judge such matters on the basis of surviving letters and journals, these two strong-willed leaders appear to have proved Darrow wrong. In one of many letters she sent to eastern friends in the late summer and fall of 1818, Molly Goodrich pictured a playful and affectionate family scene among the South Union leaders, when Youngs arrived home from the East laden with gifts and letters:

> Beloved Elder Benjamin arrived safe & in good health to the desired haven on Thursday about 5 o'clock in the evening, with his blessed little wagon loaded with the richest of blessings right from Zion; . . . About the second word I said to Elder Benjamin; was, Is it possible that you have seen Mother and the Church? Yea I have, says he, and I can make you believe it. So we did not give him much rest that night, for we made him talk till late bed time, and then we went to bed but I could not sleep one wink: & about one o'clock in the night Eldress Mercy and I got up & went & got him up also, then we talked a heap more, and went to bed again. And in the morning we were up bright and early; I went out and got into the little wagon and sit down on the pretty seat and I told the young Brethren I wanted to ride, and they took hold of it & drawed it all round the yard, & so I had a pretty ride the very first morning, and after breakfast, Elder Benjamin began to open the treasures. [27]

When Molly Goodrich died in December 1835, the grieving Benjamin Youngs sent New Lebanon an account of her death and burial, adding:

I do not know that I would err in saying, I greatly coveted her situation. . . . She went out of time like a candle that had consumed its wick without a sigh or a struggle.—She retained all her loveliness, right mind & bright senses to the last—And now thus bereaved, it almost seems as if I were left to tread the wine press alone.[28]

Within a few years, Youngs and the few other remaining eastern pioneers in the West had returned, leaving the western communities entirely to the leadership of native westerners, and ending an important era in Shaker history.

During a time when divisions and dissensions frequently threatened the continued existence of some of the fledgling western communities, the east-west correspondence among the leading sisters worked to counteract such divisions. This was a political task, clearly, though there is no way of measuring precisely its contribution to the history of the communities' growth and development. From the point of view of the transplanted eastern sisters themselves, regular communication with the eastern Shaker establishment about concrete daily life issues must have made the daunting project of replicating eastern authority structures in the wild new communities seem almost feasible.

NOTES

1. The first three Shakers to journey to Ohio were Issachar Bates, John Meacham, and Benjamin S. Youngs. They were sent in January 1805 with a letter from the New Lebanon Church to those engaged in the Kentucky revival.
2. Letter from David Darrow and John Meacham, Turtle Creek, to New Lebanon, June 5, 1806 (OClWHi IV A 66).
3. Ruth Farrington, Ruth Darrow, Prudence Farrington, Molly Goodrich, Martha Sanford, and Lucy Smith arrived in 1806; they were joined by Lucy Bacon, Susannah (later Anna) Cole, and Rachel (formerly Ruth) Johnson in 1807; and Hopewell Curtis, Hortency Goodrich, and Mercy Pickett in 1809.
4. Christiane Fischer provides an able discussion of common themes in Anglo-American pioneer women's writings from a somewhat later period. She includes the longing for female companionship, loneliness, insecurity, anxiety, homesickness, and dismay at primitive conditions (Fischer, Let Them Speak for Themselves: Women in the American West, 1849–1900 [New York: E. P. Dutton, 1978]).
5. Marjorie Procter-Smith has made the point that "in their communal structure, the Shaker woman pioneer had the advantage over her non-Shaker counterpart" (Women in Shaker Community and Worship, 55–56). The early letters in this correspondence suggest that though they did not experience isolation, they had the opposite problem of overcrowding and lack of privacy.
6. A letter from Seth Y. Wells to Freegift Wells at Union Village, March 21, 1836, details this eastern aid (OClWHi IV A 36).

7. Benjamin S. Youngs to New Lebanon Ministry, August 27, 1825 (OClWHi IV B 19).

8. Rachel Johnson, who came from the Gathering Order at Watervliet, was an exception to the rule. Her lack of Church Family upbringing was actually to interfere with her promotion to first eldress in the western lead ministry, decades later.

9. Molly Goodrich mentions this expectation in Letter 7 of this chapter. All of the eastern missionaries had a standing invitation to return to their original communities in the East if at any time they felt "their gift was out"—that they were unable to make the kind of wholehearted contribution expected of them in obedience to those placed above them in the leadership hierarchy. (But this was tantamount to admitting failure to perform one's duty as expected.)

10. Prudence Farrington died after less than a year in Ohio; Lucy Bacon returned to New Lebanon after only five years; and Ruth Darrow died in her seventh year in the West.

11. Ruth Farrington had been appointed the leading ministry eldress in the West, the partner of David Darrow, before she left New Lebanon. She served in that role until her death at Union Village, Ohio, in October 1821. Molly Goodrich, first ministry eldress at the South Union, Kentucky community from its gathering until her death in 1835, served twenty-nine years in the West. Eldresses Lucy Smith, Mercy Pickett, Hopewell Curtis, Ruth Johnson, and Anna Cole all ultimately retired (some more willingly than others) to the eastern Shaker communities, after twenty-one, twenty-six, twenty-six, twenty-nine, and thirty-four years in the West, respectively.

12. Molly Goodrich was finally allowed to come east with her ministry partner Benjamin S. Youngs in 1827. New Lebanon's reluctance to allow the missionaries to revisit the East may have reflected their fear that intercommunity rivalry would only increase if certain community leaders were allowed the privilege of private talks with New Lebanon.

13. The names of the first group of six eastern sisters to go to Ohio had been submitted to David Darrow, John Meacham, and Benjamin S. Youngs for approval in a letter of February 1, 1806. However, when the western brethren asked for some specific sisters and not others, New Lebanon apparently felt that it was too late to change the selection without hurting feelings (see New Lebanon ministry letter to David Darrow and John Meacham dated April 18, 1806) (OClWHi IV A 31).

14. David Darrow was particularly outspoken in his judgments of individuals, but there are also critical evaluations from John Meacham and more diplomatic comments by Benjamin S. Youngs, in the early correspondence between Ohio and New Lebanon.

15. The earliest of the gathered Shaker communities in the West were Union Village, Ohio (formed in 1806 at Turtle Creek); Pleasant Hill, Kentucky (formed in 1809 in Shawnee Run); South Union, Kentucky (formed 1809–1811, at Gasper); and Busro or West Union, Indiana (formed in 1810–1811, on the Wabash River). Though New Lebanon made suggestions, it was also said explicitly that Lucy Wright "feels to submit the distribution of them to you" (New Lebanon ministry letter to Ohio elders, Eldress Ruth, and family, February 23, 1809 [OClWHi IV A 31]).

16. David Darrow and Ruth Farrington to Ministry, New Lebanon, November 27, 1809 (OClWHi IV A 66).

17. John Meacham to Lucy Wright, August 21, 1810 (OClWHi IV A 52).

18. Lucy Smith to Lucy Wright, August 21, 1810 (OClWHi IV A 52).

19. The leadership correspondence of the first three decades of western Shakerism reveals that a surprisingly high proportion of the easterners who became leaders in the West were ultimately removed from their positions as a result of allegations

of incompetence or spiritual disobedience or rebellion against their authority by factions of their own communities. The most notable of the recalled easterners were Pleasant Hill's Father John Meacham (recalled in 1818 when he "lost his gift") and Mother Lucy Smith (first exiled to Union Village in 1828, and then recalled to New Lebanon in 1829).

20. Perhaps because of this feeling about writing, Ruth Farrington remains nearly completely in the shadow of David Darrow, who acted as the principal correspondent from Union Village to New Lebanon over her entire western tenure.

21. Laurel Ulrich's useful notion of the "deputy husband" role for northern New England women in the colonial period (discussed in the general introduction, above, in reference to Ann Lee's claim to head the new church) has clear application within Shaker communities during these years.

22. I have not been able to locate this letter from Eldress Ruth to "Sister Lucy," which is referred to in a letter from Rufus Bishop of the New Lebanon lead ministry to the Union Village lead ministry, dated April 13, 1829 (OClWHi IV B 7).

23. An unusually large number of letters between Molly Goodrich and her eastern friends and relatives survives in eastern Shaker archives. I have drawn liberally on these for inclusion in this section and as the basis for many of the generalizations made in this essay.

24. Molly Goodrich to Lucy Wright, September 10, 1807 (OClWHi IV A 67).

25. Benjamin S. Youngs made a comment in a letter to Lucy Wright and the New Lebanon ministry dated May 1, 1813, about what he saw as the lesser interest of the black Shakers at South Union in "self-denial and the cross" (OClWHi IV A 60). In the summer of 1816, before the signing of the South Union Shaker Covenant, the heads of families "were spoken to on the subject of freeing their slaves." Only one family dissented, and the dissenting family head left the community on September 22, 1816, selling his four slaves, who signified their desire to remain as Believers, to the community (Benjamin S. Youngs's Journal, KyBW).

26. Darrow wrote in August 1814 to New Lebanon (OClWHi IV A 68).

27. Molly Goodrich to Sisters Hannah [Shapley] and Asenath [Clark], New Lebanon, August 10, 1818 (OClWHi IV B 19).

28. Benjamin S. Youngs, South Union, to New Lebanon ministry, December 22, 1835 (OClWHi IV A 61). Youngs was also referring to the loss of other "old friends" in the western leadership, through their return to the East. But his description of his own illness immediately following Goodrich's funeral also suggests the depths of his personal bereavement.

Letter 1. "I know that nothing but love could have induced me to write to those I never saw." Jennie Luckie McNemar, Turtle Creek, Ohio, to the sisters in New Lebanon, September 25, 1805.[1]

> [A recent western convert to Shakerism writes
> to the Shaker sisters in the East of her spiritual
> progress and her desire to have contact with the
> sisterhood.]

Dear Sisters,

I have long had a desire to see you, although unworthy of the privilege; from the good report I have had of you, I should exceedingly rejoice to see some of you here. I feel a union of spirit to all Zion's travellers and am willing to run that I may obtain. I feel thankful to God for the opening of the everlasting gospel amongst us which goes to the destruction of all sin. We have witnessed a great work of God in this land, and many of us thought we had almost attained the end of our calling, but alas, that wicked which [raiseth?] itself above all that is called God still remained in the Lord's temple, the flesh lusting against the spirit and the spirit against the flesh. And these being contrary the one to the other we could not do the things that we would. But I feel thankful to God that sin is brought to light which did so easily beset us and has so long grieved and quenched the spirit of God and kept our souls lean and barren. I cannot say my flesh is all destroyed or that I am already perfect, but this one thing I can say, that to be redeemed and purified from all sin is my daily labor. My determination is to bear the yoke of Christ and learn of him who is meek and holy and conform to him who did no evil, and in this I find rest to my soul.

I doubt not but you rejoice to hear of so many coming out of the City of Destruction and setting their faces Zionward, and would gladly obey that heavenly vision that would call you over to help us. But the Lord knows how to manage his own work, and it is good for us to be resigned to his will. I believe he will be at no loss for instruments to carry on his work as fast as the way opens. Satan has reigned long but God has begun to cut short his power and will finish his work in righteousness till every Believer is an ark to bear about the testimony of God's truth. As yet we can only see in part and are entangled with many fetters, while you enjoy the full liberty of the King's Daughters. I hope you will remember us as little babes just beginning to learn of Christ. This much we have already learned, as little children to love one another, and I know that nothing but love could have induced me to write to those I never saw. And if my freedom is acceptable I should be thankful for a recompense of the same by the first opportunity. May the Lord prosper you all and continue to make Zion a praise in the earth.

I am yours in the best of bonds,

Jenny Luckie McNemar

NOTE

1. Source: OClWHi IV A 66. Jennie McNemar's husband, Richard McNemar, was a New Light preacher who helped convert many of his congregation to Shakerism on the heels of the Kentucky revival. He was later an important Shaker leader— a western missionary, writer, and elder. He appended a paragraph postscript to this letter (and may in fact have been the scribe for the whole letter). Jennie Luckie McNemar converted to Shakerism shortly after her husband, in April 1805.

Letter 2. "Our journey was long and tedious and very wearisome." Ruth Farrington, Martha Sanford, Lucy Smith, Prudence Farrington, Molly Goodrich, and Ruth Darrow, Ohio, to the elder sisters in the First Family, New Lebanon, August 16, 1806.[1]

> [Three months after arriving in Ohio, the first group of eastern Shaker sisters write from Ohio to the elder sisters in the New Lebanon Church Family, describing the difficulties of the journey across the mountains and the shock of encountering primitive conditions of life in Ohio.]

Beloved Sisters that still feels near and dear to us,

We now take this opportunity to write to you something of what we have experienced since we left New Lebanon, as we well remember that you requested us to write to you the particulars concerning our journey. We now feel thankful to give you something of an understanding of what we have passed through since we left you, as far as we are able. Our journey was long and tedious and very wearisome, much more than anyone could imagine except they experienced it. We got no rest or but very little by day or by night; the mountains were long and tedious. We came to the mountains the third week on Tuesday. That day we came over the mountains called Blue Mountains; then we put up and washed our clothes. From thence over the Catetonna Mountain, Tuscarora Dieling Hill, Hogana Mountain, Laurel Hill, Chesnut Ridge—we were seven days acrossing these mountains. All these mountains is what you call the Allegheny, but there is but one that is properly called the Allegheny in that country. This mountain was about the smoothest of any of the mountains we crossed, but some of them was very long and rough, nothing but rocks and stones, for you could scarcely see the ground. We travelled afoot up all these mountains chiefly and some agoing down them, for they were so exceeding rough that we could not ride. The mountain called Laurel Hill was two miles up and three miles down; we came to it just before night. We travelled up the mountain and then put up, and in the morning we travelled afoot three miles down the mountain before breakfast—it was more like going down stairs than any thing we can compare it to. Some of the great chests pitch[ed] forward and split the bottom very much, but we did not meet with the loss of anything in the chests.

But we think that all these mountains are not equal to the road we met with after we got into the state of Ohio, for the extreme mud and mire is beyond our communication to you. For miles together there was no cessation of deep mud holes and short pitches—first the horses would go down to their bellies, then they would rise and the forewheels of the wagon would go down to such a degree that the forebows of the wagon cover would strike the horses' backs. It appeared many a time that nothing visible held up the wagons, but God in his mercy protected and kept us from all danger. For we feel sensible that we were under a measure of protection and blessing of God, for which reason we feel thankful. Furthermore we travelled afoot as much as our strength would admit of, for the horses were not able to draw us—we travelled up all the mountains and hills, or the most part of them in the whole in our journey. Dear sisters, if you should see the mountains and hills, rocks and stones, mud and mire, holes and swamps that we passed through and been over, you would not think strange that we tell you that our journey was long and wearisome.

In relation to our support, our food and drink was not so good and nourishing as it had been heretofore. It was dry and salt; we got no fresh meat or fish but two or three times in the whole of our journey. We did not buy but seven meals of victuals on our journey; we did not cook but one meal a day in general. Our bread lasted seven days and our butter three weeks and our dried beef and biscuit and cheese to the end of our journey.

In the forepart of our journey we had a comfortable entertainment, or as comfortable as could be expected among the wicked dirty world, but the latter part of our journey we had pinching times. Sometimes we could get beds to sleep on and sometimes we could not. The first log house we put up at to stay all night there was upwards of fifty moving people—we lodging in the chamber. It was very open, something like a barn. It rained very hard that night and it came in upon our beds and wet us very much. We took our lodging in the wilderness one night—it was in the midst of that extreme muddy travelling—and in the morning we travelled three miles. It appeared so dangerous that we could not ride. And then we put up in the woods and got breakfast. We made a fire and took long forks and briled [broiled] some pork and made some tea, and everyone took a piece of bread and pork and did eat and felt freshed, took courage and went on.

Furthermore we did not meet with any danger or difficulty in crossing the waters except the banks were very steep where the wagons went down in to the boats. Crossed eleven ferries and waded ten large cricks [creeks]; the water in general was so deep that it covered the hubs of the forewheels of the wagons. If some of them had been two inches deeper the water would have run into the wagons and damaged our loading. Furthermore we think that the weather was agreeable as could be expected considering the season of the year. In the whole of our journey it rained ten days out of forty-one—some days it rained all day and some days there was only showers.

We arrived at Wheeling the fourth week, on Friday. Wheeling lays upon the Ohio river. There we proposed to stop and wash our clothes the second time, but when we went into town we could not find one tavern that had housekeeping. Therefore we concluded to cross the river and go on, but there was a Quaker man by the name of Col. Zanes came to us and invited us to go to his house. So we accepted and went. He treated us very kindly and made us welcome to anything he had. The next day washed our clothes and refreshed our selves and wrote a letter back to Lebanon. And the next morning, which was Sabbath day, we crossed the Ohio river and went on.

The sixth week, on Tuesday, we arrived at Chillecotha, and about a mile after we left the town, just before sunset, there we met the brethren from Ohio, Issachar [Bates], Malcolm [Worley] and Calvin [Morrell]. It was a very happy meeting. We met them with joy and thankfulness, for all felt it to be the very right time for them to meet us. The next day they took some of our loading into their wagon and Issachar and Calvin went on before us with their axes cutting new roads and making bridges. For it was a continual swamp for three days after they met us, but the last day the road was better. We arrived at Malcolm's Saturday in the afternoon, May the 31st, Elder David and Elder John and all the brethren receiving us kindly, and Malcolm and Peggy [Worley], and made us welcome home.

Now perhaps you would like to know something how we began our work and labor in Ohio. It is as follows: Sabbath day in the afternoon we went to meeting. On Monday we walked out to see our new house and to see our little cabin, which is the house we are to move into. On Tuesday we went to another little cabin, which was about half a mile from Malcolm's, and did our washing—because there was not sufficient water in Malcolm's well. On Wednesday we ironed our clothes; on Thursday we moved into our little cabin.

The bigness of it is eighteen feet by twenty, one room below and one chamber. Our chamber floor is loose boards laid down. Our chamber is very full of large cracks, much more open than your barns, but we have stopped the large cracks with sticks of wood, corking them with tow. We have one window in the house which contains six lights, but two of them was broken out. We have another little hut about three rods from the door which was formerly a smokehouse. This is where we do our cooking. It is nothing but logs laid up and a roof put on. The fireplace is on the ground in one corner with a large stone set up for the chimney back and a hole cut out of the roof for the smoke to go out. Our conveniences for cooking is small but our family is large; and besides our own family we have workmen to cook for continually that works on the new house. In the whole we have nearly twenty to cook for in general, and in harvest time we had upwards of twenty and sometimes thirty, and continual comers and goers daily; there is no cessation. All those we have to cook for in our said kitchen without any handirons and other things accordingly.

Furthermore, the second and third and fourth week after we came to Ohio we did all our washing in the woods about two miles from home by a little creek because our well was dry—but the brethren dug a new well by the new house as quick as possible. But we have all our washing to do outdoors, only a shelter of bushes over us, and we do all our ironing in the room where we all live, which makes it very uncomfortable—for the weather is very warm here; we think it is quite as warm here as it is at New Lebanon. Likewise we found our brethren very needy of sisters' help. Their clothes needed repairing very much, and some of them appeared to us quite weak and feeble in body, especially Elder David, for everything being different, their manner of cooking and diet was so different that he could not get that nourishment and support as to make him comfortable. But they were taken care of as well as could be expected. We have all been quite unwell more or less since we left New Lebanon, but we have been able to keep about for the most part of the time.

Dear sisters, we have not had one day of rest since we left you. We work very hard indeed. We used to think that we knew what hardship was, and truly we did, but we knew nothing about it to what we know now. We do not write these things to you in way of complaining, but we feel reconciled to that work and gift of God that is allotted for us. For we learn in whatever state we are in therewith to be content. But we feel a desire that you may have a right understanding of our circumstance.

In relation to the property that we brought with us, we do not feel that any of it will be useless or unprofitable, but we feel thankful for the charity and bountiful blessings which we received from you when we come from home in both things spiritual and temporal. And we still desire your love and charity and prayers to God for us, for we feel poor and needy. We desire that you would not forget us but remember us, for we remember you and love you every one in particular.

We have written to you in short, for the time would fail us to write to you as we should be glad to write. But we expect that the brethren will be able to inform you more particular than we can write. We have written to you chiefly in relation to our journey and concerning temporal things, but we feel thankful to inform you that we have found a people that loves the gospel and has got the gifts and power of God among them in divers manners. And some of them has powerful gifts of God in shaking, turning, leaping, and clapping their hands and shouting, and some has the gift of tongues. We have written to the sisters in particular because they requested us to write, but we remember the brethren and love them all every one. And we desire to be remembered by all, both brethren and sisters. And in your prayers to God let us not be forgotten, for we feel poor and needy. This letter is closed with our love and remembrance to all our beloved brethren and sisters in the gospel.

Ruth, Martha, Lucy, Prudence, Molly, Ruth

P.S. Our cabin is shingled with palisades bound on with weight poles without any nails or pegs. Likewise the floor is a puncheon floor laid down without any nails or pegs about it. We have not washed our clothes in the half bushel nor ironed our caps on the dye tub, but we have met with that which is much more inconvenient. We have wrote our letter in our cabin chamber where[2] light comes in only through the cracks and a little hole cut out through the logs about a foot square, and our table was a box cover laid in the lap. This is the sisters' lodging chamber, and when it rains it comes in by streams through every direction—sometimes in the night first thing we know the rain comes in upon us.

The first meal of victuals we ate in our little cabin was on Thursday. We cooked some beef which we brought from home with us and made some cakes and made some tea. Our table was a long bench and a very rough one too; it was nothing but an old plank with some legs put in. But in a short time we received a table from one of our young believing brethren.

NOTES

1. Source: OClWHi IV A 66. Also see the more formal letter from these sisters to Lucy Wright, and her response (chapter 2, letters 6 and 7).
2. MS has "there is no" before "light."

Letter 3. "Dear sisters, you cannot sense your happiness in the Church, neither can I tell you what is here in Ohio." Susanna (later Anna) Cole, Warren County, Ohio, to New Lebanon, New York, September 7, 1807.[1]

> [One of the second group of eastern Shaker sis-
> ters describes in detail "this dreadful road," the
> overland trail journey to Ohio.]

Dearly beloved and much respected Elders, Brethren, and Sisters,

I feel thankful for this opportunity to manifest my love in a measure to you, well remembering the comfort, peace, and union that we have taken together from time to time in this your peaceable habitation. Although my day with you seems to be past, yet the remembrance of it remains fresh in my mind of your love, kindness, charity, blessings, and prayers while with you; and since I have felt many times my heart filled with love and mine eyes with tears, sensibly feeling your prayers and fervency to God for me. And I thank you all kindly for your remembrance and still desire your prayers to God for me, that I may be able to do the will of God in a distant land. I feel poor and needy, yet I feel reconciled to the cross, not looking to please myself. Dear sisters, you cannot sense your happiness in the Church, neither can I tell you what is here in Ohio. But I believe God is to work here.

In relation to our journey, we got on as well as could be expected through such a rough road, and we are in a comfortable state of health and have been for the most part of the time since we left you—although we was unwell in the way but did not lie by till we had a touch of the dysentery and did take some pills that helped us. This disorder was very frequent amongst the inhabitants of the land.

After Deacon Samuel left us, the way began to grow rough and still increased. We walked more or less every day while on the land. It is not in my power to give you an idea of this dreadful road that we have travelled unless you were eyewitness. These roads are cut almost all into deep ruts eighteen and twenty inches deep and eight or ten of these to be counted across the road, in many places up and down long hills where it looked in danger of a person's life to be in a carriage, mud and slough holes which we in no wise could shun. We thought many times we travelled seven miles to gain three by turning from one side of the road to the other, and all we gained by it was we did not get so deep in the mud but what we got out again, yet many times picking our way well as we could and we should be in the mud over shoe sometimes, no way to get along but travel along upon the logs in the bushes. For the way was so bad, a great part of it, we thought ourselves well off to get the wagon along by holding it up and we all on foot. And when we got to the mountains we found but a little of the way that we could ride.

The second week, on Saturday, we crossed the first mountain. The next day being exceeding hot as though we should scorch, we sisters walked fourteen miles and rid [rode] three that day. During the time crossing the mountains, which was one week, we sisters walked twelve and fourteen miles each day and sometimes more. And when we came to the hills, they was still worse, for these hills were so slippery and steep that our horses fell down on their knees frequently and on broadside in their tackling, and we could scarcely stand on our feet. There was but one day in ten that it rained not, from the time we got to the mountains until we got to Wheeling.

One morning we went nine miles to breakfast and walked eight miles of it and rid every place that we thought we could.[2] We rid for that mile, for Nathan was exceeding kind and would urge us to get into the wagon, said he hoped we could ride a little. When we got in, sometimes we could ride twenty rods, sometimes thirty and forty and then come to such bad places that we could not ride. Then it would take both of the brethren to hold up the wagon. We could not see our road many rods before us, it was so up and down and cracked, and people would tell us we did not know anything about bad roads: when we come to cross the river we should know what bad roads was. We said if we find worse roads we cannot get along.

In [the] third week of our journey, Tuesday, we get [got] to Wheeling. Now we was all very weary and much spent. I thought that I had been tired before, but this far exceeded. We all judged that we sisters walked 150 miles by this time. People inquired where we was bound and advised us to go down the river, telling us they did not think we could get through without much trouble by land. They was very kind and several of them stood ready to assist us had we desired it, but our feeling was to go on by land, expecting some of the brethren to meet us; so crossed the river and went on about five miles. We had rose a hill which was one mile up and steep too where we see [saw] Constant [Mosely] and John Casson rising the other side of the hill. We was much rejoiced to see each other and they soon told [told] their minds and we was all ready to unite and turned back, although three miles off. This way was what was called bottom land in this country, which is a black sod mud and water up to the horses' bellies, mile after mile. This Tuesday we crossed one creek seventeen times in going nine miles, which was sometimes several rods wide and up to the [in?] of the wagon—twenty-five rivers and creeks we crossed that day.

Wednesday we returned to Wheeling again and waited at the tavern for the brethren to get a boat and make ready for us till sometime in the afternoon. Then we walked down, very hot, and as we had strong invitations to go to Col. Zean's [Zane's], we now went, and they treated us very kindly and went and made us a dish of tea and gave us such things as we needed. And we felt much refreshed and returned to the boat, went on board about five o'clock.

We had a thunder shower at evening, a violent shower and heavy thunder and sharp lightning. In the morning we bailed out seventy-two pails of water, as there was a loose floor and the water settled between. We sisters had a bundle of straw and a blanket over it in the wagon box for our bed. We kept much drier than the brethren did, but when we took our clothes to put on in the mornings they felt damp as if prepared for ironing by the fog and rain. We had a fire in one corner of the boat. We had a spider teakettle and teapot. Here we cooked for seven people and put on our womanly spirits and eat, drank, and cooked with the river water. It was very nasty and [ricly?] by the abundance of rain and filth. We landed Friday of the fifth week and went on and put up at a private house.

Saturday in the forepart of the day Daniel [Mosely] met us with great joy to help us through, for which we felt thankful, and went on rejoicing to Elder David's, where the gates was opened for us, and the elders, brethren, and sisters met us to the wagon and saluted us and welcomed us to their habitation and conducted us into their house in a very kind manner. We wept and rejoiced together not a little. We rested and gave Mother's love and those that are with her and all the elders, brethren, and sisters, which they thankfully received and thanked us for.

They soon told us that Ruth was sick, asked us to see her. We found her with a violent dysentery, high fever, and inflammation of the stomach and many bad symptoms, which attended her without much signs of recovery until the Saturday following, which was the eleventh day of her disorder. She began to mend and has been gaining ever since.

The young Believers likewise received us very kindly and welcomed us to this country. They appear to be zealous and powerful. As I have had some opportunity of seeing a number of them from a distance, they are continually coming and going from the east, west, north, and south, between twenty and thirty here at a time to cook for and take care of. There has been but one day since we have been here that there was not more or less here from a distance, and likewise joiners to work on the house. What time they have all mixed up together, sometimes there is hardly a place but what they are in labors with some one.

But what struck me more than any thing else was to see Elder David and Eldress Ruth come so low to fallen man.[3] It did not look like man's work but the mighty work of God. There is not a minister since hardly to be found in the parts.

I close my letter with my kind love to all the brethren and sisters.

Farewell,

Susanna Cole

Eldress Ruth and the rest of the sisters return their kind thanks for your love and remembrance and desire it may continue with us. They heartily thank Rhoda and Joanna in particular for their presents. Likewise they send kind love to all in particular.

NOTES

1. Source: OClWHi IV A 67.
2. The MS text here has "a number of spells," which seems to be a false start.

3. Apparently she is referring to the fact that under frontier conditions the Shaker ministry could not maintain their usual distance from the visiting "world."

Letter 4. "There is neither door nor partition upon the loft." Rachel Johnson, Miami County, Ohio, to Deborah [Woodworth?] and Susanna [Ellis], [Gathering Family eldresses, New Lebanon], September 12, 1807.[1]

> [Another new arrival from the East writes home
> to describe the primitive organization of meals
> and laundry chores and the new dwelling house
> in which there is very little privacy and no
> separation between novice Believers and "old
> Believers."]

Dear beloved Elder Sisters Deborah and Susanna,

I now send you a few lines to let you know how we get along in this western land. We have three and four and more sittings to eat. We all mix up together, young Believers and old. Elder David, Elder John, and Eldress Ruth as often eat at the second and third setting as any way, with a panel of young Believers—and the rest of us two [too?] sometimes to one sitting and sometimes to another, as one can get a chance. We have great washes. We have a shed where we pound and rub our clothes. We boil suds and rinse them in the open sun.

We have great meetings, public meeting twice a week, when the young sisters are under exercise. Sometimes they get us into their arms and make us hardly fit to be seen. It is so hot and so many people here that the sisters make use of white muslin looseback gowns, sometimes white jackets on weekday meetings. The first of our house is finished, white oak floors without planing, to two lofts, four smoky fireplaces on each loft. Our garret we have for a lodging room with seven beds chiefly on the floor. There is neither door nor partition upon the loft. We have some blankets hung up between the brethren's beds and ours. The middle loft is all open. They are to work on it. And there is people coming and going frequently from east, west, north, and south. Yet I don't feel discouraged but feel as though my help was needed. I feel poor and needy and desire that I may be remembered in your prayers.

I close these lines with my kind love to you all.

Farewell, this from

Rachel

NOTE

1. Source: OClWHi IV A 67.

Letter 5. "Dear sister, we often think of you and those who are with you."
Cassandana Goodrich, Hancock, Massachusetts, to Molly Goodrich, South
Union, Kentucky, August 8, 1812.[1]

> [Eldress Cassandana Goodrich of Hancock
> writes to her natural sister Molly Goodrich, who
> has recently become first eldress at South Union,
> reminding her that "great patience is required of
> all who are called into the vineyard."]

Beloved Sister Molly,

With joy and thankfulness of heart I received your kind and satisfactory
letters of May 26 and August 4th, informing me of your present situation
and welfare, which is cause of great consolation to me and those that are
with me and likewise to all the elders, brethren, and sisters in the Church.
Your letter was read in the Church at this place the day that we received
it and the next morning was sent to Mother at Lebanon.

Loving sister, I understand that you are at a great distance from us,
among a people who have had but little privilege in learning the way of
God and are much uncultivated in almost every sense and that you have
much labor, tribulation, and suffering to pass through in order to gain a
little where there is so much evil. And this I believe is the case. It is through
much tribulation that the gospel can be firmly established in any part of
this lost world, and as you are called to be a weapon of war in this great
and glorious warfare, I am thankful to hear that it is your labor to do all
the good that you are able and to honor the gift and calling of God wherein
you are called and patiently endure those outward afflictions which are of
but short duration.

Dear Sister Molly, there is nothing that you could have written to me
could bring more satisfaction to my feelings than the above determination
to stand with fortitude in defense of the true and living way of God, which
will make you an heir of glory and a terror to the wicked. And it is my
desire that you may always keep this determination and be careful to hear-
ken and obey the voice of God which hath called you to follow the Lamb
whithersoever he goeth; and that the rising generation may call you lovely,
blessed, and holy. My loving little Sister Molly, I am thankful to hear that
you have a goodly number of young Believers and children at South Union
who feel very near and dear to you. You must be patient with them and

let them have time to grow for a season, and after awhile they will begin
to bear fruit that will add some consolation to your labors. Perhaps it may
feel to you like waiting for the growth of a tree that requires many years
in order to bring forth fruit to perfection; and so it is, and great patience
is required of all who are called into the vineyard.

Dear sister, we often think of you and those who are with you and
speak one to another concerning you, our good brethren and sisters in the
West; and not only so, but we sincerely pray that you may be under the
special notice and blessing of God, that you may be endowed with that
wisdom and power of God that will overcome all your enemies. And as
the testimony of eternal truth must finally bear the sway, I have no reason
to doubt but you will come off conquerors and overcome all your adver-
saries. Be of good cheer, my little sister, and remember that the conquest
depends upon faithfully enduring to the end. And when we have finished
the work that we are called of God to perform in this world and leave these
earthly tabernacles, then we may see each other and converse together
upon what we have passed through in this world for the sake of keeping
the way of God and helping others that they might share with us in the
same blessing. And so I shall rest contented respecting my beloved Sister
Molly for you to be in that place where you can do the most good to yourself
and others. And whether I ever shall see your face again in this world, that
is uncertain to me. Be that as it may, all my desire is that we may do the
will of God in this world, that we may be the heirs of eternal life in the
world which is to come.

As to matters here, I think I shall not write much at this time as there
have been a number of letters written, and one from me to thee which was
delivered to Peter [Pease] before we received your letter and Brother Joseph
Allen's.

Your aged mother Anna [Goodrich] retains her sense, her health, and
strength remarkably well for a woman of her age and feels composed and
reconciled for you to continue where you are, so long as it is the gift of
God. She sends her kind love and thanks to you for your notice to her in
your letter to me. We are all in our usual state of health at present. So I
shall close these lines with my sincere love and remembrance to thee. And
likewise Elder Nathaniel [Deming], Brother Nathan and Sister Sarah [Mark-
ham?] together with me send their kind love and thanks to thee and to
Elder Benjamin; also to Brother Joseph [Allen] and Sister Mercy [Pickett].

From your kind Sister Dane Farewell

NOTE

1. Source: OClWHi IV B 35.

Letter 6. "Perhaps Eldress Dane would like to hear something about the situation of things here." Molly Goodrich, South Union, Kentucky, to Cassandana Goodrich, Hancock, Massachusetts, May 5, 1813.[1]

> [Molly Goodrich thanks her natural sister, Cassandana Goodrich, for letters of nearly a year before and gives news of the increase in population at South Union.]

Respected Eldress Dane,

It was with much satisfaction and thankfulness that I received the two letters sent from thee by Brother Peter. Yea, I felt very thankful for the two kind and loving letters full of good counsel and kind encouragement. And now I undertake to write a little, although it has been a long time since I received those letters. I hope Eldress Dane will not think it was through an indifferent feeling that I have not written before, but with patience I have been obliged to wait till the time come, and now with pleasure I embrace the privilege.

We were at Union Village in Ohio when Brother Peter arrived there from the Church, and you may be sure it was a time of much joy and thankfulness to hear and receive such fresh information from our precious Mother and elders, brethren, and sisters in the East. I feel unable to express what consolation it gives us to know and feel that we are remembered in love and union by those who are in Zion, for our dependence is there. O Eldress Dane, did you know what a precious little letter we received from our blessed Mother. It was a balsam indeed and a feast of fat things well refined. I set more by it than I should by a paper that come from the United States Bank.

Dear Eldress Dane, let me tell you once more that I feel thankful for your kind notice to me in every respect. It did me good, and I believe I stand in need of all the help and strength that I can get to support me in my heavy burdens. My determination is the same [as] it was when I wrote to you before, but whether I shall be always able to abide in this gift I cannot tell. But if I do all I can, I believe that I shall be accepted. I well remember the promise that Mother gave us, before we left her; she said if we would be faithful and do all the good we could, when our gift was out, then we might return again into the ark of safety. And that promise is engraved on the tablet of my heart, but I do not mean to take any advantage by it and shun the cross, but still it gives me confidence to believe that if I should return home again, I should not be shut out. Now I do not believe that you want me to come back again, neither do I believe that you want to hear me complain of my weakness or inability nor of my sufferings and tribulations which I have to pass through. But I believe you would a great deal rather hear of my being able to do good and to work in the vineyard of the Lord, if it is a 1000 miles off and even in the west end of it, and stick by the stuff even if you should never see my face again.[2]—This is my faith, too, if I am only able to hold out. But my weakness of body is a great discouragement to me, although I cannot complain at this time for I have had better health this winter past than I have had for three years past. I think I have said sufficient on this subject.

Perhaps Eldress Dane would like to hear something about the situation of things here and how we are getting along by this time. The number of the Believers have increased considerably since last summer, and they have increased some in faith and obedience. They are quite poor yet in temporal things and very much distressed for house room, but they are beginning to build. There is about ninety persons in the family where we live, and the size of the house is twenty-eight by thirty-six. And besides it is all the meeting house we have for public meetings and the public house for travellers, both Believers and the world, to gather to, and I think it is the most public place for travellers of the world of any place that ever I lived at. You must think of necessity we have to experience a great deal of confusion and distress, but we hope for better times by and by. We have another large family of upwards of fifty in number, and our school family is about 150 in number, upwards of 130 children and about twenty of them too young to learn their books. Besides these families we have a number of little out-families round about.

Now dear sister, it is almost time for me to close my letter. What more shall I say? If I should say that I loved you, that you well knew before. If I should tell you that I would be thankful to see you, that you will not dispute. If I should tell you that I loved all my good old friends and wanted to see them properly, that you would believe to be true. And if I should tell you that I had just to bear my cross about the whole of it, that you will know is true. Therefore I don't see as I can tell you much news about it.

Good Eldress Dane, I will be a good child and learn wisdom and prudence as fast as I am able.[3] Therefore, don't forget little Molly. I do not believe you will forget good children, neither do I believe Elder Nathaniel will forget good children. Elder Nathaniel knows that I love him sincerely, and so I do Brother Nathan and Sister Sarah too.

My Sister Mercy [Pickett] will not let me forget her; she desires to be remembered in the tender ties of love and union.

Be so kind as to receive my little letter of love. I feel thankful that my other letter was so kindly received by those that I do so highly love and esteem.

So farewell kindly till I see you, and then I will talk a heap more.

From your little sister,

Molly Goodrich

N.B. I thankfully received the pretty little present of the good creation of God, which Eldress Dane sent me, for which I return my kindest and sincere thanks. I will labor to make a good use of it you may depend. The little round bright eye made little Molly smile.

P.S. Eldress Dane, I have written some letters in return to letters and presents which was sent to me in your order, and I am willing you should do as you think best in relation to the disposal of them. And if I have done amiss, I shall be willing to be taught better. Now I want the last word in my letter to be love.

NOTES

1. Source: OClWHi IV B 35.
2. This is a direct allusion to Eldress Cassandana's phrase in her August 6 letter: "we are placed one at one end of the vineyard, and the other almost at the other end."
3. Again, Molly Goodrich echoes a phrase in the letter she is answering, in which Cassandana Goodrich said, "I recommend you to the dictates of wisdom and prudence."

Letter 7. "I want you to be so kind as to send us particular word about our precious Mother." Molly Goodrich, South Union, to Ruth Landon, New Lebanon, November 28, 1816.[1]

> [Molly Goodrich reminds second ministry eldress Ruth Landon that it has been eleven years since she was sent west. Expressing dutiful resignation at not yet being invited east for a visit, she tells a bit about the work the sisters in the West do, and gives news of the South Union family reorganization.]

My loving Sister Ruth,

I want very much to talk a few words with you once more, for it has been so long since I saw you that instead of having the privilege of seeing you I feel as if I cannot do any longer without talking a little with you on paper, which will in some measure answer the same purpose. It has been now nearly eleven years since I left my good home and my precious Mother and all my pretty brethren and sisters, although when I left New Lebanon I had no other expectation but that I should see you all again in three or four years. But so it is, the longer I stay the more I have to do, and the tighter I get bound, and what shall I do about it? Sometimes I feel as if I wanted to be at my good old home very much, so bad I hardly know how to stand it. But I consider to be out of a gift would be an uncomfortable state for me whether here or there, and so I labor to be contented in my calling. But still I think, oh, if I could only see the beautiful face of my pretty Mother once more or even touch the hem of her garment as you so often do, how happy I should be in it! But I know if I do her will, which is the will of God, I shall be happy whether I ever see her again or not.

Now my dear sister, I have one little request to make—that is, if the request is not too bold. I want you to be so kind as to send us particular word about our precious Mother, about her health and just how she looks and how large she is and her exact age and just what clothes she wears and how she lives and how much she has altered since we saw her—yea, how she walks about and visits her pretty children. And when you tell us all about it, it will make us laugh and cry too, both. This you know we cannot always help. For we do want to have you tell us a heap about our dear Mother and that will do us ever so much good. For you know that little children love to be pleased, and there is nothing pleases children so much as to be about their Mother and to have her give them good cakes to eat. And if they cannot see her, they want to hear about her the oftener. Now good sister, if you will get Mother's liberty and answer my request, it will be a precious good little cake; and also do not forget to let us know particularly about Elder Abiathar and Sister Ruth. And if I have been too bold or used too much freedom in my little petition, you must only whip me and then I expect to find forgiveness, as I mean to bear it patiently. I often feel as though I should be glad to write about a heap of things, but you know I am in a distant land and must feel straitened lest I should say something that might not be acceptable.

At this time we are in our usual state of health and as comfortable as would be expected in our present situation. We still live in a house with a family which makes it rather uncomfortable[2]—but we have two comfortable rooms, and the children are as kind to us as they know how to be. The family consists of about forty in number, mostly young people, the eldest about thirty-six and the youngest about ten. Generally speaking it is a comfortable family. Also we have taken about forty of our oldest children out of the school order and have made a new family with them. They are from the age of about twelve or fourteen to eighteen, and they make a very pretty family of youth. They have older brethren and sisters who live with them to teach and to take care of them and protect them. So we think that in a few years more we shall have a goodly number of young people in this place, if they should all keep their faith and do well. But sometimes we have to suffer the tribulation of seeing some nasty old flesh-mongers going off to the world and dragging off innocent children and the poor little creatures crying and begging to stay, but the merciless old wretches have no pity nor compassion on them. But no doubt the time will come when they will have to bear the judgment of their own doings and when the people of God will be released.

Now my dear sister, it is time that I should bring my letter to a close, as I had no thought of writing so much when I began—only to make my little request about our precious Mother. And as I went on I thought you might wish to hear a little how we were coming on; but oh, if you will only take a little pains to step over the mountains and see us, what a happy meeting it would be, and then you will know a great heap about it. Indeed we have looked pretty strongly all last summer for some of our dear friends, but they have not come yet, so I reckon we will have to wait a while longer like patient children.

Sister Mercy and myself desires the privilege to send our best love and remembrance to our ever blessed Mother, Elder Abiathar, and Sister Ruth.

Farewell from Molly

P.S. I think I must tell you a little about our employment. We have a plenty to do, both in things spiritual and temporal; we do not see any place for being idle. Besides other labors, we do a heap of work with our hands. Sister Mercy is very industrious indeed, I tell her sometimes she is too worldly minded. She spins nearly 100 runs every year, besides she hunts up all the old rags she can find and cuts them up for carpets and gives them to the little school girls to sew and then to the big girls to weave, and then she has them sold to get such like things as we stand in need of. Likewise little me does a heap of work. I have spun thirty runs of wool this season, besides a heap of knitting and sewing and a plenty of other employments such as walking and talking, etc., etc., and we labor to do the children all the good we are able.

NOTES

1. Source: OClWHi IV A 60.
2. The South Union ministry still lodged at this time in one of the communal families, rather than in its own quarters in the meeting house, as did the New Lebanon ministry.

Letter 8. "The sisters here have a little mulatto child to raise by hand." Molly Goodrich, South Union, Kentucky, to Daniel Goodrich, Junior, Hancock, Massachusetts, November 30, 1816.[1]

> [Eldress Molly Goodrich responds to a letter
> from her natural brother, Daniel Goodrich, Ju-
> nior, an elder at the Hancock community. She
> tells several stories about interesting new mem-
> bers of the South Union community, including
> a 77-year-old woman and a mixed race infant.]

My good friend and Brother Daniel,

I do not recollect as I have written one line to thee since I have been in this western country—therefore I have a desire to have a little conversation with thee once more, for it seems that after I have served seven years, I shall have to serve out seven more before I shall get the chance to go home and see my beautiful Mother and all my pretty brethren and sisters. I often think, oh! had I but wings like a little bird, how quick I would fly and light in your habitation, and then how I would chatter with all the pretty doves! But so it is, I have not only to be reconciled but thankful to labor in that part of the vineyard of Christ allotted for me and to labor to bring forth good fruit, which if I do, no doubt I shall be rewarded for all the crosses and trials I have to pass through. So it is of no use to complain. But I do want to see you all exceedingly. But as that cannot be at present, to hear from all our dear friends by letter is a great privilege indeed.

The particular information in your last letter was very satisfactory. It did us a great deal of good to hear from the aged brethren and sisters. It is very remarkable, to be sure, how they live and keep along so comfortable as they do. Also, it is a lovely thing to hear of the middle-aged and youth growing and flourishing in the way of God, and above all to hear that our beautiful Mother looks just like Mother and that her children look just like Mother's lovely children. To be sure this makes a handsome and lovely family—and don't you think that we claim a right in that family too? O yea, that we do, and good Elder Nathaniel will say so too. If we will be right good children, we shall eat and drink at Mother's table.

Now concerning information, I thought of relating a little curious circumstance which might perhaps be some change among the rest of the letters. In the first place I have to inform you that there is one soul more added to the faith. About three weeks ago there came an aged woman here from Northern Carolina the distance of six or seven hundred miles on purpose to get among the Believers. She said that she had heard a great many more evil reports than good ones, but she had read *The Testimony* [*of Christ's Second Appearing*] and she believed we were the people of God and she wanted to get among us before she died. One of her sons brought her and he has faith too but is bound to a very wicked family. She said that she did not come because she had no home, for any of her children would be glad to take care of her as long as she lived, but because she wanted to flee out of Babylon. What makes it remarkable, she has left all her children and come six or seven hundred miles and is seventy-seven years of age. And she is very small—she measures four feet and three inches and weighs eighty pounds. She appears very well satisfied and is very zealous to come to meeting. She makes us think of little Zacchaeus of old when he had to "climb the tree, his lord to see," for she acts pretty much like him in order to see in time of meeting. She came to see us and I gave her a cap and Mercy a handkerchief—we told her to wear them when she came to meeting. She was exceedingly pleased and said, "God bless you, dear honey." She is quite bright and sensible for her age and is a pretty little child. Her name is Anna Darby, but we call her Granny.

Now I have to relate to Eldress Dane and Sister Sarah one little circumstance more. The sisters here have a little mulatto child to raise by hand. The way it came was this. Last Christmas there was a young woman here before she had the child and was in a heap of trouble and wanted to confess her sins. She had faith two years before this happened, but her parents would not let her come. And when she got in this situation they were glad to let her come, in order to escape the dishonor that it would bring on them if she stayed in the world, and thought by this means the people in their neighborhood would never find it out—for they lived seventy miles from this place and were counted honorable people in the world. And considering the girl had faith long before this and wanted to be a Believer, but was hindered, we thought it was right to show her charity. And she had a privilege to confess her sins, which she did honestly, and appeared like making a right pretty Believer—this was about Christmas. In February she had her child and lived but just three weeks after it and left her poor little yellow papoose behind. And the sisters could not bear to send it to the girl's mother because they knew that it would be so exceedingly abused, and so they chose to keep it and nurse it. And now it is a fine, smart, fat child about ten months old. Its name is Juliet, after its mother, whose name is Juliet Mackaby and a smart likely young woman.

When her mother heard of her death, the wicked old creature said she was glad of it, and if they brought the child there she would kick it out of doors as quick as she would a rattlesnake. And this same woman has faith and so have all the family. About two years before this happened, one of her sons came here and stayed about two month. He was a very pretty boy and had good faith and pretty love to the Believers and wanted to stay with them exceedingly, but this same cruel woman would not let him stay. When she came here and took him away we talked very pointed to her and told her that if she did not let her children obey their faith, something would happen to them that would make her sorry for it. And after all that could be said to her she hardened her heart and took her own way. But we think she will not show her head here again very shortly, lest she should see something here that she did not want to see. The child is nursed by the sisters that take care of the little children that is too young to go to school, such as are three and four years old.

So now my two little stories about our two little babies are ended—the one being seventy-seven years old, and the other a little yellow papoose of ten months. And as these little stories have been pretty long, I must tell you some short ones and I think it will be time to quit.

Once in a while Mercy and I take a walk to the school about half a mile off and there walk and talk about among the sisters and children. And then sometimes we go from there a little ways through the groves and across the road to see our family of black people and do the same there. And our family that is nearer home we visit some oftener. And then once in a while too we all take a ride on horseback or in a carriage to see our family of Believers four mile off, and there we stay sometimes till the next day and then return, and go to work at home. And so you see how we are doing. And now dear brother, lest I should talk too much and weary you, I must begin to bring my letter to a close, ever wishing to be remembered by all my dear friends, for the love and remembrance of our blessed Mother and elders and all our dear brethren and sisters [are] the sweetest cakes[2] we ever got. We do not let them kind of cakes ever get dry nor moldy, but they are always fresh and new. I well remember the good counsel Eldress Dane sent to me in her last letter, and I expect to keep it till she sends me another good little cake. I close by sending my best love, together with Sister Mercy, to the beloved ministry in particular, and to as many of their little household as they feel a gift in.

Farewell

From Molly

To Elder Nathaniel, my love I do send,
And to Eldress Dane, my kind loving friend,
And good Brother Daniel, my love you must keep,
And good Sister Sarah, I send you a heap.

N.B. Brother Daniel, the little anecdote about the two hay poles that you mentioned was quite diverting. We concluded if you had little me there, you would have another little hay pole of the same stamp—my weight is about ninety and Elder Benjamin is very near the same. Brother Joseph and Sister Mercy is a heap larger. And we always find a plenty to do to keep us as busy as bees. When you see this paper, I reckon you will say, "Little Molly is yet alive," and when you have said this, be sure to give my kind love and remembrance to all the aged brethren and sisters.

Molly

NOTES

1. Source: OClWHi IV A 60.
2. "Cakes" are not literally food in this correspondence, but playful metaphors for the love sent by the parental New Lebanon leaders, Lucy Wright and her associates, to their spiritual children in the West.

Letter 9. "Now my pretty Sister Molly I am agoing to try to tell you about our good Mother." Ruth Landon, New Lebanon, to Molly Goodrich, South Union, Kentucky, February 21, 1817.[1]

[In answer to Molly Goodrich's request, Ruth Landon gives a full description of Mother Lucy Wright, adding details about herself. She also tells of a recent New Lebanon ministry visit to the dying ministry eldress of the Harvard, Massachusetts, community, Hannah Kendall.]

My dear Sister Molly,

I now with heart and mind full of love and remembrance of thee, my good and faithful sister, take pen in hand to talk a little with you. Firstly, I kindly thank you for the pretty letter you sent to me. I feel much pleased with it and shall try to give you satisfaction in answer to it, though I have not time to write lengthy.

In the first place, I will relate our journey to the eastern Churches this summer past. June the 3rd, 1816, Mother, Elder Abiathar, Brother Rufus [Bishop] and I set out for Harvard, Shirley, Canterbury, and New Enfield. We made our first stop at Shirley. There we found Mother Hannah [Kendall] very feeble but thankful to see us. Her sufferings increased continually. We tarried there two days. Then we, in company with Mother Hannah and her two children, started for Harvard. Her spirit was swift and her sufferings great. We travelled as fast as our horses were able to go. When we reached Harvard, she was taken out of the carriage and led into the meeting house. Her sufferings the night following was beyond our description. Her groans were so heavy, they seemed to jar the house.

This was a sorrowful scene to us. Our Mother said, "This is one of my nearest and dearest friends—but she has done her work and I am willing she should go." In the morning she was more quiet and remained so while we stayed there. She appeared as simple as an infant child. She would often speak thus, "I have done—I have done." Beholding her face in a glass, says, "Oh! you are going to your Mother [at last?],"—it seemed she was ready for her journey. We tarried there four days. When taking leave of Mother Hannah, she said, "We shall meet together again. Father William told me he had seen Hannah Kendall's name written in the Lamb's Book of Life in capital letters of gold. This has been a great comfort to me," says Mother Hannah. We all wept with her, then bade her farewell for time.

We then started for Canterbury, reached there the second day, and found the ministry and people all comfortable and very glad to see us. Had a very agreeable visit at both places. Returned to Watervliet the fourth week, all in good health.

Now my pretty Sister Molly, I am agoing to try to tell you about our good Mother, but I am afraid I have not skill enough to do it complete. Mother, Elder Abiathar, and Ruth lodge in the meeting house, eat breakfast there, then go to our shop and there attend to the duties of the day, sometimes talking, sometimes thinking, sometimes get almost beyond thinking.

Mother visits the elders often, sometimes the brethren and sisters, which pleases them much. We go to Watervliet four or five times in a year, stay four weeks at a time. We sometimes go to Hancock, spend the day with the ministry. There they feel dependent on Mother and the Church here, for union and strength.

Respecting Mother's health, she is [as] well at this [time] as she has been for two years past, and that is somewhat feeble. She is considerably less than she was when you saw her last. She is very spry and nimble, looks some older. She is some gray, though not to be seen when her cap is on. She is clothed with meekness and love, does not appear to be broken with age, walks about much as she used to do. Mother's winter dress for everyday wear is a drugget gown, made in the same style or form of that which was sent to Rachel Johnson, worsted for Sabbath. Her everyday summer dress, dark blue striped, and Sabbath, light striped, such as we used to wear in short gowns; handkerchiefs white for Sabbath, summer and winter. Sometimes she wears silk and blue cotton in the winter season and wears very thin caps in warm weather. She looks very beautiful to every good Believer because she is holy, just, and true, ever laboring to comfort and encourage her children. She often speaks about Molly and Mercy, says, "I hope they will have wisdom and patience according to their lot and place in the house of God." We feel as though we never could bear to part with Mother, but by and by the time will come. But we have learned it is best to take comfort as we go and not look forward for tribulation.

Now what shall I say more? Oh, let me think, you wanted to know how Elder Abiathar looks. I think he has not altered much, looks some older. He is middling healthy and sometimes very pleasant and never very cross and always good. As to myself, middling healthy, look and feel something old, considerably gray, not much broken yet in memory, etc. It seems to me I must tell you a little about the good elders here in the old hive where you have eaten so much honey. The elder brother is very bright and lively; the elder sister is very good and steady. Brother Rufus [Bishop] and Sister Olive [Spencer] makes very good and choice elders. The family has as much faith in their elders as they ever had. Thus much I can say for them: they have labored and strove to keep the way of God and have been a great comfort and strength to Mother. I think I must begin to close my letter. Perhaps I have written as much as you will have patience to read.

Mother, Elder Abiathar, and myself (Ruth) send our kind love and remembrance to Elder Benjamin, Brother Joseph Allen, Eldress Molly Goodrich, and Sister Mercy Pickett.

From Mother's Ruth

N.B. If it would do any good, I would apologize about the writing and spelling of my letter, but I guess you can find it all yourself if you try hard enough. If you laugh about it, Mercy must send me word and I will send the next letter to her. She and I have just learning enough to know we have but little—which is better than none at all. So farewell

R.

P.S. One thing more I must tell of. Mother's arm is so far recovered she can comb her own hair. Also the ministry from Alfred visited us while we were at Canterbury; all well at that time.

N.B. Eldress Anna Cogswell has been very feeble for a long time. It is doubtful whether she will ever recover. She has stood in her lot about three years and has had a profitable gift.

R.

NOTE

1. Source: OClWHi IV B 35.

Letter 10. "Every line I read my heart leaped for joy." Molly Goodrich, South Union, to Ruth Landon, New Lebanon, May 10, 1817.[1]

> [Molly Goodrich thanks Ruth Landon for her re-
> cent letter describing Mother Lucy and asks for
> a copy of her cap pattern. She also responds to
> news about the aging New Lebanon sisters she
> had known.]

My dear Sister Ruth, my Mother's Ruth,

With the greatest pleasure I take pen in hand to inform you that I received your very kind and instructive letter into my little hands with gratitude and thankfulness. I could hardly wait to open the seals, and every line I read my heart leaped for joy. I cannot express by word nor letter how much delighted I was to receive such particular and satisfactory account of my precious Mother and good elders. Indeed, Sister Ruth, I think you had skill enough to suit me very completely. Yea, you brought our precious Mother so near; oh, how pretty she did look! You made us feel very thankful when you told us how she retained her health and strength so as to perform such a journey as she did the summer past. But oh what a blessed thing it would be if she could only perform such a journey and visit all her little children in our part of the world. I think it would be such a meeting as never was before—it would feel as though heaven was opened in very deed. But we do not look for such a thing to take place as ever to see

Mother here in the body, and if we can only get to see her and feel her lovely spirit by your communications once in a while we shall labor therewith to be contented. Sister Ruth says, "We do not feel as though we could ever bear to part with Mother," and we feel so too, and it is our desire and prayer that Mother might be blessed with health and long life for the good and comfort of her dear children far and near.

We was very sorry to hear of the sufferings and death of Mother Hannah, knowing that her dear children must feel great grief to part with their precious Mother.[2] Oh, do keep our dear Mother as long as ever you can; an hundred years will not be more than half long enough, as she will still be getting more children and they will all want her to live as long as they do. Sometimes the young Believers here ask me how Mother looks? And I tell them that she is the prettiest woman they ever saw with their eyes, and that will make them laugh and say, "Oh, how I wish that I could see her here!" O my good and faithful sister, I thank you very kindly for your pretty information and want you to be so kind as to thank my kind Mother and Elder Abiather too for their union with it. Oh, how I wish I could take a look at that old hive once more where I have eat so much honey, but I don't care so much about seeing the old hive as I do about seeing the bees that are in it and getting the honey.

My best love and remembrance together with Sister Mercy's I send to our ever blessed Mother and to her lovely children who are with her.

Elder Benjammin and Brother Joseph desires that their best love and remembrance might have a place in this little letter too.

A kind farewell

From Molly

P.S. Sister Ruth—I feel much pleased to hear that Mother wears thin caps in warm weather, for I have felt much need of them in this warm country and have worn them some but have felt straitened, but now feel released in the matter. The little pattern you sent me in your letter, I take to be the same kind of cloth Mother wears in warm weather and the exact pattern of the strap of her cap, though no mention was made about it.

Now Sister Ruth, I have got something else to ask for! The next letter you write to me, I want you to be so kind as to cut the paper just in the shape of Mother's cap pattern and write on that, and then I shall get a letter and a cap pattern all in one—Oh, do let me think, there is one thing more. How I do wish I could get one of Mother's pretty caps already made up and folded in a letter! I would be willing to pay two whole round silver dollars postage any time for such a letter.[3]

I am very sorry to hear that Eldress Anna [Cogswell] still continues to be so feeble. I remember she used to be very weakly and I did not expect she would live as long as she has. I should be glad to hear more about her when it is convenient. I remember Sister Elizabeth [Goodrich] used to be very weakly, and I do not recollect as I have heard one word about her since I left New Lebanon.

Molly

NOTES

1. Source: OClWHi IV A 60.
2. Hannah Kendall, ministry eldress of the Harvard and Shirley communities, died August 18, 1816. She was the original Mother of these communities, appointed shortly after Ann Lee's death to help with the gathering of scattered Believers in the Harvard, Massachusetts, area.
3. At this time the recipient of the letter paid the postage charge.

Letter 11. "Dear Sisters Molly and Mercy, I cannot communicate to you with my pen Mother's appearance at that time." Elizabeth Goodrich, Second Order, Watervliet, to Molly Goodrich and Mercy Pickett, South Union, September 21, 1817.[1]

> [Elizabeth Goodrich,[2] another natural sister of Molly Goodrich, writes her a lengthy letter describing some of Mother Lucy's gifts, her own experience of miraculous healing by Lucy Wright, and a recent visit to the Watervliet community by the President of the United States, James Monroe.]

Beloved Eldress Molly and Sister Mercy,

As the great distance between Watervliet and Jasper[3] renders it difficult for us to have much correspondence together, we feel the more anxious to hear of your welfare, of your increase and prosperity in that land. And we believe also that it must be a consolation to you once in a while to hear from the Church and people of God in your native country. And we think it will be agreeable to you to hear from our ever blessed Mother (Lucy) and kind Sister Ruth as anything we can say.

Our ever faithful Mother visits us as often as when you lived in the Church. She always comes with an increase of the power and wisdom of God, which is very refreshing to our souls. Mother administered a very precious gift not long since to all her children, which was for us to walk so upright and to be so watchful in all our goings forth, as neither to give offense nor take offense. She said if we kept this gift we would be on Christian ground and would be in safety, but if we did not keep it we would get on the enemy's ground and be in a dangerous situation. This gift brings great peace and comfort to all who keep it.

Eldress Molly, we find the way of God grows very strait but none too strait for good Believers. When Mother was here in July, she came into our meeting on the Sabbath afternoon and appeared to be filled with the power and glory of God and spake these words: "When I set out to obey the gospel, I set out a free soul, and I have remained free ever since." She walked back and forth between the brethren and sisters and spoke to some in particular as she walked.

Dear Sisters Molly and Mercy, I cannot communicate to you with my pen Mother's appearance at that time. But so far as I can say, she appeared to be free from everything that obstructed her union and communion with God and angels. Could you have seen Mother at this time, you would have had a feast that would have satisfied you for some time. But as your calling deprives you of those personal interviews with the ministry which we are blest with, I think it must be very comforting to hear and sense how heavenly and refreshing such privileges are to us. Notwithstanding, we feel no disposition to boast, but feel great cause of gratitude to God that our lot has fallen where we can enjoy these blessings.

Dear sisters, we often think of you in a distant land, how you are deprived of seeing our ever blessed Parent, Elder Abiathar and Eldress Ruth, when we so often enjoy that blessing. I fear many times that we are not so thankful to God as would become those who enjoy such repeated blessings. Dear sisters, we remember you in our prayers to God. Our Parents teaches us to pray for the people of God in the western country, that they may be able to do the will of God in all things, that God's blessing and protection may ever be with them, that they may be able to honor the gospel in a distant land. We know you must have great tribulation and suffering to pass through; we pray God to give you patience, wisdom, and strength according to your day. We believe it to be our privilege and duty to pray for one another.

We feel at this time very thankful and happy to inform you that the ministry are in a comfortable state of health notwithstanding the great labor they have continually upon them. You would be surprised to see with what fortitude and presence of mind our blessed Mother appears under every circumstance she has to pass through; and our desire and prayer to God is that He would lengthen out her days and years for the strength and consolation of all her children.

Now Eldress Molly, I think it will be agreeable to your feelings to hear of my situation, where I live, etc. I now live at the Second Order, what used to be called the Second Family, or formerly the elderly people, but at this time they may more properly be termed a family of youngerly people, although there are a number of aged people in the family. Yet there are twenty-one young brethren and sisters between nine and thirty years of age. The whole number of our family, both brethren and sisters, is forty.

Levi Pease, David Hawkins, are the elder brethren; Prudence Spencer and myself are the elder sisters in the family. I came to live with Prudence the 16th of May 1815. Previous to my coming, Mother sent for me to come to her shop and told me that I was needed at the Second Order, that I could do more good there than I could where I then lived. I felt reconciled to Mother's gift and willing to go where I could do the most good.

Now dear sister, I will inform you in relation to my health and how it has been with me for several years past. Near the first of August 1807, I was taken with such a violent pain in my right arm between my shoulder and elbow that within the space of two days I was entirely deprived of the use of it and it continued useless for three years and had frequent turns of convulsions attended with such violent turns of shaking that no one was able to hold my arm still. Sister Molly, it was in such extreme pain during this period that I could not feel comfortable in any situation whatever, although every effort was made to relieve my distress and every necessary aid that was within the power of my attendants was administered, yet it was without effect. After living about three years in this distressed situation, my left arm was taken much like the other, and within three days I had not an arm to help myself with. Now sister, you may be sure this was a trying scene to me to think of living so, for I could not raise either of my arms out of my lap for six weeks, after which time I began to move my fingers a little. I continued to gain slowly from that time. While in this situation you may depend that I felt like an object of pity, and I believe all the brethren and sisters pitied me from their heart. Everyone seemed to try to do something to relieve my affliction. One day Mother came into the room where I was and spake these words: "Elizabeth, your arms will get well; you will yet get so well that you will be able to cook for me." From that time I had the fullest faith that I should recover.

Now Sister Molly, Mother's words have been verified, for I have had the privilege of cooking for the ministry about three years since I recovered. I can do almost any kind of work if I am temperate. Now I want to tell you that my only interest is in the gospel, and that my union and relation with my blessed Parents, my good elders, and my good brethren and sisters is my only treasure. And what more could I desire but a thankful heart to God for so great a blessing?

I think I will stop talking about myself and tell you a little story about the President of the United States. He has made a short visit among the Believers at New Enfield while on his route from the eastern, the northern, and western lakes. Elder Nathaniel [Deming] and his order were at that time at New Enfield on a visit. Arrangements were made by the ministry previous to the President's arrival, and Daniel Goodrich was appointed to go and meet him and conduct him to their settlement. When he arrived, Daniel made him welcome. He alighted from his carriage and was conducted to the dwelling house. Father Job [Bishop], Mother Hannah [Goodrich] and all the elders, brethren and sisters, were assembled in the meeting room, about seventy in number. Chairs being placed, the President and his aides took seats. He asked after their health and was very free in conversation and appeared to have a desire for their prosperity.

After some conversation, he was invited to walk into the garden. He accepted the invitation and rose together with the bishops,[4] elders, deacons, brethren, and sisters and walked through the garden, the brethren taking one alley and the sisters the other until they came to the head of the garden, where the sisters wheeled and changed alleys. Then all marched back, the sisters walking a little before the brethren, while about 100 spectators from the adjacent places stood with their hats under their arms viewing the procession. The President had designed to go into their machine shop and take a view of their mechanical work, but on his return from the garden one of his attendants informed him that the time had expired which was allotted for their stay at that place and that they must be on their journey in order to fulfil their appointments. The President then addressed the Believers apparently in an affectionate manner and said he was sincerely sorry that he could not spend more time with them. He also desired that the blessing of God might rest upon them, and then he took his leave, etc.

It is a general time of health with but few exceptions. Eldress Molly, we can inform you with pleasure that we are once more blessed with a visit from the ministry, yea, they are now with us and desire that their love may be conveyed in this letter to the elders, deacons, brethren, and sisters at Jasper. Also, the elders, deacons, brethren, and sisters of the First Order, together with the brethren and sisters of our family, [who] unitedly desire that their love may be conveyed with the love of the ministry, to the elders, brethren, and sisters at South Union with their desires for your increase, strength, and prosperity in the way of God.

Farewell. Be so kind as to write to us as soon as may be convenient. We want to hear from you very much.

Elizabeth Goodrich

NOTES

1. Source: OClWHi IV B 35.
2. Elder Sister Elizabeth Goodrich died at Watervliet in January 1818, at the age of forty-two, only a few months after writing this letter.
3. Jasper was the original name of the South Union Settlement.

4. Bishops are those Shaker leaders who functioned as the lead ministry for several communities at once, such as the Hancock and Shirley, Massachusetts, and Enfield, Connecticut, communities.

Letter 12. "Nobody left at home but us two poor little sisters." Molly Goodrich, South Union, to Archibald Meacham, West Union, Indiana, May 22, 1818.[1]

[Molly Goodrich responds to the West Union community's request for the help of the South Union brethren, in Benjamin's absence. She writes firmly but diplomatically to Elder Archibald Meacham that no one is presently available to help the West Union community with its brickmaking.]

Beloved Elder Archibald and those with thee,

We received your letter dated April 8th a few days ago, and we were very thankful to hear from you and that you were all in usual health and prosperity. We concluded by your letter that you had not received Elder Benjamin's last letter to you, we think it was dated about the last of March, informing you that he was going to start a journey for New Lebanon shortly—and accordingly he did; on the 7th of April he left South Union and started to Pleasant Hill, and he left Pleasant Hill on the 13th inst. in company with Father John and Elder Comstock for New Lebanon. And now beloved elders, you will see by this letter that Elder Benjamin is not here, and we do not expect to see him till sometime next fall.

Now in relation to Elder Archibald's request that one of the brethren would come to West Union and assist about making brick, it appears very difficult at this time as Elder Benjamin is gone and we cannot feel as though any of the brethren here would be suitable to go for that purpose, considering all things, except John McComb. And as he has the charge of a family and a great deal depends on him, it appears difficult to spare him at this critical time without a great deal of loss. We are very sorry, you may be sure, to disappoint you, for it has always been a pleasure to us to oblige you whenever we had it in our power. The brethren have a very heavy job on hands this season. They have began to build a mill on Drake's Creek. Doubtless Elder Issachar remembers where it is. And if they don't get it started before the waters rise next winter, they will be in a proper bad fix, hardly able to save themselves from sinking. They have not been able to do a stroke of work to the meeting house since Elder Issachar [Bates] was here, and we don't expect they will till next July. So you see a little of their situation. But all this would not hinder a brother going to assist you, was any of them able excepting the one we have mentioned. We well remember that Elder Benjamin gave Elder Issachar encouragement of assistance about brickmaking when he was here, but he little thought then that he would be gone this summer.

Now kind elders, what more shall we say? We will only add how sorry we are that you could not see Elder Benjamin before he went home to see Mother. I don't know but we mentioned it twenty times and said, "Oh, how disappointed Eldress Martha [Sanford] will be," but it was out of our power to let you know it, for after he received Mother's letter, he started in three weeks.

We are in usual health and common prosperity with few exceptions. We are getting along as well as we can, but you may be sure we feel lonesome: Elder Benjamin is gone and Elder Joseph [Allen] goes to Drake's Creek to assist about the mill very often and nobody left at home but us two poor little sisters. And now we think you will pity us a little. The day we wrote this letter Frederick Rapp arrived here from Harmony.[2] We gave the letter into his hands to carry as far as their own post office, if he had no other opportunity to convey it to you. We hope you will receive it safe and we would be glad if you would be so kind as to write to us shortly after you receive this.

Receive with these few lines our best and dear remembrance. Elder Issachar, I have enclosed to you the little farewell hymn which was composed when Elder Benjamin started his journey, as I thought you would like to hear it.

So kindly farewell,

From Molly and company

NOTES

1. Source: OClWHi IV B 19, 173.
2. The "Harmonian" (Harmonist) Society was a celibate religious community originally founded in 1805 by the German nonconformist preacher George Rapp, in Pennsylvania. The Harmonists moved to the Wabash Valley in Indiana in June 1814 and created the town of Harmony (later sold to Robert Owen, in 1824). In 1825, the Harmonists, or Rappites, moved to Economy, Pennsylvania, near Pittsburgh (Charles Nordhoff, *The Communistic Societies of the United States*, 63–95).

Letter 13. "Anna and Polly go there sometimes and see good Mother and Sister Ruth." Anna Cogswell, New Lebanon North House, to Molly Goodrich, South Union, June 14, 1818.[1]

[In a spritely and detailed long letter, Anna
Cogswell portrays her own life as the busy
eldress responsible for recent converts at New
Lebanon and describes the rooms and work life
of Lucy Wright and Ruth Landon.]

Beloved Eldress Molly,

Twelve years have now passed since we have seen each other's visible
appearance, and during all this time I have never found that our spirits
have been separated nor our union broken; and by the late arrival of some
distant visitors, I find that our union has rather increased. In what little I
have had of conversing with Elder Benjamin, I have taken the liberty to ask
a great many questions about thee, my dear sister, and I think you have
passed through considerable, to be sure, since you have seen little Anna,
and perhaps a considerable part of your experience was not exactly your
own choosing. But be that as it may, if I should undertake to pity you now
and feel very sorry, I could not alter it, and then again I do not suppose
that it is your wish to have the different scenes recalled to memory. Perhaps
as I have heard a little about my Sister Molly, she will be wanting to ask
how Anna gets along, and what is her occupation? I think if I could be
with you about six weeks and talk all the time steady I could tell you a
little about it, but a few lines I can here state if you think them worth
reading.

I have lived at the North House four years last March[2] (which I think
will be full far enough back to tell about) and since I have lived here I have
enough to do, I can assure you, to keep me out of idleness. There are
generally about eighty-eight persons in our family who are most all young
people and need not a little attention; and we have generally more or less
company either of the world or Believers which makes some labor.

We have another family of about twenty members at the Mill place, but
there are three of the old Believers there, viz. Jeremiah Talcott, Phebe Smith,
and Anna Davis, who take a great burden off of us in being helps. But we
go and visit them once in a while, and as we come along up the hill there
is another small family, fifteen in number, where we have to stay a spell,
walk around and talk, etc. James Farnham and Deborah Woodworth has
the care of this family and are also helps to go journeys, etc. We come
home and get a little rest (sometimes), in a few days go down to the Patterson house and see some young Believers there.

Not long before something breaks out at the old Darrow House[3] among
some that are believing there and some that don't know much about it.
Then we get up old Dick and the little wagon and I drive it myself and go
and see them, and when this is done, all our order is visited and poor
Anna, who is rather feeble, gets tired. Scarcely has she got rested before

it is time for somebody to go on the tiptop of the mountains to see some young Believers there, but as yet I have not had quite fat enough on my bones to go pounding over the stumps in a wagon; this generally falls to poor Polly. I went there last February in a sleigh when the snow was about four feet deep upon a level or thereabouts, so that we went riding about the lots to shun the snow banks, and we often rode over the tops of the fences and stone walls. We melted snow to get water to drink and after we got a pailful thawed and set it down in the corner, it would there freeze again. The family where we stayed mostly being rather poor on it for knives, the same knife they stirred their victuals with when cooking often fell to my lot to eat without being washed, and not a little of whatever was cooked froze on to the blade; whether it was pudding, turnips, or onions, it made no difference to me as long as it there stuck. However, my appetite being rather poor I had not so much use for a knife as if it had been better.

But to tell a little more, we go about from house to house and try to do what little good we can, have meetings, etc. Then on our way home, we stop in Cheshire and see a very few Believers, but what there is are very good and clever and are wealthy people and give us good refreshment and good clean beds to sleep in, have a little meeting with them. From fifty to 300 spectators attend, a great deal of singing to be done here, always sing, sing, till our throats are parched dry. The next day we leave them and come home.

One time we went there on purpose to have a meeting, having repeatedly been requested by the world's people. Accordingly Elder Ebenezer, Brother Calvin, Sister Polly and myself, and two young sisters that used to live there went over and appointed a meeting at Benjamin Brown's, a young Believer, Lucy Bennett's nephew. But the world, fearing we would be crowded, desired us to hold our meeting in a large upper room in a store about two miles distant. We consented and went to the place appointed. When we got there, we discovered their intention, for the room we found was a ball chamber, and they had cleaned the floor very clean, sanded it and strung laurels and ground pine over head, expecting to be sure that we would dance. There was about 600 people attended, and after their hearing about three hours sound doctrine, meeting was dismissed without any dancing, which greatly disappointed them.[4]

Dear sister, I believe you are tired by this time. Be patient, I am most through. We have, besides these young Believers mentioned, a few scattering ones that we labor to strengthen by writing them short epistles. Some of them are in Wilmington, Vermont, fifty miles off, and a half dozen more in Saybrook, Connecticut, 110 miles off—pretty ones too if the wolves have not got them by this time. Besides attend[ing] to what I have mentioned I get some time to work. I spin, knit, and sew, make a great many shirts, caps, etc.

Now by this time, Eldress Molly, you will begin to think, "If Anna is in the 'good old hive'," as you expressed in your letter, "she has a little to do of what I have had a great deal of since I came to Ohio and Kentucky." But dear sister, do you call poor little Anna in the old hive, when she is flying about with a young swarm? Dear, nay. It is true I am near the place, so I can go there once in a while and see the good old bees, how busy, peaceable and happy they live. But the best of it all is to go and see the clean little cell, which is neater than wax in the midst of the beehive. Did you ever see it, Molly? I shall expect you to answer me in your next letter. I mean where our pretty Mother works and where pretty Sister Ruth works and in the other room where Elder Abiathar works. Eldress Molly and Sister Mercy, was you ever there? Why then I will [show?] you.—

Anna and Polly go there sometimes and see good Mother and Sister Ruth. Sometimes they are at work making shirts, sometimes making pillow cases, sometimes knitting, and Mother hems a great heap of pocket handkerchief[s] and sister makes a good many caps, and a great deal more work they do. Their shop always looks neat and clean as anything can. The floor is narrow boards, not the head of a nail to be seen, and it shines like a mahogany table that has just been waxed and rubbed. The wall is very white, and the stove is smooth and the hearth scoured bright and swept clean and everything looks as nice as you can think. Sometimes we stay half the afternoon, and Saloma comes in with a little pitcher of tea and some good home victuals such as pie, cake, biscuit, or bread and butter, etc., and sits it on Mother's table and we eat right there in Mother's room. Sometimes Mother gives us some fruit, sometimes some dried plums that little Polly Billing has fixed for her. And what is the very best of all she gives us is, when we need it she gives us a good whipping,[5] and then we can step home spry!

Now Eldress Molly, [I?] believe in your whole packet of letters you will say this letter is the worst of all. And we cannot blame [you] for saying so. But we suppose that Elder Benjamin will have matters of so much [more] importance than our trifling affairs that he will hardly mention us. However, we perceive that you still thought of us by the presents, the pretty little bottle you sent me, which was wrapped up so careful that not one drop had leaked out, and the little satchel that you sent to Polly (of which I suppose she will have something to say). And in return as a token of my love and remembrance, I have sent Eldress Molly some cloth (I spun the filling for the cloth myself and have had it two years for a gown), a white pocket handkerchief, a tape needle, a hair pin, and a little tumbler of preserves. The little tumbler I bought myself in Boston almost three years ago and when you drink in it, perhaps you will sometimes think of your old friend and sister.

N.B. one tape needle is for Sister Mercy, and please to accept with these my best love.

N. B. From Anna one pocket handkerchief for Elder Benjamin.

P.S.[6] I think, Eldress Molly, that after Eldress Anna has written such a lengthy letter that I must take the liberty to fill up the postscript and try to explain something she has stated in hers about the little "satchel." Hannah Shapley came into our shop one day and gave Eldress Anna a little bunch rolled up in a white rag very curious and careful. She took it and began to rip off the things. I, being very anxious to see what was in it, began to take the things as they fell. First came off a piece of paper, then a little white rag, then the little satchel, which I told her then and there was mine—but nay she could not spare it because it came from Molly. Well, then she took off another rag while Hannah and I sat laughing to see it go on. By this time we spied some cotton and began to tell her that Eldress Molly had sent her pod of cotton to show the productions of the country. But while we were there thus talking, we spied a little brown thing, which we concluded was a butterfly egg, and began to laugh very heartily. But she still kept ripping till out come a little bottle safe and sound, which pleased all very much. But neither the bottle nor the satchel could I get, although I begged very hard; but the rags and the cotton and the leather bag she very freely gave me, and thus I remained till about a week after she received her letter from Eldress Molly. She began to read along and I began to find that my dear Eldress Molly did remember me too. "There," said I, "I knew the little satchel was mine." "Well," says she, "if you will wait till morning you shall have the little nasty thing." And now, Eldress Molly, I kindly thank you for it. I think it is quite as pretty as the bottle, and especially it made me feel so nice because [you] did remember little Polly too. And now as a token of my love and esteem I have for Eldress Molly made her a new cap, a checked handkerchief, and sent a little block of silk to do the nice work on your cotton and worsted gown. The little block Elder Abiathar whittled out. And I have sent a hair pin to Sister Mercy. Please to accept of my best love and sincere good wishes.

Polly Billing

N.B. The cap was cut exact by Eldress Anna's pattern. I should like to hear if it fitted.

From little Polly

NOTES

1. Source: OClWHi IV B 19.
2. Anna Cogswell had been one of the New Lebanon North Family elders since 1814, along with Ebenezer Bishop, Calvin Green, and Polly Lawrence.
3. David Darrow's original farmhouse in New Lebanon was used by the New Lebanon Gathering Order as one of the smaller out-family houses.

4. Apparently the Shakers refused to satisfy the idle curiosity of the non-Shaker "world," about their famous dancing.
5. "Whipping" is meant metaphorically and humorously; a tongue-lashing.
6. Polly Billing is the author of the postscript, according to this text.

Letter 14. "I wish you would just step over the mountains into Kentucky." Molly Goodrich, South Union, to Calvin Green, New Lebanon, November 22, 1818.[1]

[Molly Goodrich congratulates New Lebanon North Family elder Calvin Green on the recent growth of Shakerism in the East. She emphasizes the greater difficulty of implanting Shaker life in the slave state of Kentucky, where "the air" is "impregnated with that careless, idle, indifferent spirit which is imbibed into creatures through that sense of slavery."]

Beloved Brother Calvin,

I received your long letter so full of intelligence by Elder Benjamin, and you may be sure I was very thankful for it. I know it has been a long time since we conversed together either by tongue or pen, but be assured, dear brother, I have not forgotten that we were once acquainted and had a good deal of gospel union. I never can forget my good companions in the gospel, whom I was raised with from my childhood, for they feel very near and dear to me. And although we are separated so far distant in body, yet that precious union which we gained in the spirit will abide forever. It would be very satisfying to me to see the pretty faces of all my good old friends once more in this life and to enjoy their sweet company. But for the gospel's sake I feel resigned to bear the present separation, on the conditions of our blessed Mother's will and pleasure and my interest with her faithful children.

O my brother, do you know what a cross it is to be so far away from home as never to see it in thirteen years? Only think of this! How would you feel, if you knew you would not get to see your pretty Mother and dear brethren and sisters again in twelve or thirteen years and after all not even to know whether you would ever see them again in this world or not? Aye, aye, here is cross enough in good earnest! And I shall not pity poor Calvin as bad as I do poor Molly, until he has tried such a tour as this! Or at least half a tour, and then see if he don't think poor little me has got a heap the biggest cross. Now if you don't believe this, if you will just step over here in some of your evening walks, I think I can make you believe it without much trouble. But anyhow! Come and see us if you can.

Concerning the information you wrote in your letter about the number and increase of Believers since I left that country, I think it is very extraordinary [illegible] thankful and well pleased with the fruits of your labors. It appears as though you have been very busy in every respect, both spiritual and temporal. Elder Benjamin says you have, and I really believe it. He says I would hardly know the place or the people, but I think I should know the good old hive yet and the bees that are in it, at least a part of them. There may be some of the young swarm that I would not know immediately, but I would soon find them out if I only had the chance. It is really very satisfactory to hear you tell about gathering Believers here and there and almost everywhere, and especially about your new country, Savoy!² It is quite remarkable—also to hear Eldress Anna [Cogswell] tell about it too, it is very pleasing. She calls it the tiptop of the Green Mountains.³ Aye aye, many such a trip as that have I had since I crossed the Allegheny! But if I should undertake to relate my travels, it would be too long and tedious. Therefore I must omit it until I can see you face to face, and then perhaps I may tell you all about it. At present I do not go much abroad, but I stay mostly at home. And we are laboring to gather the oldest Believers in this place into some gift and order. My farthest visits among Believers is four miles off and sometimes fifteen from where we live. It is four years this fall since I have been a journey of any great distance.

Now dear brother, if you should happen to get out of business, I wish you would just step over the mountains into Kentucky and labor there about eight years, and then you would have a chance to know the difference between a free country and a slave country. You may be sure the difference is very great in almost every respect. It is a great deal harder to bring them to a sense of their duty and to really feel interested in things either spiritual or temporal, as the people of the East do! It seems sometimes as though the very air, so to speak, was impregnated with that careless, idle, indifferent spirit which is imbibed into creatures through that sense of slavery. It feels a heap harder to them to be really industrious, neat, and clean, and to be really subject and obedient to what they are taught.⁴ Considering these things, we can have more charity for the Believers here for they have good faith as a body and really love us a heap.

Now, Brother Calvin, you see my little letter is nearly at a close. And if you have tribulation to pass through, think of us away off yonder. And when you come to see us, we shall support a heap of union together, and I expect it will take us a long time to tell over our experience and travels. And what will crown it all will be the comfortable reflection that we have passed through all these various scenes with patience and fortitude. So I close my letter, full of love and good desires to all the elders in your order and to all the good young Believers as far as you feel a gift.

N.B. Give my kind love and thanks to Brother Jeremiah for the pretty little scallop shell he sent me, and also to Brother Richard Bushnell for those pretty combs.

Farewell from little Molly

NOTES

1. Source: OClWHi IV A 60.
2. The Savoy, Massachusetts, revival, which began in 1817, resulted first in a small "out" community there. Ultimately it brought eighty new members to move to New Lebanon.
3. This phrase is echoed from Anna Cogswell's own letter of June.
4. This refers to the white population of Kentucky, who had grown reliant on slave labor. (Molly Goodrich was not alone in expressing this view of the difficulty of teaching western-bred Shakers obedience to authority. Benjamin S. Youngs made the same point in a letter to New Lebanon in 1827, offering to resign and let the westerners try to govern themselves.)

Letter 15. "We have been learning the good ones to take care of the bad ones." Ruth Farrington, Union Village, Ohio, to Rachel Spencer, New Lebanon Church Family, April 21, 1819.[1]

> [Western lead ministry Eldress Ruth Farrington
> writes a long letter accompanying a gift of bon-
> nets for the New Lebanon ministry sisters and
> Church Family eldresses. Apologizing for her
> former silence, which she blames on her "lack
> of letter learning," she mixes information about
> the styles of the sisters' garments with news of
> the spiritual progress being made by the western
> sisters under her care.]

Kind Elder Sister Rachel,

I want to talk a little with thee at this time, yet I am so poor a hand to talk with my pen that I fear I shall make out but poorly; however, I will try to do as well as I can. It is now this day thirteen long years since I have seen thy face, but how many thousands of times I have thought of thee since I cannot tell. But I will tell thee what would be the most pleasing to me at present, that is only to have one privilege that thou hast enjoyed ever since I saw thee last—that is to see my precious good Mother's face once more in the body. Now Sister Rachel, thou cannot think how I have felt in all our trying labors for the want of that privilege that thou hast continually enjoyed—that is to see my Mother. But as I cannot have so great a blessing as that I must content myself by doing my duty as faithfully as I can and hope my Mother will accept me in so doing.

Now I want to talk a great deal more and tell thee some of my feelings. I think I have kept my first faith and love, that is, to obey my elders in all things and keep myself pure from every wicked thing. In so doing I have kept my justification. I still remember the good counsel my pretty Mother gave me when I was coming to this country and have strove to keep it according to my little wisdom and understanding—that is to do to others as I would they should do to me. I think I have kept it.

Now I want to talk some more. Mother hath many children in this part of the globe that needs to be nursed continually. Some are strong, others are weak and sickly, for they keep coming in continually full of the flesh. So we make the strong ones take care of the weak ones and they are very charitable indeed for they do give bountiful to the weak ones that are poor that believe[2]—also to the world. And last year they sent us as much as 400 dollars worth in articles to West Union, such things as they could not get there. This spring they will send more than that to South Union. So I love them for their good works of charity and I want thee to love Mother's good children here as well as I do. We teach them the way to be good is to do good—is not that right? Now dear sister, I hope thou wilt not think I mention these things by way of boasting—by no means. I only do it that thee may see the fruits of Mother's gospel in this western land. I love all Mother's good obedient children wherever I have visited them in this part of the vineyard—and the vineyard is middling large thee may depend, so that it would weary thee stoutly to inspect every part of it and pull out all the evil weeds that are growing in it.

Now good sister, I want to talk a heap more about our little affairs here. So I think to begin first on our new fashion of bonnets, as thou knowest that we old Shaker women are always after some new fashions. We first began to make them for sun bonnets out of any kind of cloth or color that they had, and the sisters soon liked them so much better then the old manner that we now make all our bonnets after this plan or fashion.

We have sent one to each of the elder sisters in this country—they like them very well. Now we send six to thee (as we wanted to send something) that you might believe that we had not forgotten our good sisters in the East that hath been so very bountiful and charitable to us ever since we have been here—for which we always remember to give thanks to you all, for we know it is the fruits of Mother's gospel. Now if our pretty Mother will accept of one of these bonnets and Sister Ruth another we will be thankful. And if thee and Sister Olive will accept of two more we will also be thankful. The other two we should be glad that Eldress Dana and Sarah had. And we should be glad to know whether my precious Mother and all my pretty sisters there liked them or not. The color we do not like, as we should prefer a fur color better.

Now kind sister, I want to talk a little freely on some spiritual things, which is the most important of all to me. I want thee to tell my pretty Mother, Elder Abiathar and Sister Ruth, the elder brother and Brother Rufus and Sister Olive, Brother Samuel and Eliza, Sister Mary and Lucy, and all the rest of Mother's good children that we desire their prayers to God for us that we may finish our work in righteousness and true and faithful obedience to Mother's gospel, so as to be accepted at last. And as it hath been a long time since I have talked with thee and know not when I shall have another opportunity, I must talk freely at this time.

I understand Mother's gospel is love, that is to love Mother and all her faithful children. Now Mother hath many children here that claims a relation to her by faith, a number very good, and some dreadful bad. So we have aplenty of work to do all the time. But we have been learning the good ones to take care of the bad ones, to purge and separate the flesh from the spirit—this has taken off a great burden from us.

Now I want to tell thee one thing more—I do love Mother's young daughters here because they are filled with Mother's good spirit. They speak with new tongues[3] and are full of spiritual songs and lively in the works of God. Indeed they are zealous in every good work and obedient, so I say I love them and I believe Mother loveth them, and thee too and all Mother's good children in the East.

Sister Rachel, thou hast lived where the candle of the Lord and Mother hath continually shined upon thee ever since I saw thee last. I have been here in the wilderness, toting and travelling about in the mud thirteen years, so that I suppose it will be difficult for thee to understand my language now. As I told thee in the beginning, I was but a poor hand to talk with my pen, so I think I had better close with only a few lines more.

Now sister, is it impossible for me to tell thee with my pen all the trials and difficulties that we have had to surmount and travel through since we saw our good sisters in the East. But we have had our good wise Father [David Darrow] to lead and conduct us through so far. Had it not been for that I hardly know where we should [have] been by this time. And he keeps his strength remarkable and sometimes I think his power, wisdom, and gift increases. And we hope it will increase until the gospel is so established here that it can never fail or be overcome, world without end.

Sister Rachel, we feel well pleased with the new manner of caps. I think it a great improvement and thank thee kindly. Also we like the gowns, we like the cloaks, we like the aprons, we like the shoes, and kindly thank our good sisters for the whole. But we cut our aprons whole before and like them better. Now good sisters, I should be glad to know what ye call them: whether aprons or tires[4]—as we have received both names from our sisters in the East. We generally choose to call them aprons.

Now beloved sister, I must take my leave of thee for the present and close my lengthy discourse by sending abundance of love to everybody that loves Mother and will obey her. For my love hath increased, thee may depend, since I saw thee last, and I will tell thee how it runs if thou wilt be so kind as to deliver it. First of all, to my precious good Mother, Elder Abiathar, and Sister Ruth. Next to all the good elders, and lastly to everyone that will love and obey Mother's gospel. So, kindly farewell, sister, for the present. Written by the hand of thy good friend Ruth—and a lover of Mother's gospel.

P.S. Now sister, I will tell thee one thing more and then I must close lest I burden thee. The above scrables [scribbles?] I have wrote with three pens (with my own hand)—made and given to me before I left the Church—that I have kept safe till now. The name of the person that gave them I do forget. So sister, thee may judge by that that I have been very prudent of pens, ink, and paper since I have been here. And it has not been for the want of love to my good sisters in the East, thee may depend, but for the lack of letter learning.

Beloved Sister Rachel, I find I cannot put all the conversation I want to talk with thee about at this time on one sheet of paper. It is not half large enough—indeed it would fill a number of sheets—so I have concluded to tuck in this little scrap also.

Thee may remember that when Brother Peter came from the Church in 1812, that thee did send Father David a pretty little speckled snuff box full of excellent snuff. He has taken a pinch of it almost every morning since when he has been at home, and finds it helped his eyes and head according to thy direction. Now it is almost run out, so I send the pretty box back again by the hand that brought it and if thou will be so kind as to fill it again and send it to us, Father says he will pay thee for the whole, that is, in thankfulness, which is all the pay we have to give for all your goodness and charity to us. And we think it will be accepted.

Ruth

P.S. The little blue bag and ball in it is for my Mother. The two bonnets marked with "Sm" are the smallest size; the other four are of one size.[5] The reason why we made a part of the bonnets without linings is the sisters here likes them better so. I suppose you will say, "Who made these bonnets?" It was our little Sister Charlotte Morril that made these. She makes or sews rather the best. There is a great many sisters here that sews proper well—I think so. So farewell in love to thee and all the rest of my good friends in the gospel of Mother's dispensation or of God almighty in this day.

Sister Rachel, there is one thing more we would like to know, whether the sisters wear white gowns or not. Please to inform us when Brother Peter returns here again.

R

NOTES

1. Source: OClWHi IV A 69.
2. This refers to gifts sent from Union Village Believers to those in the struggling Kentucky and Indiana communities.
3. One of the rare indications in letters from this period that spontaneous spiritual gifts and ecstatic worship activity continued in the West.
4. This is spelled "tiers" here, which may indicate that its root is "tie."
5. This is my best guess at interpreting "the two Bonnets marked with—one em and Sm—are the smallest size the other four are of one size, etc., etc."

Letter 16. "You requested to know something about our gowns and tires." Rachel Spencer, New Lebanon Church Family, to Ruth Farrington, Union Village, Ohio, July 1819.[1]

> [Eldress Rachel Spencer passes on some of Lucy
> Wright's recently recorded sayings and gives in-
> formation about the clothing styles of the New
> Lebanon sisterhood.]

Beloved Mother Ruth,

I cordially received the kind interesting letter together with the pretty presents you sent by the hand of Brother Peter. I was thankful to hear from my good friend at this time. And oh, could I but see your lovely face once more in this world I would soon tell thee all about it and disclose my feelings much easier and quicker then it could possibly be done with pen and ink, but as this privilege cannot be granted I must content myself with writing a few lines to thee.

The time has felt very long since we were separated, but you have been often, yea, very often in my remembrance, and I shall never forget you nor the many happy days we have spent together. And I oftentimes think of you while I am enjoying this "greatest of all blessings," as you expressed it in your letter, which is to be with my precious Parent and continually enjoy her presence. This I do esteem to the greatest of all favors. But I do believe Mother can feel for all her faithful children and doth pour out her abundant blessings daily upon them wherever they be, whether at home or abroad, for her love and charity can never fail. She is endowed with wisdom and understanding. Now is it possible for me to express how beautiful and lovely she is? Her countenance glows with truth and grace, and she often addresses us with humility and meekness, and clothes her children with this beautiful garment of humiliation and says we must be little and simple in order to feel the gospel, that a great big spirit can never inherit the kingdom of God. And we must labor for a meek, humble spirit and not only labor for it but have it and always keep it to the end of our days. That if we are only little enough, we shall all find a place in the kingdom of heaven.

Sometimes Mother comes into our meetings and appears heavy and sorrowful and oftentimes weeps. And at other times she is so full of love and joy that she fills everyone with her lovely spirit. And now, my good sister, don't you think I can sense what a privilege I have here at the fountainhead right under my Mother's wings from day to day? That I can, yea, but I find I do not get free from the cross by my great privilege of coming the nearest to the foundation. Nay, quite the reverse, I have to come down to it and give up all my own ways and will and subject my self in every respect and perhaps find as much mortification, and feel as great a degree of tribulation in proportion as my privilege is greater.

And I can guess, too, something how you feel away over the other side of them great mountains almost a thousand miles off of Mother. I know indeed this must feel tough, to be sure, to any one to have to wade through tribulation and pass through all these heart-trying scenes year after year and then after all that not find any way to get to Mother to unbosom your grief—this must feel hard. I have thought of these things a great many times and how I should feel if I was in your place. But we have one thing to comfort ourselves with: after we have passed through all these trying scenes here below and finished the work we are called to do we shall receive that everlasting treasure which is laid up for the faithful.

I feel thankful to hear of the growth and increase of the gospel in that part of the vineyard and that Mother has got so many faithful sons and daughters growing and increasing in purity and holiness. And it is my fervent prayers and desires that the gospel may spread and increase until all souls may learn the way of truth and righteousness. But when the gospel net is spread it gathers in all, both good and bad, and then there has to be a separation between the precious and the vile. For none can abide but those who are faithful and honest-hearted.

There has been a considerable number set out to obey the gospel within a few years in this part of the vineyard. Some appear to be very good Believers, and a great many more have pretended that are after nothing but the loaves and fishes. But when they begin to feel the burning truth, they fall off like withered branches.

And now, my good sister, you told me what a sight of pretty children Mother has got away there in the West and what beautiful gifts they have, and how you loved them pretty children there and you wanted me to love them as well as you do. Now how shall I convince you that I do? For I suppose you think it would be almost imposible for me to feel so near a feeling as you can. But let that be as it may, I do love my precious good Mother, and so far as I have partook of Mother's love and abide in it, so far I love all that she loves. And I certainly do love all Mother's good faithful obedient children wherever they be and I know that my love increases daily to the way and work of God. Nor have I found any time to be idle since you left this place, but the further I progress in the way of God, the straiter I find it to be, and the more there is required of me. And Mother often tells us the way of God is always new, that it never grows old, that it will always grow brighter and brighter. And the further souls advance in it, the more and more beautiful and lovely it will appear to everyone that is faithful.

And now, my good sister, if you should only come back once more into the good old hive, I do not know as you would hardly know it, for there has been a great many alterations here since you left this place, and we have gathered in a considerable number of youth and children. And there has been a good many that lived here when you did that is now gone to their long homes. Our family at present consists of 108 members, and they are of all classes and all ages, from eighty-four down to seven years of age. And you may depend I find enough to do to keep me busy all the while. The number of Believers in this place and at Watervliet is estimated between 600 and 700, besides a number that has lately believed in other places round about that has not been gathered in as yet, some at Savoy, some in Wilmington, and a few at Saybrook. But how many will hold out to the end is very uncertain.

Now I think is time for me to change my discourse and say something about them pretty bonnets you sent us. Mother and Sister Ruth was much pleased with theirs, likewise Sister Olive and myself, for which we all unitedly send our kindest thanks. We thought they looked quite pretty and was made very neat. And we do not know but the sisters here will like them for sunbonnets when we have made sufficient trial of them. But as we have all got good silk bonnets made in uniform, we do not think it would be prudent to alter our fashion. Also Sister Ruth sends her thanks for the Harmonian cap Sister Hortency sent.[2] She was quite pleased with it; she showed it to all the sisters both in Lebanon and at Hancock, and we thought it was a curious odd thing. Some said they should not want to join the Harmonian Society for the sake of getting such caps to wear. And the most difficulty any of us found with it was in getting it put on right.

And in relation to clothing, you requested to know something about our gowns and tires. We have cut them straight before several years and it is immaterial to us what name they go by, whether tires or aprons, but we have called them tires in general. As to our summer gowns we wear light-colored striped for our uniform dress, the same we had when you lived here. And the families without the Church have white gowns for a uniform dress. They think they are easier to keep in order than striped would be, as they attend public meeting and travel in the mud and dust considerable and get them very dirty. They think they can wash and boil them and whiten them if needed, whereas they could not if they were blue and white.

And now, my kind sister, I think it is almost time for me to begin to draw to a close. But before I finish I must tell you one more pretty little story which I think will sweeten all the rest. The 30th of last May, Sabbath day P.M., between five and six o'clock, our pretty Mother, good Elder Abiathar, and kind Sister Ruth went all over the house, into every room where the brethren and sisters were supporting union. And Mother had in her hand a pretty oval box filled with maple sugar with two teaspoons in it. And she said, "Here is a box of sugar that Mother Ruth has sent me all the way from Ohio." And she bid us all to arise and eat, which we all accordingly did and gathered around her like a swarm of bees. Each one got as much as a teaspoon full, and I daresay there never was a swarm of bees extracted so much sweet at one time before. And you may be sure we ate this in remembrance of thee. Every countenance looked pleasant, every heart was filled with gratitude, and every tongue manifested thankfulness at this time. And we thought it was the nicest we had ever seen of the kind. Now we could all taste of the sweet that grew in Ohio, but what had made it still sweeter was because we received it through such pure clean hands. It felt more precious to us than mountains of gold, nor can kings or princes taste of such delicious fare. It was sweeter than the manna that the children of Israel feasted on, yea, or the shewbread that was reserved for the priests only.

Now as my paper is almost filled I think it is time for me to stop. And that is not all, I am some afraid I shall weary your patience. So I must close with sending my unfeigned love desiring that you would be so kind as to impart a good portion of it to Father David, Brother Solomon, and Sister Rachel, for I do love you all with that love which can never be erased through time nor through eternity.

N.B. I do not know but you will think strange that I have not wrote something in relation to dearly beloved Mother's sufferings.[3] But I concluded that Brother Peter would be able to give you a correct information, so I have passed over it in silence. But you may be assured I have had as much tribulation of late as my little vessel could hold.

NOTES

1. Source: OClWHi IV A 33.
2. The western Shakers had some friendly intercourse with the Harmonists (Rappites), as indicated by the sisterhood's copying their cap pattern and sending it on to New Lebanon.
3. Lucy Wright was ill at this time, but recovered and continued as active head of the Society until shortly before her death, February 7, 1821.

Letter 17. "It seemed as if the end of all things had come." Ruth Landon, New Lebanon, to Molly Goodrich, South Union, February 22, 1821.[1]

> [Ruth Landon, now first in the New Lebanon
> lead ministry sisterhood, writes a personal letter
> to Molly Goodrich about Lucy Wright's death
> and the succession of leadership in the New
> Lebanon lead ministry.]

Dearly beloved and much respected Eldress Molly,

Having fresh in remembrance that thou hast been a beloved child of our good Mother and one that I have always placed much confidence in, I feel to improve this opportunity to write a few lines to let you know a little how it has fared with me, while passing through those troubled waters that cast up so many rolling waves of tribulation.

I think sometimes, "If I could but see little Molly, how I should love to tell her how beautiful and how honorable our good Mother finished her work here below." But as that cannot be, you must try to be content with my illiterate scratching.

The first week she was confined in the meeting house she did appear to be very sick. We improved the time in conversing together about our gospel friends. I thought I had never felt so much comfort with her in so short a time before. Yet I believed the time was near at hand that she must leave us. Her sensation was bright, regular, and full of the gift of God. She did not appear to be broken in her understanding. When she was taken worse I gave her up to go to God. This felt very hard for me to do, you must believe. She appeared to be the most like a little sick lamb. When I perceived she was dying, I kneeled down by her bedside, wet her mouth. She placed her eyes on me and appeared to know me so long as she could see. O my dear sister, it is impossible for my tongue to say what I felt at the time, but I strove to be all the help I could be. I put her cap on her head, kissed her face, and wept aloud. It seemed as if the end of all things had come.

Mother is gone, what shall we do? Every good Believer felt borne down with tribulation, considering we have none forward of us in this world to help us. We must swim or sink and drown in our sorrows; these considerations caused all to cry to God to show mercy and protect us from evil. Remembering what Mother had taught us: if we kept a meek humble spirit, there would always be some way that God would make known his mind and will to us and we should find increasing light and blessing—but if we went to striving who should be the greatest, we would fall into confusion and distress and be like sheep scattered on the mountain and be destroyed by the unseen enemy.

Now it is with great satisfaction I inform you that we have been blessed with a good degree of peace and union. All appear to unite and bless Mother's appointment.[2] The people of God have all been very kind to me; they have blessed me and prayed to God for me, for which I feel thankful. I feel fully satisfied with my companions in the ministry, though I did not pick them for myself. I love them and believe they love me. They are good; they live to God, loving mercy and dealing justly. We live together in peace and union. And I can as really feel that Mother is with us as ever I could when she was here in the body. And evil has to pass by us; we mean to keep no room for it.

O my dear sister, I think I must begin to close my little letter, hoping my dear friend will remember when she reads it that I never had any letter learning to polish me. But I hope I have learned obedience to my faith.

One thing more I would mention. Elder Abiathar lives in Watervliet and is as comfortable as we can expect. He is a very old man of his years and is much broken in his understanding, yet he has always been faithful and true to the gospel.

Please accept these few lines and this cap of Mother's, with my never-failing love to thee.

Farewell, from

Mother's Ruth

NOTES

1. Source: OClWHi IV B 35. I have corrected the date of the manuscript copy (given as February 22, 1822). Wright died on February 7, 1821, and it seems very unlikely that Ruth Landon delayed a year in notifying Molly Goodrich.
2. Eldress Ruth is announcing that Lucy Wright's choice of successors (including herself) has been unanimously approved at New Lebanon.

Letter 18. "This is the room little Molly lives in and you are welcome here, my good sisters." Molly Goodrich, South Union, to Elizabeth Youngs and Ann Bowser, South House, Watervliet, November 2, 1822.[1]

> [Molly Goodrich gives an unusually detailed de-
> scription of the buildings and grounds at South
> Union, in the form of an imagined tour for the
> visiting Gathering Order eldresses from Water-
> vliet.]

Beloved and respected Sisters Elizabeth and Ann,

I received your pretty letter of July 18th and now return my kind and most hearty thanks for the abundance of precious love and good information it contained. No one could feel more rejoiced than I would once more to see and be in the embraces of my worthy and precious friend good Eldress Ruth—and many more of my choice and precious gospel friends in the East whom it would greatly rejoice my heart to see. . . .

Now as you wished to know a little about our meeting house, where it stands and which end I live in, I will tell you. If you will only step along down this way and keep on the course of them pretty smooth lines which Elder Benjamin has drawn on the little map till you get near the southwest corner, then I will go with you on to the top of one of our high nobs about a mile north from South Union. And then you will be able to see exactly where it stands and soon after to know what end I live in. But most likely you are too much engaged on the east side of the mountain to come over them all, however smooth the road may appear. But still, you wish to know how I am situated and this I will now tell you, so that you may know how to find me, at least in spirit, and in what end of the meeting house I live in and where it stands.

For about sixty miles before you get to South Union you come over extensive plains called barrens and in places pretty thickly settled, the general course coming from the northeast toward the southwest. The main street at South Union through which the great public road passes is due east and west for about a mile. When you are very near to South Union you pass through a grove of timbered land, and coming on to some rising ground just past this spot of woods, you at once have a view of South Union (though not of all of it, because of little groves and rows of trees which look as if they might have been planted).

Now you are at the east end of the street or straight road leading due west for about a mile, and you are about three quarters of a mile from the meeting house. While you are on this little rising ground, you begin first to discover an extensive open space of large cultivated fields, both to the right and left, reaching about a mile from the north on your right and the south on your left. A little before you on very level ground you discover to your right hand a cluster of ordinary buildings about eight or ten rods from the road. And a little forward between the road and buildings is a circle of large trees surrounding a spring of water in the form of a basin about as large as your new house.

You are now half a mile from the meeting house. Passing on a little further, you discover on your left hand another cluster of buildings in a grove and at eighteen or twenty rods distant from the road, and some of them near the road, and among the latter a new brick house which the young Believers are building. (To the right and left thus far is all occupied by the young Believers.)

Coming on you discover away forward and off to the right hand and across the fields another cluster of buildings something like a little village by itself. This is the North Family. And before you on the right hand is a large garden and a brick house. This is the First Family. It is here, and not before (owing to the row of trees on the south side of the road), that you come in full view of the meeting house, and you are right at it at once. . . .

Now, step on the walk and come into the yard at the west gate, then come round to the west end of the house, walk up the steps. Here is the door. Come, walk in my friends; here's an entry—now walk upstairs toward the north. . . . There stop and look.

On your left hand is a door leading into the dining room which stands on the middle of the floor. On the other side is a passage and door just like this. Now step five or six steps further and you come into a considerably spacious hall, leaving the dining room just behind you at your left. Immediately before you, in the southwest corner of the hall, you see a small room taken off about ten feet square, but you see no door as yet into this little room. To your right hand is a door; come, let us go in here. This is the west end of the house and the southwest corner room. This is the room little Molly lives in, and you are welcome here, my good sisters, yea, welcome a thousand times.

See here, on the east side of the room, between the door we just came in at and the wall, is the door into the little room we have just seen in the hall—this is my clothes room. It has a window from the south. In the northeast corner of the room behind the door you came in at is another door—this leads into a large clothes room which is between this room and the front room. And at the north corner of the front room is a door into a little convenient closet, immediately over the platform of the stairs as you came up. The other end of the house is exactly like this. The dining room is twelve by sixteen feet. It has two windows (one on each end) which borrows light from opposite windows, and that gives light aplenty.

Now let us look out of the window toward the west. To your right hand across the street is a framed house containing about seventy-five persons. This is a part of the First Family belonging to the brick house before mentioned. Between this frame house and the brick house is where the large brick house (dwelling) is on hand and right opposite the meeting house. Now look past the framed house toward the northwest, about 100 yards, and you see away through the trees a cluster of log buildings. This is the office. It stands a little off from the road. And beyond this again, if you look narrowly between the tops of the trees about 300 yards further, you see water. This is Jasper Spring, where our mills and machinery stands.

Now let us look a little straight forward on this side of the road, and there is a garden close by. It belongs to the framed house family. It runs from the road toward the south. Just beyond the garden and toward the southwest you see a large young orchard or about 1000 trees just beginning to bear. Toward the middle of this orchard is a Connecticut Greening and a Spritzenburger and Bow apple from Niskeyuna. This last apple they call Eldress Molly's apple and what they call the other two, as they came from the East, you may easily guess.[2]

Now come, let us go to the south window of my room. On the back or south side of the meeting house, besides the meeting lot, you see a strip of garden ground. This has in it early lettuce, strawberries, medical herbs and grass seeds of various kinds, and beyond this you see a vineyard of about an acre from which we procure some wine. Beyond this vineyard and directly south you see a patch of cotton, and beyond this is our grave-yard. Every funeral we can plainly see the brethren and sisters as they go and come from this south window.

Now, my good sisters in the gospel, I have conducted you and shown you everything consistently within my reach. Now I must suppose you are tired by this time. Come, let us sit down and rest and smoke a pipe of union[3] and talk about any little thing you wish to know. If I mistake not, you asked about our health. I will tell you we are in as good health as we could reasonably look for, although I am rather weakly. Yet I generally keep about pretty spry. Elder Benjamin looks quite well and hearty to what he did before he went home to the East. And it seems that he sucked and eat so much sweet milk, cream, butter, and honey and everything else that was good, that he has been fattening ever since.

And now, my dear sisters, don't you think that poor little Molly ought to have a privilege to go home and suck some too? And Sister Elizabeth, if you will be my friend and intercede for me the next time you see Eldress Ruth and Sister Asenath and get a privilege for me to go home and see all my good friends once more, I promise you that I will love you so long as I live and forever afterward.

Now here sits good Sister Mercy along with us, and she says she wants [to] go home too, for she is getting in years almost fifty-two years of age, and she is afraid if she don't go home before long, that she never will get to see her good old friends in this life; for she wishes a thousand times that she might once more enjoy their company. . . .

Now, dear sisters, what shall we talk about next, as we expect you feel your visit nearly out and would wish to be returning home? Now I will tell you if you will only get my little request granted, I expect that my kind elders at New Lebanon whom I used to be so well acquainted with, viz. Elder Sister Rachel and my pretty Sister Olive together with the union of my good friend Elder Brother John and my dear friend and Brother David, that they will let me go to Watervliet and pay you a visit.

N.B. Now, Sister Elizabeth, you see my paper is nearly full, and if you have got any satisfaction by opening your mind to me, I shall be very thankful. And you need not be troubled with Elder Benjamin's apologies at this time, but he thinks if you are not troubled with his long letters all will be well. And besides all this, if we can only have the satisfaction to hear that you have received our letters and that they have been no burden to you, we shall not feel troubled, but on the contrary we shall feel more than satisfied.

So I close with much love and kind farewell,

This from your friend Molly Goodrich

Enclosed are two little songs composed by some of our children here. They are a present from Sister Mercy with her kind love and remembrance of her visit with her friends at Watervliet fourteen years ago. One is a quick song.

Mercy

NOTES

1. Source: OClWHi IV B 19.
2. This seems to refer to the fact that different members of the South Union ministry had brought apple seeds or grafts from eastern communities, including Watervliet (formerly Niskeyuna) and perhaps Hancock, Massachusetts, and Enfield, Connecticut. As she is writing to Elizabeth Youngs, Goodrich may perhaps be alluding to one or more of the "other" apple trees as Benjamin S. Youngs's.
3. "Smoke a pipe of union" refers to the custom of Shaker "union meetings" of smoking together. Sisters as well as brethren smoked tobacco in pipes in the early years of Shakerism. Tobacco was one of the items prohibited by spirit message at New Lebanon in the 1840s.

Letter 19. "As to my lameness and all my other infirmities, they have fled away together." Elizabeth Youngs, Second Order, Watervliet, to Molly Goodrich, South Union, January 26, 1829.[1]

> [Elizabeth Youngs, now retired from the elder-
> ship, writes to Molly Goodrich about her "gift
> of healing" at the hands of New Lebanon lead
> ministry eldress Ruth Landon.]

Dearly beloved Eldress Molly,

With much pleasure I have taken my pen in hand to answer your very kind and pretty letter which I received dated December 13th, 1827. It came safe to hand the same month. You must be assured, Eldress Molly, the information you had the goodness and freedom to send to us were very acceptable and thankfully received. We were thankful to hear that you had a prosperous journey and was protected by kind heaven till you arrived safe to your destined home;[2] we were glad to hear that the brethren and sisters had been faithful to keep the word of God in your absence. You may be assured, Eldress Molly, that we were not a little comforted, for we feel deeply interested in your welfare.

The beautiful hymn the brethren and sisters sung on their bended knees I believe was very solemn and heavenly. Dearly loved Eldress Molly, did you feel as though I had forgotten you? Or that I had no remembrance of Elder Benjamin, my best of gospel friends? Nay, Eldress Molly, you did not believe this to be the case. For not many days or hours have passed since the moment I saw Elder Benjamin and you last, but you have been fresh in my memory. Your very free, kind and loving visit with us at the South House has left a near and dear impression on my mind that time nor distance can never erase.

I know you had reason to feel as though I had slighted your kind request, which was that I should inform you in relation to my health as soon as convenient. But the way has never been opened till now for me to write.

Now if you will only be so kind as to forgive me this time, I will certainly do better in future. But, Eldress Molly, if you do not feel as though you could forgive me, I will write to Elder Benjamin and I really believe that he will.

My health continued to fail after you left us till I felt myself unable to bear so great a burden. I felt interested in the work of God and that the one who was chosen to stand in the door ought to be able to stand the storms by day and by night and to be able in body and spirit to do their duty to God, to their own souls, and to their brethren and sisters. Finding no way for me to gain my health, I felt a gift to pray to God as earnest as ever I did in my life, that I might be released in some way agreeable to his will, and I believe the Lord heard me. After the ministry had borne with me longer than I could reasonably have expected, they felt a gift for me to retire to my former home, the Second Order. I moved September 16th, 1827.

But my change made no alteration for the better till the month of May 1828. Our beloved ministry were on a visit at Watervliet. Eldress Ruth felt a gift to visit me, and a blessed visit it was, for she had a special gift of God to raise me from death unto life, yea, she had a healing gift for me and I received the resurrection power of life from her. I felt in a few hours after she left me like an infant child born into the world to receive life and breath and grow thereby. In a few days my strength came to me gradually so that I was able to go the rounds of duty with the sisters, such as washing, milking, spinning, and working in the kitchen and the like. And now I am as heavy as I was at eighteen years of age, and I can labor in the work of God as springy as the Prophet Habakkuk when he said the Lord had made his feet like hind's feet. As to my lameness and all my other infirmities, they have fled away together. The Lord has looked on my affliction; in judgement he has remembered mercy.

O my beloved Eldress Molly, I cannot describe to you through the medium of my pen what joy and thanksgiving filled my soul, yea, inexpressible comfort and gratitude to God for his loving kindness which he has always manifested to me through the ministry and elders. Praises and thanksgiving often fills my soul so that I am lost to every other object. And now I have sat myself down by the springs of Zion to rest, yea, and I feel rested, for I do know that I have the bread of life to eat and the waters of life to drink which nourishes and refreshes my poor and needy soul. Ages will roll away before I can pay the debt I owe to God and his people. But the greatest of all my joy and consolation is that I can pray to God who will (I believe) hear me if I am truly resigned to every dispensation of his providence.

I feel interested in the work of God and love it, for the gospel feels very precious to me and I feel exceeding thankful that I was called by the gospel when I was young and have been made able to keep my precious faith to the present time. My privilege is great and I am sensible of it. I never mean to stop short of final redemption from a carnal nature, for I do know from experience the foundation that is laid in Zion. The order of God that is established will protect and keep every soul from evil in every situation if they will only yield perfect obedience. This is the rock whereon if a man build his house, he never can fail. . . .

It is now a healthy season at Watervliet and a time of peace and prosperity. There have been a number of deaths here since your last visit there with us. . . .

N.B. We have received information that Anna Cogswell is gone. She died February 4th 1829. . . .

The consumption appears to have made its way in among our young class of people and has laid claim to many of our most beloved and promising youth; this feels very grievous to our feelings, but still it is a consolation that they have died in the faith of the gospel and a hope of a reward for their labors from which they have rested.

Now, beloved Eldress Molly, I must draw to a close. I have deposited a great treasure of love and a good cake from the ministry in Elder Benjamin's letter, and I hope that you will have your full share of it, and good Sister Mercy too, for I can assure you that the brethren and sisters here love you very much; many of them sent a warm share of love and respect to you—Good Sister Tabitha, Hannah Weight, and many more. I also feel a desire that my best love may find a place in your heart, and be so kind as to give my best love to Elder Benjamin and Sister Mercy, Brother Matthew, Brother Eli, Sister Prudence, and as many more as you may feel to.

Now do be so kind as to correspond [with] me a little once in a while so that we may feel our union, for this is very precious to gospel friends.

Eldress Molly, I hope you will be so kind as to forgive my failings in my letter. I have not written any of any consequence for three or four years past, and my communication being so long after my first date was in consequence of my move.

N.B. Eldress Molly, if Elder Benjamin should feel a gift to answer these letters, I wish he would be so kind as to direct to Frederick Wicker, Office.

Farewell,

Elizabeth Youngs

NOTES

1. Source: OClWHi IV B 35.
2. After twenty-one years in the West, Molly Goodrich had finally been allowed to visit the eastern Shaker societies in the summer of 1827, along with Benjamin S. Youngs, Matthew Houston, and Prudence Houston.

Letter 20. "He was a good child, and we considered him a promising youth." Molly Goodrich, on behalf of the ministry at South Union, to the ministry at New Lebanon, September 27, 1831.[1]

> [With Elder Benjamin Youngs ill, Molly Goodrich writes to the New Lebanon lead ministry in answer to their request, giving some of the history of a former South Union Shaker who apparently went to sea and then returned to Shaker life in the New York community.]

Beloved and esteemed Ministry,

This morning we received a letter from you, dated Watervliet September 12th, which seems to require an answer. In the first place, it seems as though we ought to make some apology for not writing any sooner, but we hardly know what to say. The last letter we received from you did not appear to require any immediate answer, and as Brother Seth wrote shortly afterward and had an answer immediately, Elder Benjamin postponed writing some on that account, expecting another letter from Brother Seth in the course of the summer. Likewise communications had been sent here and there in the course of a year or eighteen months past, all of which we supposed you would see.

Now in relation to our poor Brother Milton [Robinson], the reason why we have not written to the ministry before on the subject is this—after he arrived at New Lebanon, he wrote a letter to Elder Benjamin, informing him all about his trip and where he was there, and requested some counsel what to do in relation to his returning home again.

Accordingly Elder Benjamin immediately wrote him a letter and gave him all the good advice and consolation he could and further expressly told him, seeing things had turned out as they had, that we could not decide whether he should return home again or not, but told him that we felt perfectly satisfied to leave the matter entirely to the gift and direction of the ministry and elders at New Lebanon. And when we had done this we felt to let the matter rest, as we knew of nothing more that we could do, and we did not expect by his letters that he would be ever able to return again to South Union. And accordingly about a month ago, we received a letter from him informing us that considering his low state of health, it was felt best by the ministry there for him to make New Lebanon his home. And we can inform you that we felt perfectly satisfied with the conclusion. And we do feel very thankful to the ministry and elders, deacons, brethren, and sisters all, for receiving poor Milton into their bosom and making him welcome home. For we consider it the hand of Providence to him, seeing he strayed away from home as he did, to light down into the ark of safety, where he could be protected and comfortably provided for both soul and body.

In relation to Milton's character, he was a good child and we considered him a promising youth. But as to his taking his own way in going to sea, we did not approve of that, but considering his motives we can forgive him, and we wish that he might die in peace and in good union with all Mother's children.

Now one more essential apology for not writing is this. Elder Benjamin has been quite feeble all summer and for six weeks past has been pretty much confined to his bed, by reason of a fall which hurt his side very much and of course threw him into fevers, and [he] is at this time not able to write or walk any distance, and we cannot tell when he will get over it. So you see, beloved ministry, we are in affliction and by that means some-what excusable for our neglect. But be assured that our feelings are warm as ever to our precious gospel friends, and we would not have them feel any other wise toward us for all this world. And we are striving to keep the gospel and to do the best we can, but it is through much tribulation.

The ministry from Union Village, Ohio, made us a visit in the month of July. They stayed with us about two weeks. Their visit was very com-forting and agreeable. Elder Solomon [King] expected Elder Benjamin to visit Pleasant Hill this fall, but this, too, has become out of the question.

It has been very sickly here for two months past, many cases of heavy fevers, but at present it appears to be subsiding.

Precious friends, we return our kind thanks for the beautiful letter we just received from you and for the information it contained. Also for the letter we received dated February 17, 1830.

Also we should be very thankful to hear when the dwelling house at Lebanon is completed, and when the family moves into it, and how they like it, etc.

Beloved ministry, be so kind as to accept these few lines (as we are unable to write much at this time) together with our best love, and be so kind as to give it to the elders and to as many as you think proper. And we do earnestly desire your remembrance and prayers.

Ministry, South Union

N.B. Brother Rufus, concerning R. Wickliffe's speech,[2] Elder Benjamin says there has been a few copies in pamphlet form printed in Ohio, but they were not correct. But he is in hopes that he will be able to have some correct and revised copies printed this fall or winter, and if so he will be sure to send you some, and anything else that you would wish of him that would be any satisfaction to his good friends.

Dear brother, I thank you very kindly for sending me that beautiful hymn last February, also for your kind expressions of remembrance, for it felt like something right new, and I had not get anything particular from my good old friends at Lebanon for several years.

Molly

N.B. We have sent a little fine marking silk to our dear friends as a token of our love and respect, thinking it would not [add] much to the weight of the packet.

Molly and Mercy

NOTES

1. Source: OClWHi IV A 61.
2. A reference to the pro-Shaker speech made in the Kentucky senate by Robert Wickliffe, whom Julia Neal calls "Pleasant Hill's neighbor," in early 1831. Despite the efforts of Richard McNemar and Wickliffe, a bill to repeal several anti-Shaker statutes at this time failed (Neal, *The Kentucky Shakers*, 60).

Letter 21. "But alas! I have not got the wings of a bird." Molly Goodrich, South Union, to Rufus Bishop, New Lebanon, March 25, 1833.[1]

> [Molly Goodrich writes in a chatty, humorous
> style to New Lebanon lead ministry elder Rufus
> Bishop, thanking him for his gift of verses and
> sending some of her own. She compares herself
> to a dove that returns in imagination to New

Lebanon, and asks for more specific news of the
new dwelling house there.]

Beloved Brother Rufus,

With joy I received the beautiful little verse you sent me enclosed in
your letter of September last. I kept it till Christmas times, and then I gave
it to Prudence; she picked off the notes and learned it to the brethren and
sisters, and in our Christmas meeting at ten o'clock in the forenoon in the
meeting house, this song was nicely sung and marched at the close of our
meeting, in thankful hearts, and a sweet remembrance of the kind notice
of our precious gospel relations at New Lebanon, whom we always feel as
the Mother Church.

Brother Rufus, I thank you kindly for your notice to me and am thankful, yea, it does me good that I can get the chance to thank any bee in the
old hive once in a while for a drop of honey. And I always feel thankful
to all my old friends at New Lebanon, although I have not had a line from
any of them for this four years past, except from yourself. I could complain
but I reckon it's not worth while.

Enclosed I send this little song as a token of my best love and respect.

From Molly

While meditating on my good old home, I sometimes think, oh, that I
was a little dove! how soon I would fly there and light down upon the very
spot. And then I would go to the doors or windows, and peck, peck, till
they would let me in. And then I would go all about among my dear friends
and see where they was, and how pretty they look, and what they are
doing, and all about it, etc.. And then my kind friends would give me some
dinner, and let me smoke a pipe of union with them, and tell me about
this, that, and the other, and show me a heap of pretty things. And then
they would sing me some beautiful and heavenly songs and give me some
kind encouragement and good exhortations, and fill my weary spirit with
some comfort, and then I would fly home again to the old camp, and feel
as much refreshed as though I had been to heaven. But alas, I have not got
the wings of a bird, so I must control myself to dig, dig, at home, let it be
ever so crossing. Now you will say, "This is little Molly," and so it is, and
I do wish you would be so kind as to be a little more liberal with her and
give her once in a while some little sweet cakes to eat, and a little basket
of good fruit to eat, such as you know pleases little children. And you may
be sure she will be so thankful.

My good friends don't think that I am saucy, in using my little simili-
tudes, for I feel very far from it. Do remember me.

M

N.B. We have understood that the First Family's new dwelling house at New Lebanon was the beauty of beauties. And now, my good friends, this is the very house that I want to eat my dinner in, and then have my union smoke and then learn some pretty songs, etc., etc., as I said on the other side of the sheet. But seeing I cannot accomplish this desirable visit, pray be so kind as to inform us all about that house, both inside and outside, and what the conveniences of the kitchen are, and how many brethren and sisters can eat at the kitchen tables at a time, and how they are situated in their rooms, etc. I do not wish to bring too great a burden on my good old friends nor have anything written but what is thought best and proper by the ministry and elders.

Molly

NOTE

1. Source: OClWHi IV A 61.

Letter 22. "Eldress Mercy has been a good and faithful soul here for upwards of twenty-three years." Molly Goodrich, South Union, to Ruth Landon and Asenath Clark, New Lebanon, May 5, 1835.[1]

> [Molly Goodrich announces Mercy Pickett's retirement.]

Beloved and much esteemed Eldress Ruth and Sister Asenath,

I cannot let this good opportunity pass without writing you a few lines, although I have neither health nor ability to write much at this time.[2]

In the first place, I will inform you that I received your lovely letter dated April 1st, 1835. And be assured my dear friends I never was more thankful for a letter in all my life.[3] I had been looking and hoping that Eldress Ruth and Sister Asenath would think of poor little me enough to send me a letter in these trying times, and to be sure, the looked-for letter did come. And it was brim full of love, good will, kind and tender, respectful, and benevolent feelings and a great deal of good instruction and spiritual communications, all of which I feel very thankful for and will labor to be worthy of some more notice whenever it comes convenient.

Now what shall I say about my good old companion, dear Sister Mercy, as it is very uncertain that I shall ever see her again in the body. You may be sure I feel it to the center, but still I believe it is all for the best; therefore I have to be reconciled. Eldress Mercy has been a good and faithful soul here for upwards of twenty-three years, and I have no doubt she will receive the reward of the righteous. And we all feel to bless her and hope she will arrive safely home to the bosom of her dear old friends. We have labored to fix her out as comfortably as we knew how, and if there should be anything lacking, it will not be for the want of good will. I enclose in this letter her farewell, which will speak the feelings of all the Believers in South Union.

In relation to Elder Benjamin, it is expected by all the people here that he will return again. His health is very delicate, but we hope for the better and we all desire and earnestly pray that he may regain his health and be able to return again safe and sound to the children who love him and need him.

Now, my dear friends, what more shall I say? Why, to be sure, I could say a great deal if it would do any good. You all very well know that I love you with an everlasting love and I would give all this world if I had it in possession to see all your lovely faces once more. But as that cannot be at present, I must try to be reconciled. And considering I, with all the rest at South Union, had such a precious privilege last summer with the two lovely messengers from New Lebanon,[4] I ought not to complain. For surely it was a feast of delicious things, well seasoned with good love and everything that was pretty. But dear me, what will we do, for we want such another visit worse than ever. But I fear you will never let good Brother Rufus come to this rough country again. I am very sorry to hear that he has not yet regained his health and strength, but I pray that he may and live many years to do good. For truly we count him worthy of much love and respect. And there is our good Father, Elder Ebenezer. Although he has not been at South Union in body, yet we know he has been here in spirit, and he feels very precious to us all, and I wish him health and long life too.

Now my good and affectionate friends, Eldress Ruth and Sister Asenath, I have not language to express myself to you, for you know you have my whole heart.

So with these few lines be so kind as to receive my best love and thankfulness to the blessed ministry all. And as far as you may feel, to all the good elders, deacons, brethren and sisters, for I do desire and I very much need the prayers of all my good friends.

Molly Goodrich

N.B. Take particular notice, my much esteemed and good Brother Rufus, I enclose in this letter a little present as a token of my respectful feelings to thee. I would have been glad to have written a clever letter to thee, but I know you are well acquainted in similar circumstances of my busy situation at this time. But dear brother, don't forget poor me this summer. Just a line or two will feel worth a mountain of gold

To little Molly

2nd N.B. You can hardly think how thankful and very much pleased our sisters were, and indeed the brethren too, that our good friends in the East were so well satisfied with their ingenuity in manufacturing silk, etc. Yea, the notice and thanks you have given them in all your letters is of more value to them in their feelings than all the silk was worth. They would have been glad to have sent a good deal at this time, but they had wove up all they made last year. But out of their little store they have sent some more to their good kind benefactors and gospel friends in the East, feeling a reward in so doing.

M

3rd. N.B. I have sent a satchel and some little notions and some silk in it, one or two to Lebanon, etc. And another to Watervliet and one to Eldress Esther at Port Bay.

I have sent nothing to Harvard, nor Canterbury, etc., but if you feel to give them anything, I shall be well pleased.

Molly Goodrich

NOTES

1. Source: OClWHi IV B 19.
2. This letter was written to be carried to New Lebanon by the visiting westerners Benjamin S. Youngs, Harvey Eads, and the retiring Mercy Pickett.
3. Pickett's retirement had been approved in a letter to her from the New Lebanon ministry eldresses dated March 21, 1835. A second letter, dated the next day, was sent to Molly Goodrich.
4. She refers to the western visit of Rufus Bishop and Issac N. Youngs, of June 1834.

Letter 23. "Farms and gardens at this time are suffering much on account of the vast quantity of rain which has fallen." Eldress Molly Goodrich, South Union, to Benjamin S. Youngs and company (on a visit to Watervliet and New Lebanon), June 25, 1835.[1]

> [Molly Goodrich writes to Benjamin S. Youngs, Harvey Eads, and Mercy Pickett, who have recently arrived in the East. She emphasizes the progress of the harvest at South Union, despite poor weather.]

Beloved and respected Elder Benjamin and company,

Agreeable to your request, and according to our agreement when you left here that we should write you every two weeks (at least for a while), we now take pen in hand to write you the third letter since your departure, which is just seven weeks today. And we are pretty sure to keep good account of every long week that passes.

In the first place we are happy to inform you that we received your letter dated 29 May written in part at Utica, but was not finished until you arrived safely among your good friends at Watervliet (post marked June 3rd). And you may be sure, beloved companions, it was heart cheering and reviving news to us to hear that you had accomplished in safety and under a blessing that long and wearisome journey.

Also, we received a lovely and very satisfying letter from Eldress Dana dated May 28th. Please tell her that little Molly thanks her and all the rest of her good friends very kindly for that peculiar favor. And now I can tell you of another kind favor, good and acceptable—that is, last Monday morning, June 22, we received a beautiful letter from under the hand of Eldress Elizabeth, stating all about our good friends, when they arrived at Watervliet, and considerable about their visiting, etc. And it came in such a good time that all past neglects were forgotten. I thank you a heap, in the language of your country, and Eldress Elizabeth for your valuable letter.

And take notice, the spiritual and affecting little close in her letter shall be closely observed by me. So my beloved sister, you shall have little Molly's spirit with yours, in comfort and in sorrow, and your God shall be my God and your people shall be my people, knit together in the bonds of imperishable love. All the brethren and sisters who had the privilege of hearing this letter were much pleased with it, and more especially because Elder Benjamin had some few pencil lines at the close of the letter. But some say, "Is that going to answer for a letter from Elder Benjamin?" "I reckon so," says another. But says a third, "Stop, stop, that won't do." "Well, but," says another, "that's all you'll get from Watervliet," etc. Others will say, "I wonder what is the reason that Brother Harvey don't write more? What has become of his Muse? Oh! he has so much to hear and see, it's a chance if he hasn't forgotten all about us at South Union," etc., etc. But now in earnest, if we don't get some good letters before long we shall be very much disappointed.[2]

We will now give you a brief statement of temporal concerns. Farms and gardens at this time are suffering much on account of the vast quantity of rain which has fallen. During the last seven weeks the weather has been invariably showery with scarcely enough clear sunshine to dry the earth and allow some chance to kill the weeds. Of late the clouds seem to make this part of the country a kind of a center or place to pour out their contents. They do not seem to be confined to one regular channel but will come from the four quarters, generally accompanied with much lightning and thunder. Sometimes we have storms of considerable violence but have suffered no essential loss by them as yet. The meadows and grain fields in the more luxurious parts have been blown down considerable, but if the weather would only hold up long enough for them to be taken care of, we should feel no disposition to complain.

On Monday the 22nd the brethren and sisters of the Center Family generally united in pulling the flax, twelve acres in all, and beautiful flax it was, tall, well-linted and thick on the ground. But the storms had whirled it and laid it to the ground a good deal, on which account it was pulled greener than is usual, lest it should take the second growth. But the weather since has been so wet and unfavorable there really seems to be danger of its being altogether lost; but we still trust not.

Harvest has been on hand more or less for the last ten days, this being Saturday the 27th—cutting clover, rye, pulling flax, etc. But on Thursday the 25th they commenced cutting the wheat, which, though thin and a little affected by the spot, is considered good, the heads being well filled and the grains large and plump. On the whole, it is thought we will have a greater amount and better wheat than we had last year. But as the case is with the flax, the difficulty lies in having an opportunity, or privilege, to take care of it. The brickmaking, of course, has advanced but little, and it is expected if we should have open weather that the brick yard hands will give their assistance in taking care of the grain, at least during the press and pinch, while their help is needed.

The gardens still hold out a pretty fair prospect for seed of almost all the kinds that are common, but we are much concerned lest the wet weather should continue and make difficulty in saving them. The seed from Scotland arrived here on the 15th. Some of each kind were immediately put into the ground, which have come up well sprouted, strong, and looked thrifty. The brethren so far seem to be well pleased with them.

The sisters are still advancing in their line of business with their usual zeal and industry and support a good degree of comfortable feelings and pretty good union. A number of them are now engaged combing and spinning wool.

Their silkworms are turning out as well as they could expect. The first crop produced fifty-two pounds of cocoons. They think [it] is an excellent turnout for the number of worms. The second crop they think will produce equally as well.

It is a general time of health and common prosperity we may say, both spiritually and temporally, for all the faithful are striving to keep the gospel and they do keep it, too, according to the best of their understanding. Meetings are kept up pretty regularly. And they are always thankful to get a letter from Elder Benjamin and company to read in meeting and from any of their good friends in the East. It does them a heap of good.

As to my own health, it is as good as usual and I am as comfortable every way as could reasonably be expected. I rise at five o'clock in the morning or a little before and take breakfast at half past six, with little Sarah [Rice?] by my side.[3] Brother [Samuel] Robinson is very kind and takes good care of every thing about the place, and so are all the rest of the brethren and sisters, whenever need requires.

Now Elder Benjamin and Brother Harvey, receive with this letter our united love and sincere desires for your health, blessing, and prosperity, and a safe return home to your bosom friends at South Union whenever your work is done in the East. And we desire that Eldress Mercy will receive a good share of our love and everlasting remembrance. We are thankful to hear that she survived her journey. Also the same to Eldress Hopewell [Curtis]. And Elder Issachar [Bates],[4] you know, must always have a good share of Benjamin's mess from South Union. And now to finish this lettter as it ought to be, we want Elder Benjamin to be faithful in delivering our love and respect to the ministry, elders, deacons, brethren, and sisters in every place where opportunity offers. We do sincerely desire an interest in their love and prayers.

Farewell from your affectionate Sister Molly, and in behalf of all at South Union.

N.B. Sister Sally Eads is still able to attend to all the rounds of her various duties, as you will see by her little verses.

Molly

NOTES

1. Source: OClWHi IV B 19.
2. Benjamin S. Youngs and Harvey Eads wrote to South Union from New Lebanon, June 17, 1835, giving details of their trip from Watervliet to New Lebanon, but the letter was not mailed until July 18, because Youngs had to spend some time in Saratoga Springs trying to recover from an illness.
3. After Molly Goodrich's death, Sarah Rice was one of the South Union ministry eldresses.
4. Eldress Hopewell Curtis and Elder Issachar Bates were also retiring to the East at this time and had journeyed with the South Union company.

Letter 24. "Farewell in love to one and all, my dear gospel relation." Mercy Pickett, in New Lebanon, to Molly Goodrich, South Union, August 26, 1835.[1]

> [After her arrival in New Lebanon, former South
> Union Eldress Mercy Pickett writes a farewell
> letter to her former partner in the South Union
> ministry.]

Beloved and much respected Eldress Molly,

I think it likely you would be glad to hear something from your old friend and companion. Well, I will try and to give you some information as it respects our journey. I enjoyed my health very well considering the long distance we travelled. As to the particulars of our journey, Elder Benjamin will be better able to tell you to your satisfaction than I can by writing. However, we arrived at Watervliet on Saturday the 30th of May, a little before dark, where we were kindly received and made welcome to their delightful habitation. We had a very agreeable visit with all Mother's good children in that place, and [?] of hearing them express their faith and their love and zeal for the way and work of God, and their thankfulness for the gospel.

This ends our visit in this place.

On Tuesday the ninth of June we left Watervliet and started for New Lebanon in company with Brother Frederick Wicker and Daniel Copley. We got to the office a little before sunset. Here we were received with kindness and made welcome by all, and I believe it was from the heart as well as in the mouth, for it was the general word from every one, "You are welcome home." The next morning the ministry came to see us, and you may be sure their smiling beautiful countenances, their heavenly and solemn looks, and their godly deportment—altogether it was delightful to behold. They made us welcome in the most feeling manner to the privilege of partaking of the blessings of the increase of the gospel and work of God in the Church, which feels to me like a very precious privilege.

But I felt that I had come to judgment and justly so, for I had been gone a great while and the requirement of God upon me to give an account of myself in my long absence from this place, it felt to me like a privilege, and I did it conscientiously before God. In the afternoon one of the sisters from the Second Family came and conducted Sister Hopewell and myself home. Here we met with a great many of our good old friends and former acquaintances, besides these a great many that we never saw before. All seemed to say, "Welcome home, we are glad to see you, you are welcome, we are glad you have come home, you have been gone a great while, and at a great distance; you have spent your time and strength in trying to help others that needed help; you are welcome to all that we possess; this is your home; we want you to be free and feel at home; you are welcome to all we have." This was the general salutation from old and young. The elders are very kind; they teach us to love and bless each other and neither give nor take offense. They are meek and humble, and such they teach others.

Now, Eldress Molly, don't you think I have great cause to be thankful and humble? I think you will say, "Yea," and I say so too. I feel myself unworthy many times of the kindness, freedom, and love and charity that I find in our beloved ministry and elders. Their very countenances and all their words and actions show that they do maintain the pure gospel of Mother; they do both by precept and example. They teach it to the people that all our words and actions must come into judgement, that we must come to judgment ourselves before we are able to teach others.

I went to the office and have taken care of Elder Benjamin about five weeks.[2] The ministry and elders all appear to feel a good regard for Elder Benjamin and the gift he has kept and ministered throughout all his labors; and I believe it is their earnest desire that he might be supported and strengthened in his gift.[3] They have paid great attention to him through his sufferings and in his critical situation since he has been in this place; and it is my prayer that he may be protected and blessed on his way and be able to meet you with a blessing.

Now Eldress Molly, you will conclude from these few broken lines that my eyesight is some better than it was, though not very good yet. So not to weary your patience I close with the never failing love of the good elders, brethren, and sisters, together with Sister Hopewell's and my own to all and every one at South Union, earnestly desiring their blessing and prosperity in the gospel.

Farewell in love to one and all, my dear gospel relation. This from your old friend and sister,

Mercy Pickett

NOTES

1. Source: OClWHi IV B 19.
2. Because she was the sister who knew him best, it was thought appropriate to assign Mercy Pickett to nurse Benjamin S. Youngs during his illness.
3. Mercy Pickett believes that Elder Benjamin will be sent back to the South Union community as elder, rather than be retained in retirement at New Lebanon.

4. "THE HEAVENS ARE OPEN"
Women's Perspectives on Midcentury Spiritualism

INTRODUCTION

From the days of Ann Lee through the Civil War, the United Society of Believers in Christ's Second Appearing depended on religious revivals to bring in new members in large numbers from the outside world, to replace those who died or left dissatisfied. Internal revivals, which were sometimes related to outbreaks of religious enthusiasm among neighbors of Shaker communities, also made significant contributions to the renewal of Shaker religion and community life.[1]

Revivals were times of dramatic social upheaval and religious excitement when one's feelings about other members of the community as well as oneself could be radically transformed, as happened for Elizabeth Lovegrove in 1827 during a New Lebanon community revival: "O how lovely how pleasant was every countenance, it appeared to me that the heavens was opened and I was worshipping with the Angelic host."[2] Internal revivals also provided opportunities, of course, for public confessions of ill will, jealousy, and feelings of inadequacy in living up to the stringent version of Christian ideals held up by Shaker ideology.

As a rule, Shakerism's internal revivals, like those in the outside world, were relatively short-lived. After several months the excitement would die down of its own accord and religious life would return to its normal routines. One of the many unusual features of the midcentury spiritualistic revival documented in this section was its institutionalization. Working in a partnership with an officially sanctioned group of spirit instruments, central Shaker leadership artificially prolonged for roughly fifteen years what began as a highly chaotic expression of the visionary imaginations of a group of young women at Watervliet.[3]

A great variety of spiritualistic expressive forms were generated during this revival. Most were fundamentally performance forms: songs, spoken messages, narrated dream visions, prophetic pronouncements made in meetings, and rituals of purification and renewal. A great many of these were reduced to writing by witnesses or by the performers themselves. There were also longer, written spiritualistic documents which took hours or days for the writing medium to commit to paper. The spiritualistic literature of the revival, when read in the light of records kept by the leadership, offers an unusual window on the private spirituality of some individual Believers. At the same time it casts light on a series of political and social struggles going on within the Shaker communities between old and young, liberal and conservative, leaders and common members, and women and men.[4]

The visionary and trance activity which apparently began spontaneously in 1837 was speedily shaped into a Society-wide revival with multiple purposes, reflecting its multiple constituencies. Women and men participated in characteristically different ways in "Mother Ann's work," as it was later called. The differences shed light on the evolution of gender ideology in Shaker religious culture two generations after the death of Ann Lee.[5]

I. M. Lewis has made the very useful observation that spirit possession is frequently used by the relatively powerless—especially women—for the "oblique" expression of discontent or rebellion against subordination; it is also used by religious leaders seeking to "strengthen legitimate authority."[6] The Shaker midcentury revival began with an early "protest" phase, in which the spirits possessed children, particularly girls, and lower-status sisters, then settled into a far longer phase dominated by central leadership interests (as served by officially appointed mediums with higher status, including many men). The younger and less prominent sisters may have initially turned to spiritualism as an occasion for some behavioral license that contrasted with their highly routinized and regulated work and religious lives. However, the majority of the Shaker women who gravitated toward the role of spirit instrument (and remained within the communities) ultimately worked under central leadership guidance to renew Shakerism as an ascetic religion. During the fifteen years of the revival, female spirit instruments did carve out an enlarged role for women as visible leaders in worship. They also created a set of spiritualistic expressive traditions that endured primarily within the sisterhood for many years after the officially-sanctioned spirit inspirations had ceased.[7]

The Spontaneous Visionary Phase of the Midcentury Revival

The onset of spiritualistic trance activity at the Watervliet Second and South Families was in August 1837. By September 24, lead ministry elder Rufus Bishop was writing with excitement:

. . . for a number of weeks past the meetings have been wonderful, even
to the astonishment of believers as well as unbelievers. In addition to the
gifts of shaking, turning, bowing etc., some souls seemed to be traversing
the invisible world, at times viewing the happified state of the Saints in
light, and when permitted, singing and dancing with them, some of
whom had been their former companions in the gospel. . . . [8]

The ministry elders visited the families where the trance activity had
started and witnessed impressive trance states in several young women
visionists. Rufus Bishop was initially concerned with the credibility of the
visionists' reports on their visits to the spirit world and was careful to note:

There was undeniable proof of what they asserted to have seen and heard,
for there was generally two or more in these trances at a time, and tho'
they opened their visions separately to their Elders without any knowledge of what each other had said, yet their narratives agreed perfectly as
to the souls they had seen in the spiritual world, their conversation that
passed on both sides, the manner of dress, songs, exercise in the meetings, and the various mansions in the spiritual world. . . . Some believers
acknowledge that they have heretofore had doubts concerning the truth
and reality of such gifts, but they will now say they must believe their
own eyes.

Bishop saw the obvious risk to the Shaker system of government by the
appointed successors of Ann Lee, if the authenticity of such gifts were to
be acknowledged by the lead ministry. As early as October 1, he was advising the Second Family how such "supernatural gifts" must be understood and how spirit instruments must regard their powers:

I . . . labored to give the family some good counsel concerning these
supernatural gifts . . . which was no doubt given for the purpose of
strengthening their faith in the work of God, & of the certainty of a state
of rewards & punishment beyond the grave, &c. I warned them against
letting their sense rise or taking the honor of those gifts to themselves,
& assured them that they must keep their joining to the elders & to the
living body or they would suffer great loss, &c. &c.

Initially cautious, Bishop counselled the elders of the Second Family
about "their duties in governing the meetings" and asked the elders of both
families where visionists had emerged to record the visions in writing (October 9 and October 23).

Bishop also saw in this ecstatic activity the potential for a Society-wide
renewal of dedication to Shaker principles. In a clear effort to encourage
the spread of such activity throughout the Shaker world, he visited the
New Lebanon Shaker families and read the first written accounts of the
Watervliet visions to the elders there. He also spread the word through the
ministry correspondence with other communities. Not surprisingly, then,
by April 19, 1838, he could report "great manifestations of the gifts & power

of God in every Society, & I believe every family of the Eastern Believers."
By July 21, word had reached New Lebanon that "the same good work has
begun at South Union & Pleasant Hill."

The visionists' trances and accounts of their spiritual travels in the world
beyond death had brought them not only unusual attention from the lead
ministry elder Rufus Bishop and their family leaders, but also from "the
world," through the public meetings, as Bishop's journal indicates.

> Feb. 4 A great concourse of spectators today. . . . Eldress Elizabeth,
> Ellyet, Ann Mariah, Eliza Chadwick & others spake much to the specta-
> tors, & no doubt but they spake right, for they spake as they were moved
> by the spirit, but I could hear but few of their words, as there was such
> rustling among the world for the purpose of getting a better chance to
> hear what was said, & to see such as were in trances on the floor.

Undoubtedly aware of their unusual new power over their peers, the
visionists began to deliver in family meetings a series of personalized accusatory messages in the name of Mother Ann to individual Shakers who
needed reform. Bishop's journal suggests the satisfaction the central leadership may have felt at seeing unrepentant skeptics and lukewarm Shakers
change their behavior as a result of such "warring gifts" from the spirits:

> Wed. Feb 7 To day Eliza Elleyett & Ann Mariah delivered their first mes-
> sage to Gideon Cole, but he was obstinate as a bull. . . . The 3 Sisters
> above named had 2 more gifts with Gideon in the afternoon & evening.
> The latter was after he had retired to rest, but he had to get up & receive
> what gift they had in Mother's name, which seemed to undermine him
> considerable, & well he might feel lowered, for Eliza, who had the gifts
> for him could, by the revelation, tell him of sins which he had committed
> something like 15 years before she was born.

> Thurs. 8 The Visionists lodged at the Second Order last night, & contin-
> ued labors with Gideon until he became as simple & obedient as a child.
> This is casting out devils in very deed, and when they finished with him
> he hardly seemed like the same man that they had begun with.[9]

The younger visionists developed a remarkable repertoire of physical
activities which took place during trance, such as whirling in place "like
tops," often for long periods of time. Some of their physical gestures could
be read as "signs" for aspects of their spiritual activity. On September 2,
1838, for example, just a year into the revival, Rufus Bishop described
witnessing this impressive spiritualistic pantomime:

> five of the Second's girls were in trances. . . . These innocent children
> seemed to sign out the state of the damned! They were frequently bent
> into hoops backward, insomuch that the tops of their heads actually
> pressed against the hollow of their feet!!! . . . and what makes these op-
> erations appear more wonderful, they will sometimes go, or rather roll
> from the top to the bottom of the stairs, bent as above described without

receiving any injury whatever. One of them asked Mother why they had to visit hell so often; She said it was not for anything which they had yet done, but that they might know what they would have to suffer if they were wicked.

In her discussion of the underlying reasons for the revival, Priscilla Brewer describes the mid-1830s as a time of "crisis" in eastern Shakerism, when the communities were under stress because of economic hard times. She traces ongoing tensions within the communities, particularly emphasizing the dispute between Shaker followers of diet-reformer Sylvester Graham and dietary traditionalists who wished to continue eating butter and pork. She points out the serious loss of members suffered at New Lebanon in the years immediately preceding the revival—particularly among young men from the Church Family.[10] To these special problems of the 1830s we might add the routine stress of suppressing internal community antagonisms in a religious society based on a stringent ideology of perfect love among all Believers.

Some of the visionists evidently enjoyed exposing the misbehavior or lukewarm spiritual condition of members of their own Shaker families. Though girls and women were the first visionists and were prominent instruments of the early "warring gifts" directed against individuals, the role also appealed to some of the brethren. Philemon Stewart of New Lebanon, who had begun to act as "a useful and conspicuous instrument in the heart searching work" by April 1838, was responsible for conveying messages from Mother Ann critical of the prominent New Lebanon former elder and writer Calvin Green. Green was one of those forced by the spirits to make a public confession of errors in May 1838.[11]

Sometimes one visionist might turn a "warring gift" against another, as in the case of "A Visionary Dream Concerning Ann Eliza Goodwin" (1840), included in this chapter. The young sister Harriet Goodwin obviously used the visionary dream form to air a grievance against Addah Zillah Potter, one of the leading spirit instruments in the Church Family sisterhood.[12] Goodwin seems to have held Zillah Potter at least partly responsible for bringing false charges that led to the defection of her sister Ann Eliza Goodwin, another spirit instrument, from the New Lebanon community in August 1838. In the dream vision, "a woman dressed in Shaker dress" is unable to get in to heaven, and so returns to earth and confronts Zillah Potter with her misdeeds:

> You have abused me! you have laid things to me that I was not guilty of; you have carried false reports about me to the elders, in order to cover your own sins.

The misbehavior exposed through spirit instrumentality included, significantly, skepticism about the authenticity of the spiritual gifts.[13] Skeptical

talk out of the earshot of the elders was "heard" by the spirits and sometimes held up to public scrutiny, as in a message received in February 1842
at Watervliet:

> I dare say the Elders have a hand in putting them [the instruments] up
> to it, in some way or other; to see if they cannot frighten some body
> enough, to make them confess a sin or two. And as for these songs that
> they say are given by the Spirits, what silly things they are! I could make
> better songs myself, if I should try, and I believe I shall. I can tell them
> that they came from the Spirits, and I dare say they will all believe me.[14]

The departure of some of the early visionists was a particular spur to
further skepticism. Ellyet Gibbs, one of the first to act as instruments for
the spirits, was also one of the first to leave the community during this
turbulent time. She and Eliza Chadwick are recorded as "eloping" from
Watervliet to Albany on June 6, 1838, by Bishop; Gibbs returned for the
summer but left finally in September.[15]

The lead ministry had initially expressed pleasure at the willingness of
young women and girls (and a few boys) to act as spirit instruments, because their presumed innocence and natural incapacities made the authenticity of the gifts seem less questionable:[16]

> For we consider that there is a greater proof of the divine agency in these
> gifts than there would have been if the Ministry or Elders had been the
> immediate instruments; because in that case the caviler might ascribe
> some part of those gifts to priestcraft, etc. But in the present circum-
> stances, those who were eye & ear witnesses of those frequent and won-
> derful manifestations of divine power, & knew the illiterate & bashful
> state of those youth and children, could no more ascribe those gifts to
> deception & fraud, than they could Balaam's Ass when she rebuked her
> master.[17]

When instruments began to fall from grace, however, the other instruments and the central leadership reminded the disillusioned that earthly
vessels sometimes proved unworthy of the spirits that filled them. Rufus
Bishop wrote frequent admonitions to the leaders of other communities to
"keep awake" and to "distinguish clearly between the genuine spirit of
Mother and that which is counterfeit."[18] By 1840, the central ministry was
also attempting to control for potentially subversive messages by requiring
that they be written down and checked by the leadership before being
spoken in meeting.[19]

Some elders themselves took on the spirit medium role, despite Bishop's
initial recognition that this might lead some to suspect leadership manipulation of the spirits.[20] But by and large the mediums were not drawn from
the ranks of established leaders. Inevitably, there were some Shaker leaders
who saw the opportunity of manipulating the instruments for their own

political purposes, in power struggles within their families or communities. The best known case is the spirit-inspired expulsion of Richard McNemar from leadership at the Union Village Ohio Society in 1839, apparently to satisfy the newly arrived eastern Shaker elder, Freegift Wells. Margaret O'Brien, a young instrument, was implicated in the expulsion. The New Lebanon lead ministry ultimately responded when notified of McNemar's humiliation, by using another spirit medium from Watervliet to produce a vision of McNemar's reinstatement.[21]

The alliance between the central leadership and the spirits was established in part because the central ministry and elders naturally encouraged those instruments who seemed most attuned to leadership wishes,[22] and in part because the instruments who became dominant themselves knew how to anticipate their elders' wishes. In his ministerial journal, we can see some of the visionists beginning to form alliances with Rufus Bishop, though he himself seems unconscious of it. An example is an entry from October 21, 1838, when Bishop was at Watervliet:

> Sabbath 21   I went to the 1st Order's forenoon meeting—towards the close Sarah Simons said she had Love from Mother to us, I told her we wanted as much of Mother's love as we could get—She came out between the brethren & sisters & stooped down & seemed to dip love from a fountain with her right hand & reel it on to her left. She said Mother said we must come low to get it. . . . She said Mother had a golden chain that was composed of the orders of God, & some of the links had been broken, and it must be mended—And whoever had broken a link, or an order, must mend it by confession & repentance. She then closed her gift with these words—"Mother is going to the Meeting house with brother Rufus."

Bishop does not seem to have suspected the spirit instruments of manipulating his credulity—though others, in retrospect, came easily to this interpretation.[23] The strong support of Rufus Bishop in the first years of the revival was crucial both to its overall continuation and to the selection of the particular forms of spirit inspiration that were allowed to flourish.

Shaker Women as Speaking Mediums

In April 1838 the course of the revival took a distinct new turn when Philemon Stewart, a brother from the New Lebanon Church Family's Second Order,[24] began to speak for Mother Ann. By September, Stewart had more influence perhaps than any other single spirit instrument, because of his penchant for the long, solemn "prophetic" type of spirit message communicating the need for community reform and because of his ability to form an alliance with Rufus Bishop of the New Lebanon lead ministry. He was promoted to the First Order, and he continued to function as one

of the most prolific speakers and writers of the prophetic style spirit message over the next ten years. He ultimately delivered himself of hundreds
of pages of spirit-inspired writings recommending specific policy changes
on temporal behavioral issues such as diet and health reform (the use of
tea, coffee and pork was banned, for example). New sets of rules for governing the relationship between the sexes also came through him.[25] Stewart's is a very clear case of how the role of spirit instrument could be
employed by a Believer with strong ideas about how the community should
be governed as a means of gaining political power outside (or in addition
to) the eldership role.[26]

Although no single woman seems to have rivalled Stewart as a major
prophet of new community social policies, many sisters did function prominently as officially appointed mediums. They expressed the wishes of Ann
Lee, Lucy Wright, and other Shaker ancestors, and they took the role of
Holy Mother Wisdom in visiting the communities and "sealing" or blessing
the faithful, in the early 1840s. Sisters were also active recipients of rules
for correct behavior in the realms of daily life that most affected the sisterhood.

An excellent example of spirit-inspired behavioral rules brought by a
female medium is "Mother Lucy's Word to the Sisters" (March 12, 1841).
Through the prominent Church Family spirit instrument, Anna Dodgson,
Mother Lucy's spirit notes that the recently received "Book of Holy Orders
of the Church, Written by Father Joseph" (February 18, 1841) was "rather
blind in respect to the sisters."[27] She proceeds to give the sisterhood a
highly detailed set of instructions for regulating their domestic work lives
in a way that will more closely embody the austere and self-denying communal spirit of early Shakerism.

We hear in these rules a critique of such practices as the sisters' cooking
extra meals for each other; young girls refusing to be appropriately super-
vised in their work by more experienced sisters; complaints being made
over the competence of those entrusted with washing "nice clothes." (The
placating tone of the spirit speaker—"I do not wish to be unreasonable"—
suggests that the spirit instrument anticipated that some of these new rules
would be received without much enthusiasm by the sisterhood.)

Interestingly, the spirit instrument also speaks in the same message for
Olive Spencer, a beloved Church Family eldress who had died in 1834.
Spencer appears as a kind of intermediary spirit who seconds the instruc-
tions of Mother Lucy's spirit and "takes the blame" for the relaxation of
rules in recent years that allowed selfish and worldly practices to creep in.
(The instrument appears to anticipate some of the sisters commenting to
each other as these rules were issued that "what was good enough for Elder
Sister Olive is good enough for me.")

The journals of the religious meetings in the eastern communities in
the 1840s generally show women assuming the role of speaking medium

in greater numbers and with more enthusiasm than men, in all phases of the revival. In the excerpts from the Watervliet First Order Church Journal of 1842–1843 included in this chapter, we see the prominence of the sisters in one particularly interesting phase of the spiritualistic revival: the enactment of visits from spirits of "other" races.[28]

Ann Lee had originally taught and acted on the belief that neither death nor geographic separation could prevent those in need of the saving gospel from hearing it. Midcentury spiritualism dramatized this doctrine for all to see. Spirits of peoples from all over the world, living and dead, were represented as being drawn to the Shakers to learn how to find salvation. There was a particular emphasis on Native Americans, but Africans and other "exotic" peoples also made their appearances through spirit instruments over several weeks each in the nightly meetings. They told and acted out the stories of their lives and expressed gratitude for exposure to Shaker insights. (Obviously some of the younger and lukewarm Shakers themselves were also expected to be learning Shaker truths through witnessing and participating in this enactment of missionary work with foreign peoples.)

An 1843 visitor described how such a spiritualistic meeting at Watervliet looked to an outsider. When the elders "invited the Indians to come in,"

> one of the Sisters . . . informed us, that she saw them all around, and amongst the Brothers and Sisters. The Elders then urged upon the members the duty of "taking them in" whereupon eight or nine of the Sisters became possessed of the Spirits of Indian Squaws and about six of the Brothers became Indians: then ensued a regular "Pow Wow," with whooping, yelling, and strange antics, such as would require a Dickens to describe.

One of the "lessons" that the "Indians" needed to learn from the Shakers was the necessity of sex segregation, apparently.

> The Sisters and Brothers squatted down on the floor together, Indian fashion, and the Elders and Eldresses endeavoured to keep them asunder. At the same time, telling the Indians that they must be separated from the Squaws, and otherwise instructing them in the rules of Shakerism . . . thus continued the performance till about ten o'clock when the Chief Elder desired the Indians to go away, and they would find some one waiting, to conduct them to the Shakers in the Heavenly world. At this announcement every man and woman became themselves again, and all retired to rest.[29]

The Shaker sisters at Watervliet seem to have thrown themselves into the spiritualistic enactment of racial "otherness" and victimization with unusual passion. The brethren were typically more reluctant to "abase" themselves by miming "primitive" behavior in this way, according to Rufus

Bishop: "Often the squaw comes first & has to beg the brothers for one of
them to take Indian into his heart . . . "[30] Though racial and ethnic stereotypes of the period abound in the accounts of this spirit-inspired behavior,
it is worth noting that considerable anger at the history of the "white man's"
treatment of Native American women and children was also expressed by
the female spirit instruments:

> They can readily tell the names of their near relations and how many
> papoos they had, and how the white man burnt them all to death in their
> wigwams, & how many years since, & how old they were when they
> were *burnt to det*, as they express themselves . . . "[31]

A whole series of new rituals were created during the revival. Their
purpose was to involve the whole community in a rededication to early
ascetic ideals. Those sisters who were "anointed" as official mouthpieces
for the spirits functioned in prominent roles in these as well as in regular
family worship meetings.

Female spirit instruments figure very prominently in an account of a
"mountain meeting" ritual at the Hancock community in the fall of 1843,
excerpted in this chapter. This was a semiannual day-long event created in
1842, in which the whole community proceeded to a special sanctified
outdoor meeting ground on a hilltop for a spiritual feast and purification
ceremony.[32] There is an interesting flexibility here in the gender of the
instruments who speak for different spirits. Both Martha VanValen and
Elder Joseph Wicker speak for the Savior and Mother Ann, for example.
We can also see spirit-inspired sisters taking an unusually active proselytizing role in addressing the spectators who had gathered out of curiosity
to watch this Shaker event.

This account of the mountain meeting at Hancock helps us imagine
how impressed the spectators of Shaker spiritualistic rituals must have
been. On this occasion, for example, invisible trumpets were distributed
and played, "living water" was offered for bathing in and drinking, spiritual
garments were distributed to everyone present, crumbs from the table of
the Heavenly Father and slices of the Bread of Life were eaten, doves
brought "rolls" (invisible scrolls) of writing for the elders, and angels were
seen flying protectively overhead. The Hancock seceder David Lamson
found such unusual rituals easy to lampoon after he had become disillusioned with Shakerism.[33] For the Believer who did not turn skeptic, spiritualistic rituals like this one dramatized and made nearly visible a whole
complex of Shaker cultural symbols for the rewards of holy living.

The Hancock Sweeping Gift (described as performed in 1843 in this
chapter) is another ritual spawned by midcentury spiritualism which featured the sisterhood in a prominent role. Marjorie Procter-Smith cites it as
an example of the many ways in which Shaker religious culture during the

period of Mother Ann's work "raised the everyday activities of Shaker sisters to the level of spiritual activity." Bands of Shaker sisters and brethren were assembled to march separately through the buildings where they lived and worked, stopping at various stations to hear angels speak through instruments about the need to "make our dwellings clean," and to sprinkle invisible fire and wield invisible brooms. Marjorie Procter-Smith has argued that in such ritual purification activity, "the daily labor of cleaning, which was primarily the work of women, was made into a metaphor of spiritual purification."[34] Whether such symbolic elevation of the domestic realm through these rituals was experienced as empowering by the female participants is a question that still remains open.

Dramatizing the Female Side of God

As was discussed in chapter 1, the Shaker idea of a dual-gender godhead was first articulated in print by Benjamin S. Youngs in *The Testimony of Christ's Second Appearing* (1808). This idea remained an abstraction until the spiritualistic revival of the 1840s, when actual female spirit instruments appointed in each society began to enact the role of Holy Mother Wisdom. Messages from Holy Mother Wisdom were received at New Lebanon as early as 1840, and in 1841 there were preannounced formal "visitation" ceremonies in all the Shaker communities. On these occasions Holy Mother Wisdom in a sacred pantomime "sealed" and "crowned" those Shakers who could be certified as good Believers by their elders. The seceder David Lamson described one such ceremonial at Hancock in detail, hoping to shock readers at Shaker "blasphemy."[35] We also have the testimony of a woman who left the Watervliet community in the later 1840s and wrote about her experience:

> What now seem blasphemies were then to me solemn and awful truths. The dual God, male and female, called Heavenly Father and Holy Mother Wisdom, Christ being the son and Ann Lee the daughter in the new creation, were to come among us and draw a dividing line between the precious and the vile, the former to receive blessings, the latter curses, and doomed to be cut off as vessels of wrath fit for destruction. . . . Some received extraordinary promises and predictions of great usefulness as pillars of Zion, and among the rest I, a little child, was "sealed" and clothed with a garment of Divine love, and a star of great magnitude and brightness was placed on my brow, as a token that I was ever to remain one of the chosen few.[36]

Holy Mother Wisdom also spoke through writing instruments. In "Holy Mother Wisdom's Fold," an undated manuscript spirit message apparently from the early 1840s, for example, Wisdom is represented as telling the story of her own place in the Christian drama of creation and the human fall from innocence. She tells of her own coeternal existence and partnership with the Almighty Father; of Lucifer's jealousy of her first companion, the Angel of Love, and his failed efforts to supplant Love; and of the subsequent vengeful efforts of the fallen angels to destroy Wisdom—foiled because the Almighty Father hid her under his protective wings.

This message received by a female instrument has a strong tendency to absolve the woman from some of the traditional Christian blame for the fall. Her story opens:

> Well do you know my Beloved One that the female is called the cause of Mans fall But I say she was the means made use of whereby they fell

When she tells how the fallen angels take out their malice on Eve, she emphasizes the negligence of Adam:

> Wheare was the Man that had been placed with her for her protection Why he was asleep.

A massive collection of Holy Mother Wisdom's sayings during the early 1840s ultimately became the basis for a spirit-inspired book published by Shaker leadership under the title *The Divine Book of Holy and Eternal Wisdom* (1849).[37] The logic of gender dualism compelled the Society to recruit a woman to act as spirit-inspired author of the volume designed to reveal Holy Mother Wisdom's existence and views to the outside world. Paulina Bates of Watervliet was selected to act as Holy Mother Wisdom's instrument in this publication venture. As a writing instrument, Bates was released from other routine work of the sisterhood and given a room of her own to work in, "in the most still and retired part of the dwellinghouse, to resort to, whenever she was summoned by the trumpet of the holy Angel, to receive the word of God," as the preface to the book by her elders indicates.[38]

Seth Youngs Wells and Calvin Green, the male Shaker leaders who had been in charge of preparing all Shaker publications since the time of Lucy Wright, edited Paulina Bates's draft anthology of messages for publication. They felt that heavy rewriting was required. Green tells us in his manuscript autobiography that although Holy Mother Wisdom wanted her message to come initially through a female instrument, she acknowledged that the editing should be done by the more literate males:

> But Holy Wisdom by Inspiration said that "she could not create new faculties in those Instuments which were chosen, but all that any spirit could do was to Inspire the faculties that were created in them—Hence tho they might be the most suitable to bring forth an original inspired message yet the language & arrangement might be deficient; & often may be improved

to be better understood—This department is more adapted to the male sex."[39]

In the "Testimony of the Inspired Writer of this Book," with which the excerpts in this chapter begin, Paulina Bates attempts to convince her reader of the authenticity of her gift, but in doing so she perhaps "protests too much" for a modern reader. She claims not only not to have been manipulated by the elders in any way, but also to have been totally ignorant of Shaker theological writings, despite her long life in the community:

> Neither have I ever been influenced by what was laid down in the pub- lications of Believers in any one point. For although I had lived among Believers eighteen years, yet I never read one of their publications once through, nor have I ever read but very little in them, and that little was when I first came among the people, which soon passed out of my rec- ollection and was as though I had never read it.[40]

The Divine Book of Holy and Eternal Wisdom clearly defines Holy Mother Wisdom's derivative and secondary role in the creation and redemption.[41] In a speech attributed to God the Father, we hear that

> the woman was created to be the glory of the man. This I the God of heaven decreed when I stretched forth with my almighty hand, & brought forth the lesser power, the bright & adorned Wisdom, who is as one brought up at my side, the glory of the greater power, yet subject in all things. How then is the Son of Man to appear in his glory, except he appear in and with the woman, whom I created to be the bright glory of man, yet subject in all things?[42]

In this chapter, excerpts are included from a long explanation offered by Holy Mother Wisdom of the creation, fall, and redemption. In this of- ficially sanctioned and highly male-edited version of Wisdom's story, we find no protest against woman-blaming of the sort we saw in the manu- script "Holy Mother Wisdom's Fold" (quoted above). Orthodox Shaker gen- der dualism had by this time led theologians to the theory that even Lucifer must have had a female partner, a "mother of harlots." She plays her part in Holy Mother Wisdom's narrative as "the mother spirit of the power of opposition," the "co-worker" and "helper meet" of "the father of all abomi- nations." Thus a female principle is still blamed for bringing evil into the universe—even if she can only act in a subordinate capacity!

In a final excerpt from Bates's volume, "Particular Instructions to Fe- males,"[43] Holy Mother Wisdom's voice advises women in the world how to remain as little carnal as possible while in the married state:

> Listen and understand: Ye are not called to become defiled and polluted and to wallow in fleshly gratifications as a sow walloweth in the mire in

order to fulfill the marriage covenant and rear up an offspring to him
[man] and become a crown of glory to his existence. Nay, in no wise. I,
Wisdom, will teach you a far better way to act the part of a mother and
a bosom friend to your companion.

Wisdom even suggests wily feminine behavior by which wives will be
able to control men for their own good:

Thou mayst be artful in thy insinuations, to gather the feet of thy husband
within his own dwelling, lest he wander in by and forbidden paths, and
this, too, to thy sorrow and bitterness in the time to come.

Wisdom also urges non-Shaker women to "use all your influence to
suppress the haunts of iniquity and debauchery," and at the same time try
"to do good to those of [your] sex, that lie buried in ruinous habits." This
is advice which reminds us that Shaker leaders were aware of reform movements in the outside world—in this case, of the female moral reform movement which began in the growing cities of the eastern United States in the
1830s.[44]

Bates's text was published in 1849, when skepticism and apathy within
Shaker communities had already seriously undermined the effectiveness
of the revival. Heavily rewritten to express the theological and social ideology of the central ministry at this time—including a conservative, traditional gender ideology—it will disappoint the modern reader who is
searching for a Shaker sister's independent perspective on Shaker religion.
Yet it is of great interest in showing the degree to which a thoroughgoing
but nonfeminist gender dualism had penetrated Shaker theology and social
ideology by midcentury.

Feminist scholars of religion are currently debating the importance of
the Holy Mother Wisdom figure of the midcentury revival to Shaker women
and men. The most positive view of the possible spiritual and emotional
impact on Believers of the ritual drama of Holy Mother Wisdom's visits is
offered by Marjorie Procter-Smith, drawing on current feminist critiques of
patriarchal religion. For Procter-Smith,

Each woman and man in the community received at the hands of a woman, a gift directly from God, the mark of Holy Mother Wisdom, and
heard from the lips of a woman words of judgment or blessing. Whereas
during the years before the revival women were visible in the dance, but
largely silent during preaching and exhortation, during the revival, and
especially during rituals associated with Holy Mother Wisdom, women
became not only more prominently visible, but more audible as well.[45]

But what of Believers' inner experience of this radical reconceptualiza-
tion of the male God of traditional Christianity? Linda Mercadante has read
through a set of sixty testimonials written in 1843 in the eastern commu-

nities of Enfield, Connecticut, Harvard, Massachusetts, and Watervliet and New Lebanon, New York, in order to look closely at how Holy Mother Wisdom might have been felt or seen by actual Shaker women and men. She has pointed out that "few of them actually use female images of God," and "in three of the four communities the name of Holy Mother Wisdom is absent from the majority of the testimonies."[46] Several writers at the Harvard community who had functioned as instruments for Holy Mother Wisdom (including male instruments) did write about experiences of being, in Mercadante's reading, "personally enlivened by the Mother Spirit." But the infrequent references to Holy Mother Wisdom by members of other communities she found to be "formulaic rather than personalized." Mercadante concludes her analysis:

> It is clear that average Shakers did not simply adopt the doctrinal perspective whole even as they were surrounded by it and encouraged to appropriate it for their own. It is ironic that the gender-inclusive doctrine of God was formulated largely by males, yet the liberty taken by many males and females was to refrain from using it. . . . Perhaps Lamson was correct in suspecting that the visitations, however well-intentioned, did not arise from the spiritual experience of the leadership (or, it should be added, of the general membership), but were instead orchestrated by the leaders for the benefit of the rank and file.[47]

Spiritualistic Culture in the Female Sphere

Underneath the "high" officially sanctioned public spiritualism represented by the prophetic pronouncements and community rituals of the 1840s, there was always another stream of spirit communication. This flowed primarily through female spirit instruments[48] and served to express (and perhaps recreate) feelings of connectedness between individual living Shakers and their spiritual ancestors and recently departed friends and companions. Encouraging gift messages in a variety of invisible and visible forms came from protective beings in the spirit world, male and female, and functioned to praise Believers for faithfully living the self-denying life that would lead to salvation.

Mary Hazard recorded some of the songs and messages and invisible symbolic tokens given to her and other sisters in the New Lebanon Church Family between 1839 and 1842 in a small, beautifully calligraphed booklet, "Precious Crumbs of Heavenly Food." Despite the conventional language employed by the instrument to represent the speech of exalted beings, we get occasional glimpses of individual relationships among the sisters from such messages. For example, the "Words of Comfort from Mother Ann," dated January 13, 1841, describes Mary Hazard as "sitting by a window, bearing a grave and solemn countenance, as if very weary and borne down with the burdens of this life." Perhaps the spirit instrument who brought this message was a friend in the sisterhood who recognized Mary Hazard's moment of genuine need.

The sisters who wrote for the spirits sometimes took the opportunity to exercise their artistic talents. In "New Years Verses for the New Lebanon Sisters" (1846), a set of symbolic spiritual gifts from Mother Ann (crown, watch, cup, key, robe, and others) is given to each of the fifteen members of the Church Family sisterhood, accompanied by individualized verses in which the same essential message is artfully varied. Similarly, a few members of the Hancock and New Lebanon sisterhoods enhanced their role as writers of spirit messages by creating some fine symbolic drawings, using pen and ink and watercolor. Some of these were produced well into the late 1850s, after all the official rites of the revival had been disestablished, and a new generation of male leaders at New Lebanon and elsewhere were debating with puzzlement and some rancor whether the revival's spiritualistic excesses had produced more losses than gains.[49]

The Legacy of the Midcentury Revival for Shaker Religion

The midcentury revival left a mixed legacy for Shaker culture and religion. The politicized spiritualism of the midcentury revival initially enabled Shaker communities to enact conflicts among Believers that could not otherwise be expressed legitimately. The leadership perceived the danger of allowing the spirits to speak for discontented individuals and factions, and many, perhaps most, Believers were aware of the leadership's efforts to transform spirit inspiration into a tool for social and doctrinal control. Disillusion and loss of membership—especially among males—were among the negative results of the New Lebanon leadership's decision in the late 1830s to pronounce that spirit inspiration authentic which was approved by the ministry and elders.

Yet the fundamental basis of spiritualism—the belief in the ability of the living and dead to communicate—remained a vital current in Shaker religion throughout the nineteenth century. It took new direction when the "spirit rappers" from the outside world began to visit interested eastern Shaker communities in the 1850s.[50] A less politicized and less entirely Shaker form of spiritualism provided both religious excitement and comfort for the bereaved, well into the twentieth century.

Among the seeds of later nineteenth-century Shaker visionary activity and spiritualism are the expressive traditions of the domestic gift-giving spiritualistic culture primarily developed by the sisterhood during the revival and never abandoned in disillusion. In a journal entry for December 1, 1857, Anna White of New Lebanon shows us the feeling which this current of midcentury Shaker spiritualism enabled the sisterhood to express:

Death has visited us—Our much loved Sister Eunice has left this mundane sphere to dwell in the land of Spirits—the fell destroyer laid her low and that form we loved so well is deposited in the cold cold grave never shall we behold her pleasant visage or be partakers of the good she imparted from temporal labors. All shared in them alike—milk butter & cheese 3 times a day—she faithfully performed her duties in that line to the satisfaction of all.—It is very near 8 years that she worked in the Dairy. . . . Still we have the pleasure of knowing that she can administer that food to us that will nourish and strengthen the immortal part. May she hover around as a guardian angel aiding & bestowing power to the needy from her bright home in Heaven—Farewell dear Sister in love . . . [51]

NOTES

1. An internal revival occurred in 1807 at the Harvard community, in response to a letter from Lucy Wright (Procter-Smith, *Women in Shaker Community and Worship*, 181, quoting Clara Endicott Sears, *Gleanings from Old Shaker Journals*, 188–89). Another took place in 1819–1820 at Pleasant Hill (see letters from Pleasant Hill ministry to New Lebanon, January 25 and February 23, 1820, OClWHi IV A 52). A third, in 1827 in New Lebanon, may have begun in a revival outside the Shaker communities, in Berkshire county, Massachusetts, and New Hampshire (Priscilla Brewer, *Shaker Communities, Shaker Lives*, 106).

2. Elizabeth Lovegrove's "Journal of the Revival" plentifully documents both positive and negative aspects of the 1827 revival within Shaker communities (OClWHi V B 93 and 94).

3. Historians of Shakerism acknowledge the difficulty of establishing an end date for the "era of Manifestations," as it was later called by the Shakers themselves. Brewer uses 1844 as the end of a "first phase" and discusses the 1844–1858 period as a fading out of the ritualized spiritualism developed in the early phase (*SCSL*, 136).

4. In this emphasis on the politics of revivalism, I join Priscilla Brewer, who sees the events as "a religious response to deeply felt insecurities" (*SCSL*, 115). Brewer especially emphasizes the different interests of the older and younger generations in her analysis of the politics of Shaker spiritualism (116).

5. Many analysts of Shakerism have commented on the numerical predominance of women as spirit instruments during the revival. Louis Kern, in *An Ordered Love*, tends to see ecstatic religion as an expression of suppressed erotic feeling. He views Shaker women as more drawn to this mode because they had fewer other physical outlets than men, because of the sisters' confinement to the domestic sphere in their work lives. Marjorie Procter-Smith has commented critically on this interpretation as failing to take seriously the religious experience of the instruments (*Women in Shaker Community and Worship*, 194–95).

6. I. M. Lewis, *Ecstatic Religion* (2d ed., 1989), pp. 28–30. Lewis distinguishes "peripheral" from "central" possession cults, on the basis of the social status of those possessed and the function of the spirit-possessed behavior. Marjorie Procter-Smith, among others, has applied Lewis's concept of "peripheral possession" to the onset of the Shaker midcentury revival among young girls and women (*Women in Shaker Community and Worship*, 206).

7. Both Marjorie Procter-Smith and Linda Mercadante have critically assessed the impact of the revival on Shaker gender theory and on Shaker women. In this

introduction I draw on their work and that of Ann Braude, who has studied non-Shaker spiritualism.

8. Bishop, "A Daily Journal of Passing Events," 1838–1839 (NN Item 1). All further quotations from Bishop in the text and notes for this chapter are taken from this source, unless otherwise noted.

9. Bishop clearly approved of the visionists' "labors" with lukewarm older Shakers. "Considering the state that these aged people had been in for many years, especially Gideon, entirely out of union in every sense of the word, & filled up with opposition to the order of God, some thought the change wrought upon him was as great a miracle as the raising of a dead body. But whether he, or any of them will keep what they have gained, is yet to be proved" (February 9, 1838).

10. Brewer, SCSL, 112–14.

11. Bishop's journal suggests that Stewart was accusing Green of "feeling & acting against order & government" (May 9, 1838). Stewart's messages from Mother Ann at this time stressed "the confession of sin. It was recommended for old believers, who had come to a stand so that they could not live or work together in union, to open their whole lives, & so take a new start" (May 12, 1838).

12. The Goodwin sisters joined the New Lebanon Church Family on December 19, 1833, and would have been ages 10 and 14 when the revival began in 1837. Both were active spirit instruments. In an entry for August 1838, Isaac N. Youngs's "Personal Diary" (NOC) records his shock at the apostasy of Ann Goodwin: "I learn that Ann Goodwin has gone off!! She had abundance of gifts, visions etc.—but all has not saved her!"

13. Among those who seem to have been skeptical or resistant to the particular direction the revival was taking were Gilbert Avery, later to be a lead ministry elder (Procter-Smith, *Women in Shaker Community and Worship*, 192), and Calvin Green, already a twenty-five-year veteran preacher and former Gathering Order elder. Though Bishop's "Daily Journal of Passing Events" records Calvin Green's public chastisement as a result of messages from Mother Ann, delivered by Philemon Stewart in April 1838, Green himself makes no reference to this humiliation in his description of his role in the revival in his "Biographic Memoir." Green went on to deliver many prophetic messages himself, speaking or writing for the prophets Elisha, Joel, Daniel, Zechariah, and Elijah.

14. "A True Picture! South House Wisdom's Valley, February 24, 1842," in Spirit Messages, vol. 4, no. 35, MWiW.

15. "Eloping" here simply means absconding—no lesbian relationship is implied. Elleyet Gibbs of the Watervliet Second Family left the community September 23, 1839; Elizabeth Oaks of the Hancock community left October 30, 1839; other prominent spirit instruments who defected and thus cast doubt on the authenticity of their gifts include John Allen and Mary Wicks, of New Lebanon, and Sarah Simons of Watervliet. (New Lebanon ministry to Union Village, November 30, 1846, OClWHi IV B 5). Also see Daniel Patterson, *The Shaker Spiritual*, 401–404.

16. Eleven-year-old Warren Chase brought some messages from Mother "to some of the children" on May 18, 1838, according to Bishop. Ann Braude's *Radical Spirits* includes a fine discussion of the congruence between latter nineteenth-century U.S. stereotypes of femininity and the role of spirit medium (chap. 4, "The Meaning of Mediumship, 82–116).

17. New Lebanon ministry to Pleasant Hill ministry, December 4, 1837 (OClWHi IV B 8).

18. Cited in Brewer, SCSL, 125.

19. Andrews, *The People Called Shakers*, 174.

20. Brewer (SCSL 250 n. 19) cites a document in the Andrews collection, "Orders

Given by Mother Lucy, Feburary 12, 1839," which was received by Eldress Cassand-ana Goodrich; and Joseph Wicker was a Hancock elder who also acted as an instrument.

21. Hazel Spencer Phillips, *Richard the Shaker*, 115.

22. Brewer, *SCSL*, 123.

23. In the 1850s and 1860s, after Rufus Bishop's death in 1852 had diminished the support for officially endorsed ritualistic spiritualism, disagreements were expressed retrospectively with the dietary reform rules received by Philemon Stewart in the form of a spirit message. Bishop was seen in retrospect by Watervliet elder Freegift Wells as "too tender hearted" and therefore as having been taken advantage of by "fanatics" like Philemon Stewart. (See OClWHi VII B 270, one of several writings from the 1850s by Wells, "protesting the rules against the use of tea, coffee and pork.")

24. The large New Lebanon Church Family consisted at this time of two separate communal families, called the First Order and Second Order. Though all members had signed the covenant, thus dedicating their property and labor to the use of the Church, those in the First Order may have been considered spiritually more advanced than those in the Second Order.

25. Stewart was the instrument who wrote the "Holy Laws of Zion Given by Almighty God through Father James" in 1840. This included the prohibition on pork, tobacco, and liquor. He was also the author of the first major publication derived from this revival, *A Sacred Roll and Book* (1843). Soon after the death of Rufus Bishop in 1852, Stewart lost the support of the New Lebanon lead ministry brethren, Amos Stewart and Daniel Boler. His efforts to continue to function as a bearer of prophetic messages of behavioral reform in the 1850s and 1860s were thwarted, in his view, by the next generation of central ministry leaders.

26. Priscilla Brewer views Philemon Stewart as someone who "may have been using the excitement of the revival to carve out a position of authority . . . outside the Eldership," *SCSL*, 125–26.

27. Brewer cites a MS version of the "Holy Orders of the Church" in the Andrews Collection (DeWint, SA 750).

28. Brewer suggests that this phase of the revival may be seen as "the Shaker response to the foreign & home missionary movements that involved so many young people in the World during this period," *SCSL*, 129.

29. MacDonald manuscript, quoted in Andrews, *The People Called Shakers*, 169–70.

30. The seceder Hervey Elkins also described pressure from the elders to "take upon me an Indian, a Norwegian or an Arabian spirit," because "they regarded the inspiration of simple and unsophisticated spirits, as a stepping stone to a higher revelation" and such gifts "tended to simplify and humiliate the haughty spirits of the self-exalted and vain" (Elkins, as quoted in Mercadante, *Gender, Doctrine, and God*, 125).

31. Rufus Bishop, Watervliet, to the ministry at Union Village, November 3, 1842 (OClWHi, IV B 9). Edward Deming Andrews discusses Shaker identification with Native Americans in *The People Called Shakers*, 169–71.

32. In 1842 all Shaker communities were instructed to follow the lead of New Lebanon in consecrating a mountaintop meeting area where an engraved stone marker was placed and community-wide purification rites were conducted twice yearly on dates established by New Lebanon spirit instruments. Detailed records of the proceedings were kept in many of the communities during the 1840s. See "Hancock Mountain Meeting," in this chapter, for an example.

33. From the point of view of a disillusioned former insider, David Lamson de-

scribed a ceremony at Hancock in 1844 in which prospective Shakers living in the Gathering Family were inducted into the gift of Holy Mother Wisdom. Lamson called Martha VanValen and Judith Collins "the chief prophetesses in the society." In Lamson's account, as in the Shaker one excerpted for this chapter, Martha VanValen also acted as the medium for Holy Mother Wisdom (*Two Years' Experience among the Shakers* [1848]).

34. Marjorie Procter-Smith, *Women in Shaker Community and Worship*, 200.

35. Lamson was offended by both the idea and the representation in spiritualistic ritual of a female aspect of the godhead. He predicted that some of his readers "will consider this gift not only as a solemn mockery, but as really blasphemous" (95).

36. ["Daughtie"], "Fifteen Years A Shakeress," in *The Galaxy* (1872), 37–38. The "seal" of Holy Mother Wisdom was represented in watercolor drawings by Shaker artists in November 1847 (Daniel Patterson, *Gift Drawing and Gift Song*, 87–89).

37. This was the second spirit-inspired book to be published by the Shakers. The first was Philemon Stewart's *A Sacred Roll and Book* (1843).

38. Bates, *Divine Book of Holy and Eternal Wisdom*, 694–95. For an analysis of the paradoxical way in which feminine stereotypes were both adhered to and subverted in the role of the female spirit instrument in later nineteenth-century spiritualism, see Ann Braude, *Radical Spirits* (especially chapter 4, "The Meaning of Mediumship," 82–116).

39. Green, "Biographic Memoir," 356. He says he first found the material dauntingly disorderly, "& altho the matters were truthfully written, yet many things were not so clearly expressed as to be understood by the uninspired. . . . " (357).

40. Bates was not alone in writing defensively about the authenticity of the spirit inspiration: there is a stream of defensive argumentation about its authenticity by Shaker leaders in correspondence and journals from the time of the first visions in 1837. There was good reason to anticipate skepticism in the outside world, of course. David Lamson's *Two Years' Experience* had accused Shaker spirit instruments of being mouthpieces of the elders in 1848, just the year before Bates's book was published.

41. As Linda Mercadante has pointed out, "In the *Divine Book* Bates gives the clearest exposition of hierarchy in the Godhead yet encountered in the theology surveyed" (including the 1808 *Testimony of Christ's Second Appearing* and the 1827 *A Summary View of the Millennial Church*) (Mercadante, *Gender, Doctrine, and God*, 106).

42. Bates, Divine Book of Holy and Eternal Wisdom, 298. For a systematic discussion of the dual-gender Shaker godhead, see Mercadante, *Gender, Doctrine, and God*, 74–115.

43. Marjorie Procter-Smith comments that here "Holy Mother Wisdom turns her attention to domestic matters in a manner fully consistent with the mid-nineteenth century "cult of domesticity" (*Women in Shaker Community and Worship*, 204–206).

44. Carroll Smith-Rosenberg analyzes the New York Female Moral Reform Society's history in relationship to the origins of the broader women's rights movement in "Beauty, the Beast, and the Militant Woman: Sex Roles and Sexual Standards in Jacksonian America," *American Quarterly*, 23, 4 (Fall 1971), 562–84.

45. Procter-Smith, *Women in Shaker Community and Worship*, 200.

46. Mercadante, *Gender, Doctrine, and God*, 119–31. These testimonials were solicited by Shaker communal family leadership, probably at the request of the ministry. Members were required to testify to their faith in the recently published collection of spirit-inspired writings by Philemon Stewart. The testimonies are thus far from spontaneous statements of religious experience.

47. Mercadante, 143–45.

48. Louis Kern analyzed the spirit messages by type and gender in Stewart's *Sacred Roll and Book* and found that "in visions accompanied by gifts, almost all the intermediaries were women" (*An Ordered Love*, 106).

49. The work of the sisters in translating some of the visionary experiences into permanent graphic form is now being examined by feminist scholars of art and religion. See especially Jane Crosthwaite, "The Spirit Drawings of Hannah Cohoon: Window on the Shakers and Their Folk Art," *Communal Societies*, 7 (1987), 1–15; and Sally M. Promey, *Spiritual Spectacles: Vision and Image in Mid-Nineteenth-Century Shakerism* (Bloomington: Indiana University Press, forthcoming). Daniel Patterson has identified at least one gift drawing in Mary Hazard's hand "in one of the many tunebooks she wrote and signed" (Daniel W. Patterson, *Gift Drawing and Song: A Study of Two Shaker Forms of Inspiration*, 71).

50. Rufus Bishop, ever hopeful about the spirits, confirmed his belief in the "spirit rappers" in a letter of March 17, 1851; and by December 15, 1851, spirit rappers had visited the Enfield, Hancock, and New Lebanon communities to hold seances. For the next several years Shaker leaders debated vigorously among themselves about the validity of the non-Shaker spiritualist movement. From the 1870s through the turn of the century, a faction of highly committed "progressive reformers" led by Frederick Evans, Antoinette Doolittle, and others at the socially progressive New Lebanon North Family, continued their association with the outside spiritualist movement.

51. "Records" kept by Anna White 1855–1880, NN Item 11.

THE ONSET OF THE REVIVAL (WATERVLIET
CHURCH FAMILY MEETING JOURNAL,
1 8 3 8 – 1 8 4 0)[1]

The two instruments that Mother called were two young sisters, viz., Nancy White and Sarah Simons. These instruments' first labors were to purify and search their own hearts. Nancy commenced January 17th and Sarah [the] 27th of the same month. They had many operations and made some addresses in public, but chiefly what was spoken, was by signs or in tongues, and was given in a manner that would not be retained, except some individual messages, until September when many songs were given. . . .

Saturday, October 12th, half past eight o'clock. Mother came to our meeting and through the instrument (N. W.) said as follows: "I visited all the rooms in retiring time to see who was asleep and in what posture you sat in. I have now come to meeting, but I cannot breathe the air that is here, but I will go away! Tomorrow I will come again and see how you feel." . . .

Sabbath 13th A.M. nine o'clock. Mother administered the gift for us to sit straight in ranks in retiring time, facing each other, and try to keep a gift. She also said, "I want all the brethren and sisters should receive my love." She said we must take her cup and drink of it. Mother said, "If you will sing that song 'Pretty children, come and drink, out of Mother's gold cup,' yea, I will dance with you, for I am here in spirit with you, as much as anybody was ever upon earth." (Instrument Sarah Simons)[2] . . .

Thursday, December 27th, evening meeting. Mother Ann, in this meeting (through S. S.) spoke as follows: "You must keep up with the increasing work of God. . . . " Then she said, "I have a gift in relation to eating." She said we must eat on our knees four times a week for the present, viz., Tuesday morning, Thursday morning, Saturday night, and both meals on the Sabbath.

Monday evening, December 31st, 9 o'clock. Mother said (through S. S.): "All that have had any connection with those that have left the way of God must bring it to the light, or it would be a loss to their souls, and they would have their judgments!" . . .

Sabbath, January 20th [1839], P. M. The Church, including the First and Second Orders, assembled at the meeting house, in company with the beloved ministry. A number (four) of the members of the Legislature attended our meeting this afternoon at the meeting house.

Those that were inspired and gifted in vision or spiritual sight could plainly see the "line that was drawn between the world and the Believers." The spirits who particularly manifested themselves on this occasion were Washington, Lafayette, Clinton, and Adams. Lafayette said, "We are joined to the Tree of Life." (Instrument Sarah Simons) . . .

February 14. At the close of our meeting this evening, Mother Ann, through one of her instruments, communicated to us and bestowed upon us her love. She said she felt a particular gift of encouragement for us. "And," says Mother, "I know it is a trying time with you on account of sickness, but take courage and press forward in the increasing work of God. Partake ye freely of my love and blessing." (Instrument Sarah Simons) . . .

Sabbath, March 10th. Mary Robinson, an aged sister who had deceased this morning between the hours of six and seven, attended our meeting (in the spirit) and addressed the assembly (through a young sister)[3] as follows: "Although my spirit has left the body, I am not alone. I have found Mother and obtained the privilege of making some communications to the brethren and sisters. I desire the family would all receive my thanks, love, and blessing, for I feel as if I could not leave this house until I had returned my thanks to you all." She furthermore begged the forgiveness of all, if she had hurt or grieved the feelings of any one . . . (Instrument Sarah Simons) . . .

Saturday, March 16th, P. M. . . . The spirit of Mother was present in our worship and spoke as follows, "O dear brethren and sisters, pray for strength. . . . Here I suffered in the body: yea, yea, in this place; I suffered for poor souls! And I have suffered since I left the body and shall continue to suffer till all nations, kindred, and tongues shall hear the sound of this gospel. . . . " (Moriah Gillet) . . .

Sabbath, March 31st, A. M. . . . In the first place then we received a very satisfactory, blessed, and interesting gift from Father Joseph, which was administered particularly to the young brethren, under forty years of age.[4] One of the young sisters under divine influence came forward . . . and immediately the inspired sister reached out both of her hands, as if to grasp something, and exclaimed, "Here's a beautiful box, containing a great variety of heavenly gifts, to wit, the gift of revelation; the gift of exhortation; the gift of prophecy, of vision and songs; the gifts of spiritual sight, of sense and feeling; the gift of speaking in new tongues; the gift of the interpretation of tongues; the gift of outward operations, bowing and turning; the gifts of humiliation and the searching power of God; and the gifts of faith and obedience."

Each individual under forty years of age was to receive and be benefited by these gifts, according to their faith and zeal to labor for and improve in them. . . . The box containing the above gift was given to the elder brother, and Father Joseph said that "All the young brethren who desire to receive and partake of any of these gifts may do so by going to the elder brother and asking in faith for whatever gift they most need or desire." . . . (Instrument Sarah Simons)

After the foregoing was accomplished, the inspired sister stated that Mother Ann said she had planted a beautiful tree in this place while she was here in the body and that the tree bore twelve kinds of fruit, viz., charity, meakness, patience, forebearance, and longsuffering, etc. And on the top of the tree was a fruit called love, which was very beautiful and overspread all the other branches of the tree, giving grace to every other virtue.[5]

Mother wants the brethren and sisters to partake largely of the gift of love, for it is a gift very much needed in this family. Mother says she will have nothing to do with any other kind of fruit but what was and is found to grow upon this tree, which is the Tree of Life. (Nancy White) . . .

Wednesday, April 3, 1839. Mother manifested herself through one of the young sisters; and after obtaining permission of the elders to speak her feelings, she said, "I do not want you, brethren and sisters, to be inquiring of one another about the gifts that have been given."[6]

Here the inspired sister began to sign out what expressions displeased Mother, thus: "Don't you begin to see visions yet! I should think you might begin to see visions! Come, sing me a new song; I want to hear you sing a new song right off! Can't you tell me who is here with me? I want to know who is here and I should think you might tell!"

Mother says, "Such conversation as this, used by way of derision or lightness, grieves my spirit. . . ." Mother says, "I do not want to accuse any one; but I felt to speak on this wise, to caution you, brethren and sisters. . . . The spirit of evil is striving to destroy the good seed that is among you . . . " (Nancy White) . . .

August 4 . . . Thus saith Mother: "In union with the elders, I have a few words to say. There have been many doubts, and still there are many, why those that are chosen as instruments and have had great gifts given to them should not endure to the end, but should finally fall away.[7]

"Dear brethren and sisters, it is not the vessel but the gift, the mighty power of God, that you must respect. . . . Some, to be sure, I have chosen and I visit them with my compelling power; but you must not look in them for perfection more than in others, for the gift is not theirs . . . " (Instrument Sephronia H. Smith)

Saturday, October 26, P. M. . . . Thus saith Father William: "It is not with flesh and blood that I would wish to contend (i.e., no names would I wish to mention at present); but it is with the spirit of opposition that has found a resting place here. But it does not show itself as it is. If it did, we should know how to meet it, but it is covered, yea, brethren and sisters, I say it is completely under cover.

" . . . Some will say, I could receive a gift if it was administered through such a one or such a one, and I should have more faith in it. . . .

"Again, this opposite spirit will say, 'Some have failed.' But what of that," says Father? "Will a man, having a handful of bank bills, and one, two, or more prove counterfeit, throw them all away? The answer is readily, nay. Brethren and sisters, have you not all had spiritual swords given to you? And will you not use them? Will you not try to rid this house of the spirit of opposition that has found a resting place here?" (Instrument Moriah Gillet) . . .

Wednesday, February 12 [1840], P. M. "A short address from Mother Lucy, given and read in the presence of Eldress Ruth and Sister Asenath and the elder sisters to some of the sisters that are chosen as instruments."

The roll was brought and given to one of the sisters. She took it and read as follows: "You must be obedient to the good counsel that ye have received from the ministry and elders at this time, for in obedience to your ministry and elders you will find protection. For it is through them that you receive strength and support. Yea, you must bow low, low, very low, for when I carry my gifts around I want my instruments to be in that situation they can receive them at the first offer. If you will be obedient to my anointed lead, I will not suffer one of you to fall from the work of God. . . . When my finger touches your head, your arm, or your shoulder, and causes the cold chills to run from your head to your feet, then believe it is the power of God." . . . Then Mother, through the one that had been reading aloud, said, "I have something for all of you, viz., a gift of love for each one. . . . Now," says Mother, "If you are faithful to improve in the gifts that I have given you, you will be blessed with more." (Read by Moriah Gillet, Instrument). . . .

Saturday evening, March 7, eight o'clock. An instrument (Abigail M.) came forward and said, "Father Joseph and Mother Lucy have come to attend meeting with us and they have brought with them a multitude of young Believers from the spiritual world. These had never known that there was such a people on earth! And now they have the privilege granted them to come and see us." Then Father Joseph (by the instrument) placed in the alley between the brethren and sisters a basket of grapes for each one to take a cluster. This was done. Then the inspired said, "There still is some clusters of grapes left in the basket and Father Joseph wants the brethren and sisters, each one, to put a bud from their union branch (which they got last Sabbath) into the basket, as a present to the young Believers to take home with them. It will please them to take with them something from where Mother lived while on earth. And also, any that have received two pocket handkerchiefs may put one of them neatly over the basket, so as to cover the fruit." Next the inspired received two balls of union cords, one for elder brother and one for elder sister, and each went round; one went round all the brethren and the other went round all the sisters, to bind and encircle them in these cords of union. . . .

Sabbath, March 8, 1840, nine o'clock meeting. In this meeting Mother gave Jesse Harwood a chain. She put it round his neck and fastened it to his arms and, says Mother, "I will help you and strengthen you so that you may be a help to other souls."

Then Nathan Slosson was called forward to receive Mother's blessing. The instrument Sarah Simons said, "There stands by Nathan the spirit of Christ, nearly as tall as himself. It is the spirit of meekness and simplicity, which has always attended him; and Mother says he shall have rich rewards for his faithfulness." (Instrument Sarah Simons)[8]. . . .

Saturday, March 21. [Father Joseph, through Betsy Harrison]: "I have been around," says Father "to your shops, to the barns, and places of business, and I have found that which is disowned and improper to be among the people of God, and it brings great tribulation upon your heavenly parents! . . . Remember there is an all-seeing eye that sees and knows all things. And that is your heavenly Father. . . . There are some here," says Father, "that say: 'Well, we have often heard the time of separation is coming—and why don't it?' I tell you," says Father, "all these gifts and signs will come to pass . . . " (Betsy Harrison) . . .

Monday, March 23. . . . Then another instrument came forward into the alley under very mild and gentle operations and exclaimed, "Elder Sister, how pretty I feel! I never felt so happy before! Mother has clothed me with a robe of purity. I feel none of the spirit of opposition now. I do not feel pride or bondage! I am willing to do anything Mother wants me to do." She then delivered a short message from Mother, as follows: "The Church shall be purified . . . and," says Mother "when the spirit of opposition is purged out, my gifts will be administered through pure vessels."[9] (Instrument Sephronia H. Smith) . . .

Wednesday, May 13, P. M. . . . Father Joseph came to one of the young sisters, and by inspiration she spoke as follows, "Father Joseph has brought a book containing the orders of this family[10] and wishes Brother Rufus to take it." (This he accordingly did.) In the course of meeting, Mother requested to have something read to the family out of the book. Accordingly, one of the gifted was called upon, and the book presented to her, from which she read as follows: "It is against order to support union with those that have turned their backs to the way of God. If it is necessary to have any business done with them, let it be done by the deacons, in union with the elders, and no one else is to meddle with it or have anything to say about it. If inadvertently it should happen, or necessity require any of the private members to have any conversation with anyone of this kind, it must be confessed to the elders verbatim before assembling with the family in meeting."[11] After the reading of the above, the book was closed by Father Joseph and returned to Brother Rufus . . .

Thursday, May 14, P. M. . . . Father [Joseph] called upon an inspired one to ask Brother Rufus to lay the book of orders on the floor. This being done, Father then said, "Are all of the brethren and sisters willing I should open this book where I feel to?" The answer was "yea." He then opened it and said to the inspired one, "Read." She then read as follows: "It is contrary to order to have more than one newspaper taken by the family, and that must be kept at the office unless there is something that is necessary for the family to know, and then it must be given to the elders and they may do as they feel to be proper. . . . [12] Reserve such as will be useful to the young, but not such as will fill their minds with evil. The excuse is this: 'Oh! They must have something that is pleasing to the mind to take up the sense to learn them to read, and something to fill up their odd moments.' What! let them have that which will fill their minds with all manner of evil to learn them to read? such as fighting, quarrelling, deception, and lies? . . . I tell you, if things remain as they are now, there will not be one of them saved, nay, not one! For they have got already that instilled into their minds that would bid defiance to the ministry and elders, and nothing but the mighty power of God can erase it from them. . . . I will ask the elders, has the family been any more orderly and obedient to you or any more subject to the deacons, since that library was erected? If not, what good does it do? . . . O Jesse! See to the young, them that you have the particular charge of. I have had a hand in placing you there and expect to support you in it, let the feelings be what they may. Do, Jesse! Search the Children's Order and see what is there. And you, Moriah, attend to your duty, for both males and females need searching. . . . "

A Vision seen at Watervliet, Sabbath P.M., May 17, 1840.

In the time of retiring (says the visionist) there came into the room where I was a number of spirits. They came near to me and filled me with the power of God. I knew them not. They held in their hands a bright covering, or robe. This they spread over me, and immediately I was lost as to the things of time. I then saw a large sister come in, who appeared to me like one in the body. She placed herself a little behind me, bearing toward my right side, and reached out her arm to me. Wishing to know how a spirit felt, I took hold of her arm. "Take care," she said, and pointed to a place on her arm that had been broken, and acted as though she wanted I should notice it. I then felt of her arm again and I could feel the place where it had been broken very plain. She appeared very urgent that I should notice her arm. I then inquired her name. She smiled and said, "It is Hannah." I then asked the same question again, but she only replied, "It is Hannah." Thinking she was a spirit seeking after some gift, I asked her if she knew how to get her arm cured. At this she smiled and appeared to be pleased at my asking such a question, but gave me no answer. I asked again. She smiled and said, "Hark! Hark! I think I hear the sound of a trumpet and a distant sound of angels singing." I answered I would listen, if I could only hear them. I then listened and heard the sound of their horn at a distance. She (Hannah) then said, "Mother gave me liberty to come see you and make myself known and stay till I should hear the sound of a trumpet. Then I must be ready to join a company that are going to march to your meeting with Father and Mother at the head. For," added she, "Mother says a large company of holy angels are going to attend your meeting this afternoon . . . " I then came to myself. (Instrument Ann Buckingham)

On the same day, at six o'clock P. M., she came to another sister and went to see the elders. While there (through the instrument Sephronia H. Smith) she said a great deal, but it could be understood only in part, as it was spoken in an unknown language. In the course of the week, she came to the same sister again. She talked a great deal was very urgent to let it be known what she wanted; but still she was not understood. She went to another instrument (viz., Moriah Gillet). She told her, that her name was called Hannah Goodrich. She told her that she had been to others and she was glad that she had found her out.

Hannah told Moriah Gillet that Mother had given her liberty to come and see her children here and make herself known. Also gave her liberty to gather all the good she could to take to her people, which she said were a good distance off. "For," says she, "Mother has given me the charge of a people, and I want to beg some of the presents that Mother has given her children here to take to them. . . . " All that were present gave to her very freely. She said she should visit us again. It might be well to remark here, that many who were acquainted with her while in the body are living and say her arm was broken by an accident. . . .

Sabbath, May 24, nine o'clock A. M. [Sephronia H. Smith]: Mother brought a roll. She said it was for the ministry, written by the hand of the Eternal Father (to be read in afternoon meeting).

Afternoon, two o'clock. Both orders of the church together with the good ministry assembled at the meeting house. . . . Several instruments were called upon to come forward, but it seemed the enemy was present and was a hindrance to the gift. However, the good prevailed and the inspired read with great power as follows: "What is Man? . . . How often hath it repented me that I made Man! . . . And were it not for that One, and for that Second One, who have kept my commandments and drawn a straight line in the earth, and for the sake of these my peoples who have followed their example, I would sweep the earth!" . . . Then Mother Ann called on them to treasure up this word of the Eternal Father. (Moriah Gillet)

Mother, through another instrument, said, "The reason why it was so hard to read this roll was because information had been given this morning that it should be read this afternoon; and the enemy has taken the advantage of this and he has come to eat up and devour the word of God." Father Joseph, through the same instrument, said, "There should be record kept of gifts and orders of God that are given. I have been looking around, to see if I can find any one for this gift to rest upon, some one that is suitable, but I find no one that is prepared. But I hope," says Father, "ere long some one will become sufficiently purified to keep a true record of these things, for one should be kept."[13] (Sephronia H. Smith.) . . .

Sabbath, August 30, A. M. In this morning's meeting, an inspired one came forth and turned powerfully for some time, then stooped down and for several minutes wrote on the floor. Meanwhile, another inspired came forth and also turned a great deal (say 300 times or more) and spoke as follows: . . . "Mother says, 'Let no one judge the power of God! The time is short! Let no one judge the power of God and think there is enough of it! And too much of it! as some think, and say,' Mother says." (Sephronia H. Smith) . . .

NOTES

1. Source: "A Copy of the Messages, Gifts, & Communications Given by Inspiration in the Church at Watervliet or Wisdom's Valley. Including the Years 1838, 1839, and a part of the year 1840. Part I, Part II, Part III" (N). This manuscript has a preface naming the two male and three female instruments who were chosen by the ministry and elders to "gather up and record the sacred word of God": David A. Buckingham, Frederick S. Wicker, Ann Buckingham, Angeline Annas, and Sephronia H. Smith. The record was based on "scraps, or writings on loose papers, which the Instruments themselves penned, while under the influence of the Spirit."
2. The manuscript gives the spirit instruments' names or initials in parentheses. Where I have been sure of the instrument's full name, I have supplied it.
3. During Mother Ann's work, funeral services included the receipt of inspired communications from the dead. In all likelihood, this ritual derived from memories of the contacts Ann Lee and the elders were thought to have had with spirits of the dead.
4. The males are clearly being encouraged or even pressured to enter into the spirit of the proceedings with the same enthusiasm as the females.
5. The allegorical tree bearing many different kinds of fruits and flowers simultaneously appears in the Shaker spirit drawings of the 1850s.
6. This is an indication of how early the ritualized spiritualism of the later 1830s began to be mocked and taken lightly by some Believers. Many warnings from the spirits and heavenly parents against such mockery were recorded.
7. Among the Shakers who left the communities during the era of Mother Ann's work were quite a few that had been appointed as instruments of the spirits or "heavenly parents."
8. This is a good example of the individual gift message, most frequently expressing praise and encouragement of the individual Believer.
9. This message suggests that while some spirit instruments clearly spoke the line of obedience to the community and family leaderships, others were perceived as fomenting "opposition."
10. This reference to Father Joseph's book of orders for the Watervliet Church

Family occurs six months before a dated manuscript, "The Holy Orders of the Church, Written by Father Joseph" (New Lebanon, Feb. 18, 1841) [De Wint SA 750].

11. Evidently apostates and some family members were in communication with each other.

12. An announcement was made at this time by spirit instrument that "Books, papers, & pamphlets . . . composed & printed by the world" were to be collected and taken to the office to be examined and disposed of by ministry, elders, deacons.

13. This seems to be the first public announcement of the decision to keep written records of all the spirit-inspired messages (May 1840).

A VISIONARY DREAM CONCERNING ANN ELIZA GOODWIN (1840)[1]

A Visionary Dream. July 1840.

One night while asleep, I dreamed I was on the road to heaven. It was a very smooth, pretty road, but many stones, stumps, and rocks appeared in my way. But I had not gone far before I began to hear a groaning, and as I advanced forward I kept hearing it still louder; and soon I arrived to heaven's first gate. Here I found a woman dressed in a Shaker dress.[2] She stood upon her knees, crying with a loud voice, "O Father! Heavenly Father! Do open the door of thy holy sanctuary that I may enter in." But no answer was made. She then cried again and again for the space of two hours. But no answer had she yet received. She then raised both hands in revenge and arose and started to come back to the earth again. She walked by a very smooth, pretty road but did not step one step in it. The road she was in was very broad and very uneven. I followed on behind her till we came to the Second House. Here she knocked at Zillah's door,[3] but no answer was made. She then spoke these words with great fury: "You have abused me! you have laid things to me that I was not guilty of; you have carried false reports about me to the elders, in order to cover your own sins. You have accused the children of that which they were not guilty of, and made them lie and say they had done things that they never had done. And if they would not say they had done what you accused them of, you would whip them, pull their hair, and make them go both cold and hungry. This I have seen you do when I knew you was in a passion, and this I can testify against you before both God and man." Then she knocked again and again on Zillah's door, but no answer was yet made her. But soon two brethren arose, came out of the bedroom joining [adjoining?] Zillah's room, and opened the door.[4] She then exclaimed, "O Zillah! Zillah! In my first fall, in this place I felt against you."

I then waked up.

Harriet Goodwin

NOTES

1. Source: "A Book of Rolls" (1839–1841), NOC #12,317, vol. 14. Harriet Goodwin, the spirit instrument who received this visionary dream, was a member of the New Lebanon Church Family Second Order. Another "vision concerning Ann Eliza Goodwin" written by Harriet Goodwin in September 1839 is listed in the table of contents, but the pages on which it should appear have been removed from the volume, as have two other messages.

2. From context it is clear that this is the visionist's sister, Ann Eliza Goodwin, who left the community in August 1838, after a year in which she was a very active spirit instrument.

3. Addah Zillah Potter was one of the earliest and most prominent of the New Lebanon Church Family visionists. This "Book of Rolls" includes seven of her messages.

4. In Shaker dwelling houses, sisters and brothers lived in retiring rooms with several other members of the same sex, but a sisters' room might be next door to a brothers' room. Sisters were responsible for caring for the clothing of brethren and for cleaning in the brethren's rooms.

MOTHER LUCY'S WORD TO THE SISTERS (1841)[1]

Part One

Concerning Food and Raiment.

Dearly beloved Sisters,

As I took the "Book of Holy Orders"[2] and searched and read it, I saw it had left many things rather blind in respect to the sisters. Therefore I have labored to write a few lines for your satisfaction and also to speak of some things with which I have felt very much dissatisfied.

In the first place, I will tell you how I feel in regard to extra meals and messes eat [eaten] among sisters. I do not wish, neither is it my feeling to be unreasonable, but I think when the sisters want an extra meal got, tea made, etc., because they are unwell or in any way out of health, they should have it in union with the physicians and elders. But if a sister is sick and under the physicians' care, then the physicians will see to all these things, and that will be sufficient.

But if any of the sisters need an extra meal on account of hard work, the deaconesses must see that it is provided for them. Sisters must not offer to go and get meals for each other without the consent of the elders, deaconesses, or physicians, according as the nature of the case may require.

But if the sisters want some bread and water, gruel, porridge, or any little thing of that kind, they may make it themselves or may ask some one to get for them without further liberty. But go to the table in order as much as you possibly can. You had much better have something that you can eat put onto the table, than to eat extra meals tucked round here and there. And remember, dear sisters, twice in a day is sufficient for any one to drink tea.[3] . . .

But, dear sisters, I hope you will not take the dark room for your place to gather into to eat one-sided meals of any description, unless the weather is very cold and you are very much out of health. And never put a brother there to eat on any condition whatever.

If the physicians think that any of the brethren need any gruel, bread and water, or anything of the kind for a meal, or for several put on to the table, the physicians may ask one of the sisters that has the care in the kitchen, or some one, to see that it is made and put onto the table for the brother. But one side of this, sisters are not [to?] carry on any messing nor fussing for brethren.

Part Second

Concerning the Kitchen Work.

Dear sisters,

I am not altogether satisfied with your proceedings in the kitchen. I think many times your work would go better and there would a greater blessing attend you, especially the young sisters, if one or two of the older sisters that work in the kitchen depended on taking the care and management of the work. Not have every young sister that goes into the kitchen think they must do exactly as they please with the branch they are entrusted with; and no one has any right to speak a word to them but the deaconesses, and hardly they. . . .

And another thing I am not satisfied with is the dinner you get for the washers. I think six kinds of food, besides applesauce and pickles, is dinner sufficient. . . .

Dear sisters, I have passed to and fro among you many times, and I heard a great deal that has been said in respect to buying cloth for your gowns, aprons, and handkerchiefs. I do not wonder that it appears extravagant and more than you can afford to buy indigo to color so much blue as you desire to wear.

When I was alive copperas was good enough for me to wear and I think that copperas, or some substantial bark color (if you can find any such), is good enough for you. If you would make your kitchen gowns and aprons of copperas and white, or some such color, and make your nice cloth of blue and white, and color your blue handsome, it would be all the variety you would need or desire.

But you need not use copperas for neck handkerchiefs or pocket handkerchiefs. Make them of blue and white. I have no objection to your using red for aprons or for gowns, if you will not go to an extreme, having your clothes as red as bright red flannel. And every one that has got a gown or apron of this description, I hope you will wear them out as soon as you can. . . .

Now, dear sisters, I believe if you will attend to this, you will get along and be able to do your own weaving and feel as well as you have a few years past, buying cloth that would hardly pay for making up and having to support so much variation in your dress. . . .

And now, dear sisters, in regard to your washing and ironing. I do not see any need of sisters going to the wash house to wash a pair of footings, a shirt, a gown, an apron, handkerchief, or some such thing. When sisters want things of this kind washed and are not washers themselves, they should hand them to some one that is a washer; and whoever takes them should see that they are washed according to what they are. But no one ought to take the advantage to ask the girls, or some one that will be apt to be faulted for spending their time to do such things for them. And you should attend to the same rule about clothes that have been whitened.

And no one should have a private stock of ironing, unless it is their gowns, coats, or a large batch of whitening. . . .

Some one or ones ought to oversee the washing and ironing and know that it is done well and done as it ought to be. Then sisters would not feel so scarce as they do now about sending nice clothes to the wash. . . .

Again, dear sisters, I think the late manner you have got into of pleating your old drugget and worsted gowns in small pleats, and not pressing them down, is very suitable for what it is for. But I do not like to see them worn into meeting Sabbath days—it breaks the uniform and does not look pretty. But don't, dear sisters, pleat any new gowns in this manner.

And I do not like to see you stand bent over the ironing table laying box pleats in your dark-colored and everyday cotton gowns. I think that four or five half pleats on a side in your cotton gowns look much the prettiest on you. As for your white gowns, don't make box pleats in them. And they look the prettiest not to iron the pleats at all. As for your light-colored, if you feel as though you must make six box pleats in them, I do not forbid you, but I do not like to see it.

Now, dear sisters, remember I am in every deed your Mother and friend. I do not wish to be unreasonable, but I do really desire your prosperity and increase, and that the young and rising generation may learn good economy. . . .

Mother Lucy.

Elder Sister Olive says, "O dearly beloved, fear not, for this is indeed the word of your Mother. I have many times felt afraid that you would (I mean the young would) entirely run out many rules and counsels that have formerly been given regarding kitchen work, washing and ironing, coloring, and such like.

"I do not want anyone to rise up and say, 'Elder Sister Olive did not like copperas color when she was alive.' What if I did not like it? and what if I do not like it now? I united with Mother and say, in your present circumstances copperas will be a very profitable color for you to use. And I desire you not to murmur nor complain, but use that or some such color instead of using so much blue, for I do think you have made an extravagant use of indigo, and blue and white cloth.

"Do not, dear sisters, take anything that you have ever heard me say while in time, to contradict this, the word of your Mother, or any word that ye may have heard from her previous to this. For I acknowledge and say before you all, dear sisters, that in many things I was greatly in the fault. . . .

"And know ye, I have in no wise escaped tribulation. When I met my Mother in eternity, she said to me, 'Olive, why have you stored to yourself while in time treasures which belong to the children of sin?' . . .

"On the first of March, 1840, Mother Lucy came to me and said, 'Olive, you may now prepare yourself to walk with me in tribulation, and you shall in no wise be released, nor find rest to your soul, till everything that Mother does not own in her first church on earth is condemned, and the same is made known to the ministry and elders. For you did your part at bringing in these worldly treasures; therefore, you must do your part in getting them out.

"Thus I have walked in tribulation. And for many months, know ye, I found no rest to my spirit. So never again, dear sisters, hold any thing that is not owned, neither in your hands nor in your hearts, because I gave it to you when I was upon earth. Or because I had something that was like it. Remember, this will never again be any excuse for you.

"So receive ye now my best love and know I am still your friend."

Olive Spencer.

Now, dearly beloved eldresses and deaconesses, I wish you to consider all these little things that I have spoken about, and act your wisdom and judgment concerning them.

From Mother Lucy.

Instrument Anna Dodgson.

NOTES

1. Source: "Betsy Bates Book, A Record of Individual & Private Messages, Spoken by Divine Inspiration" (NOC 9786 #12,333, vol. 26). This message is dated March 12, 1841.
2. "The Book of Holy Orders" was a spirit-inspired set of rules recently received

through Philemon Stewart of New Lebanon and promulgated by the lead ministry as authoritative.

3. A spirit-inspired message received through Philemon Stewart in the fall of 1841 forbidding the use of pork, and later tea and coffee, aroused much controversy within Shaker communities during the 1840s.

VISITS FROM ALIEN SPIRITS AT WATERVLIET (CHURCH FAMILY MEETING JOURNAL, 1842 – 1843)[1]

October 1842. [The New Lebanon lead ministry arrived October 6, saying that they brought four tribes of native spirits with them.]

They said these poor natives begged very hard for the privilege to come to Wisdom's Valley,[2] which was granted them. And they said it was their request that we should open our hearts and take them in.

But we heard nothing from these poor natives until the 16th of October, when Ruth Green became inspired and spoke for Mariah Wantay. She said she had confessed her sins to the Holy Mount[3] to Shiny Mother's Olive with her face on the floor, and she felt very thankful for her privilege among Mother's children. She said she was 175 years old now; she was ninety-three when she was killed by the white man. Her Indian's name was Peter, and they had six children, Eliza, Mary, Thomas, Lucy, Henry, and William. Eliza and Mary was killed by the white man; Eliza was three years old when she was killed, and Mary was six.

Emily Conkling became inspired the 30th of October, 1842, and spoke for Lucy Wanapahoo. She said she had confessed her sins to Mariah Wantay and she was her sister. She says she was killed by the white man, but does not tell in what manner. She had five children; her Indian's name was Canelas Wanapahoo; and here follows the names of the children: Joseph, Polly, Philip, Molly, and Sally Moriah. The youngest is five years old. Lucy was about 150.

Nancy White became inspired the same day and spoke for a little squaw by the name of Nancy. She said she was killed when about nine years old by a white man, and she had a brother William.

November 3. Sarah Simons[4] became inspired and spoke for Fanny Wampoo, and her Indian's name was Moses Wampoo. They had eight children. . . . They too were killed by the whites. Fanny appeared very much affected and wept. She sung several beautiful songs. . . .

November 19. Betsy Harrison became inspired and spoke for Eliza Wantay that was killed when she was three years old. She said she and her sister Mary went into the woods. "And there came a white man and shoot me and my sister, and then he make a hole in the ground and put us in and cover us with leaves and brush. And then me Moder come and look for us but she no find us, but we see her all the while." Eliza said she was now 135 years old. She is a very bright, active little squaw. . . .

November 13. . . .[5] Mary Gillet became inspired and spoke for Margaret Wondo, about 20 years old. She said there was two white men came to her in the woods and broke both of her wrists and then killed her. . . .

November 7. While in meeting this evening Mariah Wantay said she had a present for all the brethren and sisters to receive. It is a pair of moccasins. And then Fanny said she had got a pair of leggons [leggings?] for each one: "And if you will wear these we think you will dance better than you do. . . . "

November 15. Moriah said "Me will write many pretty things for you yet". . . . Fanny said, "I often come and look at you when you are asleep, and see them little angels flying all around you, and they drop little shiny things all over you, and some they drop in your mouth . . . "[6]

November 21. Lucy Wanapahoo said she had been to tea [with] Shiny Moder, "And she gave me two noggins, one for Shiny Fader and one for Shiny Moder; dare be tuf in de noggin to rub on the white boy and girl what make de Indian and squaw come in, if day be right." . . .

November 25. This evening . . . Lucy Wanapahoo came in and said that there was a woman come to the tent today by the name of Hannah Saytroit [?]. She was a Turk, and there was twenty-five of them. . . . Then Lucy went away and the woman took up her abode in the same instrument, E. C. . . .

Then she seated herself on the floor crosslegged, and while smoking her pipe she asked many questions about our religion, etc.

November 29. This afternoon we got a meal[7] for the squaws. There was sixteen of them. We roasted potatoes, cooked beef, and made succotash. They appeared much pleased . . . Sarah McBride was inspired. The squaw's name was Asenath Wampoo, daughter of Fanny Wampoo. . . .

November 30. The brethren went in pursuit of the Indians this forenoon. I understood they was quite successful in finding them.[8] And there was one Indian came to George Price that had not confessed his sins and knew nothing of God. George became inspired today . . . Willard and W. G. [Willoughby Green?] became inspired. . . .

November 28. . . . There was near a dozen sisters inspired this evening, and we received much love from the natives. One of them said, "Shiny Moder tay dat you don't receive anyting in dis manifestation from her, only what you receive through the Indian and the Squaw" . . .

December 2. We had succotash for dinner to day and baked potatoes. And about one o'clock we called in the natives. There was seven males and fourteen females. They seated themselves on the floor and eat [ate] their victuals and appeared very thankful. . . .

December 9. [Evening meeting, with Second Order] Loren Wicks became inspired. He said he was a chief from Choctaw, his name was John Wampoo. . . . Near all the younger part of the brethren and sisters were inspired. . . .

December 19. This afternoon fifteen of the brethren went in pursuit of the natives, and I understand they found as many as six tribes. They were gone between two and three hours and when they returned they came hooting on their way. . . .

December 22. . . . John Wampoo said he had brought a wigwam filled with love. So the brethren took those that had not took the Indians in,[9] and put them one at a time into the wigwam, and a number of them received the Indians. . . .

December 26. . . . Lydia Annas became inspired and took in one of the Africans. Her name was Philanthrope; we could not understand her language. Willard became inspired and took in the Sioux chief. . . . Some of the natives appeared quite unwilling to have the Africans have a privilege here, so they held a debate upon the subject.

December 27. As the natives was crowding so hard upon us and felt that their time was short with us, we thought we would go to the meeting house, which we did at eight o'clock, and continued there two hours and fifteen minutes. John Wampoo said he had brought a wigwam filled with Africans. He then related a vision which he saw. He said he saw a large river and all the different nations swimming therein; one had as good a right to the gospel as another, etc.[10] Frederick became inspired and took in one of the Africans. His name was Jack. He was about thirty-five years old. He said he had two masters; the first one was kind to him and gave him some education, but the other was cruel and whipped him to death. . . . Lucy Wampoo brought each of the elders a crown, which she said was taken from Mother Ann's crown. . . .

December 29. This evening while at supper there was one of the Africans came to one of the instruments (Sarah Simons). The instrument left the table and ran in hopes of getting rid of her, but she soon took possession of the body but did not incline to say much. She said her name was Phebe. . . . She lived in Africa and was related to the royal family. She said she came when she heard the great sound, and had confessed her sins to the natives. . . . The natives did not like the Africans at all and could not keep silent. . . .

January 8 [1843]. . . . Peter related a vision which he saw respecting the red men and white men. How the white man drove the red men off the ground, etc. Peter called upon Samuel to witness to the vision which he had related. But Samuel said his heart overflowed, so he was unable to speak now. But afterward he witnessed to the truth of it. . . .

January 15. . . . Samuel called the attention of the natives and said he thought they ought to be as willing that the Africans should have a privilege as themselves. He said "Shiny Mother no look at skin, but she look to the soul". . . . There was a good many Africans attended with us, and two Hottentots.

January 16, Monday evening. . . . It was thought best by our beloved lead for us to take our leave of the natives for the present, which we did, but not without a cross.[11] This truly was a heartrending scene. They said they never had met with anything that felt like this before. They all returned their hearty thanks for what they had received and promised us that they would be good forever; and they also promised that they would watch the valley and keep off the pale faces and let us know when danger was near, etc. They said Christ and Mother Ann, Father William, Father Joseph, and Mother Lucy were present. . . .

Friday, February 10. . . . This evening we went to meeting, and there was a goodly number of natives came to attend with us. Peter said the natives have had a great privilege here to learn the ways of God, and now they must be willing to go and give place to other nations that are seeking after salvation . . . So he said the natives must withdraw, but he expected some of them would be needed to help other nations. So when called for they might come. He said those nations that are coming are not to tarry over five weeks, etc. . . .

February 24, Friday evening. Peter the Indian chief came and said the French had got to leave here next Wednesday and make room for the Afghans and Arabians . . . He said the valley was filled with all kind of creatures; some of them was only part human, they were strange looking creatures, etc. . . .

April 8, Saturday evening. . . . The Holy Angel of Eternal Truth filled an instrument with his mighty power and prophesied by signs, . . . after which he made known the following words . . . "Know ye I am the same Holy Angel of Eternal Truth who accompanied your Holy Mother Wisdom and witnessed to her holy word, and with pleasure did I seal her blessing upon you . . .[12] Your Heavenly Father doth require that your work be hastened. Therefore hath he sent in this vessel which I have brought a gift for all the instruments to make known the feelings of the spirits they receive, in a language that ye can understand. Eternal Truth (Sephronia H. Smith) . . .

April 11, Tuesday. While in the meeting house after hearing the sacred book read that is preparing to be printed and published to the world,[13] we received the love and blessing of our eternal and heavenly Parents. . . . There was several of the instruments spoke for our eternal and heavenly Parents, but chief of their discourses was directed to Brother Philemon Stewart, as he was the instrument that wrote the book and read it to us; he received much love and blessing from them and also many good promises that he should be blessed and strengthened in the good work that he was engaged in. . . .

April 19, Wednesday. . . . Another instrument said there has two angels come each bearing a young and very beautiful nomatus tree about three feet high. The angels then informed the instrument that these two trees were a present from the two Anointed Ones to the Church upon the Holy Mount and in Wisdom's Valley. The angel then said, "When they are sufficiently grown to maturity, there will be found upon them twelve different kinds of ripe fruit, with as many of flowers and of leaves at all seasons of the year.[14] And upon every leaf of the tree there will be something written, which may be read, or made known by those having the gift of revelation, inspiration, or sight. The quantity written upon the different leaves will vary from one word to a long sentence," etc. . . . [15]

April 26, Wednesday. One of the instruments came hopping out into the alley. Elder Brother asked him if he had ever been here before. He answered, "Nay, never." He said, "I have life, breath, and voice. I am that I am, I am not him that was to come; I neither stand nor walk, but he that cometh after me can both stand and walk, and he has breath and voice. I am he that went before, not him that was to come; I am that I am, I was sent here by the great I am." He then said, "Do you know who I am?" We, the elders whom he asked, answered "Nay."[16] He then said, "Are you willing I should come again?" The answer was "yea," etc. (A. W.)

There was many signs given which appeared very marvelous and some talking in unknown tongues. We then went out to the fountain, and the brethren set out the nomatus tree. There was two leaves picked from the tree, one for the elder brother and one for the elder sister, and there was a few words written upon them. . . .

Upon one side of the leaf was a representation of the seal of Holy Mother, and upon the other side, the representation of a rose. Around the rose, upon four different sides, were written the following words in the form of a diamond:

> Industry of mind and body,
> Do strongly here combine,
> To form a robe of brightness,
> That will the sun outshine.

Copied May 1st, 1843

NOTES

1. Source: "Account of meetings during which the participants were inspired or experienced visions (1842–1843)," OClWHi V B 322. The writer of this journal was probably the second elder or eldress in the Watervliet Church Family. See entry for April 26, above.

2. Wisdom's Valley was the spirit-given name for the Watervliet community during the era of spiritualistic revival.

3. Holy Mount was the spiritual name of the New Lebanon community.

4. Sarah Simons, a leading instrument for many years, ultimately left the community.

5. Earlier events in November are inserted here in the manuscript after later events. This suggests that the scribe was copying the contents of loose sheets into the permanent record represented by the bound journal. Mary Gillet is probably a natural sister of Moriah Gillet, who had already acted as a spirit instrument in the Watervliet Church Family for several years.

6. These "little shiny things" dropped by the angels were invisible, spiritual Shaker representations of manna.

7. This meal was also invisible or spiritual food.

8. Pressure was being brought to bear on the Shaker brethren to "take the spirits in."

9. "Those who had not yet taken the Indians in" refers to those brethren who had not yet enacted the part of Indian spirits in the meetings.

10. This was the period of radical abolitionist agitation in the world outside Shaker communities, and it seems clear that some abolitionist sentiment (as well as anti-African racism) is being expressed here in the vocabulary of ritual spiritualism.

11. This is one of many indications in the documents of the spiritual revival that the ministry and elders exercised direct control over the spirit-inspired events, especially when things appeared to be getting out of hand.

12. The first visit of Holy Mother Wisdom, during which this "sealing" of individuals with her blessing took place, was in April 1841. Rufus Bishop, in a letter dated May 20, 1841, instructed the New Hampshire Shaker communities to prepare for her visit: "You will understand by the enclosed Communication that Holy Mother Wisdom will visit every Society of Believers in the land, in the course of the present year; and that she will set a mark on every soul, from the greatest to the least. . . . " (OClWHi IV B 9).

13. This was Philemon Stewart's *Sacred Roll and Book* (1843).

14. Mystical symbolic trees, sometimes identified with the biblical Tree of Life, recurred in Shaker visionary expressions, culminating in the watercolor spirit drawings of the 1850s. According to a spirit message received by Watervliet Second Family spirit instrument Phebe Ann Smith, the Garden of Eden and Tree of Life were actually situated in Watervliet ("Garden of Eden, Watervliet 2nd June 1842, by Pheby Ann Smith," NOC #13,486). The visionary "nomatus tree" referred to here was to be "planted" near the "fountain" in the Watervliet mountaintop feast ground as part of the preparation for the spring ceremonial there.

15. Messages written on leaf-shaped cut-out paper survive in Shaker archives, as do spirit drawings of the "seal of Holy Mother." See Andrews and Andrews, *Visions of the Heavenly Sphere*, and Patterson, *Gift Drawing and Gift Song*.

16. This indicates that the record of spiritual events was being kept by someone in the elders' order.

THE HANCOCK SWEEPING GIFT (1843)[1]

The following account of the gift of the roaring angel went through at the Second Family, September 22, 1843.

Firstly. The sister band commenced their march at eight o'clock through their shops and outbuildings and likewise the brethren through their shops.

Two. The sister band proceeds on in duty and to them was handed forth by Mother Ann's six messengers a cup of gospel fire and the indignation of God against evil. The band also was required by Mother to feel the quickening power of shaking. And with the sword and the rod Elder Sister united her spirit with its keenness, and at the same time enjoining upon the band to be faithful in the requirement by repeating these words, "I want nothing left in me that God disowns, and sisters do not do this work by the halves, but be thorough and make our dwellings clean."

Three. While performing the duty of singing the selected songs with marching throughout the buildings, there was present a bowl of fire to be sprinkled through the children's apartment, and in this Elder Sister was faithful and keen to discharge her duty.

Four. The band proceeded on to the dairy house, went into the upper rooms and sung on the march. After singing, the holy angel opens his mouth, saying: "I behold the anger of the Lord is kindled greatly against the wicked inhabitors who dwell in Zion. For lo, I see iniquity has grown strong; yea, fear overhangs this dwelling, and hope lingers afar off." In this place the band received each a broom from Mother; and her word was, "Sweep the floors clean."

Five. Again a word from Mother by the holy angel: "In the day of God's fierce wrath bow low, very low, that the hand of his judgment may pass lightly over you. For this is a day that will refine you as with fire and cleanse you as with fuller's soap." A space of remission till one o'clock, then the brethren and sisters commenced again, singing through the dooryard gardens and fields. A remission again until after supper.

Six. Then commenced the march again in the dwelling house, going into the garrets firstly. The Sisters then kneeled in solemn prayer to God, soon began to sing while marching to the next loft below. Here was presented fire by the holy angel to be sprinkled through; this was done. The brethren band and the sisters met with singing in the second hall below and in the different apartments went forth in the forementioned gifts.

Seven. Brethren and sisters proceeded down to the kitchen and cellars. There was given a cup of indignation of God, as a swift witness against an ungodly appetite, from the holy angel. Here was expressed by one of the sisters, to war all disorders; this was done. The keenness of the rod was felt through the lower apartments of our dwelling house.

Eight. When the gift closed, the elders caused the family to assemble in the meeting room, there sang the songs of blessing at evening. The elders cautioned the brethren and sisters with care to be more tidy and cleanly in deed and in truth: not because one day was set apart for a day of cleansing to let that suffice, but continue in striving to be clean and keep so from day to day, and be more like the gospel and advance heavenward.

Entered on record October 20, 1843.

NOTE

1. Source: "A Record of Messages and Communications given by Divine Inspiration, in the Second Family City of Peace," DeWint SA1073, chap. 33.

HANCOCK MOUNTAIN MEETING (1843)[1]

City of Peace,[2] September 24, 1843.

Sabbath morning, half past eight. The brethren and sisters in the City of Peace who were able in every family began their march to the holy Mount Sinai to receive heavenly blessings.

The brethren and sisters sang as they marched most part of the way. When we arrived at the walnut grove, we halted, and after placing ourselves, the brethren on the east side and the sisters on the west, Brother Joseph Wicker[3] spoke from the Savior, saying: "Beloved, thus saith the Savior, 'I have met with you this day to bless you. I have prepared the holy things of God to bestow upon your children. Yea, I will lead them to my lovely fountain, where they can drink and bathe in my holy waters, and all who have come with vessels clean and hearts prepared, I will fill with choice blessings.' " . . .

We then sang, "On Yonder Holy Mount, etc."

Instrument (Martha VanValen)[4] said, "It is true that the blessed Savior has met with us this day, and also the Angel of the Lord God. There is a cloud of eternal brightness spread over us. It is the testimony of blessed Mother Ann's gospel, and it will extend to the ends of the earth. If you desire the gifts and power of God, bow low in humiliation, down in the valley, and ye will find the favor of God." She said, "There is one here who can tell the number of spirits that are assembled here upon this holy spot with their trumpets to sound forth the word of God." Mary Ann Wollison said, "There are 15,000 angels who are flying over us."

Instrument (Joseph Patten) said, "Yea, and many seraphs with them. . . . "

Instrument (Martha VanValen) said, "Father Calvin is marching around among us. He has a gift of freedom for everyone. Receive ye this gift, then ye can go forth in whatever gift ye feel. Let not a man-fearing spirit, or a man-pleasing spirit, hinder or deprive you from enjoying or receiving the gifts and power of God this day. If ye are in possession of this, ye must shake it off." We all shook powerfully. Instrument (Joseph Patten) was under powerful operations most of the time.

. . . Sister Dana [Cassandana Brewster][5] held a powerful testimony against all sin and against bondage. She said, "I desire everyone would labor for the gifts and power of God and let not the spirit of the wicked leap upon you (there being a number of the world present). Let nothing hinder you from receiving the blessings which are for you. Labor to gain power and victory over everything that belongs to an evil nature." She also said Eldress Dana desired that everyone would go forth in the strength and the power of the gospel and labor for the spirit of conviction.

Instrument (Martha VanValen) said from the Savior, "Cleanse your hearts, and you will be accepted by the Heavenly Father. Do you believe in the promises which have been made unto you?" We answered, "Yea." She then said, "My dear children, *Ha la vin cy*,[6] I have called you up here to bless you, and in my lovingkindness I will bless you this day, that ye may find an increase in the holy things of God. There are those here who hunger and thirst, those who are willing to do the will of their Heavenly Father. You will feel that this day which ye never felt in your lives, if ye labor faithfully." We then received each of us a bright shining trumpet from the Holy Angel, that we might sound forth the testimony of the Lord Jesus Christ. We sounded our trumpets. Instrument (Judith Collins) played a song, and M. S. [Mary Smith?] sang. She said the Holy Angel Vikilan is here and he has brought a gift of love and blessing for everyone who have come here with an honest and upright heart. "I will cause to be written everything that passes this day. I will give unto the faithful ones the resurrection power of life, which will cause their spirits to live . . . "

One of the instruments (Joseph Wicker) said, "Our beloved Mother Ann has come and desires all her children to receive her love by four low bows." This we received very thankfully and returned our thanks for the same.

Instrument (Martha VanValen) gave each of us a bright and shining cross from the Savior and said, "Gather your senses, ye little ones, as ye ascend this holy hill to Mount Sinai. Reach forth your hands that ye may receive the blessings of heaven. Bow low, and ye will receive that which will satisfy your souls." We then began our march and sang, "To Mount Sinai We Are Going, etc."

When we arrived at the gate, we bowed as we entered, then marched up to the fountain,[7] and placed ourselves around it. The Savior's instrument (Joseph Wicker) then said, "Beloved, how will ye that I should treat your children this day? Should I treat them in lovingkindness?" They answered, "Yea." He proceeded, "I have caused you, dear children, to come here to this holy Mount Sinai that your souls may be filled with the blessings of heaven. Draw near and kneel around my holy fountain. Drink and bathe in this holy water; drink in faith. All ye who are justified may bathe in this living water; it will give you strength to serve the true and living God. There are lovely angels who will carry to those who are not present and cannot get near to this lovely fountain." We drank and bathed faithfully.

Elder Nathaniel [Deming] said, "It is evident the Lord has called us here this day that we may receive his holy blessing. . . . Let no cavilling feelings dwell within any soul. If any dispute the call of God in preparing this holy ground, they may look in the sacred writings. There they will find what was prophesied in the days of old. The Lord will lead us in the way we know not of. The way of love, the way of peace, the way of truth and righteousness will always remain. The work of God will be increasing daily, and our souls will be filled. The word of God has gone forth in mercy and judgment, and it will continue to sound until every heart is reached. Let not one soul be careless, for ye will see stranger things than ye have seen. Though the world may rage and fight against this testimony of truth, yet the Lord will bless every faithful soul. Let not any think because they can't see into every gift that is, they will not believe it to be a gift . . . "

One of the instruments (Nancy Oakes) then said, "O my Father, my lovely Elder Nathaniel, my faithful shepherd, heaven blesses you. The Holy Angel of the Lord blesses you, the wings of heaven fly around as a blessing, my soul blesses you. If ever my soul felt a blessing, I feel it this morning". . . .

Instrument (Adeline W.) said, "I feel that I am in the presence of the Lord God. I am a poor worm of the dust and stand before many who are clothed in white. I will look toward my Heavenly Father for a blessing."

Instrument (Joseph Wicker) said, "Saith the Savior, 'Ye may raise a mighty shout in victory'." We shouted twice and clapped our hands. Instrument (Martha VanValen) gave us a gift of strength from Mother Ann and also a mantle of love, strength, and power for Elder Nathaniel from the Holy Angel, and said, "You are clothed from the crown of your head to the soles of your feet."

Mary Ann Wollison gave Sister Dana two baskets of garments, one for the brethren and one for the sisters. Sister Dana gave Brother Grove the basket to give to the brethren and she gave to the sisters. The brethren and sisters were very lively; it appeared that there were some native spirits with us, for there was much talking and jabbering among some of them and a number of native songs sung and danced. There were diverse operations, such as turning, bowing, leaping, and shouting. Lucy R. spoke considerable to the young sisters, not much recollected, but ran thus, "The Lord will pour his blessing upon everyone who will be faithful and endure to the end."[8]

Instrument (Simon Maybee) said, "The spirit desired us to sing the song concerning Mother Ann when she was in prison" (we accordingly did). He said, "How thankful we ought to feel for such a good Mother, who was willing to suffer for our sakes. Yea, willing to be persecuted that through her the gospel we might receive. We are not in prison, and how little we have to suffer. I say how thankful we ought to feel for such a good Mother."

Elder Nathaniel said, "We are God's chosen people; we are called by a heavenly calling; we are called to be heirs of the heavenly kingdom. We must do that work that will stand when we are called into eternity. This work is for many, but the other work is for few. If we do not fulfill our calling, if we are destitute of that humiliating power, what shall we do? When we are weighed in the balance we shall be found wanting."

David Osborn said he had a few words to speak concerning what was said in the grove. He said, "There are 4,500,000 spirits here with us this day. The kings and the prophets and apostles are here with us. . . . "

Instrument (Martha VanValen) gave a particular blessing to Brother John Tiffany (who was very feeble) from Father James. She also said, "Don't you see the heavenly manna flowing all around? Ye who are worthy may eat your fill. Here are the crumbs which I have gathered from my Heavenly Father's table." We partook in thankfulness.

Instrument (Joseph Wicker) said from the Savior, "Hold out your glasses and receive holy wine." We also drank water from the fountain. . . .

One of the instruments (Nancy Riley) was led by the power of God down to the company of the world who was standing on the outside of the yard. One of the other instruments (Martha VanValen) went with her; they were both under operations. A number of the sisters followed them. A number of the world who were present were relations of the instrument (Nancy Riley). She spoke very powerfully to them and invited them to come and confess and forsake their sins and unite in the cross of Christ, for they never would find salvation in any other way.

Another instrument (Sarah Smith) then came forward and spoke in tongues in a very affecting manner, and prayed for them. We all kneeled, and there was liberty for them to kneel if they chose; the women kneeled. When she had finished her gift in tongues, she said, "The holy angels are inviting you to come and partake with us. Oh how lovely, how lovely they are." Another instrument (J. O.) said, "It is the trumpet of the Lord that is sounding. It is the voice of God that is calling you this day. Receive these words, dear children of this world." When they had got through with their gifts, Elder William held a powerful testimony to the spectators.

He explained to them the need of confessing and forsaking their sins and following Christ in the regeneration. He spoke some concerning those who had been operated upon by the divine spirit to speak to them. He said, "I do not think strange that the young people feel for their fellow beings. They think you have not been baptized with the fire of the gospel, which will save you from sin, and they feel engaged in this work and feel to help others all they can."

Instrument (Joseph Wicker) then said, "The singers may now place themselves around the fountain, and we will march around this holy ground." We sang and marched four songs. . . .

Instrument (Simon Maybee) said, " 'Beloved children,' saith the Holy Angel, 'hear ye this my word, concerning the holy ground on which ye stand. Ye are called to worship God in spirit and in truth. I have reserved this [little] spot to myself, saith the Lord, kept it pure and holy, not polluted with sin. Yea, I have reserved it for my holy people, whom I delight to bless, and all my beloved ones who love to serve me, them will I bless. From this place my word shall go forth to the ends of the earth, yea, to all nations, and the time is short that remaineth. Thousands will flock here to hear the word of God. Some will hear my word and obey it, and some will hear and disregard it. Such ones, I will meet with my judgments. And some of you will live to see it,' saith the Lord through the Holy Angel. 'Go ye on rejoicing, all ye faithful children of Mother.' " . . .

Instrument (Martha VanValen) said, "Holy Mother Wisdom's doves have come with a blessing for us. Ye very well remember when ye were here before that these holy doves came with a blessing, and in the day when trials roll on, yea, when the wicked shall afflict, Holy Mother's blessing will rest upon every faithful soul."

We sang the dove song which came from Holy Mother.

Instrument (Nancy Oakes) said, "Behold the chariots that are coming from the Holy Mount, they come on wings of fire." "Yea," says instrument (Joseph Patten), "A flame of fire cometh from behind them." Martha said, "They are loaded with precious treasures."

Instrument (Joseph Wicker) said, " 'Ye are required,' saith the Savior, 'to turn your faces towards the Holy Mount and shout three times and bow low three times.' " We obeyed. . . .

Instrument (Joseph Patten) gave us the love of Eliphalet Slossen and William Torrey,[9] and said they had attended meeting with us. . . .

Instrument (Nancy Oakes) said, "Father William has brought a loaf of living bread already sliced; there is a slice for each one.[10] It is on the north side of this fountain." This we received and returned our thanks for the same. We then received a blessing from Father Joseph.

Instrument (Joseph Wicker) said, "Here is a loaf of pretty white bread from Mother Ann. It is cut in small pieces, one for each. The pieces are cut and piled in the same shape that the loaf was before it was cut. It is placed on a silver platter." When we had received this precious treasure, the instrument said, "It is the gift for us to load this platter with our thankful feelings for what we have received," which we did heartily. . . .

Instrument (Martha VanValen) said, "Does anyone see the cross?" "Yea," said Nancy Oakes, "I have seen it for some time."[11] "True," said Martha, "The Cross of Christ is placed over this lovely stone." Sarah Harrison said, "There is a dove flying around with a roll in its mouth for Sister Dana." She saw it light upon the top of the stone at the head of the fountain. She received the roll and gave it to Sister Dana. . . .

Instrument (Martha VanValen) said, "It is the gift from Mother Ann for all the young brethren and sisters to come forward and manifest their thankfulness for the way of God and for the privilege of coming to this holy mount this day." They came and obeyed. There were many of the older brethren and sisters who spoke very feelingly and manifested their thankfulness for Mother's gospel while in the time of our meeting. . . .

We then received comfort from Mother Ann to carry home with us and a golden sack from Mother Lucy to put it in.

We then prepared to return. We struck a march and marched on. When we arrived at the walnut grove, we halted. The instrument (Joseph Wicker) said, "Brethren and sisters, the band of angels who have accompanied us this day will now take their leave of us, and before they leave they will sing us a farewell, and then we may sing them one." The instrument then sang a beautiful farewell from the spirits, words not gathered. . . . We then marched on toward the City of Peace. When we arrived home it was half past two.

NOTES

1. Source: "Record of a Meeting held on Mt. Sinai by the Church and Families of the City of Peace," in "Record of Meetings Held on Mt. Sinai," MeSl, 109–31.
2. City of Peace is the spirit-inspired name for the Hancock Shaker community during this period and Mount Sinai is the spiritual name of the hill upon which the meeting ground and sacred stone stood.
3. Joseph Wicker, here speaking for Christ, was a prominent male spirit instrument and also the second elder of the Hancock Church Family First Order at this time. Though in David Lamson's book he is called "their chief prophet," he is also somewhat cynically referred to as "old Jo Wicker" (David Lamson, *Two Years' Experience among the Shakers* [1848]).
4. The manuscript gives either full names of spirit instruments or their initials in parentheses. I have supplied the instrument's full name in place of initials in most cases.
5. Cassandana Brewster was assistant lead eldress, with Cassandana Goodrich at this time.
6. This represents Shaker spirit language.
7. Invisible fountains (hexagonal plots of land) were part of the "holy mountain" meeting spots.
8. This shows the problem the scribe had in recording the entire ceremony, perhaps in part from memory.
9. These were two elderly Shaker brothers who had recently died—Slossen in November 1842 and Torrey in August 1843.
10. A nice instance of a female instrument choosing a spiritual symbol from the sisterhood's daily life.
11. It was a frequent practice for one spirit instrument to confirm the spiritual vision of another.

HOLY MOTHER WISDOM'S FOLD (N.D.)[1]

Beloved Daughter of thy Mother and one that is Anointed to lead my People What is writen within this fold I write myself it is information concerning a matter that has laid concealed for ages I shall fold this and put it in the bottom of this box, there to remain until the instrument unto whom I shall give the gift to read it be called Then will the Angel that protects this Box bring it forth for She (the Angel) understands the whole Matter I will give my Angel word that this be read exactly as it is written by men

Beloved Daughter I am willing that you should read this to some of your Sisters if you want to but I am not willing to have it made a publick matter I would say let not any under thirty years of age hear this if there were not a few that I should be willing between that age and twenty[2] therefore I will leave it to your judgment for you will know yourself Beloved one when you read it that it will not do for all to hear But if ever you do read it [to] any one or more caution them not to talk about it for fear that some delicate feeling might be hurt In confidence My Child I write this unto you From Holy Holy Mother Wisdom These words was writen on the outside of the fold

Beloved Daughter Long Year [Yea] very long has this thing which I am about to reveal unto you My Beloved Child been concealed And it was my wisdom that it should But the time has come and with liberty from my Heavenly Father I will tell you some thing that has never been revealed to Mortals before

My Son the Saviour of Mankind understood this from the beginning of time with Man But the Fathers command to him was tel no Man this thing for it is my Secret Will that no other than a Female should reveal this Mistry and that cannot be done unless the Holy one makes herself known upon Earth to Mortals Well do you know My Beloved One that the Female is called the cause of Mans fall But I say she was the means made use of whereby they fell For because Satan could not be greater than the Almighty and gain a place with me therefor he did make use of a Female in hope thereby to distrou both Men & Angels I wil tel you the beginning I am first with the Almighty I am His Glory and with Him I hold counsel continualy and there is naught done that is done without me Legions of Angels did the Almighty God of Heaven call into existence in the world of Spirits to be at my command and placing them in true Order He said unto them Behold my Glory obey thou Here [her] word Here is no member of any Order ether in Heaven or on Earth that can travel in the way of God and find protection without being obedient Neither can any soul either in Heaven or on Earth travel in the way of God and find Salvation if they possess Envy and jeliousy Beloved One many times I have said to thy Holy Mother Ann O that thy Children could sense the depth of their Sin For that sin was Lucifer the Angel of the Morning cast from my presence and with him went Leegions never more to Behold My face in peace throughout the endless ages of Eternity

The Angels in Heaven being placed in Order to be at my command the Angel of Love came and went before the Angel of the Morning and in consequence of that one nearer to Me O fateful consequence that For soon did the Angel of the Morning yea Lucifer the Angel of Light say unto them that come next unto himself Behold and see the Glory of the Lord Almighty Himself hath placed the Angel of Love before me next unto her And can I bear that I that carry the candle of the Morning I the Almighty hath given power to say unto the sun in the Morning shine or can say to that Planet remain thou in darkness this day or a certain length of time and it is at my command This power hath the Almighty God of Heaven given unto me And why should I be content to give place to *him* who is only the Angel of Love his power is not so great as mine I can command day Light and darkness And he only commands the tender feelings and is said to be the Angel of Love Thus my Beloved you see that Envy and jeliousy had taken possession of his breast But in this state he might have ben reclaimed had he not commited that sin which cannot be forgiven Viz judged the Almighty and bid defiance to his Glory How can I saith Lucifer to his Atributs I who have so much power given unto me bear to see the Holy one of God look with so much compassion on the Angel of Love and the Almighty Himself says She doith well dose the Almighty do me justice Sure he dose not therefore I will take the darkness of the night (that is some underhanded means) and I will cast the Angel of Love from before me and sertainly then I shall come next unto Her for my power is great there is none in Heaven like unto me for the Almighty Himself hath given me his power and then I shall be first with the Holy one

Mistaken one for by my Wisdom I discovered this thing and by the power of God it was made known in Heaven Gabriel a mighty Angel of God the Lord did set in Order to drive Lucifer and all that had looked upon me with an eye of jealousy or envy from before the throne of God unto a place prepared for them These are they which is called the Devil and his Angels Myself the Almighty God hid under his wings until the commotion ceased which was great in Heaven and under the wings of his Love I have been concealed ever sence from being known by evil or comprehended by the faln nature of man until I was discouvered by the faithful that had took up there cross and obeyed the Gospel of Mother Ann this is the Mistry that could not be revealed until the fulfillment of time the time is now fulfilled and I have made myself known unto a people that I own a people that live a life of self denial and the cross that obey the Gospel that my beloved Son & Daughter planted upon Earth

But I will return to my subject Lucifer and his angels after being drove out from the presence of God gave themselves up to do evil therefore evil took possession of them and they became all evil and sought to distroy good yea saught to distroy me the Holy one But I was concealed and could not be found At length two was formed male & Female The fallen Angels being discouraged in relation to me I being in Heaven combined together to distroy this Female and altho an Angel was placed to gard them the spirit of jealousy and envy combined together and wreathing with malace for me he could not find made to one that he through art and subtelty could find. Wheare was the Man that had been placed with her for her protection Why he was asleep Beloved one the last time that I returned from the Earth to my Heavenly Father with sorrow I had to say O my Heavenly Father Mankind in a state of Nature and after the Order of the World are asleepe yet for there breast is filled with Envy and jealousy and there is no protection for a Female because they know not my Gospel

Beloved child the time will come that every knee will have to bow and every toung will have to confess Me the Glory of the living God but this must remain concealled a little longer from the wise of the world for my ways they cannot understand therefore I have hid my word from them and give it unto a people that is chosen of the Lord

With this receave my love yea receave my blessing thou chosen vessel of the Lord. From Holy Mother to the Eldress Sister

The word of the Angel to the writer

I am a little Angel that delighteth to do My Mothers will I have read unto thee and thou hast written all of the words to this fold there is two more folds in the box but they are not for thee bow low in Humility before God for thy work is not yet done

This is my word unto thee the instrument

NOTES

1. Source: "A Fold Written by Holy Holy Mother Wisdom to be conveyed to the Eldress Sister of the First Order Watervliet in a box" (n.d.). (NN, Item 100). Original spelling, capitalization, and punctuation preserved.
2. The suggested restriction on the age of the sisters to whom this message could be read may indicate that the younger ones were more likely to react with skepticism or levity.

PAULINA BATES'S *DIVINE BOOK OF HOLY AND ETERNAL WISDOM* (1849)[1]

Testimony of the inspired writer of this book

Being impressed upon by an invisible hand to write, in my own name, a testimony concerning my own experience as an inspired instrument, I feel it my duty as well as my privilege so to do. Not that I feel any pleasure in having my name or testimony go abroad in the earth, but knowing it to be the will of my Heavenly Father, I cheerfully comply with that which would otherwise be extremely crossing to my natural feelings. . . .

But be it known unto all people that I have never been the framer, in the least, of the words which have gone forth from my pen in the name of my Heavenly Father or in the name of any holy or heavenly spirit. For seldom have I been permitted to know the subject which I was called to write upon, only as it was given, word by word; and many times I have written one or two pages before I had the least idea of what it would finally amount to. Then perhaps it would explain itself upon a point which had never entered my heart and bring forward ideas as foreign to my mind as anything could be.

Neither have I ever been influenced by what was laid down in the publications of Believers in any one point. For although I had lived among Believers eighteen years, yet I never read one of their publications once through, nor have I ever read but very little in them, and that little was when I first came among the people, which soon passed out of my recollection and was as though I had never read it.

But I have never read any part of the publications of Believers in which the scriptures were explained, with that intention, until since I wrote the word of the Lord contained in this book. Then, feeling an impression one day to look into some of the books which contained the principles of Believers, and also their explanations of the scriptures to prove the same, I was greatly surprised to see their agreement with what I had written and was thankful that I had been as ignorant of their writings and of the scriptures as I was, believing the hand of Divine Providence was in it, that I might not be influenced by such knowledge. . . .

My knowledge of the scriptures was also very limited. In many instances I have been called to write and explain passages of scripture when I did not know until it was revealed to me of there being such passages in the Bible. For this cause I cannot but feel thankful, considering it not only as a confirmation to myself, but an evidence to others, that it could proceed from nothing short of divine revelation.

And since I have been called to write the word of God by inspiration, I have considered it a blessing that I had no more knowledge of the scriptures, believing that the providence of God had so directed that I might be the more fully confirmed that it was a real gift of God that so readily brought the scriptures to my view and unfolded them in my sight. For had I been as well versed in the scriptures as some of my brethren and sisters, I should have been the more fearful lest I might be influenced by my knowledge.

So I could see in all the dealings of the Lord with me that He had chosen the weak things to confound the mighty and the base things of the world, and things that are despised, and things which are not to confound things that are mighty in their own eyes and wise as respects the wisdom of this world. And I thank my Heavenly Father that I have been sufficiently foolish in his sight to be one of that number who should receive the revelation of his divine will. . . .

As to being influenced by my elders, which may hereafter be conjectured by some, I will state the truth, which is as follows: Whenever I received a call by the trumpet of the holy angel to arise and receive the word of the Lord, I have generally gone and informed my elders that I had such a call but knew not the subject upon which I was called to write. And their advice was always to this effect: That I must always be obedient to the word of the Lord and be willing to suffer to do his will, and that I must give myself up freely into his hands, feeling that of myself I was nothing more than clay in the hands of the potter, to be shapen to his will.

And thus did the elders remain wholly ignorant of what I was writing upon until the subject was finished, except when the subject was lengthy and employed my time for many days. Then as I closed my writing for the day I usually went and read to them what I had written, and they always encouraged me to be faithful and be willing to spend and be spent in doing whatever was made known to me to be my duty.

But I was never flattered by my elders to think that I had done or was doing some great thing. Neither was I discouraged by them, that what I was doing was false or improper or contrary to the faith of Believers, or otherwise. But they let it remain as it was, using great care not to influence me one way nor the other, but always encouraged me to fear God and walk humbly in his presence, that He would uphold me in all that I was called to pass through in his name.

Thus have I spoken more fully upon this subject, being aware that many conjectures and suspicions will probably be circulated with a view to slander and defame the leaders of God's people by accusing them of influencing the young and unstable, causing them to act and speak those things which otherwise they never would have done. . . .

And whatever may be suggested and reported hereafter to favor the belief that the leaders of the people have been influential in shaping or managing to their minds the present outpouring of the spirit of God among his people, I can say for one, I know to the contrary of this, and I am not afraid to become responsible before God for all the errors which my elders have committed of this kind.

What I have written upon this subject, I have written; but I know not why I should be influenced to write as I have, for it was not in my heart to write thus. But thus it is written, and truth it is, and truth it will ever stand, and I am not afraid to meet it, neither in heaven nor on earth. And as I feel conscious that I have discharged my duty as it respects this testimony in my own name, I add no more.

Paulina Bates. November 15, 1849.[2]

Holy Mother Wisdom declares herself to be, in nature and essence,
One with Eternal Power . . . [3]

God, in the beginning, designed an extensive work that his almighty power might be made manifest. And in order to perform and accomplish this it became necessary that those of his offspring, or the workmanship of his hands, should be tried and proved for the work. In this trial the spirit of disobedience was introduced and made manifest and found its way into the heart of one who lifted up his heel against his Maker and Creator.

And that light, power and understanding which were given him of God became as total darkness, which caused him to become the prince of darkness, working in direct opposition to the Father of all light and understanding.

And thus was the opposite spirit revealed and brought forth in the creation and set up in opposition to all good; and the God of heaven suffered it so to be, that all the works of his hands might by their free agency be proved, and none but the willing and obedient might abide in his kingdom of purity, peace, and holiness.

Men are willing to believe in a God of the male order; they are willing to believe that there are myriads of angels, but all in the male order; willing to believe in the Savior of man, but alone in the male order.

Hence ariseth the belief in many that the female is not in possession of a living soul, but merely a machine for the use and benefit of man in this terrestrial state of existence. And this is not to be wondered at so long as even those who have hope of eternal life acknowledge no other agency, either good or evil, except in the line of the male only.

But this is altogether a mistaken idea, for the Deity consists of two, male and female, and from these twain proceed all goodness, purity, and holiness. So also in the power of opposition stand male and female, the authors of all impurity, unholiness, uncleanness, and filthiness of every name and nature. And from these twain come the filthy fruits of lust and all evil.

Ye read of the mother of harlots, but ye know not her origin. She was, from the beginning, the mother spirit of the power of opposition, and the spirit in her likeness became coworker together with the prince and author of all unrighteousness, impurity, and unholiness in this fallen world. For without the aid of the helper meet, the female agency, the great adversary, the father of all abominations, could never have accomplished his designs and set up his kingdom in direct opposition to the kingdom of all purity and holiness.

And thus ye may understand that in the beginning, before the earth was created, there existed the two opposite kingdoms of good and evil, the one headed by the eternal Father and coworker, Holy and Eternal Mother Wisdom, while the other was headed by the everlasting prince of darkness and coworker, the foul and abominable mother of harlots. [[St. John's vision of the mother of harlots was but a figure of this spirit. See Revelation 27:5. Eds.]] And this I do declare to be the source and origin of lust and vile affections, which is the corrupt seed that engenders vile off-spring. . . .

These things remained a mystery in that day and in all former ages, and the truth was hidden from their eyes; for the time had not come for the Mother Spirit to be revealed in and through the likeness of sinful flesh.

The Father had sent forth his likeness in his beloved son Jesus Christ, the Savior of the world. But because his likeness, according to their vain and exalted imaginations, did not favor the image of God, they condemned him as an imposter and would not that he should reign over them, but crucified him; therefore they were but little benefited in that day by the coming of the Son of God.

But this did not disannul the purposes of God in reclaiming the world by the new birth, for God in his wisdom knew that the man was not without the woman in the work of spiritual offspring, any more than in the natural. But God's work was progressive; and as he hasteth not to force his purposes faster than sound wisdom directs, he suffered the world to fall back into gross errors by their own free agency.

Hence, instead of becoming the subjects of the Prince of Peace, they became, in a great measure, the subjects of war, bloodshed, and carnage, under the banner of the mighty prince of darkness, the author of lust, pride, and ambition in the world; for from thence proceed all war, strife, and envy.

And as the male is not without the female in the work of God, so in like manner is the male not without the female in the works of the devil. For while the male subjects of his kingdom have been giving vent to their malignant natures, inflamed by the spirit which cometh of lust, to go forth and make war with their fellow beings, the female subjects of the mother, the princess of harlots, have been busily engaged to build up the kingdom of this world, which proceedeth from the lust of the flesh, the lust of the eye, and the pride of life.[4]

And who among the daughters of the fall have not sipped more or less at the sensual and self-pleasing fountain which originates from the father of all sensuality and is brought forth by the mother, the beguiling and bewitching spirit of the female?

So ye may see that in Adam and Eve all mankind fell by the bewitching and enticing snares of the powers of darkness; and that the coming of the Son in the likeness and image of the Father, through the hardness of their hearts, availeth them but little.

The world even to this day, more or less, remains under the power of the prince and princess of darkness, and lust hath been the goddess which men have served and that, too, through the agency of the female; for man would be utterly unable to serve this god alone to the satisfaction of the carnal desires.

The work of the regeneration is to be the means by which the seed of the woman will bruise the serpent's head, through the children of the second Eve. . . .[5]

As the time hath fully come for God to set up his everlasting kingdom in which He alone shall be worshipped and served, and the time hath also fully come for all idols to be put down, and God alone and that which floweth from his Almighty Spirit shall be served, honored, and glorified; how can this be accomplished without the power of the second Eve, whose seed shall bruise the serpent's head? (see Gen. iii. 15).

Now the serpent, in the form of the tempter of which ye read, was not made manifest in the appearance of a snake. But he is called the subtle deceiver, a serpent, because of the crooked insinuations which were made use of, through the agency of fallen angels that had become the ministers of lustful and vile gratifications, of which ye can all witness who have ever become partakers of it, to be a bewitching, seducing spirit, calculated to lead its captives into many by and crooked paths.

This being the case, I would now ask of you, one and all, how and in what manner is the seed of the woman to bruise the serpent's head? How is he to be conquered and overcome unless the ax be laid at the root of the corrupt tree and the fountain and source of all fleshly and vile insinuations be cut off?[6] yea, unless that propensity of nature in which men glory more than in that which is of God be wholly destroyed? . . .

I say, as the first man and woman through the subtlety of the serpent failed to show forth the likeness of God upon earth, and as this was his decree, that he would be glorified by the children of men, how could this be accomplished unless the same sex which first received the bane of destruction to man's innocence and simplicity should be the first to receive the weapons whereby this base and fallen nature might be effectually slain in herself, and in her faithful children?[7]

Truly in this and in no other way may the purposes of God be fulfilled and the woman arise from a state of sin and disgrace to that honor and glory for which she was created in the beginning. And thus it is accomplished.

The Wisdom of God is revealed from on high and the image of her eternal brightness is brought forth in the female of God's own choice, endowed with sufficient power from on high to undermine and lay low all the crooks and windings of the subtle charmer and beguiler of the innocence of the first man and woman, and to bring forth living souls who are able to bruise the serpent's head and daily trample his vile and artful insinuations under their feet.

And this is the work allotted to the woman, because the woman was the first to receive this beguiling and serpentine influence of the charmer, and she hath been influential in the ministration of the same spirit from that day to this. And through her bewitching influence hath this charmer spread her ravages far and wide over the whole earth, and millions have fallen victims to her delusive charms. . . .

And although my spirit and power have long been in a great measure withdrawn from the sons and daughters of men, because of the darkness infused by the power of the adversary, who knew full well what a deadly foe my holy influence would yet prove to his kingdom and power, and he strove with his utmost zeal and power to suppress and if possible annihilate the name of the Mother Spirit, both in heaven and on earth;

Yet this the God of heaven suffered to be so for good and wise purposes, which He will yet overrrule so as to work for good and will further promote the increase and dominion of my kingdom of peace and holiness. And although the devil with his angels has strove mightily to suppress the testimony of the woman, in my likeness clothed with the brightness of the sun,[8] and hath cast out of his mouth floods of slanderous reports and persecuting venom with the intent, if possible, to bury and swallow up the name and nature of the work of God through the female;

Yet by the power of the Most High, whose power is above all power, when executed, will God always devise ways and means through his Wisdom to help the woman. For the name of the female will never more be buried and lost in the ruins of Satan's despoiled work, for the power of heaven forbid it.

Therefore the power of the devil can never more accomplish it, for the woman hath truly become the glory of the man and by her heavenly wisdom is able to compass a man and also to undermine the very nature and cause of man's fall. And this is the work allotted to the woman, who was instrumental in leading man into loss: that she should by her wisdom in the end be the first to lead man fully out of loss (see Jeremiah 31:22).

And by the seed of the woman shall the serpent receive his deadly wound, which shall never be healed, for the mouth of the Lord through his Holy and Eternal Wisdom hath spoken it, who is now exalted in the heavens and triumpheth above all the powers of the devil.

And be it known to all nations that dwell upon the earth that I, Wisdom, have builded my house, and my maidens have I sent forth to do my work, and the gates of hell shall never more be able to prevail against it (see Proverbs 9:1, 3).

For the ancient prophecy is now fulfilling, *"And the Bride shall appear, and she coming forth shall be seen, that now is withdrawn from the earth."*

(2 Esdras 7:26). That is, in the dispensation of the Bride, Holy Mother Wisdom will come forth and be revealed in her true order and will be known, even as the Eternal Father is known. . . .

Particular instructions to females.[9]

And ye daughters of men, give ear unto my words and know that I am no other than Wisdom, the Holy and Eternal Mother of your never-dying souls, and with a mother's care and tenderness do I now address you.

O ye daughters of men, ye are called to be the glory of the man, the crown of his enjoyments and the bright morning star of his existence. Listen and understand: Ye are not called to become defiled and polluted and to wallow in fleshly gratifications as a sow walloweth in the mire in order to fulfill the marriage covenant and rear up an offspring to him and become a crown of glory to his existence. Nay, in no wise. I, Wisdom, will teach you a far better way to act the part of a mother and a bosom friend to your companion.

Rise early and look well to your household affairs. Go forth in cheerfulness and good humor and perform well your part which is allotted to you. Lay your hand to the distaff and know that it is the diligent hand which maketh rich, and idleness is the sure threshhold to destruction. Be diligent and forbear to use with a lavish hand the hard earnings of thy husband, lest he become weary of thee.

Forbear to make use of the clamorous tongue, which above all is grievous to be borne; but with the tongue which uttereth forth in the small, still voice words of love and kindness mayest thou govern in thy sphere and order all thy household affairs in wisdom and with discretion.

Thou mayst be artful in thy insinuations, to gather the feet of thy husband within his own dwelling, lest he wander in by and forbidden paths, and this, too, to thy sorrow and bitterness in the time to come.

Refrain thy feet from wandering abroad for amusement and pleasure; but rather find amusement within your own dwellings, in the nurture and tuition of thy little ones and in discharging all the necessary duties which remain incumbent upon thee. And remember withal to keep a clean habitation and let order, regularity, and cleanliness govern thy premises, even from the house top to the cellar, that the blessing of peace may attend you and the holy angels, which pass and repass, may have respect to your habitations. . . .

Ye who have a desire to do the will of your God, yet choose the path of nature and are willing to subject to his requirements, upon all such as ye are able to benefit by deeds of goodness turn your hands with all diligence, first to do good to your own household and then lend the hand of charity to your neighbor.

Use all your influence to suppress the haunts of iniquity and debauchery, and know ye that the hand of Divine Wisdom shall be with you in this. And as a token of my approbation I will register your names in my eternal book of records, as being of that number who have willingly stretched forth the hand to reclaim the vicious and, if possible, to do good to those of their sex that lie buried in ruinous habits yet have souls immortal which must forever and eternally exist.

Thus say I, Wisdom: In love and in mercy to those who are called by my name as the feminine part of man have I long stretched my wings and shed my gentle influence in the hearts of those who would receive it and caused them to gather a portion of my spirit of love and tenderness to those whose souls lie under ruinous habits and are fast sinking in the pit of endless shame and ruin. . . .

Thus have I caused my holy angels to descend, clothed with my holy and divine spirit, to work in the hearts of the daughters of men for the purpose of reclaiming those of their own sex to the path of moral virtue who have strayed and are still straying in the soul-sinking habits of making merchandise of their chastity and of selling that which ever ought to be valued by the high and the low, yea, and of all classes, the most valuable, whose worth is above rubies or fine gold.

And they that have listened and still continue to listen to the whisperings of the voice of Wisdom shall inherit the blessing of God, and thus far answer the end of their calling in outward things, and thereby recommend their souls to the mercy of God in the day which is to come.

NOTES

1. The full title is *The Divine Book of Holy and Eternal Wisdom, Revealing the Word of God, out of Whose Mouth Goeth a Sharp Sword* (Canterbury, N. H.: 1849). Excerpts below are from an Appendix, 655–58, paragraphs 1, 6–8, 10–12, 14–17, and 22–23.

2. Bates also signed a paragraph certifying that she had examined the edited version of her book and could testify that "the true sense and spirit of the divine original matter, as revealed through her, the mortal instrument, has been, by the compilers and publishers, preserved entire."

3. These excerpts are from Part VI, chap. i, 505–508, paragraphs 23–30 and 39–46.

4. Apparently the writer is adopting the Victorian view of gender-based division of public and private spheres here, in parcelling out responsibility for different kinds of "carnality." Males fight and females covet material objects.

5. These excerpts are from Part VI, chap. ii, 508–12, paragraphs 1–9 and 16–22.

6. Louis Kern points out the prominence of castration imagery in Shaker theology and suggests that there is much male sexual anxiety expressed in Shaker theology (*An Ordered Love*, 87ff).

7. This expresses the familiar Christian view of the woman as "more guilty" of

the Fall than the man and therefore more in need of redemption. Ann Lee replaces Mary as the "second Eve" (to Christ's "second Adam").

8. The scriptural "woman clothed with the sun" (Revelation 12:1) had already been identified in Shaker theology as a type of Ann Lee.

9. These excerpts are from Part VI, chap. iv, 516–19, paragraphs 6–11, 13–15 and 20–21.

MARY HAZARD'S ''PRECIOUS CRUMBS OF HEAVENLY FOOD...'' (1839–1842)[1]

A Present from Mother Ann

It is a beautiful certificate and four balls of love; they were brought by two of Mother Ann's little babes. The balls were placed by my left side and the certificate was placed on my forehead.

The following are the words written on the certificate of pure gold:

Yea, yea, oh receive, my little child, the reward of pure love and true faith. For my love I send to you at this time folded in a pretty little certificate of gold whereon is written:

My dear child, e'er long have I guarded and watched you, and to my delight and now to your joy do I say, I have found you to be a child of pure love and true faith. And oh, how I love such a soul!

Know ye, dear child, the trying scenes of your youth are known, and your trials of late are as well known; so be not discouraged; persevere on and endure steadfast to the end of your days on earth.

Be patient in your afflictions, for time will release you; but now, to comfort you, have I sent unto you this little reward of a good child of mine.

This certificate have I written with my own hand and sent it to my little worthy child. Now place it on your back, and by it shall all know you to be mine; for when you are truly good, with beauty it will shine.

From Mother Ann

To Mary Hazard   April 12th, 1840

Words of Comfort from Mother Ann,

To Mary Hazard. January 13th, 1841

O Daughter of Israel! hear ye the comforting words which I *see veen*[2] to you. I am your friend, I am your Mother in truth, a friend in time of need, a Mother in hours of trouble.

While I was marching through the peaceable dwellings of my children and viewing them with much pleasure, I paused for a moment and beheld my daughter Mary, who was sitting by a window bearing a grave and solemn countenance, as if very weary and borne down with the burdens of this life.

I spake unto her and said, "Mary, what is it that troubles thee so?" She replied, "O Mother! my troubles are great. Why was it that I was born upon this earth to be so afflicted? Oh, that I had died before this day![3] I might have escaped a great deal that I fear I shall now have to meet with."

So many were the troubles of my little Mary. But I spake again to her and said, "These troubles will soon fade and die away like the withered branches from the Tree of Life. Then heavenly joy and comfort will fill your soul."

Remember, my dear child, never since the first of your faith have you ever been forgotten by me, nor ever will be through time or eternity. Although sorrow on sorrow and crosses on crosses around you may yet roll, remember I will ever be near to the faithful soul.

Now, says Mother, this little verse I will lay upon your head. It is written upon an olive leaf.[4]

> O this my word I give to you,
> To comfort you, my little one;
> So do be faithful, just and true,
> Until your work on earth is done.
> Then in realms of sweetest joy,
> You'll meet your blessed Mother dear,
> Here mortal sufferings can't annoy,
> Nor fill the soul with *dul si mere*.
> A little song I now do lay,
> Upon thy head, my little one:
> This you may sing, my dear Mary,
> *All se ne vi, se van se von.*

This little song, says Mother Ann, that I have given to Mary is my little trumpet comforter. I sang it through the dwellings of my children on Sabbath evening, January 17th, 1841. When I found Mary, I laid it upon her head with my everlasting love and blessing, to comfort her and let her know I have not forgotten her, but still am her friend and Mother.

So fare ye well, in love. Take comfort and press on. Be not cast down nor sad, for you will soon *revon*.

From Mother Ann   To Mary Hazard

This little song[5] is the one that Mother spake of in the foregoing message. Feeling quite bad and out of health, I thought I would retire alone. Accordingly I went up garret and sat down by the window. It was nearly dark. I knew no one knew where I was or how I felt.[6] After a while I had an impression to put my hand on my head and see if there was anything for me. And immediately I received this little song.

And when my ever blessed Mother sent this word of comfort to me, it felt like a word of comfort in very deed.

A Beautiful Present from Father William to all of the Sisters over eighteen years old[7]

A very beautiful white silk neck handkerchief for each and every one of you. They are bordered with gold and have a pale blue fringe. And the picture of all your heavenly Parents' mansions is drawn on them.

And also the likeness of all your heavenly Parents, each one in their own mansion with their names written over them. These, dear children, are very beautiful indeed. I prepared them with my own hands for you and have kept them for my last and parting present. And you can receive them from the hands of your beloved elders, from whence all good shall ever flow unto you.

So receive this little present from me, your Father, as a token of my parental love. And when you feel anxious to see your heavenly Parents, you must look at your handkerchiefs. There will be the likeness of your blessed Mother Ann right in the center, and that of your loving Father William (even mine), in one corner, and Father James, Father Joseph and Mother Lucy in the other.

And as often, dear children, as you will look at this little present and think of me, your Father,[8] just so often I will remember you and send a little angel with a ball of my love to you.

This in union with all your heavenly Parents together with our everlasting, neverending love and remembrance, peace, blessing, and strength.

From Father William   January 5th, 1842

NOTES

1. Source: Andrews Collection, DeWint (SA1085).
2. *"see veen"* is an expression in the mysterious tongue, perhaps meaning "send."
3. Although the Shaker pious vocabulary was full of commonplace expressions for suffering, "wade thro tribulations," etc.—this allusion to depression of spirits or difficult circumstances has an unusually authentic sound.
4. In the mid-1840s in New Lebanon, some spirit messages were actually written on paper cut to resemble leaves.
5. The musical notation for "Trumpet Comforter" appears in the manuscript before this explanation.
6. An interesting indication of the ability of the Believers to find places to be

alone and leisure to feel sad, despite the close monitoring of their activities by elders and eldresses.

7. This gift is reminiscent of two of the later spirit drawings: "A Type of Mother Hannah's Pocket Handkerchief, Drawn by Father James for Jane Blanchard" (the work of Polly Reed of the New Lebanon Church Family, 1851); and "An Emblem of the Heavenly Sphere" (the work of Polly Collins, Hancock, 1854).

8. A similar function was fulfilled by the spirit drawings, apparently—to remind the recipients, usually members of the elders or ministry order, that their spiritual parents were watching and guiding them.

NEW YEAR'S VERSES FOR THE NEW LEBANON SISTERS (1846)[1]

December 31st, 1846

Dearly beloved Elders,

I, your ever loving Mother, have this day of the year readily laid by all other cares to immediately care for a certain class of my little ones and to fulfill unto them a promise that I through my little messenger made some long weeks ago.[2] Doubtless you and they remember the little papers of holy seed and the requirement concerning them. Now I am comforted to tell you that I am greatly satisfied with the sowing of this seed in the hearts of my little ones, and I think you are and will be rejoiced to see it spring up and grow, while they are benefited by reaping the good fruits that they bear, some four-, some seven-, some ten-fold already. And all may yet bear a hundred-fold even in time, if they will. Their perfect obedience (in the main) to my word has been echoed to me by my little messenger of tidings, and their thankful feelings and expressions of the same have oft been wafted on the wings of their little attending angels, that their Mother, their blessed Mother, has once more looked upon them in pity and remembered them in love.

Now listen a moment, and I will tell you what remains in these papers. For I have repeatedly heard their anxious whispers to know and receive whatsoever it was, but the time has only [now?] come. In each one's paper is folded a lily white robe sparkling with the eternal brightness. Also a pearl watch, a gold key, and a silver cup resembling the one given to Benjamin of old, of which that was a type. To this is added a pure emerald crown to wear upon their heads through life. These on the morrow I wish my little ones to receive from your hands, for how can I forbear to reward the contrite soul, and forever hereafter let each of my little ones remember that the truly willing and obedient shall surely reap the reward of their labors. Upon each one's paper is written a few words which is as follows. . . .

Elizaett Bates. The keys of my kingdom I've given to thee; I have crowned thee with meekness and true purity. The watch of the morning I have placed on thy neck, and from my silver cup thou shalt ever drink. So farewell in my love, says your blessed Mother Ann.

Lucy Gates. My silver cup is filled with precious drink for thee; a crown I have prepared and a robe of purity. This holy key hold fast; the morning watch is thine, and more I'll add to these, when thou hast done with time. So farewell in my blessing, says your Mother.

Matilda Reed. I have clothed you with meekness; I have crowned you with love; I have given you the keys to my kingdom above. The watch of the morning I have placed in your trust, for surely I find you true, faithful, and just. So in my peace farewell, says Mother. . . .

Anna Dodson. A shining crown most lovely, a robe that nought has spoiled, this silver cup thou hast well earned, thou true and faithful child. The key into my kingdom, hold fast; tis thine; oh cry the morning watch, thou worthy child of mine. Then when sorrows you betide, I'll walk close by your side, and ever be your guide, says your Mother. . . .

Maria Lapsley. I've crowned you with my blessing, I've clad you with my love. The morning watch of heaven your faithfulness does prove. The key of my bright kingdom I've placed in your care, that you may freely enter and ever blessing share. This silver cup of mine I've filled now for thee. Oh sup with me through time, and I will sup with thee. So farewell forever in my blessing, says Mother. . . .

Harriet Goodwin. With pleasure I say, come near unto me, for a crown of my blessing is now ready for thee. Take the keys of my kingdom, freely enter and share the pure joys of heaven, O thou child of my care. In thy right hand hold fast the watch of the morning. O drink with your Mother the blessings of heaven. Yea, come and receive this silver cup of love filled by my little dove for a worthy child of mine, for I am your Mother. . . .

Now these are my words to my little ones individually. These they can see and take pleasure in perusing, for they are visible and real. But they are worthy of all that I have bestowed upon them and it is with the greatest delight that I hand them forth. And it is my desire that they receive them as a New Year's present from the hand of their Mother, while I say to each and all of them together: O my little ones, my children dear, my jewels, diamonds, pearls, and gems, I've plucked you from a burning fire to be my royal diadems. I've planted in your hearts the precious seed of heaven; the keys of many kingdoms into your trust I've given. The silver cup of knowledge, from which your Savior drank, when death's dark raging billows he stood upon the brink, I now have given you, well filled with the same, often sup together in your Lord and Mother's name. And now to truly prove you, the objects of my care, with the morning watch I've clad you; this will true tidings bear. Receive this with my love as a reward for your true obedience and sincerity during the fifty days of sowing the seed. And now, who among you can say that you have not reaped the full crop of good and precious fruit already? If so, be comforted with me, your Mother.

NOTES

1. Source: Untitled Spiritual Gift from Mother Ann to the Sisters, New Lebanon, 1846, NOC #12,080.
2. This is an example of the written spirit communication which represents itself as continuing or completing an earlier enacted or ritualized gift.

A SELECTIVE BIBLIOGRAPHY OF PUBLISHED SOURCES

EARLY PUBLICATIONS BY SHAKERS, SECEDERS, AND OBSERVERS*

Bates, Paulina. *The Divine Book of Holy and Eternal Wisdom, Revealing the Word of God, out of Whose Mouth Goeth a Sharp Sword*. Canterbury, N. H.: United Society Called Shakers, 1849.

[Bishop, Rufus.] *Testimonies of the Life, Character, Revelations and Doctrines of Our Ever Blessed Mother Ann Lee, and the Elders with Her; through whom the Word of Eternal Life was opened in this Day of Christ's Second Appearing* . . . Hancock: Printed by J. Tallcott and J. Deming, Junrs., 1816.

Brown, Thomas. *An Account of the People Called Shakers: Their Faith, Doctrines, and Practice, Exemplified in the Life, Conversations, and Experience of the Author during the Time He Belonged to the Society. To Which is Affixed a History of Their Rise and Progress to the Present Day* . . . Troy, N.Y.: Parker and Bliss, 1812.

Chapman, Eunice. *An Account of the Conduct of the People Called Shakers: in the Case of Eunice Chapman and Her Children, Since Her Husband Became Acquainted with that People, and Joined Their Society. Written by Herself* . . . Albany, N.Y.: printed for the author, 1817.

["Daughtie."] "Fifteen Years A Shakeress," in *The Galaxy* 13 (January-April, 1872), 29–38, 191–201, 337–46, 460–70.

Dixon, William Hepworth. *New America*. Philadelphia: J. B. Lippincott and Co., 1867.

Doolittle, Mary Antoinette. *Autobiography of Mary Antoinette Doolittle. Containing a Brief History of Early Life Prior to Becoming A Member of the Shaker Community, also an Outline of Life & Experience Among the Shakers*. Mt. Lebanon, N.Y.: 1880.

Dunlavy, John. *The Manifesto, or A Declaration of the Doctrine and Practice of the Church of Christ*. Pleasant Hill, Ky.: 1818.

Dyer, Joseph. *A Compendious Narrative, Elucidating the Character, Disposition and Conduct of Mary Dyer, from the Time of her Marriage, in 1799, till she left the Society called the Shakers, in 1815* . . . Concord, N. H.: Isaac Hill, for the author, 1818.

Dyer, Mary [Marshall]. *A Brief Statement of the Sufferings of Mary Dyer, Occasioned by the Society Called Shakers. Written by Herself. To which is Added, Affidavits and Certificates* . . . Concord, N. H.: Printed by Joseph C. Spear, 1818.

———. *A Portraiture of Shakerism, Exhibiting a General View of Their Character and*

*For a comprehensive list of publications by and about Shakers, see Mary L. Richmond's two-volume work, *Shaker Literature: A Bibliography* (Hanover, N. H.: University Press of New England, 1977).

Conduct . . . Certified by Many Respectable Authorities. Concord, N. H.: for the author, 1822.

———. *Reply to the Shakers' Statement, Called a "Review of the Portraiture of Shakerism," with an Account of the Sickness and Death of Betsy Dyer; a Sketch of the Journey of the Author: and Testimonies from Several Persons . . .* Concord, N.H.: for the author, 1824.

———. *The Rise and Progress of the Serpent from the Garden of Eden to the Present Day: With a Discourse of Shakerism, Exhibiting a General View of Their Real Character and Conduct from the First Appearance of Ann Lee: also the Life and Sufferings of the Author.* Concord, N. H.: for the author, 1847.

Elkins, Hervey. *Fifteen Years in the Senior Order of Shakers: A Narration of the Facts concerning that Singular People.* Hanover, N. H.: Dartmouth Press, 1853.

Evans, Frederick W. *Compendium of the Origin, History, Principles, Rules & Regulations, Government, & Doctrines of the United Society of Believers in Christ's Second Appearing . . .* New York: D. Appleton and Co., 1859.

———. *Autobiography of a Shaker and Revelation of the Apocalypse.* Mt. Lebanon, N.Y.: 1869.

Extract from an Unpublished Manuscript on Shaker History by an Eye Witness. Boston: E. K. Allen, 1850.

Green, Calvin, and Seth Y. Wells. *A Summary View of the Millennial Church or United Society of Believers, Commonly Called Shakers, Comprising the Rise, Progress and Practical Order of the Society Together with the General Principles of Their Faith and Testimony.* Albany, N.Y.: Packard and Van Benthuysen, 1823.

Grosvenor, Roxalana. *The Shakers' Covenant (Never Before Published) with a Brief Outline of Shaker History.* Boston: W. C. Allan, 1873.

Haskett, William J. *Shakerism Unmasked: or the History of the Shakers; Including a Form Politic of Their Government as Councils, Orders, Gifts, with an Exposition of the Five Orders of Shakerism, and Ann Lee's Grand Foundation Vision . . .* Pittsfield, Mass.: the author, 1828.

Knight, Jane D. *Brief Narrative of Events Touching Various Reforms.* Albany, N.Y.: Weed, Parsons and Company, 1880.

Lamson, David. *Two Years' Experience among the Shakers: Being a Description of the Manners and Customs of That People; the Nature and Policy of Their Government; Their Marvellous Intercourse with the Spiritual World; the Object and Uses of Confession, Their Inquisition; in short, a Condensed View of Shakerism As It Is.* West Boylston, Mass.: for the author, 1848.

Leonard, William. *A Discourse on the Order and Propriety of Divine Inspiration and Revelation . . . Also a Discourse on the Second Appearing of Christ In and Through the Order of the Female . . .* Harvard, Mass: United Society, 1853.

[Lossing, Benjamin] "Visiting the Shakers in 1857." *Harper's New Monthly Magazine.* 15, 86 (July, 1857), 164–77.

Mace, Aurelia G. *The Aletheia: Spirit of Truth.* Farmington, Maine: Press of Knowlton, McLeary and Co., 1889.

McNemar, Richard. *The Kentucky Revival: or, A Short History of the Late Extraordinary Out-Pouring of the Spirit of God in the Western States of America . . .* Cincinnati, Ohio: John W. Brown, 1807.

Meacham, Joseph. *A Concise Statement of the Principles of the Only True Church, According to the Gospel of the Present Appearance of Christ . . . Together with a Letter from James Whittaker, Minister of the Gospel in this Day of Christ's Second Appearing—to his Natural Relations in England.* Bennington, Vt.: Haswell and Russell, 1790.

Nordhoff, Charles. *The Communistic Societies of the United States.* New York: Harper and Brothers, 1875.

Noyes, John Humphrey. *History of American Socialisms*. Philadelphia: J. B. Lippincott and Co., 1870.

Rathbun, Daniel. *A Letter from Daniel Rathbun, of Richmond in the County of Berkshire to James Whittacor, Chief Elder of the Church, called Shakers*. Springfield, Mass.: 1785.

Rathbun, Reuben. *Reasons Offered for Leaving the Shakers*. Pittsfield, Mass.: Chester Smith, 1800.

Rathbun, Valentine. *Some Brief Hints of a Religious Scheme, Taught and Propagated By a Number of Europeans Living in a Place Called Nisqueunia, in the State of New York*. Hartford, Conn.: 1781.

Report of the Examination of the Shakers of Canterbury and Enfield Before the New-Hampshire Legislature at the November Session, 1848 . . . Concord, N. H.: Ervin B. Tripp, 1849.

A Review of Mary M. Dyer's Publication, entitled "A Portraiture of Shakerism," . . . Concord, N. H.: Printed by Jacob B. Morse for the United Society, 1824.

Robinson, Charles Edson. *A Concise History of the United Society of Believers Called Shakers*. East Canterbury, N. H.: 1893.

"The Shakers." *Frank Leslie's Ilustrated Newspaper*. September 6 and 12, 1873.

The Shaker; The Shaker and Shakeress; The Shaker Manifesto; The Manifesto. Official monthly publication of the United Society under several different titles and editors, 1871–1899.

Silliman, Benjamin. *Peculiarities of the Shakers, Described in a Series of Letters from Lebanon Springs, in the Year 1832 . . . By a Visitor*. New York: 1832.

Stewart, Philemon. *A Sacred Roll and Book from the Lord God of Heaven to the Inhabitants on Earth . . .* Canterbury, N. H.: 1843.

Taylor, Amos. *A Narrative of the Strange Principles, Conduct and Character of the People Known by the Name of Shakers: Whose Errors have Spread in several Parts of North-America . . . In two Numbers . . .* Worcester, Mass.: Printed for the author, 1782.

Taylor, Leila S. "A Remarkable Statement," *Christian Science Journal* 75 (December 1907), 543–49.

Wells, Seth Y., and Calvin Green. *Testimonies Concerning the Character and Ministry of Mother Ann Lee and the First Witnesses of the Gospel of Christ's Second Appearing: Given by Some of the Aged Brethren and Sisters of the United Society*. New York: Packard and Van Benthuysen, 1827.

White, Anna. *The Motherhood of God*. Canaan Four Corners, N.Y.: Press of the Berkshire Industrial Farm, 1903.

White, Anna, and Leila S. Taylor. *Shakerism: Its Meaning and Message*. Columbus, Ohio: Fred J. Heer, 1904.

Wickersham, George M. *How I Came to Be a Shaker*. East Canterbury, N. H.: 1891.

Youngs, Benjamin Seth, and Calvin Green. [Alternately listed under the authorship of David Darrow, John Meacham, and Benjamin Youngs.] *The Testimony of Christ's Second Appearing, Containing a General Statement of All Things Pertaining to the Faith and Practice of the Church of God in this Latter-day . . .* Lebanon, Ohio; Press of John M'Clean, 1808. Revised and expanded editions: Albany, N.Y.: 1810; Union Village, Ohio: 1823; Albany: 1856.

MODERN SHAKER SCHOLARSHIP

Andrews, Edward Deming. *The Community Industries of the Shakers*. Albany: University of the State of New York, 1932.

——. *The Gift to Be Simple: Songs, Dances and Rituals of the American Shakers.* New York: J. J. Augustin, 1940.

——. *The People Called Shakers: A Search for the Perfect Society.* New York: Oxford University Press, 1953.

Andrews, Edward Deming, and Faith Andrews. *Visions of the Heavenly Sphere: A Study in Shaker Religious Art.* Charlottesville: University Press of Virginia, 1969.

——. *Work and Worship: The Economic Order of the Shakers.* Greenwich, Conn.: New York Graphic Society, 1974.

Barker, Sister Mildred. *Holy Land: A History of the Alfred Shakers.* Sabbathday Lake, Maine: The Shaker Press, 1986.

Bednarowski, Mary Farrell. "Outside the Mainstream: Women's Religion and Women Religious Leaders in Nineteenth-Century America." *Journal of the American Academy of Religion* 48 (1980), 207–31.

Brewer, Priscilla J. *Shaker Communities, Shaker Lives.* Hanover, N. H.: University Press of New England, 1986.

——. " 'Numbers Are Not the Thing for Us to Glory In': Demographic Perspectives on the Decline of the Shakers." *Communal Societies* 7 (1987), 25–35.

Brooks, Leonard. "Sister Aurelia Mace and Her Influence on the Ever-Growing Nature of Shakerism." *The Shaker Quarterly* 16, 2 (Summer 1988), 47–60.

Campbell, D'Ann. "Women's Lives in Utopia: The Shaker Experiment in Sexual Equality Reappraised, 1810–1860." *New England Quarterly* 51 (1978), 23–38.

Carr, Sister Frances A. "Lucy Wright: The First Mother in the Revelation and Order of the The First Organized Church." *The Shaker Quarterly* 15, 3 and 4 (Fall-Winter 1987), 93–100, 128–31.

Crosthwaite, Jane. "The Spirit Drawings of Hannah Cohoon: Window on the Shakers and Their Folk Art." *Communal Societies* 7 (1987), 1–15.

——. " 'A White and Seamless Robe': Celibacy and Equality in Shaker Art and Theology." *Colby Library Quarterly* 25, 3 (September 1989), 188–98.

Filley, Dorothy M. *Recapturing Wisdom's Valley: The Watervliet Shaker Heritage, 1775–1975.* Albany, N.Y.: Albany Institute of History and Art, 1975.

Foster, Lawrence. *Religion and Sexuality: Three American Communal Experiments of the Nineteenth Century.* New York: Oxford University Press, 1981.

Garrett, Clarke. *Spirit Possession and Popular Religion from the Camisards to the Shakers.* Baltimore: Johns Hopkins University Press, 1987.

Hadd, Brother Arnold. "And So Keep My Way Ever Holy: Roxalana Grosvenor and the Testimonies," Harvard Shaker Bicentennial, July 20, 1991.

Ham, F. Gerald. "Shakerism in the Old West." Ph.D. diss, University of Kentucky, 1962.

Hayden, Dolores. *Seven American Utopians: The Architecture of Communitarian Socialism, 1790–1975.* Cambridge, Mass.: M. I. T. Press, 1976.

Horgan, Edward R. *The Shaker Holy Land: A Community Portrait.* Harvard, Mass.: Harvard Common Press, 1982.

Humez, Jean M. "Women's Contributions to the Shaker Myth of Origins." *Harvard Divinity Bulletin* 21, 1 (1991), 12–15.

——. " 'Ye Are My Epistles': The Construction of Ann Lee Imagery in Early Shaker Sacred Literature." *Journal of Feminist Studies in Religion* (Spring 1992).

——. " 'Weary of Petticoat Government': The Specter of Female Rule in Early Nineteenth-Century Shaker Politics." *Communal Societies* 11 (Spring 1992), 1–17.

Kern, Louis J. *An Ordered Love: Sex Roles and Sexuality in Victorian American Com-*

munes—*The Shakers, the Mormons and the Oneida Community*. Chapel Hill: University of North Carolina Press, 1981.

Kitch, Sally L. *Chaste Liberation: Celibacy and Female Cultural Status*. Urbana: University of Illinois Press, 1989.

Lauer, Jeanette C., and Robert H. Lauer. "Sex Roles in Nineteenth-Century American Communal Societies." *Communal Societies* 3 (1983), 16–28.

Lauer, Robert H., and Jeannette C. Lauer. *The Spirit and the Flesh: Sex in Utopian Communities*. Metuchen, N.J.: Scarecrow Press, 1983.

Marini, Stephen A. *Radical Sects of Revolutionary New England*. Cambridge, Mass.: Harvard University Press, 1982.

———. "A New View of Mother Ann Lee and the Rise of American Shakerism." Parts I and II in *The Shaker Quarterly* 28, 2 and 3 (Summer and Fall 1990), 47–62 and 95–111.

Meader, Robert F. "The Vision of Brother Philemon." *Shaker Quarterly* 1, 1 (Spring 1970), 8–17.

Mercadante, Linda. *Gender, Doctrine, and God: The Shakers and Contemporary Theology*. Nashville: Abingdon Press, 1990.

Morse, Flo. *The Shakers and the World's People*. New York: Dodd, Mead, 1980.

Muncy, Raymond Lee. *Sex and Marriage in Utopian Communities in Nineteenth-Century America*. Baltimore: Penguin, 1974.

Neal, Julia. *By Their Fruits: The Story of Shakerism in South Union, Kentucky*. Chapel Hill: University of North Carolina Press, 1947.

———. *The Kentucky Shakers*. Lexington: University Press of Kentucky, 1977.

Neal, Mary Julia, ed. *The Journal of Eldress Nancy, Kept at the South Union, Kentucky, Shaker Colony, August 15, 1861–Sept. 4, 1864*. Nashville: The Parthenon Press, 1963.

Nickless, Karen K., and Pamela J. Nickless. "Trustees, Deacons, and Deaconesses: The Temporal Role of the Shaker Sisters 1820–1890." *Communal Societies* 7 (1987), 16–24.

Patterson, Daniel W. *The Shaker Spiritual*. Princeton, N.J.: Princeton University Press, 1979.

———. *Gift Drawing and Gift Song: A Study of Two Forms of Shaker Inspiration*. Sabbathday Lake, Maine: United Society of Shakers, 1983.

Phillips, Hazel Spencer. *Richard the Shaker*. Lebanon, Ohio: the author, 1972.

Procter-Smith, Marjorie. *Women in Shaker Community and Worship: A Feminist Analysis of the Uses of Religious Symbolism*. Lewiston, Maine: Edwin Mellen Press, 1985.

———. *Shakerism and Feminism: Reflections on Women's Religion and the Early Shakers*. Old Chatham, N.Y.: Center for Research and Education, Shaker Museum and Library, 1991.

Promey, Sally M. *Spiritual Spectacles: Vision and Image in Mid-Nineteenth-Century Shakerism*. Bloomington: Indiana University Press, forthcoming.

Sasson, Diane. *The Shaker Spiritual Narrative*. Knoxville: University of Tennessee Press, 1983.

Sears, Clara Endicott. *Gleanings from Old Shaker Journals*. Harvard, Mass.: Fruitlands Museum, 1916.

Setta, Susan M. "Woman of the Apocalypse: The Reincorporation of the Feminine through the Second Coming of Christ in Ann Lee." Ph.D. diss., Pennsylvania State University, 1979.

———. "From Ann the Christ to Holy Mother Wisdom: Changing Goddess Imagery in the Shaker Tradition." *Anima* 7 (1980), 5–13.

Stein, Stephen J. *Letters from a Young Shaker: William S. Byrd at Pleasant Hill.* Lexington: University Press of Kentucky, 1985.

———. " 'A Candid Statement of Our Principles': Early Shaker Theology in the West." *Proceedings of the American Philosophical Society* 133, 4 (1989), 503–19.

———. "Shaker Gift and Shaker Order: A Study of Religious Tension in Nineteenth-Century America." *Communal Societies* 10 (1990), 103–13.

Swain, Thomas. "The Evolving Expressions of the Religious and Theological Experiences of a Community." *Shaker Quarterly* 12, 1 (Spring 1972), 3–31; and 12, 2 (Summer 1972), 43–67.

FURTHER READING IN U.S. RELIGIOUS HISTORY

Ahlstrom, Sydney E. *A Religious History of the American People.* New Haven: Yale University Press, 1972.

Boyer, Paul, and Stephen Nissenbaum. *Salem Possessed: The Social Origins of Witchcraft.* Cambridge: Harvard University Press, 1974.

Braude, Ann D. *Radical Spirits: Spiritualism and Women's Rights in Nineteenth Century America.* Boston: Beacon Press, 1989.

Butler, Jon. *Awash in a Sea of Faith: Christianizing the American People.* Cambridge: Harvard University Press, 1990.

Cott, Nancy F. "Young Women in the Second Great Awakening in New England." *Feminist Studies* 3, 1 (Fall 1975), 15–29.

———. *The Bonds of Womanhood: 'Woman's Sphere' in New England, 1780–1835.* New Haven: Yale University Press, 1977.

Cross, Whitney. *The Burned-Over District: The Social and Intellectual History of Enthusiastic Religion in Western New York, 1800–1850.* Ithaca: Cornell University Press, 1950.

Douglas, Ann. *The Feminization of American Culture.* New York: Avon, 1977.

Dunn, Mary Maples. "Saints and Sisters: Congregational and Quaker Women in the Early Colonial Period." *American Quarterly* 30, 5 (Winter 1978), 582–601.

Epstein, Barbara Leslie. *The Politics of Domesticity: Women, Evangelism and Temperance in Nineteenth-century America.* Middletown, Conn.: Wesleyan University Press, 1981.

Falk, Nancy Auer. "Evangelical Women in Nineteenth-Century America: The Role of Women in Sunday Schools." In Nancy Auer Falk and Rita M. Gross, eds., *Unspoken Worlds: Women's Religious Lives.* Belmont, Calif.: Wadsworth, 1989, 166–78.

Gilkes, Cheryl Townsend. "Together and in Harness: Women's Traditions in the Sanctified Church." *SIGNS* 10, 4 (Summer 1985), 678–99.

Hall, David D. *Worlds of Wonder, Days of Judgment: Popular Religious Belief in Early New England.* Cambridge: Harvard University Press, 1990.

———. *Witch-Hunting in Seventeenth-Century New England: A Documentary History, 1638–1692.* Boston: Northeastern University Press, 1991.

Hatch, Nathan O. *The Democratization of American Christianity.* New Haven: Yale University Press, 1989.

Karlsen, Carol F. *The Devil in the Shape of A Woman: Witchcraft in Colonial New England.* New York: Norton, 1987.

Karlsen, Carol F., and Laurie Crumpacker, eds. *The Journal of Esther Edwards Burr.* New Haven: Yale University Press, 1984.

Koehler, Lyle. "The Case of the American Jezebels: Anne Hutchinson and Female Agitation during the Years of Antinomian Turmoil, 1636–1640." In Linda Kerber and Jane DeHart Mathews, eds., *Women's America: Refocusing the Past*, 36–51.

Lincoln, C. Eric, and Lawrence H. Mamiya. *The Black Church in the African American Experience*. Durham: Duke University Press, 1990. See especially chap. 10, "The Pulpit and the Pew: The Black Church and Women," 274–308.

McLoughlin, William C. *Revivals, Awakenings and Reform*. Chicago: University of Chicago Press, 1978.

Moore, R. Laurence. *In Search of White Crows: Spiritualism, Parapsychology and American Culture*. New York: Oxford, 1977.

Rabinowitz, Richard. *The Spiritual Self in Everyday Life: The Transformation of Personal Religious Experience in Nineteenth-Century New England*. Boston: Northeastern University Press, 1989.

Reuther, Rosemary Radford, and Rosemary Skinner Keller, eds., *Women and Religion in America*. Vol. 1, The Nineteenth Century. New York: Harper and Row, 1981. See especially Rosemary Radford Ruether, "Women in Utopian Movements," 46–100, and Barbara Brown Zikmund, "The Struggle for the Right to Preach," 193–241.

Reuther, Rosemary Radford, and Eleanor McLaughlin, eds., *Woman of Spirit: Female Leadership in the Jewish and Christian Tradition*. New York: Simon and Schuster, 1979. See especially Barbara Brown Zikmund, "The Feminist Thrust of Sectarian Christianity."

Ryan, Mary P. "A Woman's Awakening: Evangelical Religion and the Families of Utica, New York, 1800–1840." *American Quarterly* 30, 5 (Winter 1978), 602–23.

Shiels, Richard D. "The Feminization of American Congregationalism, 1730–1835." *American Quarterly* 33 (Spring 1981), 46–62.

Smith, Timothy L. *Revivalism and Social Reform*. Nashville: Abingdon Press, 1957.

Smith-Rosenberg, Carroll. *Religion and the Rise of the American City: The New York City Mission Movement, 1812–1870*. Ithaca: Cornell University Press, 1971.

———. *Disorderly Conduct: Visions of Gender in Victorian America*. New York: A. A. Knopf, 1986. See especially "The Cross and the Pedestal: Women, Anti-Ritualism and the Emergence of the American Bourgeoisie," 129–64.

Ulrich, Laurel. *Good Wives: Image and Reality in the Lives of Women in Northern New England, 1650–1750*. New York: Random House, 1982.

Welter, Barbara. *Dimity Convictions: The American Woman in the Nineteenth Century*. Athens: Ohio University Press, 1976. See especially "The Cult of True Womanhood," 21–41, and "The Feminization of American Religion," 83–102.

———. "She Hath Done What She Could: Protestant Women's Missionary Careers in Nineteenth Century America." *American Quarterly* 30 (Winter 1978), 624–38.

Wisbey, Herbert A., Jr. *Pioneer Prophetess: Jemima Wilkinson, the Publick Universal Friend*. Ithaca: Cornell University Press, 1964.

FURTHER READINGS ON WOMEN AND RELIGION

Atkinson, Clarissa. *Mystic and Pilgrim: The Book and the World of Margery Kempe*. Ithaca: Cornell University Press, 1983.

Brunn, Emilie Zum, and Georgette Epiney-Burgard. *Women Mystics in Medieval Europe*. New York: Paragon House, 1989.

Bynum, Caroline Walker. *Jesus as Mother: Studies in the Spirituality of the High Middle Ages*. Berkeley: University of California Press, 1982.

Fiorenza, Elisabeth Schussler. *In Memory of Her: A Feminist Theological Reconstruction of Christian Origins*. New York: Crossroad, 1983.

James, William. *The Varieties of Religious Experience*. New York: New American Library, 1958 (orig. ed. 1902).

Kraemer, Ross S. "Ecstasy and Possession: Women of Ancient Greece and the Cult of Dionysus." In Nancy Auer Falk and Rita M. Gross, eds., *Unspoken Worlds: Women's Religious Lives*, 45–55.

LaPorte, Jean. *The Role of Women in Early Christianity*. New York: Edwin Mellen, 1984.

Lawless, Elaine J. "Shouting for the Lord: The Power of Women's Speech in the Pentecostal Religious Service." *Journal of American Folklore* 96, 382 (1983), 434–59.

Lewis, I. M. *Ecstatic Religion: An Anthropological Study of Spirit Possession and Shamanism*. New York: Penguin, 1971.

McFague, Sallie I. "God As Mother." In Judith Plaskow and Carol Christ, eds., *Weaving the Visions: New Patterns in Feminist Spirituality*. San Francisco: Harper and Row, 1989, 139–50.

McNamara, Jo Ann. *A New Song: Celibate Women in the First Three Christian Centuries*. New York: Haworth, 1984.

Mollenkott, Virginia. *The Divine Feminine: The Biblical Imagery of God as Female*. New York: Crossroad, 1983.

Ochshorn, Judith. *The Female Experience and the Nature of the Divine*. Bloomington: Indiana University Press, 1981.

Pagels, Elaine. "What Became of God the Mother?" In Carol B. Christ and Judith Plaskow, eds., *Womanspirit Rising: A Feminist Reader in Religion*. New York: Harper and Row, 1979, 107–19.

Reuther, Rosemary Radford. *Sexism and God-Talk: Toward a Feminist Theology*. Boston: Beacon Press, 1983.

Smith, Catharine F. "Jane Lead: The Feminist Mind and Art of a Seventeenth-Century Protestant Mystic." In Rosemary Radford Reuther and Eleanor McLaughlin, eds., *Women of Spirit*, 183–98.

Taylor, Barbara. *Eve and the New Jerusalem: Socialism and Feminism in the Nineteenth Century*. New York: Pantheon, 1983.

Trible, Phyllis. *God and the Rhetoric of Sexuality*. Philadelphia: Fortress Press, 1978.

FURTHER RELATED READINGS IN U.S. WOMEN'S EARLY HISTORY AND LITERARY CULTURE

Andrews, William L. *Sisters of the Spirit: Three Black Women's Autobiographies of the Nineteenth Century*. Bloomington: Indiana University Press, 1986.

Baym, Nina. *Women's Fiction: A Guide to Novels by and about Women in America, 1820–1870*. Ithaca: Cornell University Press, 1978.

Bordin, Ruth Birgitta Anderson. *Women and Temperance: The Quest for Power and Liberty, 1873–1900*. Philadelphia: Temple University Press, 1981.

Brereton, Virginia. *From Sin to Salvation: American Women's Conversion Narratives, 1800–1980*. Bloomington: Indiana University Press, 1991.

Chambers-Schiller, Lee Virginia. *Liberty, A Better Husband: The Single Woman in America, The Generations of 1780–1840*. New Haven: Yale University Press, 1984.

Cott, Nancy F. *The Bonds of Womanhood: 'Woman's Sphere' in New England, 1780–1835*. New Haven: Yale University Press, 1977.

Culley, Margo. *A Day at A Time: The Diary Literature of American Women from 1764 to the Present*. New York: The Feminist Press at the City University of New York, 1985.

Douglas, Ann. *The Feminization of American Culture*. New York: Avon, 1977.

Dublin, Thomas, ed. *Farm to Factory: Women's Letters, 1830–1860*. New York: Columbia University Press, 1981.

Eisler, Benita. *The Lowell Offering: Writings by New England Mill Women (1840–1845)*. Philadelphia: J. B. Lippincott, 1977.

Faragher, John Mack. *Women and Men on the Overland Trail*. New Haven: Yale University Press, 1979.

Fetterly, Judith. *Provisions: A Reader from Nineteenth-Century American Women*. Bloomington: Indiana University Press, 1985.

Fischer, Christiane. *Let Them Speak for Themselves: Women in the American West, 1849–1900*. New York: E. P. Dutton, 1978.

Hampsten, Elizabeth. *Read This Only to Yourself: The Private Writings of Midwestern Women, 1880–1910*. Bloomington: Indiana University Press, 1982.

Hewitt, Nancy A. *Women's Activism and Social Change: Rochester, New York, 1822–1872*. Ithaca: Cornell University Press, 1984.

Hoffmann, Leonore, and Margo Culley, eds. *Women's Personal Narratives*. New York: MLA, 1985.

Humez, Jean M. " 'My Spirit Eye': Some Functions of Spiritual and Visionary Experience in the Lives of Five Black Women Preachers, 1810–1880." In Barbara J. Harris and JoAnn K. McNamara, eds., *Women and The Structure of Society: Selected Research from the Fifth Berkshire Conference on the History of Women*. Durham, N. C.: Duke University Press, 1984, 129–43.

Humez, Jean McMahon, ed. *Gifts of Power: The Writings of Rebecca Jackson, Black Visionary, Shaker Eldress*. Amherst: University of Massachusetts Press, 1981.

Kaufman, Polly Welts. *Women Teachers on the Frontier*. New Haven: Yale University Press, 1984.

Kelley, Mary. *Private Woman, Public Stage: Literary Domesticity in Nineteenth-Century America*. New York: Oxford University Press, 1984.

Kerber, Linda K. *Women of the Republic: Intellect and Ideology in Revolutionary America*. Chapel Hill: University of North Carolina Press, 1980.

Lerner, Gerda. "The Lady and the Mill Girl: Changes in the Status of Women in the Age of Jackson." *American Studies* 10, (Spring 1969), 5–15.

———. "Placing Women in History: Definitions and Challenges." *Feminist Studies* 3, 1–2 (Fall 1975), 5–14.

McKay, Nellie Y. "Nineteenth-Century Black Women's Spiritual Autobiographies: Religious Faith and Self-Empowerment." In The Personal Narratives Group, eds., *Interpreting Women's Lives: Feminist Theory and Personal Narratives*. Bloomington: Indiana University Press, 1989.

Myres, Sandra L. *Ho for California! Women's Overland Diaries from the Huntington Library*. San Marino, Calif.: Huntington Library, 1980.

———. *Westering Women and the Frontier Experience, 1800–1915*. Albuquerque: University of New Mexico Press, 1982.

Norton, Mary Beth. "The Paradox of 'Woman's Sphere.' " In Carol Ruth Berkin and Mary Beth Norton, eds., *Women of America: A History*. Boston: Houghton Miflin, 1979, 279–87.

Ryan, Mary P. "The Power of Women's Networks: A Case Study of Female Moral Reform in Antebellum America." *Feminist Studies* (Spring 1979).

———. *Cradle of the Middle Class: The Family in Oneida County, New York, 1780–1865*. New York: Cambridge University Press, 1981.

Shea, Daniel B., Jr. *Spiritual Autobiography in Early America*. Princeton, N.J.: Princeton University Press, 1968.

Sklar, Kathryn. *Catharine Beecher, a Study in American Domesticity*. New Haven: Yale University Press, 1973.

Smith-Rosenberg, Carroll. "The Female World of Love and Ritual: Relations between Women in Nineteenth-Century America." *SIGNS* 1, 1 (Autumn 1975).

Taves, Ann, ed. *Religion and Domestic Violence in Early New England: The Memoirs of Abigail Abbot Bailey*. Bloomington: Indiana University Press, 1989.

Vicinus, Martha. *Independent Women: Work and Community for Single Women, 1850–1920*. Chicago: University of Chicago Press, 1985.

Walker, Alice. "Gifts of Power: The Writings of Rebecca Jackson." In *In Search of Our Mother's Gardens*. New York: Harcourt Brace Jovanovich, 1983, 71–82.

Welter, Barbara. *Dimity Convictions: The American Woman in the Nineteenth Century*. Athens: Ohio University Press, 1976. See especially "The Cult of True Womanhood," 21–41, and "The Feminization of American Religion: 1800–1860," 83–102.

Winter, Metta L. " 'Heart Watching' through Journal Keeping: A Look at Quaker Diaries and Their Uses." *Women's Diaries: A Quarterly Newsletter* 1, 2 (Summer 83), 1–3.

INDEX

Accusations: against Ann Lee, 4, 6, 11 n.21; use of spiritual messages, 212–13, 215, 226 nn.9, 11

Adam, in Shaker view of the fall, 220, 262, 266 n.7

African Americans, as early Shakers, xxvi, 140–41, 144 n.25, 164

Africans, as spirit visitors, 217, 245–46, 248 n.10

Afterworld, Ann Lee's access to, 10 n. 15

Age(s): restrictions concerning those hearing spirit messages, 256, 258 n.2; spirit possession of boys, 214, 226 n.16; spirit possession of girls, xxiv, xxxiv n.26, 210, 214; of women in the 1827 *Testimonies*, 7, 11 n.26

Aggression, Shaker views on, xvi, 38 n.2, 120, 121 n.3

Albany, N.Y., 5; Ann Lee's imprisonment, 30, 38 n.2, 54

Albigensianism, xxxii n.9

Alcoholism: accusations against Ann Lee and followers, xxi, 4, 10 n.14, 73; accusations during Lucy Wright era, 67; refutation of in testimonials, 7, 47, 51, 54–55

Aliens, spiritual, visitations of, 243–48

Allen, John, 226 n.15

Allen, Joseph, 156, 174

Almighty Father, Holy Mother Wisdom's role as partner, 220–21

Ancestors: "bearing for souls" concept, 16, 28 n.2; spiritual, xxiv, 223. *See also* Manifestations, spiritual

Andrews, Edward Deming, xxxiii n.17

Andrews, Faith, xxxiii n.17

Angel of Love, as Lucifer's original partner, 220

Angels, guardian (good), as Lucy Wright concept, xxiii, 71, 84–85

Annas, Angeline, 237 n.1

Annas, Lydia, 245

Anthems, introduction of, 69

Anti-ritualism, in enthusiastic religion, xv, xxxii n.9

Apostasy ("Falling away"; "Seceders"; "Turnoffs"), 2, 4, 100 n.2, 213; during

"Mother Ann's Work," xxv, 213, 224, 226 n.12; spirit messages' influence on, 214, 226 nn.12, 15, 232, 237 n.7

Aprons, 183, 187

Ashfield, Mass., mob action at, 41–43

Authority: difficulty in achieving in Kentucky, 180, 181 n.4; gender in Shaker hierarchy, xviii–xix, xxviii n.15, 141; of Lucy Wright, xxii–xxiii, 5, 64–81; role of New England church women, xv

Avery, Gilbert, 226 n.13

Babbitt, Abiathar (elder), 83–84, 105, 166; position in hierarchy, 66, 72, 78 n.20, 79 n.21

Babbitt, Abigail, 36

Bacon, Asa, 42

Bacon, Daniel, 42

Bacon, Lucy, as missionary in the West, 119, 120, 143 n.10

Bacon, Moses, 42

Barce, Thankful, 8, 20, 22, 46–47

Barns, John, challenge of Lucy Wright's rule, 67–68, 80 n.44

Bates, Elizaett, 271

Bates, Issachar, as missionary in the West, 107, 135, 148, 173, 206

Bates, Paulina, xxviii; *Divine Book of Holy and Eternal Wisdom* (1849), xviii, xxv, 220–21, 228 nn.38, 41, 258–67

Bathrick, Eunice, xiii; oral-history anthologies of, 8, 12 n.31, 58 n.1

"Bearing for souls," salvation concept for the dead, 16, 28 n.2

Behavior, Shaker: exposure of misbehavior, 213–14; under Millenial Laws, 69, 71; pacifism, xvi, 38 n.2, 120, 121 n.3; proposed dietary reforms, 213, 216, 227 nn.23, 25, 243 n.3; during trances, xvii–xviii, 210, 211–15

Beliefs, Shaker. *See* Theology, Shaker

Bennett, Eunice, 20–21

Bennett, Joseph, 49

Bennett, Lucy, 49, 176

Bestiality, sexual practices compared to by Ann Lee, 26, 29 n.20

xxviii, xxxiii n.15, 141; and Shaker spiritualism, xiv; teaching converts to accept, 135
Communities, Shaker: founding of, 68, 79
n.31, 143 n.15; network of, xiv, xxxi n.6;
in the West, 136, 143 n.15. *See also* communities by name
Confession of sins: by Ann Lee, 29–30;
prior to separation by sexes, 50, 56 n.2;
during revivals, 210, 213, 226 n.11, 253;
as Shaker belief, xiii, xvi, xxi
Congregational churches, women's dominant role in, xv
Conkling, Emily, as instrument, 243
Consumption (tuberculosis), among young
eastern Shakers, 196
Conversion experiences, in 1827 *Testimonies*, 7–8, 44–56
Converts: ecstatic worship modes of western, 103, 135, 183, 185 n.2; first generation of women as, xiv; learning a
communal life style, 135; during Mother
Lucy era, 186; obsession with sin, 7,
44–56
Cook, Susannah (Hannah), healing testi-
mony of, 2, 13
Cooking: diet reforms, 213, 216, 227 nn.23,
25; facilities for in early Ohio, 149, 154;
Lucy Wright's views on, 93–94; Mother
Lucy's spiritual advice on, 239–40
Copley, Daniel, 207
Correspondence: gender division of, 137–
38; of Lucy Wright, 72–77, 99–132; of
western sisters, 137–44. *See also* indi-
vidual correspondents
Cory, Zipporah, xiii, 49–52; on early
Shaker alcoholism, 7, 51
Crouch, Isaac, 21
Cures, miraculous, 2–3, 9 n.7, 13–14, 48,
139–40, 171, 195–96
Curtis, Hopewell, as missionary, 118 n.4,
206, 207

Damnation: in Shaker belief, xvii, xxxii
n.14, 7; use by Ann Lee, 5
Dancing, Shaker, xiii; accusations of naked
practices, 4, 10 n.14; effect on Zipporah
Cory, 49; ritualization during Lucy
Wright era, xviii, xxiii, 69, 72, 80 n.38;
while non-Shakers present, 176, 179 n.4
Darby, Anna, 162–63
Darrow, David, 61, 109, 148
Darrow, David, correspondence
—from Lucy Wright, 73–76; on his appointment as first lead, 103–106; on John
Meacham's recall, 124–25; on those who
invite persecution, 129–32; on those who
lose the gift, 118–21; on traveling, 74,
114–15

—to Lucy Wright: on New Lebanon Mis-
sionary sisters, 111–13; on Shaker belief,
100–103
Darrow, Lucy, xxxi n.5
Darrow, Ruth, as missionary in Ohio, 108–
10, 143 n.10
Darrow House, 175, 178 n.3
Davis, Anna, 175
Davis, Jennet, 13
Dead, the, salvation of the unconverted, 10
n.16, 16, 21–22, 28 n.2
Debility, physical, as topic of correspond-
ence, 139–40
Deming, Nathaniel (elder), 117, 171, 251–53
"Deputy husband" concept, as explanation
of women's religious authority, 5, 11
n.18, 15, 144 n.21
Devil, in Shaker belief, xxxii n.14, 80 n.36;
dual-gender concept, 220–21, 261–62
Diet reforms, proposed during mid-century
revival, 213, 216, 227 nn.23, 25
Disobedience, spiritual, 143 n.19, 212–13
"Disorderly religion," appeal to women, xv–
xvi, xxxii n.9
Divine Book of Holy and Eternal Wisdom
(1849) (Bates), xviii, xxv, 220–21,
228nn.38, 41, 258–67
Dodgson, Anna, as spirit instrument, 216,
242, 271
Domestic work, xix, 228 n.43, 239 n.4; advice in the *Divine Book of Holy and Eternal Wisdom*, 265–66; role of Lucy Wright,
70; spiritual reform messages about, 216;
spiritual sweeping gift, xxiv, 218–19, 248–
49. *See also* Cooking; Washing
Donations, eastern, as help for western societies, 127–29, 134, 182, 185 n.2
Doolittle, Antoinette, 229 n.50
Drunkenness. *See* Alcoholism
Dual-genderism
—of the godhead, xxi, 2, 9 n.6, 81 n.47,
219–23; David Darrow's desire to ex-
pound on, 74, 102–103, 117 n.2; Lucy
Wright's reluctance to publish, 2, 69, 74,
115–16
—of Lucifer, 220, 221, 261–62
—in Shaker hierarchy, xvii–xix, xxviii,
xxxiii n.15, 5, 66, 99–100, 141
Dunlavy, John, as missionary in the West,
102, 112
Dwellings, Shaker, 239 n.4; spiritual sweeping of, 248–49; in Western communities,
138–39, 148–49, 150, 154, 158
Dyer, Mary Marshall, anti-Shaker accusations of, 4, 6

Eads, Harvey, 203, 206 n.2
Eads, Sally, 206

Tree of Life: spirit messages concerning, 231, 232, 237 n.5, 247, 248 n.14; as vision of Hannah Cohoon, xiii, xxxi n.7

Trials, while traveling in the way of God, 83

"True womanhood," xxviii, xxxii n.13

Turner, Gideon, 14

Turner, Jethro, 15, 81 n.44, 86–87

Turner, Mary, 2, 13–14

Turner, Samuel (elder), 75; as missionary leader in the West, 107, 112, 137

Turning (Whirling), 212, 237

"Turnoffs." *See* Apostasy

Two Years' Experience (Lamson), 228 n.40

Ulrich, Karlsen, xxxiv n.26

Ulrich, Laurel, xv, xxxiv n.26; concept of "deputy husband," 5, 11 n.18, 144 n.21

Union Village (Ohio) community: correspondence to, 72–77; as lead ministry, 73, 136

United Society of Believers in Christ's Second Appearing: internal revivals of, xvii, 44, 65, 180, 210–25; during Lucy Wright era, 64–81. *See also* "Mother Ann's Work"

Urbanization, influence on Shakers, xvii

Van Valen, Martha, 218, 227 n.33, 250–54

Visionary activity: of Ann Lee, xvii; lack of during Lucy Wright era, 69, 72, 80 n.35, 81 n.45; during mid-century revival, 210–25. *See also* Manifestations, spiritual

"Visionary Dream Concerning Ann Eliza Goodwin, A," 213

Wardley, James and Jane, as founders of the Church, 31, 38 n.3

Warfare, rejection by Shakers, xvi, 38 n.2, 120, 121 n.3

"Warring gifts," accusatory messages as, 212–13

Washing (laundering): Ann Lee on wastefulness, 24; facilities in early Ohio, 149, 150; spiritual reform messages about, 216, 241

Watervliet community: as origin of mid-century revival, 210–11, 230–37; visit by James Monroe, 169, 171–72; Wisdom Valley as spirit name for, 243, 247, 248 n.2

Welch, Ephraim, 43

Wells, David, 42

Wells, Freegift (elder), 215; rulebook of, 69, 80 n.34

Wells, Seth Y., as editor, 3, 4–5, 10 n.15, 11 nn.25, 26, 220

Welter, Barbara, xxxii n.13

West, the, eastern sisters life in, 11–13, 108–10, 133–44, 148–50, 150–53

West Union (Busro, Ind.) community: concern about, 120, 122, 124 n.3; failure of, 73, 79 n.31, 81 n.50

Whipping, use in metaphorical sense, 160, 177, 179 n.5

Whirling (Turning), during trances, 212, 237

White, Anna, 77 n.7, 224; *Shakerism: Its Meaning and Message* (1904), xxvi

White, Nancy, as instrument, 230, 232, 243

Whittaker, James (elder), xxxi n.3, 50, 53; on Ann Lee's imprisonment in England, 32–33; as head of the church, 64; recollections of by others, 57, 60

Wicker, Frederick S., 197, 207, 237 n.1

Wicker, Joseph (elder), 218; as spirit instrument, 250–55

Wickliffe, Robert, 199

Wicks, Loren, 244–45

Wicks, Mary, 226 n.15

Wight, Lucy, 8, 52–55

Wisdom Valley, as spirit name for Watervliet community, 242, 247, 248 n.2

Witchcraft, Shaker's binding of evil spirits viewed as, 28 n.17

Wollinson, Mary Ann, as spirit instrument, 250, 252

Women: church membership role, xv, xxxii n.9; as early converts from New Light Baptists, xiv; role in spiritualistic rituals, xxiv–xxv, xxxiv n.26, 210–11, 215–19, 225 n.5, 230–37; as Shaker missionaries, 108–10, 111–13, 133–44, 148–50, 150–53. *See also* Dual-genderism; Gender; Testimonials; individual names

Wood, Aaron, 43

Wood, Daniel, 31, 65

Wood, Elizabeth, 9, 58–63

Woodworth, Deborah, 154, 175

"Words of Comfort from Mother Ann," 223

World, the, escape from through communal living, xvii, 68, 79 n.29

Worley, Malcom, as missionary in the West, 102, 148

Worley, Peggy, 148

Worship

—ecstatic: among early Shakers, 1, 10 n.16, 80 n.37; among western Shakers, 103, 135, 183, 185 n.2

—during Lucy Wright era, xxiii, 69

—*See also* Dancing, Shaker; Rituals

Worster (Worcester), Abijah, 22

Wright, Lucy (Mother Lucy): during Ann Lee's last days, 27, 65, 78 n.9; birthday of, 85–86; cooking and eating views, 93–94; illness and death of, 188, 189; information about for missionary sisters, 138, 160, 165–66, 167–68, 177; leadership role, xxii–xxiii, 5, 64–81; meeting with second generation at New Lebanon, 82–85;

JEAN M. HUMEZ is Associate Professor of Women's Studies at the University of Massachusetts, Boston. She is the editor of *Gifts of Power: The Writings of Rebecca Jackson, Black Visionary, Shaker Eldress* and author of many articles on women's autobiographies and Shakerism.